W9-ABV-911

Seeing Together

*Friendship Between the
Sexes in English Writing,
from Mill to Woolf*

Seeing Together

Friendship Between the Sexes in English Writing, from Mill to Woolf

Victor Luftig

Stanford University Press
Stanford, California

Stanford University Press
Stanford, California
© 1993 by the Board of Trustees of the
Leland Stanford Junior University
Printed in the United States of America

Original printing 1993
Last figure below indicates year of this printing:
04   03   02   01   00   99   98   97   96   95

Stanford University Press publications are distributed exclusively by Stanford University Press
within the United States, Canada, Mexico, and
Central America; they are distributed exclusively
by Cambridge University Press throughout the
rest of the world.

Frontispiece: *Interior*, 1918, by Duncan Grant,
© 1978 Estate of Duncan Grant. Reproduced
with the kind permission of the Trustees of the
Ulster Museum, Belfast.

Library of Congress Cataloging-in-Publication Data

Luftig, Victor, 1959–
    Seeing together : friendship between the sexes in
English writing, from Mill to Woolf / Victor Luftig.
            p.   cm.
    Includes bibliographical references and index.
    ISBN 0-8047-2168-8 (cl.) : ISBN 0-8047-2591-8 (pbk.)
    1. English literature—19th century—History and
criticism. 2. English literature—20th century—History
and criticism. 3. Man-woman relationships in literature.
4. Friendship in literature. 5. Sex role in literature.
6. Women in literature. 7. Men in literature.
I. Title.
PR468.M36L85   1993
820.9'353—dc20   92-44199
                                                 CIP

⊗   This book is printed on acid-free paper

Acknowledgments

Victorians and Modernists concerned with heterosexual friendship struggled, often in isolation, to find the right words. My examination of their efforts has benefited throughout from the gracious assistance of teachers and colleagues who had better words than I. Among the many happy debts resulting from the composition of this book, the most conspicuous inheres in the phrase at its conceptual center: I began with a vague interest in "the language of friendship between men and women"; the terms that define the subject as it is studied in this book—the study of the *idioms* for *heterosexual friendship*—were contributed by, respectively, Lucio Ruotolo and Regenia Gagnier, who supervised its original incarnation as a Stanford University doctoral dissertation. Their generous contributions go well beyond that central phrase, and are only partly acknowledged in the endnotes. That I received helpful chapter-by-chapter commentary, not just from them, but also from Peter Stansky and Ian Watt, was the result of a system of dissertation-level instruction at Stanford that I'm afraid I rather took for granted at the time, but now recognize as having been extraordinarily beneficial for me and my fellow students.

This project began as an undergraduate essay on T. S. Eliot and Virginia Woolf at Colgate University in 1980, and I am grateful for the continued interest of Jane Lagoudis Pinchin, for whose class that essay was written. Also at its source are four other extraordinary teachers, Jonathan Kistler, Paul Luftig, David Pearlman, and Philip Restaino. Jay Fliegelman and Richard Brodhead provided support and guidance without which the work could not have been completed. In early stages of writing I received valuable assistance from William Chace, Charles Fifer, Thomas Moser, and Alexander Welsh; in the later stages, particular sections of the manuscript were thoroughly and insightfully commented on by Helen Tartar, Lynn Wardley, Mark Wollaeger, and by Regenia Gagnier again, while the anonymous reader assigned by Stanford University Press was equally gracious in responding to the whole—I am especially thankful for these most substantial contributions. Cathy Caruth, Mary Jean Corbett, Katherine Snyder, Lon Wilhelms, and others guided me to particular research sources; Agnes Albert provided personal knowledge concerning her aunt, Agnes Tobin; and I owe much of my other primary material to the diligent creativity of Stanford's Inter-Library Loan Division at Green Library, especially Sonia Moss, who got me books and pamphlets from, well, everywhere. My research assistant, Cristina Ruotolo, corrected many errors in my quotations and other information; Ellen Smith thoroughly edited the manuscript; and Siobhán Hutson helped with corrections in the proofreading. Henrietta Garnett, Patricia McLean, and Richard Shone responded graciously to my interest in Duncan Grant's *Interior*. My book writing began with the support of an Alden Dissertation Award from Stanford and ended with the support of a Morse Fellowship from Yale.

By the nature of my subject I have often depended on the informal contributions of a number of my friends, among them Daniel Jaul, Gordon O'Reilly, Margaret Callan, Kim Edwards, Marshall Eisen, Barbara Felling, Aryeh Gritzerstein, Mike Jones, David Long, Christopher Lowe, Sarah Marcham, Cindy Montgomery, Rose and Hans Parkinson, Larry and Elizabeth Schaaf, Katie Towler, John Whittier-Ferguson, and Deborah Wise, as well as my family. Perhaps most practically significant have been those friends with whom I have undertaken various collaborative efforts in writing and teaching, among them Ehud Havezelet, Jean Lee, Leslie Moore, Frank Murray, Gail Perez, Steven Reese, Ann Watters, and Mark Wollaeger. The greatest of these debts is to Heather Gordon, for our work together at Stanford's Center for Teaching and Learning taught me much of what I know and value about cooperative vision.

This book is dedicated to two teachers who saw much together, friends who have helped others see—"how describe the pure delight?"—: to Paul Luftig and, in thankful memory, Elaine Spitz.

Galway, Ireland   V.L.

Contents

A Note to the Reader

Throughout this book, I could put the word "friendship" in quotation marks nearly every time I use it; for my object of study is almost always the word "friendship," rather than some supposed social, historical, or psychological fact it might denote. But to avoid unnecessary distraction the text uses quotation marks only when calling particular attention to the fact of idiom. In the same way, friendship-between-the-sexes is distinguished from single-sex friendship—with the cumbersome phrases "heterosexual friendship," "friendship between the sexes," "friendship between men and women," "cross-sex friendship," and "male/female friendship"—only as often as seems needed. The reader should assume *friendship* to designate an *idiom* describing extramarital, extrafamilial, *heterosexual* relations; my use of each of these terms is further explained in the Introduction.

In quotations, also to avoid distraction, I have normalized punctuation in some otherwise confusing instances. Spaced ellipsis points (. . .) indicate that portions of the original text have been omitted; closed suspension points (...) are used to replicate ellipses in the original.

Seeing Together

*Friendship Between the
Sexes in English Writing,
from Mill to Woolf*

Introduction

Try to talk about friendship between the sexes, and the conversation always becomes about something else. The inevitable shift is part of what marks the topic as interesting—that it immediately summons a whole range of associations about the way people interact—and is also what defines it as an *idiomatic* problem: friendship between men and women, no matter how intensely it may be valued by how many people, is scarcely nameable as a thing unto itself. Contemporary phrasings, like their predecessors in earlier times, define male/female friendship according to what it is not. "Just friends," "only friends," "not lovers," and similar combinations all in effect describe friendship negatively; all insist that what friendship is not is sexual union or attraction; and all, in the process of making that negative declaration, invite the suspicion that what is being talked about is in fact not friendship but sex, whether unacknowledged, unrealized, or unrevealed. To begin defining friendship according to the absence of sex may be to say much about one's expectations concerning gender relations, but it is also to offer little hope for being able to say what friendship actually is.

And so, while people continue to refer to cherished opposite-sex colleagues and acquaintances as "friends," the very existence of friendship between the sexes is left in doubt. The release of the film *When Harry Met Sally . . .* in 1989 prompted general discussion in forums ranging from the *New York Times* to *USA Today* as to whether "friendship between men and women" was "possible," and the film's ads assumed an audience eager for an answer to that question.[1] Indeed, the film begins by offering its plot as testing a pair of opposing answers. Yet neither seems very promising. "We are just going to be friends, OK?" Sally defensively insists; ". . . men and women can't be friends . . . ," Harry emphatically responds, "because the sex thing is always out there, so the friendship is doomed, and that's the end of the story."[2]

It's not the end of Harry and Sally's story, of course. But it might as well be as far as "friendship" is concerned; and there seem few other sources to which one would turn for a true story of friendship between the sexes. This book developed from a sense that the words being used to discuss affectionate relations between men and women were inadequate to the diversity and significance those bonds often demonstrated. It began with a guess that writers from the not-so-distant past might provide models for testing and developing the questionable idiom of the present. The book opens by studying a period when, because of shifts in the nature of production and interaction, cooperative relations between men and women gained great prominence in public discussion, but when cross-sex "friendship" was defined, much as now, doubtfully and in terms of sexlessness. Ensuing chapters describe how that mid-Victorian definition gave way, by the end of the nineteenth century, to a dual meaning, whereby "friendship" could still denote doubtful, sexless relations but could also be used to indicate newly conspicuous extramarital sexual relations—"friendship" was coming to mean anything and everything as the working relations of the sexes changed. The final chapters focus on the years of the First World War and their aftermath: in wartime, "friendship" was suddenly made to revert to its earlier meaning of sexlessness, but without any of the earlier attendant doubts—"friendship" between the sexes was accepted, hailed, even celebrated. That didn't last long. Only in the years after World War I, when "friendship" had been gutted of any real meaning, could those who had been most dissatisfied with its earlier uses (because they wished most ardently for better ways of naming relations between the sexes) begin to develop real alternatives.

It is to those Modernist experiments, in their relation to the preceding series of Victorian tests, rejections, and reconsiderations, that this book looks for solutions to the idiomatic bind in which "friendship" finds itself today. What follows, then, is a history of the changes undergone by the idioms for friendship between the sexes during times when that relation was, as now, a matter of urgent public concern: that history issues in a practical account of how the idiomatic tests of the historical past may be brought to bear on the suspect idioms for human affections in the present.

The two positions voiced at the opening of *When Harry Met Sally* . . . , one weakly claiming "friendship," the other flatly dismissing it, were very familiar to the Victorians. A compendium entitled *A Woman's Thoughts About Women*, for instance, juxtaposed the same conflict thus: "While allowing that a treaty of friendship, 'pure and simple,' can exist between a man and a woman—under peculiar circumstances, even between a young man and a young woman—it must also be allowed that the experiment is difficult, often dangerous, so dangerous that the matter-of-fact half of the world will not believe in it at all." [3] The recent film and the Victorian book share not just skepticism but also a terminology of limitation and risk: being "*just* friends" is "doomed" in one; "friendship 'pure and simple' " is "difficult, often dangerous, so dangerous" as to be discounted in the other. The italics, quotation marks, and asides are typical of such accounts from past and present. Talking about friendship makes talk nervous; "friendship" prompts, particularly in a period when there is special tension about relations between the sexes, apologetic emphasis or absolute denial, schisms and gaps even at the level of punctuation and syntax.

That is because "friendship" marks a challenge to basic and accustomed categories for relations between the sexes. If "friendship" is uncertain that is because other possibilities, "more" than friendship or less than friendship, aren't as secure as they might seem either. "Friendship" between the sexes is, and has been for some time, a fundamental threat to the stability and separateness of the prevalent categories for gender relations; it challenges the boundaries of socially acknowledged interaction between men and women. It suggests that the labels and demarcations that distinguish courtship and ordinary working relations, for instance, are less absolute than the commonplace idioms suggest. Where discourse would validate only a few mutually exclusive categories for relations between the sexes, "friendship" invites the likelihood of exceptions, trespassing across borders that commonly accepted expressive modes would preserve.

In Victorian England, "friendship" challenged the defining lines between some of the most valued bourgeois institutions—courtship, the family home, and the place of work. On various occasions, "friendship" might be comfortably placed in any of these, for the term's instability made it easy to appropriate as a way of affirming positive relations in the processes of wooing, maintaining a marriage, or even laboring. But what bourgeois Victorians were far less ready to accept was the possibility that "friendship" might be linked to all of these areas simultaneously and so suggest overlaps between them. In Victorian texts, claims of "friendship" repeatedly introduce the threat that sexual attraction may be operating in the workplace, or the even greater threat that the cooperative dynamics of shared work might have their impact on courtship and domesticity—that the domains of work, sex, and family might all be interwoven. "Friendship" thus marks and defines the barriers to a complete and integral vocabulary for describing the relations of women and men.

Each of the ostensibly discrete arenas—the family home, the realm of courtship, and the workplace—was, in the mid-Victorian years especially, under intense pressure. Moreover, all were coming into social, economic, moral, and linguistic conflict. The industrial "reorganization of production which separated the household from the workplace"[4] had left both categories unstable—hence the famous Victorian bourgeois tendency to cultivate "Work" and "Home" as cherished abstract values,[5] and hence also the understanding that the homes of workers must conceal scenes of sexual misrule hardly different from the places of interaction between idle men and women yet undomesticated. At the same time, the expansion of literacy and communication resources made the stakes involved in the representation of gender relations ever higher.[6] The same nation whose print media seemed dedicated to the examination and discussion of sex[7] was simultaneously absorbed in the attempts by "workers, employers, and concerned observers . . . to formulate languages in which to negotiate their relationships to each other and to a changing environment."[8]

These attempts granted "friendship" varying degrees of importance. Working-class texts were far less likely to insist on the sharp categorical distinctions of their bourgeois counterparts; they were thus also less likely to muster the terms for providing "friendship" with even a negative definition. On the one hand, the obscurity of categories for gender relations among the working classes followed from a lack of access to certain kinds of information—about sexual conduct, about rights and practices specific to the sexes. On the other hand, one might guess that the representation of hetero-sexual friendship did not become a problem among the working classes until mass-media culture enforced the assimilation of certain bourgeois assumptions.[9]

Yet those assumptions underwrote the idioms and actions of the people who, while desperately struggling to maintain the sanc-tity of their own homes, continued to rule England and a great deal of the world. Though repeatedly doubted, displaced, or dis-missed, "friendship" stood in these years as a principal challenge to common understandings in bourgeois discourse surrounding every major realm of human interaction: work, affection, combat, com-munity, imagination, and so forth. The chapters that follow trace the processes by which the prevailing categories asserted themselves against friendship in Victorian and post-Victorian texts, and exam-ine the resistant idioms that were broached nevertheless, in affirma-tion of cross-sex cooperation that the dominant discourse would have overwhelmed. From John Stuart Mill and his feminist essay-writing contemporaries to Robert Browning; from late-Victorian Shelleyans, like Thomas Hardy, to Henry James; from early Mod-ern novelists like Joseph Conrad and D. H. Lawrence through the propaganda pamphlets of World War I to the anti-War and post-War creations of Virginia Woolf and her Bloomsbury comrades, the English texts examined in this book struggle to position "friend-ship" in ways that destabilize the terms according to which their educated contemporaries understood heterosexual relations.

The difficulties of representing friendship between the sexes had worried English writers for centuries—the concern generally being that a claim to friendship might conceal, or might be expected to conceal, some dangerous sexual motive. As early as the 1400's, holy men and women exchanged "letters of friendship . . . filled . . . with assurances (or warnings) that they should not be construed as letters of love."[10] Dorothy Osborne's letters to Sir William Temple, written in 1653, despaired of being able to describe their "friend-ship" to others: "Alas, how few there are that ever heard of such a thing, and fewer that understand it. . . ."[11] Near the end of the eigh-teenth century, John Gregory warned his daughters, "Thousands of women of the best hearts and finest parts have been ruined by men who approach them under the specious name of friendship," a warning roughly echoed by Mary Wollstonecraft Godwin, who declared herself "convinced" of the existence of "friendship between persons of different sexes," yet acknowledged that "nothing can more tend to destroy peace of mind. . . ." [12] Commentary on cross-sex "friendship" since the Victorian age has continued to express fear and doubt, and, most importantly, a sense that "friendship" may only weakly stave off the inevitable. One of Robert Browning's characters reports his society's expectations regarding a purported friendship between a man and a woman: " '. . . at last, e'en have it how you will, / Whatever the means, whatever the way, explodes / The consummation'—the accusers shriek." [13]

Where "friendship" is understood only to issue thus, male/female social relations must be understood to take, as their truest or sole course, the path of sexual relations. Where "friendship" defines a more complex dynamic, other possibilities emerge: my goal in this book is to help generate a more flexible vocabulary with which to describe heterosexual relations. Yet I must approach that vocabulary in ways somewhat different from those who have advanced the representation of other kinds of disestablished forms of affection. Though scholarship has helped previously suppressed relations to emerge from hiding, it reaches heterosexual "friendship" to find that it has already, and all too readily, been exposed; whereas other relations may be served by new markers, or the full reformation of old ones, to give them fresh public visibility and viability, heterosexual "friendship" requires authentication of what mainstream discourse has always acknowledged and always dismissed. Eve Kosofsky Sedgwick began her analysis of friendship between men by seeking "to hypothesize the potential unbrokenness of a continuum between homosocial and homosexual—a continuum whose visibility, for men, in our society, is radically disrupted." [14] An analysis of heterosexual friendship must instead contend with a continuum that is constantly, simplistically, and oppressively accepted as a given—the social dynamic between men and women seen as inevitably (and almost always at the expense of those in subordinate roles) giving way to the sexual, "friendship" inevitably being rendered "just friendship" by the assumption that it must indeed mask or lead to something "more"—and more compromising. Not only does the recurring question "Can men and women be 'just friends'?" assume heterosexual attraction is a universal norm; it also assumes that attraction to be universally definitive of cross-sex relations. Thus, the term "heterosocial" would need to carry a slightly different emphasis from "homosocial," drawing attention primarily to the social, public significance of dynamics whose sexual identity is hardly ever challenged.

Such emphasis would be consistent with that of past attempts to validate friendship between the sexes; but in the nominal act of displacing the sexual in favor of the social, "heterosocial" would seem destined only to recapitulate the fate of earlier idioms for male/female friendship. It is true that Victorian and post-Victorian attempts to produce viable names for friendship between the sexes are terrifically illuminating, both for the names they summon, test, and (more often than not) finally reject and for the network of social relations and structures they challenge and reposition to afford a place for friendship. But this study does not seek to authenticate "friendship," or "heterosocial" desire, or any comparable term. Though I often rely on the shorthand phrase "heterosexual friendship" when describing my subject—as a quick way of naming both a represented male/female relationship and, as is more often than not the case in the pages that follow, a represented relationship between ostensible heterosexuals—that phrase must, too, be merely provisional. The history of attempts to legitimize such idioms suggests that merely renaming relationships between men and women must finally be far less productive than invoking the actions "friends" undertake together: the best evidence of the value of friendship must be found in accounts of shared actions and processes of cooperation, not in the words designating relationships themselves.

Still, the category of heterosexual friendship is itself worth introducing, if only because it has undergone so little scholarly analysis in its own right.[15] When bourgeois heterosexuality has been examined, "friendship" has been mainly ignored. Studies of society's sexually oppressed groups, though affording much attention to single-sex friendship, have often snubbed categories like "friendship" between the sexes while asserting, for their own definitional purposes, a rather uniform model of heterosexuality. The same critic who advocates study of "the oppositional practices of women, gays, even children in the history of sexuality" may refer to "the model of heterosexuality and marriage" as if heterosexuality and marriage are inevitably continuous, never themselves in opposition.[16] If "friendship" may help show heterosexuality to be diverse, the source of various modes of resistance (as well as of authoritative conventions), it may then be figured as no more or less stable than other sexual identities and, even when studied in relative isolation (as it is in this book), available for dialectical comparison with any and all.

The two most significant critical precedents for such analysis of gender-related discourse (or in any case the two that have contributed most to the conceptualization of this book) may be found in the work of philosopher Michel Foucault and of feminist historians. Foucault's accounts of discursive authority, and of the way language participates in the enforcement and undermining of power, led him near the end of his career to the study of the processes by which "sex 'is put into discourse' "; North American feminist accounts of friendships between women, often emphasizing the way women's relationships have served as an alternative to patriarchal oppression, "always . . . have revolved around an interpretation of language," as Carroll Smith-Rosenberg has observed.[17] As an alternative to dominant forms, heterosexual friendship is here conceived both in relation to the model of discursive hegemony theorized by Foucault and in comparison with the subversive modes chronicled by Smith-Rosenberg and others.

But these two approaches to the discourse of gender relations share at best an uneasy relationship. Foucault declared that "relations of power are interwoven with other kinds of relations (production, kinship, family, sexuality) for which they play at once a conditioning and a conditioned role" and "delineate general conditions of domination." Though he also declared that "one should not assume a massive and primal condition of domination" and that, rather, "there are no relations of power without resistances," neither his general statements about subversion nor his analysis of particular challenges to authority provide full assurance that oppressed individuals may overcome the "specific technology of power" he calls "discipline."[18] Foucault's account of power has been said itself to "disciplin[e] women by robbing them of the conceptual tools required in order to theorize and overcome male domination. . . ." Jana Sawicki has noted that "Foucault does sometimes speak as though the domain of sexuality were already colonized beyond redemption."[19]

Study of heterosexual friendship affords an opportunity to decolonize that domain by challenging its boundaries. "Both Foucault and feminists have pointed to the ways in which friendship provides a model for nonhierarchical, reciprocal relations that run counter to the hierarchical modes that have dominated Western society," Irene Diamond and Lee Quinby observe in introducing their collection *Feminism and Foucault: Reflections on Resistance.* "In oral and written discussion," they note, "friendship's reciprocity takes the form of dialogue, what Foucault has called 'the work of reciprocal elucidation' in which the 'rights of each person are in some sense immanent in the discussion.' "[20] Not that "friendship" names some pure mode uncontaminated by abuse: as Victorian moralists well knew, "friendship" can conceal the most insidious kinds of subterfuge or domination. But when friendship is figured as dialogue or cooperation between men and women, expressions of sexual identity may at least be posited as coequal, rather than inherently oppositional or hierarchical; moreover, insofar as friendship acknowledges rather than (according to the mid-Victorian definition) wholly suppresses sexuality, it may treat sexual divisions as *a* factor, and a negotiable one, rather than *the* factor, definitive.

Past advocates for the study of "oppositional texts" associated with gender relations have long insisted on analysis "of the concrete ways in which opposition, in spite of its textual oppression, disruptively . . . continues to assert itself."[21] The present work locates such disruption at the level of idiom, in the contestation over specific words through which relationships might be asserted or suppressed. No name for a relationship may self-evidently prove the essential existence of that relationship. But the struggle to generate a viable name for a group of real or imagined relationships highlights the forces then marshaled against those relationships' coming into being, or coming into acceptance, as well as the sources supporting their emergence. Idiom, then, is a useful place to assess how power is both asserted and undermined: focusing on idiom, one may assert the value of past texts and the relations they describe without ignoring the social and linguistic restrictions enforced upon them.

In the study of gender relations, a focus on idiom may help avoid one of the most obvious traps. Some scholars who have considered

Victorian male/female friendship in passing have, in Alice Rossi's words, "unwittingly [fallen] in line with the Victorian writers and early twentieth-century commentators in drawing up a balance sheet of evidence of the 'did they or didn't they sleep together' variety."[22] Perhaps the worst consequence of such a tendency would be its likely prompting a re-inscription of the Victorian standards whereby "friendship" would be measured "merely" according to the exclusion of sex. On the contrary, the post-Victorian history of "friendship" suggests that its most valuable intellectual allies are often those who have been most explicit about sex's interrelation with other human dynamics—Freud most conspicuous among them, but Edward Carpenter, the "New Woman" writers, Bloomsbury, and others as well; such figures make it more possible to place "friendship" among a full range of gender-related possibilities. The best way to avoid the gossipy speculation, foolish prudery, and historical myopia that may result from a too-easy application of dualisms is to focus on "friendship" as a complex fact of language: to give careful attention to the way it is named and negotiated in particular texts and to the discursive context in which those occasions are placed. That phrases associated with heterosexual friendship from the historical past still seem familiar makes all the more important present-day recognition of the historical specificity of those idioms, as well as of similar idioms now used—of what, then and now, it has seemed possible and impossible to say.

It has often seemed all too easy to use words like "friendship" to designate conventional relationships. That is one of the main reasons why it was so hard to authenticate the term in reference to cross-sex working relationships less commonly accepted. Among the mid-Victorians, "friendship" was readily accepted as a necessary attribute to marital happiness; it also, quite separately, designated a sexless (if gravely doubted) alternative to courtship among the unmarried. (Those uses are illustrated in Chapters 1 and 2.) In the succeeding generation, beginning in the 1890's, meanings for heterosexual "friendship" proliferated, so that it might now apply both to sexless relations and to newly acknowledged models of extramarital cohabitation and sexual interaction (as illustrated in Chapters 3 and 4.) At each of these stages, "friendship" seemed drawn inexorably toward the bourgeois ways of talking about sex, sanctity, and social control: the activities that would give "friendship" a positive content were persistently drawn away from "friendship" and toward other kinds of vocabulary (words associated with sin, for instance, or with heavenly duty, or with family bonds).

But in the years of the First World War, when heterosexual cooperation seemed to serve the nation's material goals, "friendship" was suddenly and insidiously promulgated as a national virtue. "Friendship," or "comradeship," was proclaimed to be the definitive attribute of those men and women who were working together for the sake of the nation, and the sexual associations that had previously burdened the word in discussion of working relations were at once dismissed. "The sexes were meant to work together, and our factories and public offices have proved how easily they can do it," proclaimed a typical celebrant of the new "sex-comradeship," who explained, "There is no sex in brains and work. Men hated women workers before the War. They were rivals. Men admired women workers after the war began. They were equals and comrades."[23]

In this transformation of friendship from taboo to triumph (described in Chapter 5), neither stage admits of any dissension: unanimity of sentiment—at least on the part of men, on whose passions heterosexual cooperation seems principally to depend—is absolute. Such consensus depends on an implicit agreement that there is an absolute divide between sex, on the one hand, and brains and work, on the other. At the same time, wartime friendship would allow the workplace to subsume courtship and family relations, as another commentator made more explicit: "The men of the factories are not an alien race. They are our fathers, brothers, and sweethearts, just as the boys in the trenches are: and anyone who attempts to cause division between us is no friend, but a foe to the workers."[24]

"Friendship" had been co-opted on behalf of a monolithic understanding of gender relations that merely reprioritized convention in order to see happy heterosexual relations as synonymous with military cooperation: almost as if everything else was now "just sex," or "not war work." To defy this model of gender relations, highlighting the distinctions that war work was said to elide, was to be a foe to the war effort. Pacifist, promiscuous, and well-immersed in their own cooperative schemes, members of the Bloomsbury community and other anti-War artists attempted in these years to construct a model of home in which sex and work both had places. They sought not an alternative model of "friendship" but in fact an alternative *to* "friendship," one that would define extramarital and extrafamilial relations according to some other dynamic (as described in Chapter 6).

Bloomsbury's wartime productions stand as an exemplary series of "oppositional texts," contesting an enforced discourse of gender relations with a new and compelling set of idioms. No historical epoch better registers the way an unstable idiom like "friendship" may be appropriated to serve the most destructive ends, regardless of how such use goes against all commonly held understandings; but neither can any body of artistic productions better illustrate the degree to which such appropriation may be resisted and countered. In the face of a discourse that was powerfully enforced and popularly embraced, Bloomsbury developed its own ways of describing its cooperative efforts.

Most important about Bloomsbury's wartime creations was the way in which they transformed the subject/object paradigm according to which friendship's cogency would depend on what one sex made of its observations of the other. The most frequently described experience of the typical woman war worker was that of being gazed upon, while at work, by a group of men. Heterosexual cooperation, long practiced among the working class, was now suddenly acknowledged, but with the scrutiny devoted not to the fact of the work but to the appearance of one segment of the workers. Bloomsbury chose instead to emphasize scenes in which men and women each looked, but not upon each other; each chose his or her own field of vision, and the contiguity, analogy, or connection between those fields, and between the very acts of looking, defined the relationships. If "friendship" couldn't properly designate the necessary connections between the acts of working together, sleeping together, and together constructing a safe sense of place removed from the scenes of war, then accounts of shared imaginative activity that partook of all these elements yet might.

That Modernist construct, emphasizing shared, subjective, visual experience, extends models for friendship available from earlier texts: where Victorian texts like J. S. Mill's *Autobiography* and George Eliot's *Daniel Deronda* had sometimes defined heterosexual cooperation in terms of common *objects* of vision, a Modernist novel, less epistemologically secure, would define heterosexual friendship in terms of an uncertain action, "a way of looking on." [25] Such alternative idioms seem especially valuable in a time when terms like "friendship" are hopelessly compromised in application to heterosexual relations. And Bloomsbury's wartime and postwar exploration of the bonds men and women may create through seeing together serves as an especially apt demonstration of how compromised idioms for heterosexual friendship may not only be avoided but even, effectively, displaced.

One of the greatest challenges to representing friendship, as *When Harry Met Sally* . . . makes very much apparent, is a set of narrative conventions according to which friendship must always give way for the sake of narrative closure. *When Harry Met Sally* . . . is, from its title to its final scene, a romantic comedy whose narrative is impelled by attraction first suppressed, then acknowledged, then countered, then consummated: interludes showing elderly couples describing the trajectories of their courtships (one of these begins the film) disclose from the outset that "friendship" is just the name for the necessary tension that gives interest to a marriage plot. Sally summarizes it at the end: "We became friends. We were friends for a long time. And then we weren't. And then we fell in love." The film is designed so that, as a comedy, it can *only* end in sexual union. If the couple at the film's center were to remain "just friends," there would be no way for it to end happily—indeed, there might be no way for it to end at all. *When Harry Met Sally* . . . illustrates the continuing pertinence of a problem registered by a number of the texts to be studied in the ensuing pages: how can a story remain genuinely *about* friendship, rather than position friendship as a merely temporary stage on the way to something the story is more essentially about?

Narrative theorists who have examined novelistic endings have made clear just why this question is so difficult to answer. Studies by Barbara Herrnstein Smith, Alan Friedman, Rachel Blau DuPlessis and others have established that the novel, as a genre, and the Victorian novel in particular, has tended to close consistently in either marriage or in death [26]—so consistently that it may be said to have hampered Western societies' ability to tell stories directed towards any other ends. But in the thirteen years between Alexander Welsh's call for a consideration of "the relation of endedness to nineteenth-century convictions about human . . . history" and the *New York Times Magazine*'s suggestion, in 1991, that "closure" had been exhausted as an engaging scholarly topic,[27] critical discussions of closure thoroughly anatomized the Victorian novel's "sense of an ending" without demonstrating how it might positively affect human institutions.[28] The greatest achievement along this line has been Joseph Allen Boone's analysis of the way a "counter-tradition" of endings that *avoid* marriage "eludes the impositions of social and sexual conformity"; Boone describes the way such anti-endings enforce "the reader's active engagement in the unease of wedlock." But in Boone's dualistic model of tradition/counter-tradition, anticlosure must ultimately be valuable mainly for the way it "sets into motion organizational formats that *forego* the repose traditionally associated with fictional closure as well as with domestic felicity" (emphasis added), rather than that create new vocabulary for heterosexual relations.[29]

None of the novels studied here may be said to end in "friendship"; instead, they end having repositioned friendship in relation to various other heterosexual possibilities. That is, in addition to following the narrative process by which friendship is displaced or (in later works) enacted, they undertake an idiomatic process whereby "friendship" and other comparable terms are used, tested, avoided, discarded, replaced, and/or re-placed. Their contribution, then, is not to be measured in terms of whether closure has been avoided or fulfilled (any more than it is to be measured according to whether sex has been avoided or consummated) but rather in terms of the way it has become incidental to other enabling novelistic patterns.

Because these novels do not move inexorably or even continuously toward a final resolution of their idiomatic crises but rather undertake a series of distinct (often widely separated) moments of idiomatic testing, "friendship" may be said to be one of those novelistic "secrets" that Frank Kermode has described as being "at odds" with novelistic "sequence."

Whatever the comforts of sequence [and] connexity (I agree that we cannot do without them), it cannot be argued that the text which exhibits them will do nothing but contribute to them; some of it will be indifferent or even hostile to sequentiality. . . . To read a novel expecting the satisfactions of closure and the receipt of a message is what most people find enough to do. . . . Authors, indeed, however, keenly aware of other possibilities, are often anxious to help readers behave as they wish to; they 'foreground' sequence and message. This cannot be done without backgrounding something, and indeed it is not uncommon for large parts of a novel to go virtually unread; the less manifest portions of its text (its secrets) tend to remain secret, tend to resist all but abnormally attentive scrutiny. . . .[30]

As Peter Brooks has demonstrated, even the reader who is most avidly "reading for the plot" may also work toward resisting the temptations of plot and may attend very closely to particular phrasings.[31] And as "friendship" is often positioned as an alternative to marriage, its students cannot but be interested in the foreground of courtship narratives and their consummate moments of closure. Yet equal focus must go toward various more obscure moments of the kind Kermode highlights, especially those important not for their stake in the narrative but as distinct experiments in idiom[32]— moments when characters or narrators seem engaged in crises of definition regarding "friendship" and comparable terms.

Such experimental moments often seem to form a pattern in contrast to that proposed by the main narrative. For in a number of Victorian novels that build their story lines on the dynamics of sexual desire, "friendship" is associated with something different, a less thoroughly and consistently plotted dynamic that is religious, imaginative, or social rather than chiefly sexual. So that rather than functioning as a way of forestalling closure, in a kind of narrative version of coitus interruptus, analysis of friendship invites one temporarily to modulate narrative desire with a focus on discrete novelistic moments.[33] The key here will be to compare what the text momentarily affords in the way of a name, or names, for "friendship," in comparison to the products of other experimental moments before and after. Sometimes Kermode's term, "secrets," seems especially apt, for in George Eliot, Henry James, and Virginia Woolf, the most illuminating moments are those in which a key idiom is *withheld* rather than named, to avoid inevitable compromise with idiomatic and narrative conventions. And at other times, as in Grant Allen and Joseph Conrad, the "secret" may be found in a new way of naming friendship that is only incompletely understood by the characters who utter it.

But sometimes the key moment comes when "friendship" vanishes entirely. In the texts I discuss in the first half of this book, "friendship" cannot hold: the narratives of Browning's *The Ring and the Book* and Hardy's *Jude the Obscure*, to name but two, surely overwhelm "friendship" in favor of other categories. Yet the word is still fully significant to such texts. It elicits a great deal of discussion, a great deal of tension, and a great deal of fruitful experimentation, and is thus no less important. And that, for the purposes of reinvesting contemporary idiom, is the point. As Dominick LaCapra notes: "one *may* insist that even losing forces in history . . . have as much right to close attention as do dominant forces and pressures. To think otherwise is . . . to deprive oneself of the forms of language that can be a force, however weak and anticipatory, in preventing the subversion of ends by means. . . ."[34] In novelistic study of "friendship," critical obligations to the ends of narrative need to be modulated enough for the moments when "friendship" is enunciated to be studied as ends in themselves, satisfactory or unsatisfactory for what they achieve or enact rather than only for what they must eventually lead to.

As I consider "friendship," in the ensuing pages, I mean to identify words for momentary acts of insight and creation whose significance may be missed in the pursuit of other readerly goals. In a series of English texts, I highlight familiar phrasings intensely examined, and unfamiliar, potentially fruitful idioms and instances hopefully offered. My assumption throughout is that literature has, in the past, not only reflected dominant discourse but has also contributed to it and challenged it, and that it may still be made, through its consideration in classrooms, written forums, and elsewhere, to produce such results in the present. More precisely, I assume that literature is often the place where idiom is most diligently and constructively tested. If Victorian and Modernist writings do not authenticate "friendship," they may yet offer access to better words, motives, and actions.

Part I

*Contrary to Nature: Heterosexual
"Friendship" in Mid-Victorian England*

1

Problems of Representation in 1869

Mid-Victorian Phrasings

Prominent mid-Victorians celebrated friendship between men and valued, or at least acknowledged, friendship between women;[1] but when they addressed the possibility of friendship between men and women, they voiced considerably more skepticism. Though the Reverend Sidney Smith, for instance, claimed it "a great happiness to form a sincere friendship with a woman," in the same breath he complained that "a friendship among persons of different sexes rarely or never takes place in this country." Essayist Anna Jameson concurred: "Our conventional morality, or immorality, places men and women in such a relation socially as to render such friendships difficult and rare."[2] Popular novelist Dinah Mulock Craik believed that heterosexual friendship could not but meet with obstacles: while insisting that "he must take a very low view of human nature who dares say that these attachments, satirically deemed 'Platonic,' are impossible," Craik admitted that

at the same time, common sense must allow that they are more rare to find, and not the happiest always, when found; because in some degree they are contrary to nature. . . . While allowing that a treaty of friendship, "pure and simple," can exist between a man and a woman—under peculiar circumstances between a young man and a young woman—it must also be allowed that the experiment is difficult, often dangerous; so dangerous, that the matter-of-fact half of the world will not believe in it at all.[3]

In spite of all such difficulty and danger, the Victorians left much documentation of relationships that might now be casually referred to as "friendship" between the sexes; Craik's remarks, from her 1858 *A Woman's Thoughts About Women*, may help explain why

Victorians were nevertheless reluctant to accept general application of the term. For Craik, as for most Victorian commentators on gender relations, "friendship" would but insufficiently account for affinities between women and men. Modifying phrases like "Platonic" and "pure and simple," themselves dressed in apologetic quotation marks, needed to stand alongside "friendship" if the word was to have even temporary viability. Acknowledged matters of fact, available to "common sense," showed "friendship" to be "contrary to nature," to give way always to human interactions less experimental, more clearly defined.

In the middle years of Victoria's reign, those with the leisure to generalize about human conduct—the educated bourgeoisie—understood sex to be central to the "nature" of gender relations. "Nature" here dictated a narrative both inevitable and, when properly directed, desirable, in which the sexes tended to be drawn together sexually; and societal law and practice sanctioned that undeniable pull toward marital and family happiness. If by heterosexual "friendship" one meant the exclusion or subordination of sex—which is how the mid-Victorians characterized it—the word could serve only as an illusory barrier to the natural tendency. "Friendship" could signal either a "difficult, often dangerous" self-delusion or a doubtful ruse concealing illicit lust. Even were sexless friendship possible to maintain, such relationships would still be disruptive rather than fruitful, for, as Craik said, "it is always, if not wrong, rather pitiful, when any extraneous bond comes in between to forestall the entire affection that a young man ought to bring to his future wife, a young woman to her husband."[4] Friendship was discredited by the inevitability, moral probity, and exclusive rights of legitimate sexual attraction.

The Victorians were probably not the first to speak of sex as motivating all cross-gender relations or to "dedicat[e] themselves to speaking of it *ad infinitum*"; Michel Foucault has described that tendency as characteristic of "modern societies."[5] But though one must be cautious in speaking of Victorian discourse on sex as distinct "from what went before," or in speculating about "what the Victorians knew about sex,"[6] it is safe to say that by the late 1860's, English readers were used to finding the search for sex at the center of public discussion of cross-gender relations. The year 1869 serves as a useful marker, since by that year the Contagious Diseases Acts, originally invoked with the limited goal of containing prostitutes' spread of venereal ailments, had clearly come to be "extended well beyond their initial defined limits," as Judith Walkowitz has observed, and had "generated," among other things, "an avalanche of controversy and publications" about sexual relations.[7] If the educated English hadn't already been prepared to see sex as central to all extrafamilial heterosexual relations, and if they hadn't already been suspicious of any phrasing that might deny or muddle that association, then the newspapers of 1869, when the public contention over the authorities' pervasive search for contagious diseases reached new heights, provided a daily lesson.[8]

With sex believed to be omnipresent, and believed at least by some *to have to be* omnipresent, attempts to suggest any other basis for heterosexual relations seemed more unacceptable than ever. Words that seemed to describe only the most "innocent kind of nonsense" were just the kind to produce the most "incalculable damage" if misunderstood by the uninitiated, as Eliza Linton observed in her famous 1869 essays characterizing the circumstances faced by "The Girl of the Period":

[T]here are certain men who flirt only with married women, and others who flirt only with girls. . . . And there are some who are 'brothers,' and some who are 'fathers' to their young friends—suspicious fathers on the whole, not unlike Little Red Ridinghood's grandmother the wolf, with perilously bright eyes, and not a little danger to Red Ridinghood in the relationship, how delightful soever it may be to the wolf. Some are content with cousinship only—which however breaks down quite sufficient fences; and some are 'dearest friends,' no more, and find that an exceedingly useful centre from which to work onward and outward. For, if any peg will do on which to hang a discourse, so will any relationship or adoption serve the ends of flirting, if it be so willed.[9]

In a world where such dangerous possibilities abound, cynicism regarding heterosexual friendship would not lead one to be silent about it. Rather, as Linton's admonitory litany makes clear, a world where "any peg will do on which to hang a discourse" would generate an excess of terms, every one of them considered suspect.

Accordingly, Victorian commentators rejected each designation in turn. Craik and Litton cast doubt upon the panoply of familial idioms (" 'brother,' " " 'cousin,' " etc.) and upon phrases like "friendship 'pure and simple,' " while noting that " 'Platonic,' " perhaps the most ambitious designation, had become parodic. Mary Wollstonecraft Godwin had had to warn an earlier generation of girls that "nothing can more tend to destroy peace of mind" than "Platonic attachments." Now George Henry Lewes's *Dictionary of Philosophy* could say, with all Godwin's certainty and more regret, that "the celebrated Platonic love" had been "degraded to the expression of a maudlin sentiment between the sexes. Platonic love meant ideal sympathy; it now means the love of a sentimental young gentleman for a woman he cannot or will not marry." [10] Although the *Oxford English Dictionary* would still, late into the nineteenth century, define "Platonic" as "allied to love or affection of the opposite sex, of a purely spiritual character, and free from sensual desire," it relied on Lewes's skeptical pronouncement to illustrate how the word might be used. Other contemporary dictionaries similarly defined "Platonic" in terms of both high spirituality and the absence of carnality, but none denied that common usage tended to summon at best the latter and almost never, convincingly, the former. [11]

Other terms evoked even less. "Comrade," for instance, would later become a favorite of the famous 1890's Woman Who Did, but the mid-Victorians might have considered it most suspect of all, given its etymological association with cohabitation. The *OED* noted tersely about "comrade": "Less commonly said of women." As for "friend," the *OED* thought obsolete the use of the term to describe "a lover or paramour, of either sex," and said the word was "not ordinarily applied to lovers or relatives."

In the 1860's Victorians could extol heterosexual "friendship" in but one context: "friendship" or "comradeship" was commonly declared to be an essential element to happiness in marriage—a central part of that exclusive and "entire affection," in Craik's phrase, that spouses were supposed to feel for one another. "A man's best female friend," wrote the novelist Edward Bulwer Lytton, "is a wife of good sense and good heart, whom he loves, and who loves him. If he have that, he need not seek elsewhere." [12] Social activist Beatrice Webb would express this notion faithfully in closing her autobiography with a description of her "working comradeship founded in a common faith and made perfect by marriage; perhaps the most exquisite, certainly the most enduring, of all the varieties of happiness." [13] Modern scholarship may wonder how truly companionable was even the best Victorian "companionate marriage," as it has been designated by the historian Lawrence Stone—and "companionate" was another word the OED thought long obsolete[14]—but marriage was the one area in which Victorian discourse commonly credited men and women with enacting successful "friendship." Attempts to represent friendship *outside* marriage and family, and outside the compromising realm of courtship, amounted to challenges to a whole set of dualistic boundaries: not only the division between "natural" dynamics and those "contrary to nature," but also that between the private, domestic realm in which women and men were understood to meet and the public realm that was represented as exclusively male. Extramarital friendship would find no legitimate site until women achieved greater participation in the areas from which they had been excluded and until that participation was fully acknowledged. Mid-Victorian feminist energies focused mainly on the efforts of women (as have subsequent feminist histories of the period);[15] but the dismantling of courtship's hegemony over gender relations had obvious consequences for cross-gender relations as well. Geraldine Jewsbury, writing to Jane Welsh Carlyle, looked forward to "better days, when women will have a genuine, normal life of their own to lead," days that would include better relations both among women and between the sexes:

There, perhaps, will not be so many marriages, and women will be taught not to feel their destiny *manqué* if they remain single. They will be able to be friends and companions in a way they cannot be now. All the strength of their feelings and thoughts will not run into love; they will be able to associate with men, and make friends of them, without being reduced by their position to see them as lovers or husbands.[16]

In the meantime, no one, not even the OED, would ever explicitly prohibit calling men and women "friends"; individual Victorians invoked the word regularly. But it signaled little by itself—the OED noted that "friend" was used "*loosely* in various ways; e.g., applied to a mere acquaintance or in kind condescension" and that the word could also be used "*ironically*." The term gained validity only when applied in accepted contexts: the separate spheres occupied by the two sexes comprised the sites in which friendship between men and friendship between women, respectively, could be legitimated and even hailed. But in the absence of comparably acknowledged sites at which heterosexual friendship could be enacted or represented convincingly, the term passed on none of its prestige to cross-gender bonds. It was instead conceded to those who posed no bodily threat: to the very young and very old, to the disabled, and to the purely spiritual; extramarital friendship could be practiced convincingly only by children, the elderly, and ghosts.[17] "Friendship" and "Platonic" were assigned to an irretrievable past and the uncertain "better days" of the future.

Among the mid-Victorians, then, heterosexual "friendship" stood only for a set of disconcerting absences—above all, for the exclusion of sex, but also for the promise of unrealized reforms and for an unmapped domain unchecked by "nature." To those who wished to advocate heterosexual friendship or at least to invoke it in the service of some other cause, the challenge would be to define heterosexual friendship as a *presence*—to declare what it was, rather than to have to admit what it was not. That amounts to a narrative challenge: a way of telling a story about "friendship" rather than a story in which friendship cedes ground to something more natural, more visible, more socially sanctioned.

In this chapter and the next, I will examine mid-Victorian texts that have some stake in figuring positive versions of heterosexual "friendship" but that can rely on no legitimate term. Seeking to prove the inherent value of heterosexual cooperation, they contest a prohibitive discourse, through a series of idiomatic strategies that range from grandiose allusion and willful overstatement to gentle evasion and stubborn silence. *The Autobiography of John Stuart Mill* stands, itself, as a cooperative endeavor on the part of a man and a woman forced to legitimize their close and well-known premarital relationship: as co-authors in the process of recording their co-habitation, they acknowledged and sought to avoid the range of discursive traps awaiting "friendship" at mid-century. A series of texts from the pivotal year of 1869—Mill's *On the Subjection of Women*; a feminist essay collection entitled *Women's Work and Women's Culture*; and Robert Browning's *The Ring and the Book*—shows what became of attempts to characterize "friendship" according to the most obviously promising models of the time, models grounded in Victorian adulation of family relations and religious transcendence. These writings indicate how readily "friendship" could be subsumed in the categories that made its convincing representation unlikely.

If Victorian prose and poetry may serve to register the idiomatic conventions that circumscribed "friendship," the novel best illustrates how such idioms were in turn conditioned by the customary narratives of gender relations. And the novelistic career of George Eliot, the subject of Chapter 2, provides the most illustrative series of tests for the various suspect idioms. Eliot's experiments issue in mid-Victorian England's greatest achievement in representing heterosexual friendship—the assignment of a continuing, nameless, uncompromised narrative position for it. Under the circumstances, what these texts by Mill, Browning, Eliot, and others achieve toward establishing a credible ground for the unnameable is indeed extraordinary. But their particular failures, and their apologies for those failures, may be equally important; for the Victorians' least successful idioms sound familiar precisely because they still echo in current attempts to name the relationships of the Victorians, and of their descendants.

Wooing, Working, or Worshipping?
John Stuart Mill's "Friendship"

The Autobiography of John Stuart Mill invests equal energy into its profoundly ambitious claims and its apologies for the ambitiousness of those claims. Nowhere are those emphases more apparent than in the book's presentation of a close and sometimes co-habitational twenty-year "friendship" between its subject and his eventual wife, Harriet Taylor; for the *Autobiography* attempts to characterize that relationship as not only exemplary and essential to Mill's public career but also excusable and acceptable according to the conventional standards of bourgeois mid-Victorians. The *Autobiography* diligently argues that the life of the mind, when lived according to liberal ideals, might achieve many forms of legitimate satisfaction otherwise unattainable: the project's ultimate rhetorical test—and the moment in that argument that has met with the most skepticism over the years—is its claim that adherence to the life of the mind might allow an unmarried man to sustain, with supreme satisfaction, a long-standing "friendship" with a married woman.

By the time John Stuart and Harriet Taylor Mill began work on the *Autobiography*, in 1854, their relationship had long been a matter of speculation and discussion. They met in 1830, when Harriet Taylor had already been married for four years to a junior partner in a wholesale pharmaceuticals concern, and J. S. Mill had become well known as an East India Company colonial administrator and as a writer, editor, and reviewer with the potential to match the achievements of his celebrated philosopher father. Their relationship developed rapidly. In less than three years, Harriet Taylor began a trial separation from her husband, and Mill followed her to France. By the spring of 1834 the news of that rendezvous was conspicuous enough so that it was the first item the gossip-hungry Thomas and Jane Carlyle would pick up upon returning to London after two years away.[18]

By the summer of 1836, Thomas Carlyle was speculating that the unconventional relationship with Harriet Taylor must lead Mill to a melodramatic death from lovesickness (though overwork and the recent death of his father were probably the main causes for Mill's temporary decline). Carlyle wrote to a mutual acquaintance, John Sterling:

Mill, they say, writes from Nice. . . . Mrs. Taylor, it is whispered, is with him, or near him. Is it not strange, this pining away into dessication and nonentity, of our poor Mill, if it be so, as his friends all say, that his charmer is the cause of it? I have not seen any riddle of human life which I could so ill form a theory of. They are innocent says Charity: they are guilty says Scandal: then why in the name of wonder are they dying broken-hearted? Alas, tho' he speaks not, perhaps his tragedy is more tragical than that of any of us: this very item that he does not speak, that he never could speak, but was to sit imprisoned as in the thick ribbed ice, voiceless, uncommunicating, is it not the most tragical circumstance of all?[19]

Carlyle's speculation, however hyperbolic, that enforced silence might make Mill a "nonentity" usefully illustrates how "contrary to nature" and beyond articulation an apparently unconsummated heterosexual relationship might seem. The suggestion is that if Mill's affection isn't socially transgressive then it must be self-destructive. Mill survived, of course, and as his reputation grew in the 1840's through his *System of Logic* and *Principles of Political Economy*, it was John Taylor who seemed to become the nonentity: Harriet Taylor's husband would leave his house for the evening, she would stay home, and Mill would arrive. But that arrangement might well seem to endow the relationship with every troubling element that Dinah Craik had attributed to "friendship, 'pure and simple.' " The matter-of-fact half of the world—of which Carlyle, as gossip if not as philosopher, can serve as a good representative— had been skeptical and determined the relationship to be "not the happiest always when [or if] found," to put it mildly; and the extra-marital tie had certainly mitigated "the entire affection" a wife should feel for her husband, even if it did not overwhelm it entirely.[20] To credit this relationship as both happy and moral would be to deny the demands of "nature."

That denial is precisely what the Mills could be expected to articulate when they wrote about themselves. Work on the *Autobiography* immediately succeeded Mill's full-length undermining of the term "Nature" in an essay of that name: "the doctrine that man ought to follow nature," Mill declared, ". . . is equally irrational and immoral."[21] Harriet Taylor had written early in their acquaintance, "I do not believe *affection* to be natural to human beings."[22] Their account of their relationship would not prove it to have been "natural," but rather a cooperative arrangement, deliberately weighed.

Yet Carlyle's assumption—that if the early stages of their relationship were indeed celibate, they had to be characterized by some extraordinary act of sublimation—has been shared by many subsequent commentators. Ever since F. A. Hayek published *John Stuart Mill and Harriet Taylor: Their Correspondence and Subsequent Marriage*, in 1951, the relationship has received increased attention: feminist scholarship has examined it especially closely during the past two decades, toward assessing the contributions of these two founding figures. But that scholarly priority may still influence contemporary understanding of the relationship less than does a romantic pattern familiar to modern heterosexual bourgeois professionals, and perhaps implicit even in Hayek's title. Everyone likely to consider the Mills knows the common narrative of intellectual interaction that issues "naturally" in sexual consummation and, sometimes, in marriage. Everyone knows some version of that story, and everyone recognizes the motives, priorities, frustrations, and deceptions that circumscribe the story's "real" center as it works its way toward, or perversely defies, consummation. Those assumptions may not only tempt one to condescend to the

Mills and treat them anachronistically but may also obscure what would otherwise remain the central scholarly concern: not the Mills' sexual history, but what they produced as writers and how they produced it.[23]

Such assumptions always trouble heterosexual friendship's position in discourse.[24] It is almost impossible to invoke heterosexual friendship, no matter how forcefully or persuasively, without alluding also to the common assumptions that would cast it into doubt (as, for instance, in idioms ranging from "friendship 'pure and simple' " to the more familiar "just friends"). Successful representation of friendship thus means focusing readerly attention on something besides the nominal subject—that is, on something besides the relationship itself.

What the Mills wrote about their relationship, as they collaborated in describing it in the *Autobiography*, suggests an interest in such an alternative focus—though on the part of one co-author more than the other, at least at first. Most of the impetus for representing the years of friendship in any substantial way seems to have come from Harriet Taylor Mill; the ostensible autobiographer's immediate inclination appears to have been to disclose as little as possible. By January 1854, J. S. Mill wrote to his wife of three years that his incomplete draft of his "life" contained, "in a perfectly publishable state,"

a full writing out as far as anything can write out, what you are, as far as I am competent to describe you, & what I owe to you—but, besides that until revised by you it is little better than unwritten, it contains nothing about our private circumstances, further than shewing that there was an intimate friendship for many years, & you only can decide what more is necessary or desirable to say in order to stop the mouths of enemies hereafter. The fact is that there is about as much written as I *can* write without your help & we must go through this together & add the rest to it at the very first opportunity. . . . [25]

The wavering from "perfectly publishable" to "little better than unwritten" reflects both his uncertainty about the correct means of representing the particular issue and his growing understanding of the project's being fundamentally collaborative. By the time he described the same portion to her two weeks later, J. S. Mill had become even more tentative about what he had produced on his own:

of what particularly concerns *our* life there is nothing yet written, except the descriptions of you, & your effect on me; which are at all events a permanent memorial of what I know you to be, & of . . . what I owe to you *intellectually*. That, though it is the smallest part of what you are to me, is the most important to commemorate, as people are comparatively willing to suppose all the rest. But we have to consider, which we can only do together, how much of our story it is advisable to tell, in order to make head against the representations of enemies when we shall not be alive to add anything to it. If it was not to be published for 100 years I should say, tell all, simply & without reserve. As it is there must be care taken not to put arms into the hands of the enemy.[26]

In a subsequent letter, Mill further described what he had written as "show[ing] confidential friendship & strong attachment ending in marriage when you were free & ignores there having been any scandalous suspicions about us," and asked for his wife's response.[27]

His self-deprecation did not prevent her from including an element of rebuke in her reply:

I feel sure dear that the Life is not half written and that half that is written will not do. Should there not be a summary of our relationship from its commencement in 1830—I mean given in a dozen lines—so as to preclude other and different versions of our lives . . . —our summer excursions, etc. [?] This ought to be done in its genuine truth and simplicity—strong affection, intimacy of friendship, and no impropriety. It seems to me an edifying picture for those poor wretches who cannot conceive friendship but in sex—nor believe that expediency and the consideration for feelings of others can conquer sensuality. But of course this is not my reason for wishing it done. It is that every ground should be occupied by ourselves on our own subject.[28]

On a tack more aggressive than her husband's, Harriet Mill would not neglect the rumors so much as fend them off, both with "genuine truth and simplicity" (a phrase that echoes Craik's more tentative reference to "friendship 'pure and simple' ") and with comprehensiveness that would serve to overwhelm all unwelcome versions. The two alternatives are illuminating: the obstacles to representing "friendship" can elicit either silence or a kind of preventive verbosity.

But how, if they chose the latter option, could they occupy "every ground"? What words could they use? Where his manuscript claimed "our conduct . . . gave not the slightest ground for any other supposition than the true one, that our relation to each other was one of intimacy, entirely apart from sensuality," she altered the final phrase to "one of strong affection & confidential intimacy only." Where he had written "confidential intimacy," she changed that to "valuable friendship"; she added "friendship" at one point in the manuscript but elsewhere replaced that word with "acquaintance." By the time of the published version, Mill would excise a passage describing how they had

disdained, as every person *not* a slave of his animal appetites must do, the abject notion that the strongest & tenderest friendship *cannot* exist between a man and a woman *without* a sensual relation, or that any impulses of that lower character *cannot* be put aside when regard for the feelings of others, or even when only prudence and personal dignity require it.[29] (emphasis added)

Including that passage would not have been consistent with Harriet Mill's insistence on seizing "every ground" on their "own" subject; its five negatives would have gone a long way toward saying how that ground ought not to be occupied, but the sequence makes no positive claims. It thus contributes little toward valorizing a relationship that the *Autobiography* would ultimately wish to portray as nothing less than "the honour and chief blessing" of its subject's "existence."[30] The Mills needed a vocabulary that would allow them to say not only what their relationship had barred, but what it had made possible.

The vocabulary of "Platonic love" could not be a suitable option, as I have already suggested: for years, Carlyle's letters had mockingly referred to Mrs. John Taylor as "Mrs. (Platonica) Taylor" or as "[Mill's] *Platonica*," while at the same time describing her as "some young philosophic beauty," or as "a living romance heroine."[31] Nor was the word "intimacy," which John and Harriet Mill each seemed ready to employ, any less risky. The *OED* would later in the century give three definitions for the word, two of which referred at length to people's being "very familiar" and "familiarly associated," and the third of which read, simply and finally, "*euphem.* of illicit sexual intercourse."[32]

The idiomatic strategy finally chosen for the *Autobiography* is of course famous; it is indeed what has attracted much recent interest to the document. Rather than attempting to argue on behalf of an ennobling term to name the relationship, the book offers instead a series of claims about the quality and quantity of the autobiographer's intellectual debt:

What I owe, even intellectually, to her, is in its detail almost infinite. . . .

Not only during the years of our married life, but during many of the years of confidential friendship which preceded, all my published writings were as much her work as mine.

The writings . . . were not the work of one mind, but the fusion of two. . . . [33]

These are the passages that have prompted a biographical debate, founded on opposite and equally emphatic answers to questions such as, "Was Harriet Taylor as smart and influential as the *Autobiography* says?" and "Was Mill blinded by love into thinking she was?" But the Mills' correspondence, as quoted above, shows that they themselves saw these remarks as disproportionate—necessarily and deliberately disproportionate. Mill's February 1854 letter to his wife declares "what I owe to you *intellectually*" to be the "smallest part" of his debt, yet at the same time "the most important to commemorate, as people are comparatively willing to suppose all the rest." Instead of the always questionable idioms surrounding heterosexual "friendship," the *Autobiography* would apply a vocabulary associated with intellectual achievement. Exaggeration, or at least disproportionate representation, would serve the book as a progressive contribution and as a defensive tactic. Describing their intellectual interaction thus allowed the Mills to cover vulnerable ground without depending on inherently compromised terms.

That they arrived at that rhetorical alternative for a work begun in early 1854 seems no accident. The Mills, like much of the rest of intellectual England, were then reading a work that contained the most idealistic and absolutist claims for a woman's influence upon a male philosopher's career, claims linked, furthermore, to the most emphatic praise for heterosexual "friendship" ever to reach Victorian England. In early February 1854, J. S. Mill reported to his wife that he had "read through another new volume of Comte" and had found "no fresh bad in it." [34] Throughout the early 1850's, in nearly annual volumes of his *System of Positive Polity*, the French philosopher Auguste Comte was prescribing an ideal human society. He made recommendations about nearly every kind of personal interaction, but devoted his highest praise and most detailed instructions to friendship between the sexes. Indeed, he declared,

For perfect friendship, difference of sex is essential. . . . No other voluntary tie can admit of such full and unrestrained confidence. It is the source of the most unalloyed happiness that man can enjoy; for there can be no greater happiness than to live for another.[35]

Comte considered himself to be speaking from his own triumphant experience. Though history records Clotilde de Vaux, the woman Comte had so happily lived for, as an impoverished aristocrat who was less intelligent, appreciative of, and devoted to Comte than was his prostitute wife, Comte remembered her as his "Saint Clotilde, thou who wert to me in the stead of wife, of sister, and of child," his "loved pupil" and "true fellow-worker." She had died of tuberculosis within two years after they had met, but Comte claimed that all of his subsequent career had been governed by her "angel influence." And Comte surely did all he could to keep that influence strong. He derived from it a full system of private worship, which he expounded in turn into an integral part of his Positivist religion. Each "true positivist" who followed Comte's direction was enjoined to offer to the woman who was his own "personal patron," "guardian angel," or "household god" three daily prayers: the longest at "the first hour of each day to place the whole day under the protection of the best representatives of Humanity"; the shortest at noon; and a third "at the approach of sleep to protect the harmony of the brain from disturbance during the night."[36]

One of John Stuart Mill's great unheralded achievements is his diagnosis of Comte's obsession with ritual: poor Comte, said Mill, had no sense of humor. "We notice this without intending any reflection on M. Comte," Mill would explain ten years later in his book-length response to Comte, "for a profound conviction raises a person above the feeling of ridicule. But there are passages in his writings which, it really seems to us, could have been written by no man who had ever laughed." These Mill would see as resulting from Comte's typically French "mania for regulation." But Mill believed Comte's rules to be misdirected more in their means than in their ends. "There is nothing really ridiculous in the devotional practices which M. Comte recommends towards a cherished mem-óry or an ennobling ideal, when they come unprompted from the depths of individual feeling," he insisted, "but there is something ineffably ludicrous in enjoining that everybody shall practice them three times daily . . . not because his feelings require them, but for the premeditated purpose of getting his feelings up."[37]

By 1865, when Mill wrote those words, he had perhaps become forgetful of the deliberate rigor of his own devotions in the years following his beloved Harriet's death in 1858.[38] But in 1854, reading Comte's *System* and reporting on it to Harriet while he was at work on the early stages of the *Autobiography* must have prompted certain anxieties about his own project—anxieties more profound even than those suggested when the sober Mill mocked Comte's lack of a sense of humor (in what must, after all, be acknowledged one of the great cases in the history of philosophy of the pot disparaging the kettle's obscurity). In noting that an extreme elevation of woman might throw an "irresistable air of ridicule over the whole project," the Mills must have recognized Comte's book as illustrating a danger inherent in the way they were depicting themselves in the *Autobiography*. Their plainly stated claims of collaboration, like one that read,

During the two years which immediately preceded the cessation of my official life, my wife and I were working together at the 'Liberty,'

might be inconspicuous enough to trouble no one. But a more grandiose claim, such as,

Everything in my later writings to which any serious value can be attached . . . is in all essentials not my writing but hers

smacks of Comtian effusiveness. Indeed, that passage, from Mill's manuscript notes, is the one that was changed, apparently at Harriet's insistence, to one already quoted:

not only during the years of our married life, but during many of the years of confidential friendship which preceded, all my published writings were as much her work as mine.[39]

The difference between attributing the whole product to Harriet and attributing half the working process to her was immense. That difference would not necessarily determine whether the *Auto-*

biography's claims would be taken seriously or protect it from the same kind of light condescension that Mill had extended to Comte's *System*. But the decision to depict Harriet as a co-worker rather than as a "guardian angel" was, finally, what would determine whether the *Autobiography* could distinguish its ambitious claims from Comte's as both credible and progressive.[40] Though Comte explained the English popularity of his *System* according to its "immense improvements in the position of women," Mill and his feminist contemporaries recognized that Comte was generating yet one more image of the "Angel in the House," the passive, benign female figure of which England already had many images available.[41] "Positivism," wrote the feminist Frances Power Cobbe, "having allotted to woman the position of Vice Goddess, proceeds logically to make her like all other idols, an image of Repose." Mill noted that Comte would maintain "the complete subordination of the wife to the husband, and of women generally to men" in a system under which women were either "treated as grown children" or "exalted as goddesses." Under the Comtian scheme, a *Contemporary Review* columnist complained, "Woman is the object of worship . . . and yet woman . . . is to find her highest object in ministering to . . . the lords of thought." While drafting the *Autobiography*, Mill remarked on the danger of Comtian men's seeking to exploit women's "alertness & their practical sagacity for the interests of their own success." Comte himself may have been sensitive to the Victorian belief that friendship required equality, as his remark about heterosexual friendship's "excluding the possibility of rivalry" suggests; but readers like Mill could recognize that friendship figured as worship was mere oppression, not less when it appeared before or during the marriage of an active man and a passively influential woman.[42]

The *Autobiography*'s case for friendship may be distinguished from Comte's in its subtle but insistent presentation of Harriet Taylor Mill and John Stuart Mill at work together. Its reference to their "working together at the *Liberty*" made the point in passing; the comment that "all my published writings were as much her work as mine" made the point more emphatically; the declaration that "there was not a sentence . . . that was not several times gone through by us together," illustrated a positive version of cooperation that might be hoped to bar any imputation of illicitness.[43] For the image of two writers at work is erotic only in a very precise and un-Victorian sense. Further, writing was an activity Victorian convention grudgingly accepted as available to both women and men,[44] so no one would deny the Mills' overlapping (if not equal) rights to the ground at which they showed themselves meeting. Thus, the *Autobiography*'s depiction of heterosexual activity could make a positive claim for the relationship that defined it not according to compromised or exaggerated idioms but through a description of the same acceptable activity of which the book itself was a product.

The *Autobiography* could derive only so much narrative energy from deploying the act of writing as image and proof of the nature of the Mills' relationship. Even where it willingly exceeds apparent generic limits and becomes the story of two people rather than one, only a low proportion of the text can reasonably be devoted to descriptions of cooperative composition: the physical process of writing, whether it involves one person or two, doesn't often constitute an exciting or instructive plot. And the *Autobiography* would not suggest that Harriet Taylor had "any desire . . . to mingle in the turmoil & strife" of other occupations typically undertaken only by men. When Phyllis Rose, one of the commentators most sympathetic to the *Autobiography*'s depictions of the Mills' relationship, characterizes the book as a "monument in the annals of Victorian domesticity," she rightly acknowledges the precise limits of the locus in which it images cooperation: the home, even if not necessarily the version of the home the Victorians were readiest to glorify.[45] Mill's life is offered as having put into practice a model of heterosexual cooperation, but that model does not obviously extend into the world of the East India Company or Parliamentary activities that had given authority to Mill's social declarations.

Nor would Mill's more general consideration of relations between the sexes, his 1869 text *On the Subjection of Women*, move the argument much further. While he acknowledged that women's "demand for their admission into the professions and occupations hitherto closed against them becomes every year more urgent," and that "a considerable number of them have occupied themselves practically in the promotion of objects beyond their own family and household," Mill thought the "more remarkable" gains resulting from women's emancipation would be evidenced "through the influence they exercise, each in her own family. . . ." [46] The *Subjection* argued in passing for women's "admissibility to all the functions and occupations hitherto retained as the monopoly of the stronger sex" (299), but it provided close attention only to women's potential as workers in "the various arts and intellectual occupations" (319). Regarding these limited areas, he could speak from experience, even if he would not acknowledge, in the context of the *Subjection*, that he was so doing: "Hardly anything can be of greater value to a man of theory and speculation, . . . than to carry on his speculations in the companionship, and under the criticism, of a really superior woman. There is nothing comparable to it for keeping his thoughts within the limits of real things . . ." (306).

Though the problem continually acknowledged in the *Subjection* is the absence of opportunities for women beyond marriage, Mill's images of improved circumstances continually return to the married couple in the individual home. So when Mill discusses the possibility of heterosexual "friendship," he anticipates its results not in the cooperative work occasionally depicted in the *Autobiography* but instead in the achievement of a steady state of domestic happiness. The "real enriching of the two natures, each acquiring the tastes and capacities of the other in addition to its own," which "often happens between two friends of the same sex who are much associated in daily life," could become commonplace in marriage, he says, "did not the totally different bringing-up of the two sexes make it next to an impossibility to form a really well-sorted union" (334). Mill goes on to describe the resultant superior union as effacing the preliminary differences, in favor of "complete unity and unanimity as to the great objects of life." That union would be mutually absorbing: the benefits of "friendship," as Mill describes them, would be private to the couple involved and could not function as the public example the *Autobiography* had sought to describe and enact. In the *Subjection*'s description of the pre-marital years, the "objects" that unite the pair become the means only to a kind of consummation of the two characters:

When the two persons both care for great objects, and are a help and encouragement to each other in whatever regards these, the minor matters on which their tastes differ are not all-important to them; and there is a foundation for solid friendship, of an enduring character, more likely than anything else to make it, through the whole of life, a greater pleasure to each to give pleasure to the other, than to receive it. (334)

The Mill who wrote the *Subjection* was a nostalgic widower, less likely to remember the productively contentious collaboration that led to the *Autobiography* than the tacit understandings that led to a happy marriage. In its echo of the *Autobiography*'s absolving Harriet Taylor Mill from interest in professional "turmoil and strife," the *Subjection*'s closing disclaimer made clear that its topic was *not* "the need which society has of the services of women in public business . . ." (339). The *Subjection* does not figure "friendship" in the public sphere. Rather, extrapolating from the unique instance of Mill's "friendship" with the remarkable nonprofessional woman he had eventually married, it grounds "friendship" within the realm of happy marriage in a way that would have been untroubling to Craik or other mid-Victorians. As Regenia Gagnier has described, Mill's vision of a perfect marriage "is a metonymic vision of a noncoercive society to come."[47] But its perspective is that of the surviving member of a highly unconventional couple who eventually found comfort within the framework of friendship's most conventional mid-Victorian plot.

Average Specimens: *Women's Work and Women's Culture*

The argument for heterosexual cooperation was expanded "beyond the limits of the individual home" to those areas Mill shied from, in a companion volume to the *Subjection* that was published simultaneously and sometimes reviewed alongside it. Like Mill's *Autobiography*, the essay collection *Women's Work and Women's Culture* embodied heterosexual cooperation in the process of its composition; its ten essays were written by five men and five women, as reviewers were quick to recognize.[48] *Women's Work and Women's Culture* focused, like the *Subjection*, on women's lack of opportunities for advancement outside marriage and on the societal losses implicit in the failure to take advantage of women's skills. The book argued against "the social framework which makes marriage women's only concern" (Wedgwood, 261) and on behalf of their becoming "fellow workers with [men]" in service of "the one great duty of doing some good on earth" (Boyd-Kinnear, 367). Occasioned by the debate over the Married Women's Property Bill,[49] and sensitive to the sexually charged climate of the time, this explicitly anti-Comtian volume (which included Frances Power Cobbe's criticism of Comte, quoted earlier) concerned itself with a greater range of practical solutions than did Mill's. It argued for increasing women's opportunities in the areas of property owner-ship, suffrage, education, and employment. *Women's Work and Women's Culture* thus could figure cooperation at a number of specific sites outside the home and through a number of activities unavailable to Mill. Moreover, its sense of heterosexual relations being directed toward the completion of "one great duty" repre-sented a narrative alternative to the courtship plot to which Mill had partly succumbed in the *Subjection*.[50]

Throughout, the collection stressed that society suffered "spiri-tual as well as material" diminishment because courtship held ex-clusive sway over heterosexual relations (Butler, viii). England was undergoing moral loss in its domestication of women and practical loss in its failure to accomplish the "abundance of work to be done which needs men and women detached from domestic ties . . ." (Butler, xxxv). The "doctrine" that defined womanhood only ac-cording to that "which enables a woman to attract conjugal love" thus belonged "properly," Frances Power Cobbe argued, "to ages of barbarism" on two related counts: it reflected an antiquated morality and it was slowing the progress of civilization (8). "We ask that the gifts of God may not be wasted," wrote Elizabeth Wolsten-holme, "that women themselves may not be robbed of the purest joys of life, those of intellectual effort and achievement, and that society which needs their help so much may not be defrauded of their best and worthiest service" (327–28).

The broader argument of *Women's Work and Women's Cul-ture* depended much less than Mill's more personal arguments had on images of any individual man and woman in the act of co-operation. This collection was concerned with mapping areas of shared activity rather than with exemplifying or designating any ideal relationship. Thus it might avoid the dangers of putting for-ward a version of "friendship." Yet that term still remained crucial. Julia Wedgwood noted as the "most obvious, perhaps, though not the most important" consequence of the "social framework" that required courtship to be women's exclusive concern,

that it makes friendship between men and women, for average specimens of both, impossible. . . . The fact that a man with nothing particular about him should be on terms of intimate friendship with a woman with nothing particular about her, is, I venture to say, unheard of. (261)

Like Craik, Wedgwood attested to the existence of rare "instances" of heterosexual "friendship" but insisted that "they belong only to the exceptions of humanity." (She presumably thought herself one of those exceptions because of her friendship with Robert Browning; as will be discussed below, Browning may be supposed to have been less sure.) "Commonplace men and women" were not "incapable of mutual understanding," Wedgwood insisted, but a woman needed "exceptional force of character . . . to hold at bay the idea of marriage wherever it is possible . . . [T]o leave [marriage] out of sight—the only basis for friendship—is, to the average girl, whose future is a blank but for this prospect, impossible" (261).

The collective posited a variety of alternatives that might fill out that blank and permit new dynamics for heterosexual relations. In learning and in work, men and women might interact in ways that subordinated courtship and sexuality; they might instead be "drawn . . . closer in the bonds of mutual service," as John Boyd-Kinnear insisted (367). If it was true that "no one is fit for the profession of Medicine unless able to banish from its practice the personal idea of sex," as Sophia Jex-Blake reported the statement of an eminent London surgeon, then there should be no obstacle, she argued, to men and women's being trained together as doctors (114). There were already positive examples of safe and productive heterosexual interaction—Jessie Boucheret pointed to the cooperation of male and female farm laborers (40), Wolstenholme to a successful "experiment of mixed classes" in the education of young boys and girls (326). *Women's Work and Women's Culture* argued its case in terms of expanding the scope of heterosexual cooperation and being able to represent it as a norm, rather than as a rare or unacknowledged exception. For women's work was itself nothing new: "women have always had to work," Boyd-Kinnear noted; the change, from the point of view of those who were resisting it, was that women no longer worked "quietly," but were "grown querulous and discontented," and wished to work alongside men "in every trade and profession" (333).

The collection couched its own arguments for professional heterosexual interaction in ways that would be far less threatening. *Women's Work and Women's Culture* consistently appealed, in fact, to some of the recognized priorities of mid-Victorian bourgeois morality.[51] Though the essayists did wish to subvert the hegemony of marriage, they were far from hostile to the "ideal of Home." Indeed, the collection's editor, Josephine Butler, who was simultaneously leading a moral crusade against the Contagious Diseases Acts, made clear in her introduction that she was far from seeking to "revolutionize our Homes." Rather, she believed that "Home is the nursery of all virtue, the fountain-head of all true affection, and the main source of the strength of our nation" (xxv). It was the ideal of the family that served throughout the collection as the model for proper heterosexual interaction: Wedgwood pointed to "some of the most affectionate brothers and sisters" as her example of heterosexual "friendship" (261); Wolstenholme saw the best consequence of the successful experiment in coeducation as the proof that "to boys living at home with their sisters . . . companionship with girls in study, as well as in their daily life at home, would come easily and naturally" (326). Butler herself pointed to the "general intelligence of the young Geneva watchmakers who help their fathers in the trade," in order to insist "that it is very probable that the home-bond, the good ideal of domesticity, would in a great degree be restored and strengthened by the admission of daughters to the family trade or profession. When fathers, brothers, and sisters are working at one art, a sort of pride in the family excellence grows up which is a wholesome bond of union" (xliii).

Butler believed that women's increased opportunities to exhibit their skills would make them more attractive and thus "tend to the increase of marriage . . . though not very soon" (xxxiv).[52] For marriage was not in itself the "bond of union" she saw as providing the telos for proper heterosexual interaction. The truer goal would be the expansion of heterosexual relations derived from sibling and parent-child relations to include the whole "great human family" (xxxvii). Butler predicted "a great enlargement of hearts, and a free opening out and giving forth of the influences of homes, as reservoirs of blessing for the common good . . ." (xxviii). Her ultimate goal was to see heterosexual cooperation consummating in moral, national, and, most of all, religious regeneration. Wife of an Anglican clergyman and herself a passionate (if unconventional) Christian,[53] Butler used her introduction to cast the collection's argument in relation to "the great principles announced by Christ" (xiv). The collection's continual recourse to family models served a Christian argument for life's being directed toward the eventual coming together of a universal family. Butler's opening suggestions were given fullest realization in Boyd-Kinnear's concluding essay: "Let fathers and mothers count it their most solemn duty," it read, "to help and guide their children to render themselves thus worthy workers in their Father's vineyard, that so when the day is done they may receive every one the reward of their work" (361–62).

Though this rhetoric surely attempts to "occupy its grounds" thoroughly enough to bar sexual cynicism about heterosexual interactions, its interest is clearly less on presenting real-world cases of that interaction than in promising a more perfect world to which they might lead. In some ways, Butler's model represents a more egalitarian model of Comte's "perfect friendship," in which competition is eliminated not because of the passivity of one sex but because of the passivity of both. But Butler's model also resembles Mill's insofar as it ultimately positions "friendship" as a stage toward a greater end. For Mill "friendship," defined as an unmarried couple's working relations, served mainly as a conventional stage on the way to marriage; here "friendship," defined as parents', children's, and siblings' working relations, becomes almost as conventional a stage on the way to heaven.[54] Butler would make most explicit her willingness to see "friendship" giving way to a greater good in the conclusion to her *Personal Reminiscences* about the period. There, in an address to unspecified "Friends and Fellow-Workers," she recalled "many pleasant adventures, social gatherings, and sweet friendships, taking their rise in a common aim, cemented by fellowship in trial and in hope, and ripening, year by year, for the higher communion."[55]

By that late stage, a quarter century after *Women's Work and Women's Culture*, Butler had eliminated the family terms from her teleological argument; here "friendship" gives way to universal "communion," but fathers and daughters are absent. The change may be considered a necessary concession to Victorian skepticism. The familial rhetoric of *Women's Work and Women's Culture*, even if drawing on a wealth of Victorian understandings about the sanctity of the home, nevertheless represented the collection's most questionable argumentative link. Eliza Linton's warnings, in the same year, about men who would cast themselves as "fathers" and "brothers" to their female "friends" has already been noted; an even more telling reaction may be found in a contemporary transcript of the debate over the Married Women's Property Bill. The *Times* recorded Lord Penzance arguing as follows:

> A married woman, . . . being at liberty to carry on any trade, a man might be startled by the information that his wife had determined to set up a shop in the neighborhood—which at present [is] prevented by her inability to contract—and still more startled at hearing that she had entered into partnership with her cousin, who need not be a woman. (A laugh.) A husband who expected his wife to keep his home and attend to the children might find her opening a Berlin wool shop with her cousin John as partner. (Renewed laughter.) [56]

Penzance's jokes, stressing the comic insidiousness of extramarital cooperation masquerading as family, belie an anxiety slightly different from that of the usual mid-Victorian antifeminist complaints. Butler and her fellow contributors had readily acknowledged moral concerns about a sex war and economic concerns about women's fighting men for jobs; Penzance is recognizing a threat not against the male sex, or even against male wage-earners, but against man as husband, as ruler over both the marriage bed and the pocketbook.[57] The woman here empowered, financially potent and in collusion with a male partner, is not a symbol of a helpless sex fighting for the power held by its opposite; neither is she that ultimate Victorian failure, the spinster, "pinched and starved in the matter of affection and therefore glad to exchange the exclusiveness of the domestic hearth for a communism in which [she] would not feel . . . left out. . . ."[58] She is instead a married woman who has joined with a man not her husband in the economic sphere, the world of work and money, and who has not even had to leave the family entirely behind, since she can resort to the moral authority and social benefit of "cousinship."

Yet Penzance and the *Times* effectively surround her mention in titters. Unless heterosexual cooperation were established as a valid end in itself, then neither family idioms nor real evidence of working cooperation could adequately buttress it against damning imprecations about its consequences. Penzance's dismissal of both family and trade shows just how easy models of friendship were to discredit. In some ways, though it avoided some of Mill's suspect terms, *Women's Work and Women's Culture* left itself far more vulnerable to such cynicism than Mill had, for it took the risk of presenting men and women together in arenas less acceptable than those to which Mill had confined himself; and even Mill's *Subjection*, far more theoretical in approach and less daring in its examples, had caused James Fitzjames Stephen to remark on "something—I hardly know what to call it; indecent is too strong a word, but I say unpleasant in the direction of decorum—in prolonged and minute discussion about the relations of men and women."[59]

Whatever the Means, Whatever the Way: Browning's *The Ring and the Book*

If Butler's religious rhetoric hadn't been burdened by suspect familial idioms, might it have satisfied readers as wary as Stephen? Though Christian terms for affection commonly stem from the familial—George Eliot's recourse to the Methodist practice of addressing fellow congregationalists as "Sister" or "Brother" will be discussed in Chapter 2—religious rhetoric does have other idioms at its disposal, and it can point in the direction of spheres meant truly to transcend all worldly bonds.

Robert Browning's famous 1869 poem, *The Ring and the Book*, depicts a clergyman and his female parishioner attempting to prove "pure friendship" as a "simple" fact. That attempt carries enormous consequences: if the despairing priest Giuseppe and the dying young wife Pompilia can prove the legitimacy of their relationship, then Pompilia's fatal stabbing by her husband Guido will stand as a capital offense; should the relationship be proved immoral, Guido's killing of Pompilia will be understood as a just retribution by a wronged husband. Giuseppe and Pompilia's relationship seems suffused in holiness, affection, and the sympathy of the poet, while Guido's malice, if not his defiance, has the poet's scorn. But the priestly pair's effort to prove the legitimacy of their "friendship" is made in the context of assumptions like Carlyle's, Craik's, Linton's, Penzance's, and Stephen's, that any such attempt must conceal sexuality at its heart and must, eventually, at some point in its narrative, divulge that sexuality: as one of Browning's characters puts it, summarizing the common response, "Ay, but at last, e'en have it how you will, / Whatever the means, whatever the way, explodes / The consummation."[60] Moreover, those who invoke religious rhetoric on the couple's behalf quash the claim to "simple friendship" as surely as do those who make the fullest concessions to sexuality; transcendence, after all, is but another consummation. *The Ring and the Book* thus stands as the fullest measure of the discursive features that doomed mid-Victorian attempts to ground heterosexual friendship in the available legitimizing formulae.

Heterosexual friendship may be the least obviously substantiated element in the 21,000 lines of *The Ring and the Book*; certainly criticism of the poem has not generally contended with the subject, and even the present analysis cannot address it without first delving into several of the issues in which the poem envelops it. *The Ring and the Book* is best known for its innovative structure (ten dramatic monologues of comparable force and length), for its adaptation of a late-seventeenth-century Roman trial, for its series of distinctive metaphors (especially those of the poem's title), and for its frequent and obvious allusions to the private life of its author. Critical analysis of the poem has focused, from the beginning, on matters of form, symbol, and autobiography; occasional historical considerations have centered on the poem's explicit discussion of history and religion as themes, and on its Roman context.[61] Though Henry James saw the relationship of Giuseppe and Pompilia as the poem's "main substance," there have always been those who judged concentration on that relationship as, at best, a kind of sentimental absorption in a couple of trees at the expense of a vast and impressive forest.[62]

Few of those scholars who have been interested in the poem's network of personal relationships have viewed them as demonstrably Victorian. Some of the original reviewers, however, did note the way the poem's tale of a brutal husband and a helpless wife sold, ravished, and robbed within the legal confines of marriage echoed stories then prominent in political controversy. The *Saturday Review* dubbed Browning's Guido to be "every inch of him, a man of passions, reasonings, volitions, the like of which may be seen (though not in the same combination) in many of those whom we meet in our daily life"; and indeed, as Lee Holcombe has described, the 1869 press was giving readers frequent opportunity to consider the trials involving such husbands.[63] For instance, the

Times recorded in detail the brutalities described by a Susannah Palmer, as she explained to the court why she had finally struck back against her violent and "persecuting" husband; the horrors amounted, *Times* readers were told, to "a touching story which appeared to produce a strong feeling of commiseration for her among the whole audience."[64] The *Macmillan's Magazine* reviewer of *The Ring and the Book* urged readers to recognize that the poem bore analogies to such familiar texts:

> We are contented to peruse the facts and pleadings of a modern law-case; why should we not bring the same freshness of interest to bear upon this tragedy, not stripped, as happens in the newspapers, of its poetry, but invested with all the splendours of a powerful imagination, while retaining the reality of incidents and details that bear a crime of yesterday home to the hearts of every one?[65]

No kind of mid-Victorian text might arouse fresher interest than a poetic rendering of a law-case that centered on marital unhappiness and adultery. Neither might any kind of text more readily invite a way of reading especially damaging to attempts to present an extramarital relationship in terms of extrasexual priorities. The divorce courts were assuredly the most efficient Victorian machines for "putting sex into discourse": English law required that a husband suing for divorce produce clear evidence of his wife's adultery, and that a wife provide evidence of "intolerable adultery, that is, adultery accompanied by incest, bigamy, sodomy, desertion, rape or adultery coupled with . . . cruelty."[66] Browning's massive poem on such a case might be expected to offer readers a surplus of this fascinating material, though, as the *Saturday Review* had noted, in a different (and more culturally sanctioned) combination.

Furthermore, the poem's multifaceted presentation would allow those readers to exert their own interpretive assumptions in ways that newspaper trial transcripts did not. The same issue of the *Times* that presented Susannah Palmer's trial revealed the court's final verdict on her case (conviction, though with a recommendation for leniency because of the horrible circumstances); readers of *The Ring and the Book* could find, as a subsequent issue of *Macmillan's* noted, not only the usual pleasure of deducing guilt or innocence and comparing their judgments to the court's, but also the additional incentive of comparing their deductions to what they understood the poet's personal verdict to be. Thus, J. R. Mozley felt licensed to pose, as an alternative to the version "which Mr. Browning evidently means us to believe," a "counterhypothesis that Pompilia, cruelly treated no doubt by Guido, eloped with [Giuseppe] Caponsacchi in a commonplace manner, having previously corresponded with him." This theory, the review added, "cannot be said to be one that experience proves unlikely."[67]

In typical mid-Victorian fashion, that "commonplace" deduction from "experience" recognized Giuseppe as an example of an ill-concealed seducer, whose claims to be anything other than Pompilia's lover must be understood as a necessary but transparent ruse. Much modern criticism has matter-of-factly carried forward such a reading: Park Honan made the inheritance explicit when he noted, in commemoration of the poem's centennial, that Thomas Carlyle had "expressed much of the commonsense side when he said 'the girl and the handsome young priest were lovers,' and . . . research seems to confirm commonsense and Carlyle."[68]

It should not be surprising to find Carlyle standing for the "commonsense" side, given his appraisal of the Mill/Taylor relationship: he might even have recognized parallels between the earlier couple's journey to France and Giuseppe and Pompilia's flight from Guido. What Carlyle might have been less willing to recognize was the close relation between his own conventional assumptions and those of the Roman society that Browning's poem presented far from sympathetically. Ann Brady has described that society thus: "The seventeenth-century Italian world of Robert Browning's *The Ring and the Book* abounds in, is leavened by, and exudes sexual cynicism."[69] It need only be added—as Brady later implies—that the Romans' cynicism is of a recognizably Victorian kind. Giuseppe and Pompilia find themselves surrounded by a "rabble . . . rampant on the side of hearth / Home and the husband" ("Giuseppe Caponsacchi," 1538–39), eager to find sex encroaching upon any and all moral norms. The nearly universal willingness to suspect adulterous motives is evident even at Pompilia's deathbed, where she lies overcome by the wound Guido has inflicted and where further adultery would seem truly out of the question. The energies of sexual discourse run so high in this world that Pompilia's mutilated body invites rather than bars sexual insinuation.

Why, take men as they come,—an instance now,—
Of all those who have simply gone to see
Pompilia on her deathbed since four days,
Half at least are, call it how you please,
In love with her—I don't except the priests
Nor even the old confessor whose eyes run
Over at what he styles his sister's voice. . . .
Well, had they viewed her ere the paleness pushed
The last o' the red o' the rose away, while yet
Some hand, adventurous 'twixt the wind and her,
Might let the life run back and raise the flower
Rich with reward up to the guardian's face,—
Would they have kept that hand employed the same
At fumbling on with prayer-book pages? No!
Men are men: why then need I say one word
More than this, that our man the Canon here
Saw, pitied, loved Pompilia?
       ("The Other Half-Rome," 865–71, 873–82)[70]

On behalf of what Craik had called "the matter-of-fact half of the world," Browning's speaker here dismisses several legitimizing factors at once: age, religion, and even mortality seem laughable as forces against sex. In the context of the insinuations against the "old confessor," the reference to the young priest, Giuseppe, as "our man" endows him with the same motivations felt by "half at least" of the men confronted with the pretty girl. Defensive idioms of any kind seem hopeless against a commentator who is willing to "call it how you please," and happy to take or leave the word "love" as adequate to whatever degree of lust the situation contains.

"Perhaps there is no more conceptually imprecise word in English than *love*," Brady writes when discussing Browning's poem, "and none more prone to misinterpretation."[71] But there have been many positive critical readings of Giuseppe and Pompilia's relationship, and these, Brady's among them, tend to rely on a positive understanding of the word "love" when they try to counter the various degrees of cyncism expressed by "The Other Half-Rome," Mozley, Carlyle, and Honan. For the most obvious positive source to draw on in validating the relationship is that acknowledged by Mozley—Browning's own sympathy with Giuseppe, a sympathy that seems stronger still if Giuseppe is seen as a thinly disguised alter ego for a noble Browning rescuing his beloved Elizabeth. Read thus, the poem most aptly describes Giuseppe when it calls him a

> . . . true Saint George
> To slay the monster, set the Princess free,
> And have the whole High-Altar to himself. . . .
> ("Pompilia," 1324–26)

These lines offer Giuseppe two possible "loving" roles at the altar: as priest or as would-be rightful husband who would displace the evil Guido. In other words, the Saint George myth may be invoked to prove that Giuseppe's motives transcend sexuality or to serve precisely the opposite purpose.[72]

Critics arguing each alternative have commonly characterized Giuseppe and Pompilia's "love" as positively "Dantean,"[73] an analogy that itself offers two divergent possibilities. Some critics seem to think that Giuseppe's parallels with Dante and Saint George show him to be worthy of a hearty slap on the back—and show Browning to be worthy of comparable reward for his willingness to recognize sexuality as an essential part of human life. Such interpretations arrive at a conclusion little different from the J. R. Mozley review, in which Giuseppe stands as a virile, decent, but ill-fated and adulterous buck.[74] Other critics invoke Dantean love as a pattern in which sex serves only as a stage towards transcendent Good, so that the whole process of the relationship is sanctified as a "meeting of pure souls."[75] If this is not to recover the lost ideal of the truly Platonic mourned by Lewes, then it is at least to find a "mystical love-union" anticipating "a more perfect future when the love of man and woman will be mysteriously fused into the love of God," in the words of Charles Phipps.[76] (One may presume that both Butler and Comte could have sympathized with this sort of interpretation.)

This transcendent approach seems authorized by *The Ring and the Book*'s concluding gestures: in the final monologue, the narrator urges his readers to view the story in terms of religious salvation. In the meantime, the verdict on the case has been handed down by the Pope, who sees Giuseppe and Pompilia's relationship as

> . . . this gift of God who showed for once
> How He would have the world go white
> ("The Pope," 680–81)

and who thus refuses to pardon Guido. The Pope recognizes both Guido's guilt and "the uniqueness of the Canon's case, transcending as it does the normally foreseen eventualities of the Law as well as all other conventional criteria," as Phipps, the best of the Dantean commentators, has explained. Not that Browning ever simply spells out this interpretation: Richard Altick and James F. Loucks say Browning presents the case as "an ineffable experience, the meaning of which is evident only to the Pope, who plainly asserts the inadequacy of language to characterize it."[77]

When Altick and Loucks characterize the proceedings as "ineffable," they straddle at once the position sympathetic to the couple and another position that is perhaps truest to the poem's formal requirements. For *The Ring and the Book* seems, famously, to validate no single judgment; its multiple narratives leave interpretation, as Mozley suggested, and as W. David Shaw has since affirmed, to its reader.[78] What is striking about Phipps's transcendent, sympathetic reading is that it gives no more authority to Giuseppe and Pompilia's language than do the more skeptical positions of Altick and Loucks or Shaw. Whether language is "inadequate" to the experience or the experience uniquely "transcends" all aspects of the legal case, Giuseppe and Pompilia's language, their way of making their case, must be discounted just as much as the hostile articulations of figures like The Other Half-Rome. Further, in deferring to the opinion of the Pope, Dantean readers oddly duplicate the process of the obviously culpable Roman judicial system—which first determines "guilt enough / To be compatible with innocence" ("Giuseppe Caponsacchi," 1735–36), then defers to an external spiritual authority, while permitting Pompilia's murder in the interim. The Dantean model assimilates the couple's assertions about their relationship as not only inaccessible but also, finally, inconsequential.

Moreover, such an interpretation makes a very high virtue of a Victorian social and literary necessity: it celebrates that what could not be represented in fact was not represented in this poetic fiction.

Thus abandoned (because seen as transcended) are Giuseppe and Pompilia's claims that their relationship has been defined, from the time of Pompilia's flight, not according to a retrospective fantasy of heavenly transcendence, but by Giuseppe's role as "priest and friend" ("Giuseppe Caponsacchi," 1057). This is the pair of terms

to which Giuseppe and Pompilia resort on those occasions when
they seek to repudiate the incriminating associations of the term
"love." Pompilia designates Giuseppe as follows:

> There is the friend,—men will not ask about,
> But tell untruths of, and give nicknames to,
> And think my lover, most surprise of all!
> Do only hear, it is the priest they mean,
> Giuseppe Caponsacchi: a priest—love,
> And love me! Well, yet people think he did.
> I am married, he has taken priestly vows,
> They know that, and yet go on, say, the same,
> "Yes, how he loves you!" "That was love"—they say,
> When anything is answered that they ask:
> Or else "No wonder you love him"—they say.
>
> ("Pompilia", 160–70)

"You know this is not love, Sirs," Giuseppe insists, "—it is
faith" ("Giuseppe Caponsacchi," 1193). Such claims by Giuseppe
and Pompilia would seem consistent with an element of the Pope's
interpretation (and Phipps's) in which the personal relationship is
displaced by the holy one. But, as already suggested, there is no
evidence that claims based on a priest's inherent innocence would
hold any ground in the Roman society Browning depicts: The Other
Half-Rome's comments about the Canon as "our man" have already
been quoted, and his representative opposite mocks Giuseppe as
"the all-consoling Caponsacchi" and a "courtly Christian" ("Half-
Rome," 783, 791). Rome seems unabashed about doubting the
ability of priestliness to outweigh lust, or the claim of the word
"priest" to greater credibility than the word "friend." [79]

And Giuseppe and Pompilia, trying to make a legal case for their
relationship's legitimacy rather than a religious case for its sanctity, do not really seek to argue on behalf of priestly transcendence:
at one moment only does Giuseppe claim to have privileged the
priestly over the personal:

> I must not blink the priest's peculiar part,
> Nor shrink to counsel, comfort: priest and friend—
> How do we discontinue to be friends?
> I will go minister, advise her seek
> Help at the source,—above all, not despair.
>
> ("Giuseppe Caponsacchi," 1056–60)

But that moment quickly passes. In attempting to characterize his priestly role, Giuseppe and Pompilia do not seek to "discontinue to be friends." They indeed rely on forms of the word "friend" to name their relationship. It answers an obvious rhetorical need, for they are aware of having to describe situations outside the accepted domain of the priestly. They use it to acknowledge moments at which Giuseppe exceeded clerical conventions: "Now, be you candid and no priest but friend," in Pompilia's words. "This time she might have said—might, did not say, / 'You are a priest.' She said 'my friend,' " recalls Giuseppe ("Giuseppe Caponsacchi," 1353, 1382–83).

But "friend," as may be expected, has its own liabilities of the kind Roman/Victorian listeners would be only too ready to exploit. This becomes most obvious when Giuseppe pleads his right to attend Pompilia's deathbed: "a priest might be of use," Giuseppe says, "The more when he's a friend too,—and she called me / Far beyond 'friend' " ("Giuseppe Caponsacchi," 1609–11). Though the final phrase refers directly to Pompilia's having called Giuseppe her "sole friend, / Guardian and saviour" seventy lines earlier, it is deeply self-incriminating. It invites all the commonplace assumptions according to which the assertion of friendship must inherently suggest something "more," something beyond the "pure and simple." That their relationship has constituted something "more" than friendship is precisely what everyone else is all too ready to assume. The phrase "far beyond friend" concedes all argumentative ground.

There are times when Giuseppe makes such concessions part of his argumentative strategy. At a number of points he rhetorically admits the most sexually culpable reading of his experience, in an attempt to preempt the illicit entirely:

> I cite the husband's self's worst charge
> In proof of my best word for both of us.
> Be it conceded that so many times
> We took our pleasure in his palace: then,
> What need to fly at all?
>   ("The Other Half-Rome," 1177–81)

> Give colour to the very lie o' the man,
> The murderer,—make as if I loved his wife,
> In the way he called love. He is the fool there!
> Why, had there been in me the touch of taint,

I had picked up so much of knaves'-policy
As hide it, keep one hand pressed on the place
Suspected of a spot would damn us both.

    ("Giuseppe Caponsacchi," 184–89)

But for all the aggressiveness and defiance of these admissions, their most exaggerated claims only echo that of Guido's accusations. Daring listeners to think of sexuality as pervasive is not an effective ploy when the prevailing assumptions are based on an acceptance of precisely that dare. The more Giuseppe asserts, the more his listeners will accuse him of

flirting flag-like i' the face o' the world
    . . . this conspicuous love
For the lady,—oh, called innocent love, I know!
Only such scarlet fiery innocence
As most men would try muffle up in shade.

    ("The Other Half-Rome," 892–96)

Listeners "know" Giuseppe and Pompilia to be claiming "innocent love," though that is not the kind of phrase the couple is apt to use; and listeners further know what must lurk behind that understood, though unstated, claim. If, in the world of *The Ring and the Book*, viewers are slow to see friendship, perhaps it is because of their eagerness to see other possible renderings. They find no shortage of alternatives. The ones cited thus far comprise only a fraction of the competing fictions that are invoked in *The Ring and the Book* to explain Giuseppe and Pompilia's relationship. The poem makes recourse to models derived from mythical conquests and seductions, pastoral romances, Biblical allegories, and dozens of other genres.[80] Ultimately, the real contest in the poem is between those competing fictions, arrayed on two sides—those illustrating Guido's claim that the true story is in fact "the old stale unromantic way of fault" ("Tertium Quid," 1018) and those exemplifying the Pope's belief in a "gift of God." There seem to be only two possibilities, sanctity or sin, but there seem to be endless phrasings available to those who accept that they are describing either possibility.

    Giuseppe and Pompilia don't accept that restriction, nor do they adopt the strategy of "most men," to "muffle up" their relationship in silence. Instead, they attempt to uphold a practical version of the "pure and simple," insisting throughout on their flight's having been a practical "course we took for life and honour's sake / Very strange, very justifiable" ("The Other Half-Rome," 1119–20). Though their attempt to discredit false and damning imputations of "love" occasionally tempts them into matching Harriet Mill's wish to "occupy every ground on [their] own subject" (e.g., in Giuseppe's attempts to appropriate even the most damning accusatory language), they more often adhere to J.S. Mill's suggested strategy, of saying as little as possible. Their most characteristic claim is a kind of tautology: "This is the simple thing it claims to be," they insist; or elsewhere, "Each incident / Proves, I maintain, that action of the flight / For the true thing it was" ("The Other Half-Rome," 1118; "Giuseppe Caponsacchi," 1166–68). These are the narrowest possible definitional statements; they claim to be depicting a "true thing," but they admit no constitutive element to substantiate that truth, as all possible evidence seems tainted. At times Giuseppe and Pompilia employ patterns of negation as emphatic as those considered by the Mills, as when the priest declares himself absolutely "guiltless in thought, word and deed" ("Giuseppe Caponsacchi," 1860)[81] or insists

> . . . Enough that first to last
> I *never* touched her lip *nor* she my hand,
> *Nor* either of us thought a thought, much less
> Spoke a word which the Virgin might *not* hear.
> ("The Other Half-Rome," 1371–74, emphasis added)

Such locutions are at the opposite pole of "far beyond friend," which might admit anything and everything; whenever possible, Giuseppe and Pompilia admit nothing, negate all. Indeed, they make very narrow recourse to idioms that name their relationship in any way. Though they use "friend" along with "priest" to characterize Giuseppe in one aspect of his relationship to Pompilia, they do not use the word "friend" to describe Pompilia in her relation to Giuseppe. And they almost never refer to "friendship."

That is not just because of the word's usual Victorian deficiencies. In *The Ring and the Book*, "friend" is one of those words that, though "originally taken with powerful meaning," come, as Altick and Loucks have described, to be "weakened by repetition and abuse."[82] Throughout the poem, "friend" is so frequently invoked carelessly or condescendingly by others that Giuseppe and

Pompilia's occasional uses of it seem especially ill-fated. Here is an example from the narrative of The Other Half-Rome:

> . . . he was no one's friend,
> Yet presently found he could not turn about
> Nor take a step i' the case and fail to tread
> On someone's toe who either was a friend,
> Or a friend's friend, or friend's friend thrice-removed
>
> (1029–33)

Other similarly abused words are redeemed in the poem. The Pope, for instance, reauthorizes "love," at least to the satisfaction of readers like Brady, who are willing to see his final affirmations as transcending the word's frequent abuse.[83] But "friend" receives no such validation. Indeed, "friend" has a specific meaning within the poem's context that sentences it irrevocably to the secular level of the Law, which idealistic readers like Phipps want to see Giuseppe and Pompilia's relationship as transcending. For throughout The Ring and the Book, Giuseppe's role is literally that of "friend"; at a key moment, he calls attention to his legal status as *amicus curiae* and connects it to his personal role.

> I come . . .
> As friend of the court—and for pure friendship's sake
> Have told my tale to the end. . . .
> ("Giuseppe Caponsacchi," 1635–37)

Here "pure friendship," drawing sanction from the law, would seem to take on an authority otherwise scarcely available in mid-Victorian discourse.[84] Yet the law is the least probable source to sanction "friendship," a relation that falls into none of the marital, familial, or contractual relations a court would be likely to recognize. And Giuseppe's reference to his role as "friend of the court" allows him little more than an empty play on words. The phrase invokes not legal authority but marginality. An *amicus curiae* is by definition an outsider, one not legally involved in the actual transactions of the court: "friend" marks him, in effect, as legal nonentity, no more viable in marital law than is his "friendship." Though Giuseppe has come, voluntarily, to provide evidence, the court will grant him no legal connection whatever to Pompilia, just as no argument he can make for "pure friendship" will bear any relevance to the trial except as a denial of sex, as a contribution to the court's examination of whether adultery occurred. Giuseppe goes significantly unmentioned in Browning's final legal summation in Book 12. Nor is there any evidence that his and Pompilia's argument for their relationship's genesis in practical utility ever gains acceptance from any Roman interpreter.

Phipps, the critic most ready to affirm the wordly value of the relationship, calls Browning's portrayal of "the unconventional love of Caponsacchi and Pompilia . . . a symbol of revolution and emancipation from domestic, legal, and religious rationalisms" that proclaims the "legal impotence and moral bankruptcy of both Church and State." Phipps's description suggests that Browning's poem manages to resist ineffective and immoral discursive authorities. But when Phipps goes on to characterize that "love" as an "extralegal spiritual union," he but plays one authority against another, ascribing to Browning a strategy something like Butler's, whereby the relationship for which there is as yet no place in the world gets promised a redemptive place in heaven.[85] The most searching criticism of *The Ring and the Book* has inevitably found its language in a compromise between the vast array of rhetorical forms offered by the poem's speakers and the limited range of idioms available to present-day commentators wishing to describe unconventional heterosexual relationships. The critical record thus pursues Giuseppe and Pompilia to the door of their idiomatic trap. Something has always to be added to "friendship," whether through a nervous assertion that it was *only* ("pure," or "pure and simple") friendship and therefore not something else, or an eager insistence that there was something "far beyond" it—illicit sex, licit domesticity, or transcendent virtue. Thus, even the most "unconventional" kind of affection, as Phipps calls Giuseppe and Pompilia's, is continually restored to convention.

Elusive and multifaceted as Browning's poem may be, the fate of "friendship" has proven its language to be not so much "ineffable" as utterly permeable to critical practice—at least insofar as that practice is dedicated to a kind of translation of Browning's most troubled idioms into familiar ones. The wealth of resources that confirm the discursive limits of *The Ring and the Book*'s world may tempt the critic into a responsive role, elucidating each allusive framework, or an autonomous one, resisting the interpretive guides provided by Browning and—as the contemporary reviewer J. R. Mozley suggested—hazarding a model of his or her own. Neither perspective is likely to grant "friendship" much ground; for to delineate its features there are only tautologies, negations, and evasions, nothing with which to validate it by name. "I like clearly-defined situations and relations, and by temper am led to call for them abruptly and at any price," Browning explained to Julia Wedgwood during the early stages of his composition of *The Ring and the Book*. But he was not there referring to his poem; rather, he was comfortably accepting Wedgwood's decision to call their relationship to a close, even as he continued to call her his "dearest friend."[86] Wedgwood's belief, expressed in *Women's Work and Women's Culture*, that an exceptional individual might withstand the social pressures against heterosexual "friendship" would get no confirmation in *The Ring and the Book*, where Browning would resort to every means available to reassert conventional priorities and recontain the claim to "simple friendship."

Nor had the volume to which Wedgwood had contributed or its famous contemporary, Mill's *On the Subjection of Women*, entirely resisted that tendency: in those texts "friendship" yields to domesticity and transcendence as surely as it does to sin and "nature" in more skeptical ones. It seems remarkable that the writings of 1869, *The Ring and the Book* foremost among them, worked so insistently to displace a kind of relationship that could rarely be enacted in public life. But the vital representation of worldly, extramarital, extrafamilial heterosexual friendship would have disrupted all the basic categories that gave bourgeois Victorian life its incentives: a natural order of heterosexual pursuit, a sexually divided social order with distinct occupations for men and women, and a heavenly promise of unions not possible on earth. The admission of heterosexual friendship to the Victorian world would have suggested that men and women could, and even ought to, share the world productively.

The failed attempts at representing friendship seem to me most impressive for the ways in which they resist the conventional categories, even if only temporarily. Still, if mid-Victorian texts were found *always* to displace, to compromise, or to slight heterosexual friendship, then present-day readers would be left always either participating in or resigning themselves to those discouraging processes; and the implicit message about language's ability to give voice to human affections would be troubling indeed. Here literature, in particular the novel, may provide a valuable exception. For George Eliot spent her career attempting to propose affections whose value extended beyond her language's capacity to name them. In the end, her work maintains a critically negotiable space for "friendship" far more steadfastly than had any of the texts discussed thus far.

2

George Eliot's Experiments in Idiom

Novels, Narrative, and Idiom

In Chapter 1 I focused on a moment of particular idiomatic instability—1869, a time when, as Eliza Linton had said, one could "hang" gender-related discourse "on any peg," and when evocations of unconventional "friendship" continually had little credibility. Now I want to emphasize a relation between that idiomatic problem and a narrative problem. The mid-Victorians were unable to substantiate claims about heterosexual friendship, but not because they lacked words for it (quite to the contrary). Rather, the words were unconvincing and too often became assimilated into narratives in which "friendship" would give way to some other form of union: usually sinful romance, sanctioned romance, or heavenly salvation. Julia Wedgwood looked forward to a time when friendship would be more possible; she lived in a time when "friendship" seemed always on the verge of being consummated as something else.

That Victorian narrative conventions were almost inherently inimical to "friendship" should be evident from the preceding pages: texts as generically diverse as Mill's *Autobiography*, the essay collection *Women's Work and Women's Culture*, and Browning's epic poem *The Ring and the Book* each displace "friendship" in service of their controlling narratives. Nowhere was the displacement of friendship more insistently and instructively carried out than in Victorian novels, which sustained their stories to unprecedented lengths and on behalf of ambitious claims to realism and yet were expected to issue in the neatest conclusions—conclusions in which "friendship" had little chance of a place. With the novel as a form committed to consummation of various kinds, almost always ending in death, marriage, or some related alternative, the unstable and easily compromised processes of friendship would seem here most vulnerable. If even Mill's nonfiction could be suspected of the taint of illicit romance, what chance would ostensibly sexless relations have in Victorian novels?

Yet for these very reasons, the novel offered "friendship" its best chance to gain credibility. With the genre charged to reveal its society's discursive capacities and limitations,[1] novels could send the strongest signals about the representational possibilities for any social category, heterosexual friendship included. To tell a credible story about friendship, one that *remained* a story about friendship rather than succumbing to the usual narrative conventions, would be to make the most significant kind of case for the social viability of an idiom like "friendship," even for the idea's being in some sense "natural." Or, at least, a testing of the novel's defining energies might help reveal most clearly the expectations and limits that made "friendship" impossible to articulate, if impossible it was.

George Eliot's 1874 novel *Daniel Deronda* undertakes the most intense struggle with the mid-Victorian conventions that undermined representation of heterosexual friendship. It neither risks offering the dubious term "friendship" as a desirable name nor concedes its idiomatic space to other more conventional categories. *Daniel Deronda* does not successfully "occupy the ground" that figures like the Mills had sought to claim for "friendship," but it preserves that ground for future work and gives a precise sense of what kind of sustenance the yet-to-be-developed idiom would need.

Examining *Daniel Deronda* with particular attention to its treatment of heterosexual friendship makes evident why novelistic study has tended to slight the topic. As I noted in the Introduction, emphasis on narrative sequence may shift attention from categories like heterosexual friendship that tend to take a subordinate or passing role in narrative plots and that function instead as idiomatic problems *within* plots—as novelistic "secrets," in Frank Kermode's term.[2] *Daniel Deronda* furthers the development of new idioms for heterosexual relations by negating a series of alternatives, but its idiomatic negotiations are not crucial to the narrative, because the model of gender relations that gets the most complex discussion is hopelessly imagined rather than enacted: it develops as an absent fact referred to in conversation and in the narrator's speculations, not as an enacted activity serving the plot. In fact, the relationship that contributes the most toward a new idiom for heterosexual friendship is left with its story famously unresolved.

Critics analyzing the meanings of narrative sequence may elide historically specific problems of idiom. To take an example from one of the best critical analyses of the heterosexual relationships in *Daniel Deronda*: Joseph Allen Boone, in his *Tradition Counter Tradition*, implies that the novel successfully resolves all the mid-Victorian difficulties of representing "unconventional friendship." The best of many commentators to consider the social implications of *Daniel Deronda*'s " 'grand and vague' conclusion," Boone emphasizes how the novel's "discontinuous double-plot format" defies the usual pull toward marriage and leads instead to a more "uncertain" ending that "succeeds in calling into question the social order. . . ." Boone argues that "the originality of Eliot's plan in *not* making her protagonists lovers . . ." serves to "italicize the relationship that Gwendolen [Harleth] and Daniel [Deronda] *do* finally establish for what it is: an unconventional friendship of man and woman based on an equal vulnerability and noncombative concern for the other contrasting vividly" to the sanctioned oppressiveness of Victorian marriage.

Boone's conclusions about *Daniel Deronda* show why a chiefly narrative approach may only incompletely account for novelistic problems in representing gender relations. As he places *Daniel Deronda* in the context of a line of novels whose plots submit to or revolt against the narrative conventions of marital consummation, Boone must describe the book's contribution with a word, "friendship," that Eliot's readers would hardly have been convinced by, and that *Daniel Deronda* itself explicitly sets aside in favor of more complex locutions. Moreover, the novel hardly represents its central relationship as friendship or as anything else. Rather, Eliot separates the man and woman almost as soon as she defines their relation; so the events of the plot would offer little to demonstrate what the phrase "unconventional friendship" refers to. Moreover, Boone's description of an "unconventional friendship based on equal vulnerability and noncombative concern" accounts for the social constitution of the relationship only as *not* conventional and for its dynamic as *not* combative. Friendship is often described in such negative terms, in Victorian texts and in contemporary ones, but where it names passivity rather than engagement, it seems more likely to succumb to than to challenge the "social order." What, then, may a novelistic account of an "unconventional friendship" signify? "[F]reedom," says Boone of *Daniel Deronda*, "ultimately lies *outside* the secure brackets of the text."[3] If negations and deferrals are all Eliot's book may be said to achieve, it may stand as an impressive violation of literary marital conventions but it is not likely to seem an impressive positive contribution to social discourse. Yet a good deal of freedom may be said to lie inside the insecure brackets of Eliot's text, even if that freedom does not constitute a clear grounding for or articulation of "friendship." Eliot deploys, adjusts, and rejects in *Daniel Deronda* a series of models for heterosexual relations, and ultimately, neither representing nor entirely resigning "friendship," chooses silence. In fact she *insists* on silence. She circumscribes her moment of impasse with a series of buffers that demarcate what she is refusing to say but under better circumstances might. The novel suggests that its place of silence is temporary, a place that may be newly written in at some future point.

What *Daniel Deronda* achieves toward an idiom for heterosexual friendship seems especially meaningful in the context of several of Eliot's earlier works, which undertake a number of rigorous idiomatic experiments with friendship. While I share Boone's and others' interests in the structure of Eliot's plots, and in the way her novels employ and resist conventional structural models, my chief focus is the testing of idioms. For if Eliot's negotiations with "friendship" are to be posited as genuine challenges to a social order, criticism cannot be content merely to describe what Eliot can be said to *do*, as a novelist, in creating endings for her novels; there must also be some sense of what, as a constrained but inventive user of idiom, she does and does not *say*.

Marriage and the Sibling Bond: Eliot's Early Fictions

Famous and improper, George Eliot's most important relationship would seem a useful index to Victorian discourse on gender relations. But considered within her lifelong series of gender-related crises, her enduring, contented, extramarital union with George

Henry Lewes is, in fact, relatively uninstructive. The relationship's status in public discussion went from lightly enforced secrecy in the early years to complicit silence once her novels established her as an advocate of moral convention too important and effective to be compromised.[4] And she spoke of herself, most emphatically, as married. She seized her beloved's name more completely than did any legally married Victorian wife, using not only his last name (and chastising those of her acquaintances who failed to address her by it) but also, professionally, his first. She even spoke of their "profoundly serious" relation as proof of the solemnity with which she viewed wedlock. "The possibility of a constantly growing blessedness in marriage," she wrote to a newlywed in 1875, "is to me the very basis of good in our mortal life.[5] According to the terms set by the prevailing Victorian plots, including the lesson of Hetty Sorrel, the ill-fated unwed mother in Eliot's first novel, it seems that the most unconventional fact of Marian Evans's relationship with G. H. Lewes was its happy, unvarying persistence: none of the perilous vicissitudes of the unmarried woman; few doubts or dangers after an initial elopement; really very little to tell.

Mysteries and turmoil adhere to other, earlier stages of her life, both in intensely troubled relations with her father and brother and in an early recurring "pattern," described by biographer Gordon Haight as "intellectual friendship drawn by over-ready expansiveness into feelings misunderstood."[6] The idiomatic significance of these matters follows from their characteristically Victorian convergence: like the cynical men described by Eliza Linton or the ambitious women and men assembled by Josephine Butler, Marian Evans frequently applied familial terms to describe those extra-familial relations that were conventionally the most difficult to define. Invited to Devizes by R. H. Brabant in 1843 "to fill the place of his [recently married] daughter," the 24-year-old Evans soon after her arrival celebrated having been "baptised . . . Deutera, which *means* second, and *sounds* a little like daughter"; but by the end of the month she had been abruptly forced to leave, apparently because of Mrs. Brabant's enraged jealousy. After two weeks' residence at the home of François D'Albert-Durade at Geneva in 1849, she wrote home, "I love him already as if he were father and brother both." This relationship with D'Albert-Durade, a dwarf, was lifelong and without apparent complication, and its domesticity was underscored by her constant reference to his wife as "Maman." Nonetheless, he destroyed Marian Evans's early letters to him, as Haight notes, because "GE having received Mme D'Albert's permission to *tutoyer* him, he was afraid that people might attach some malevolent significance to them."[7]

Whether she also designated as "family" the two most intriguing of her early male intellectual acquaintances, John Chapman and Herbert Spencer, is uncertain.[8] Amid the plentiful documentation that Haight has provided for these relationships, little survives in Evans's own words. Still, one would hardly expect to find her writing to Spencer as "Brother Herbert" in the heartbroken letters that succeeded the "mischief" (as Spencer called it) that passed between them in 1852. Her openings in fact pass from "Dear Friend," to a note without any heading at all, to "Dear Mr. Spencer," in the course of a few weeks.[9] Family terms served her as mediating artifices of very limited function. Where she used them in her letters, they tended to serve descriptively, in passing, rather than emphatically, as, say, forms of address: a friend might be described to others as like "father and brother both," but "Dear Brother" had no part in her social correspondence. Indeed, it had no part at all in her letters for the twenty-four years during which Evans's real brother, Isaac, a moralist troubled by the circumstances surrounding her relationship with Lewes, refused communication with her.[10]

But what was untenable in urbane correspondence might prove basic to making a fiction of rural life. In George Eliot's first novel, Dinah Morris writes "Dear Brother" to address a letter to Seth Bede, a co-religionist whose marriage proposal she has lately rejected. At this key moment in George Eliot's oeuvre, she uses the term for her most troubled family relation to negotiate the difficulties of failed courtship, a crucial idiomatic test. But the moment is easy to miss, because it is executed entirely without crisis. Sibling rhetoric in *Adam Bede* is always rooted in the language of religious fellowship, and Dinah's use of "Dear Brother" conveys less about her feelings for Seth than about her commitment to the Methodism she preaches. Her distinctly "Methodist diction" carries the weight of that denomination's emphasis on "family religion" and its tendency to use family terms to establish the sanctity of daily interactions.[11] She has entered the novel addressing a sermon to her listeners as "Dear friends, brothers and sisters, whom I love as those

for whom my Lord has died . . ." (*Adam Bede*, 32); a few minutes later, she is turning Seth Bede away in order to return to her
"brethren and sisters," assuring him, "if I could think of any man
as more than a Christian brother, I think it would be you" (36).
Dinah's sisterly promise echoes the familiar formula in which
"pure and simple" friendship is the base on which love and/or
sex ("more than" friendship) is superadded; near the end of the
novel Adam Bede invokes it again when proposing to Dinah, asking if she thinks she can "love [him] better than a brother" (487).[12]
What is striking about *Adam Bede*'s deployment of this formula is
the steady assurance that the religious sentiment behind it can bar
any incursion of disruptive sexuality. When questioned about the
potential danger of her position as preacher, being "a lovely young
woman on whom men's eyes are fixed," Dinah answers, "No, I've
no room for such feelings, and I don't believe the people ever take
notice about that" (90). Not only is Dinah convinced of her successful exclusion of "such feeling,"[13] but the novel confirms similar
purity on the part of her listeners. An "old bachelor" explains that
Dinah has, without trouble, "preached to the roughest miners,"
who, by class and uniformity of sex, would presumably be most
apt to libidinousness: "Such a woman as that brings with her 'airs
from heaven' that the coarsest fellow is not insensible to" (266).
Her sibling rhetoric is able to account as well for the sensations of
the one honorable would-be suitor who emerges from among her
listeners. Seth, whose love has anyway been from the outset "hardly
distinguishable from religious feeling" (38),[14] readily accepts that it
is "better to be Dinah's friend and brother than any other woman's
husband" (383). Thus, Dinah can write her "Dear Brother" letter
with full confidence in family idioms to describe mutually satisfying
parameters for their bond:

Farewell, dear brother—and yet not farewell. For those children of God
whom it has been granted to see each other face to face and to hold communion together, and to feel the same spirit working in both can never
more be sundered, though the hills may lie between. For their souls are
enlarged for evermore by that union, and they bear one another about in
their thoughts continually as it were a new strength.—Your faithful Sister
and fellow-worker in Christ. DINAH MORRIS (318)

The novel ultimately gives this rhetoric its toughest test and
fullest possible confirmation, when it confronts Seth with Dinah's

marriage to his own real brother. Seth is unwavering, and so is everyone else: family idioms accommodate the situation in perfect harmony. When his and Adam's mother urges Seth, "She'll ne'er marry thee; thee might as well like her t' ha' thy brother," Seth responds by insisting, "I should be as thankful t' have her for a sister as thee wouldst t' have her as a daughter" (478). Adam soon ends his own brief qualms by recalling that "there was no selfish jealousy in [Seth]; he had never been jealous of his mother's fondness for Adam" (482). And in the epilogue the narrator confirms Seth's tranquillity by showing him contentedly drawing his "earthly happiness" from walking "by Dinah's side and [being] tyrannised over by Dinah's and Adam's children" (514). The only feeling Seth cannot "repress" is his regret that the married Dinah has given up her preaching, but on this matter he is ultimately "silent" (516).[15] The concluding domestic idyll that develops from Adam and Dinah's marriage seems to placate this and all other potentially disruptive concerns with ease. The concluding pages redeem the novel's instance of illegitimate sexuality by incorporating the wrong-doers in the happy household: in the final scene, Hetty Sorrel's death is recalled, and her seducer Arthur Donnithorne returns, physically debilitated, to be greeted with an invitation to visit the prospering family group.[16] It has now grown to include the two brothers, both the pious memory of their mother and the matronly Dinah who has taken her place—"Thee't like poor mother used to be," Seth tells Dinah (514)—as well as Dinah's children (a boy and a girl), and also her aunt and uncle, the Poysers. Even as Adam repeats his wife's ominous statement that "there's a sort of wrong that can never be made up for," the once-hypercritical Poysers arrive, now contented. Adam and Dinah's daughter is sent out to greet them, and with this moment the novel ends, the family extending to encompass all the novel's gender relations—in fact, all the novel's world.[17]

Significant as that gesture may seem in relation to George Eliot's more troubled private experience of family relations, it is a typical closing for the Victorian novel; Eliot could be confident that her chosen genre would prompt readers to accept an ending built around secure family ties. That such a final tableau could comfortably incorporate challenges to family bonds far more intense than those that had faced the Bedes may be demonstrated by briefly comparing the concluding scene of a very different novel exactly *Adam*

Bede's contemporary, Wilkie Collins's *The Woman in White*. By the time of its climax, the sensational plot of Collins's novel has rendered family idioms as insidious as the religious plot of *Adam Bede* renders them sacrosanct: the well-meaning Holcombe sisters have, for example, been saddled with a sequence of entirely unsuitable father figures, ranging from the passive lawyer Gilmore to their grossly ineffectual uncle to the sadistic Fosco, who is at his most "intensely paternal" when committing murder. Yet Walter Hartright, the novel's hero, claims that his "position is defined" and his "motives are acknowledged" when, in the book's finale, he comes to situate himself as Laura Holcombe's "father and brother both." And as he prepares to marry Laura, her sister Marian sees him as "my brother . . . my dearest, best friend," and so as constituting the limit of her wants. "My heart and my happiness, Walter, are with Laura and you," Marian declares. "Wait a little till there are children's voices at your fireside. I will teach them to speak for me in *their* language, and the first lesson they say to their father and mother shall be—'We can't spare our aunt!' "[18]

The book's final moment has Aunt Marian hoisting up her nephew (to whom she has become godmother, as both Gilmore and Pesca, the erstwhile member of a lethal Brotherhood, are beneficent godfathers) in the presence of his parents, a mirror image of Adam and Dinah Bede's son atop Seth's shoulders. The novels' two elevated sons stand to consolidate more than just their immediate families: Walter Hartright Jr. will inherit the earth "in the familiar manner of the landed gentry of England," and Adam Bede Jr., the carpenter's son, will gain his inheritance through his place in a universal Christian family. The children are offered as final familial compactings of all human bonds, most firm among them those between brothers and sisters (-in-law).

The commonness of such conclusions did not ensure that they would all be wholly satisfactory. D. A. Miller has since noted that a brutal legacy inheres in *The Woman in White*'s concluding "family portrait";[19] in Eliot's own time, *The Quarterly Review* complained that "Seth, the 'poor wool-gatherin' Methodist,' is left without any other consolation than that of worshipping his sister-in-law," and an unauthorized sequel entitled *Seth Bede, The Methody* insisted that Seth had the true claim as Dinah's rightful husband.[20] Moreover, all the tensions unacknowledged in *Adam Bede* seem to be inherited by Eliot's next novel, *The Mill on the Floss*. Though sibling relations are even more crucial to its plot, sibling idioms in *The Mill on the Floss* cannot produce or maintain order. Here the siblings themselves, of opposed sexes, are often hostile to one another; the would-be friend and suitor, Philip, who is constantly referred to as Maggie's "brother,"[21] is despised by her real brother Tom; and illicit passions end in a familial consummation entailing not marriage but the drowning of the brother and sister locked in "an embrace never to be parted" (459)—a union that suggests, as Tony Tanner has noted, "a final orgasmic love-death, more commonly associated with sexual lovers than with brother and sister."[22]

The sibling relationships in *Adam Bede* had generated mutually supporting narratives of religious and familial salvation; in *The Mill on the Floss*, the sibling bond seems appropriate only to the plot's beginning and end—the innocent animality of childhood and the uninhibitedness of a death scene.[23] In between, the brother / sister forms of address rely on none of *Adam Bede*'s connotations of religious fellowship or any other authenticating base. They refer instead to an unsatisfactory blood relationship and a third party's envious and futile emulation, that is, Philip's wish that Maggie may love him "as well as Tom" (160). The sibling terms fail to maintain clear relationships: roles become interchangeable. Late in the novel, Maggie dreams of "the Virgin seated in St. Ogg's boat," a dream in which "the boatman was Philip—no, not Philip, but her brother, who rowed past without looking at her," and finds herself "an outlawed soul, with no guide but the wayward choice of her own passion" (413). The real brother and his imitator having become indistinguishable, sibling idioms can provide no buffer against the tensions and confusions attendant to lust.[24]

In *The Mill on the Floss*, familial terms support neither actual brother-sister relations nor extrafamilial cross-gender relations. Hence, their failure as a vocabulary for heterosexual friendship, especially as the novel always links "friend" to the most troubled familial idioms—for instance, in Maggie's telling Philip that "it is quite impossible we can ever be more than friends—brother and sister in secret—as we have been" (295).[25] Sibling terms may only offer legitimacy to unconventional relations if siblings are understood to relate in a normative, untroubled way.

Some years later, having recently completed *Middlemarch*, Eliot

commented in a letter to her publisher that "life might be so enriched if that relation [between brother and sister] were made the
most of, as one of the highest forms of friendship." The statement
may represent an admission of failure—not only in regard to her
as yet unpublished *Brother and Sister* sonnet sequence, but also to
her failure to "make the most of" the relation in her novels.[26] In
her first two novels, she had approached brother / sister love from
very different directions. In *Adam Bede*, she had both drawn on
an existing fictive sibling vocabulary (from Methodism) and created her own fictive sibling bonds through marriage. But in her
second novel, sibling relationships, far from offering a solution to
the problem of naming complex heterosexuality, become part of
that problem; they too must be reconstituted and renamed if the
novel is to end satisfactorily. *The Mill on the Floss*'s images of
marriage—for so seem both the scene of Maggie and Tom's death
and the tombstone bearing their names that provides the book's
last words—ultimately displace the sibling relationship as surely as
various other consummations continually displaced less sanctioned
models of heterosexual relations in the period.

   Eliot's most orderly finales do tend to figure not only brother/
sister relations but heterosexual "friendship" or "companionship"
chiefly as by-products of marriage. In *Middlemarch*, she uses marriage to mediate "the delight there is in frank kindness and companionship between a man and a woman who have no passion to
hide or confess" by embodying that "delight" in Dorothea Brooke's
relation to her brother-in-law, Chettam (70–71). Even Dorothea's
"fountain of friendship towards men" is revealed through her assistance in preserving Lydgate's marriage, an effort that helps facilitate
her own (758). By the end of *Middlemarch*, Eliot happily subsumes
all her concerns with gender relations, family relations, and political relations, within marriage. At the end of her own life she would
actually live out a comparable resolution, marrying a man named
Johnnie Cross, whom for years she had called her "nephew," and
in so doing, self-consciously immersing herself in his large family
and gaining both respectability and a reconciliation with her long-
estranged brother.[27]

Priestly Passions

The idioms that describe the central relationship in *Daniel Deronda* center on neither marriage nor sibling relations. In her last novel, Eliot returned to another model for cross-gender relations that had appeared in her early fiction: Daniel and Gwendolen relate as priest and penitent, the benevolent cleric and the guidance-seeking woman—a kind of relationship on which Eliot had structured two of the three *Scenes of Clerical Life* with which she had begun her career as a writer. She had also used the model briefly but significantly in *The Mill on the Floss*; reviewing that novel in 1860, John Chapman had explained why his former tenant, associate editor, and probable paramour might have been interested in such a bond:

Clergymen are debarred from the expression at least of many passions that laymen are allowed to exhibit without the same amount of blame; these are chiefly the rougher and coarser feelings of our nature and their outward signs; the consequence is that the proceedings of the clergy are less direct, and, because less direct, more refined, and ultimately partake more of the character of female management than of the perhaps somewhat coarse energy of masculine methods; the singular fact that parsons and women can neither strike nor be stricken, exercises upon both an influence that tends to produce a similarity in their views of life and methods of observations.

We have little doubt that some such reflections as these influenced the author of "Adam Bede" in selecting the title of her first work, SCENES OF CLERICAL LIFE.[28]

The assumption voiced by Chapman, that clergymen are prevented from "expression at least" of certain passions, draws male clerics' relations with women parallel to the commonplace definitions of heterosexual "friendship": each kind of relation is defined by the absence of sexual expression. It is this quality, rather than Chapman's more complex sense of clerics' necessary androgyny, that Eliot drew upon in her early fictions.[29] In the *Scenes* and *The Mill on the Floss*, clerics are utterly passionless and relate to female sinners in a light so ethereal that it might well have answered to Lewes's professed nostalgia for the lost "Platonic."

Not that the clerics' communities readily accept Chapman's assumptions. The rural English population within which Eliot set her first published tale, "The Sad Fortunes of the Rev. Amos Barton," is every bit as skeptical about its clergyman, and the woman to whom he grows close, as is Browning's Rome. The difference is that where Browning's multiple narrators might leave readers in slight doubt as to whether popular cynicism was justified, Eliot's single narrator purports to discredit such cynicism entirely. This narrator claims a "wish to stir [the reader's] sympathy with commonplace troubles" (*Scenes*, 56), a goal in explicit opposition to that of the contemporary wave of "remarkable novels, full of striking situations, thrilling incidents, and eloquent writing" that have "appeared only within the last season" (*Scenes*, 42). An essay Eliot had written a short time before makes clear that she had in mind a number of "Evangelical" novels, in which

the hero is almost sure to be a young curate, frowned upon, perhaps, by worldly mammas, but carrying captive the hearts of their daughters, who can 'never forget *that* sermon;' tender glances are seized from the pulpit stairs instead of the opera-box; *têtes-à-têtes* are seasoned with quotations from Scripture, instead of quotations from the poets; and questions as to the state of the heroine's affections are mingled with anxieties as to the state of her soul.[30]

The "Amos Barton" narrator's announced interest in characters (mostly middle-aged) whose "passions have not manifested themselves at all after the fashion of a volcano" (42) thus runs counter to the reading public's "taste" for discourse on such passions: what is likely to interest the story's readers is that which absorbs the story's minor characters, "the good people of Milby" (37), who are apt to be "considerably disappointed" when they find the truth about the central clerical relations to be "very far from being bad as they imagined" (38).

"Amos Barton" consists largely of a community's speculations on illicit sexuality—between Reverend Barton and the Countess Czerlaski—where Eliot's narrator insists there is none. The story proceeds by chronicling a society's tendency to sexualize discourse: to seek out sex and drive it to the margins even in the absence of any factual origin.[31] Ultimately, the moral censure in "Amos Barton" falls not upon sinners but on those who had read sin where none existed. In the end, once Barton's wife has died, the narrator describes sad "men and women standing in that churchyard who had bandied vulgar jests about their pastor, and who had lightly charged him with sin," now pitying him, and later repentantly "[turning] over in their minds what they could best do to help" him (67, 68). The moment would seem as well to indict Eliot's readers, were Eliot's own story not occupied mainly with quoting those "vulgar jests"—" 'Mr. Barton may have attractions we don't know of,' said Mr. Pilgrim, who piqued himself on a talent for sarcasm" (50)—and indulging the reader's identification with the popular suspicions. "Amos Barton" continually defines its aims in comparison to the kind of story it claims not to be, first summoning then chastising the reader's disposition to read pruriently. The clerical relationship is fruitful not for what it bars but for what it invites: that a priest is involved means that the search for sex can be pursued more diligently and more urgently. The narrator says to the reader, "I hope you are not in the least inclined to put [on the relationship] that very evil interpretation" that others have (56) and so maintains a moral high ground to which the readers may rise whenever it suits them, while the narrative itself offers an immoral allure in which they can indulge in the interim.

The narrator condemns the people of Milby for providing the conventional language on which his story depends:

Nice distinctions are troublesome. It is so much easier to say that a thing is black, than to discriminate the particular shade of brown, blue, or green, to which it really belongs. It is so much easier to make up your mind that your neighbour is good for nothing, than to enter into all the circumstances that would oblige you to modify that opinion. (38)

Browning too would express a strong preference for "clearly-defined situations and relations." Though Eliot's narrator disparages the Milby community's "black" designations, Eliot herself provides few "nice distinctions"[32]—she does not "modify" such popular opinion so much as reject it.

The nearest the story comes to a positive description of the nature of Barton's relationship with the Countess is when the narrator explains why Barton does not react to his parishioners' "disapprobation": "in the first place, he still believed in the Countess as a charming and influential woman, disposed to befriend him, and, in any case, he could hardly hint departure to a lady guest who had been kind to him and his, and who might any day spontaneously announce the termination of her visit" (57). That the word "be-friend," the only term for the relationship that comes from a source other than popular gossip, should be so removed from public utter-ance—as the narrator's account of Barton's misguided, unspoken belief—is appropriate to the friendship's final, uncertain status. For it not only goes unnamed; it also goes wholly unexplained and unresolved. The Countess leaves, but that is not what ends the gos-sip. When Barton's innocent wife Milly dies, partly from the strain of the gossip, and is at once popularly accepted as a transcendent symbol of betrayed innocence, the relationship between Barton and the Countess disappears from discourse: "No one breathed the Countess's name now; for Milly's memory hallowed her husband, as of old the place was hallowed on which an angel from God had alighted" (68). Nonetheless, the forgiven Barton shortly after loses his curacy through circumstance, and he is then banished from the place, as if Eliot—not the public—must expunge all traces of the unconventional relationship.

Eliot had at hand idiomatic sources with which to develop a clerical relationship more fully when she wished to. With the sexes reversed, the preacher Dinah Morris could rely on familial terms to account for her relationship to Seth Bede and others; and when in *The Mill on the Floss* Maggie Tulliver seeks a final refuge from the familial and sexual complications that plague her, her most promising recourse is the priestly Dr. Kenn's offer of a spiritual "family knit together by Christian brotherhood" (435). But in both these novels, priestliness shares the different fortunes of familial rhetoric.[33] Where Dinah can pass easily from metaphorical "sis-ter" and preacher to sister-in-law and mother, Maggie Tulliver's recourse to her priest provides "no home—no help for the erring"; "public sentiment" is against it.

Dr. Kenn, at first enlightened only by a few hints as to the new turn which gossip and slander had taken in relation to Maggie, had recently been made more fully aware of it by an earnest remonstrance from one of his male parishioners against the indiscretion of persisting in the attempt to over-come the prevalent feeling in the parish by a course of resistance. Dr. Kenn, having a conscience void of offense in the matter, was still inclined to per-severe—was still averse to give way before a public sentiment that was odious and contemptible; but he was finally wrought upon by the consider-ation of the peculiar responsibility attached to his office, of avoiding the appearance of evil—an 'appearance' that is always dependent on the average quality of surrounding minds. Where these minds are low and gross, the area of that 'appearance' is proportionately widened. (451)

The wide-ranging gossip concerning Maggie's relation to Dr. Kenn prompts Stephen Guest's final "passionate cry of reproach" against her. Dr. Kenn's conscience may be "void of offense," but there is a clear sense that the novel's world is not: its elements of "overpowering passion" (452) create a very different plot from that of "Amos Barton." *The Mill on the Floss* claims to eschew "those wild, uncontrollable passions which create the dark shadows of misery and crime" in favor of "the most prosaic form of human life" (238), but its narrative turns on a situation as "striking," an incident as "thrilling," and a passion as avowedly "uncontrollable" as any in those "remarkable novels" Eliot's earlier narrator had dismissed. When sexual attraction asserts itself strongly as either rumor or fact, even Eliot's priests might discover refuge at no place on earth.

But her offhand dispatching of Barton's relationship with the Countess, as an incidental consequence to Milly's heavenly ascent, suggests that Eliot had in mind an alternative place toward which clerics and their female confessors might direct their energies. In "Janet's Repentance," the third and last of the *Scenes*, Eliot offers her version of the successful clerical relationship. Mrs. Janet Dempster's contact with the Reverend Edgar Tryan saves her from alcoholism and the miseries of an unhappy marriage, and the course of their relationship runs as free from acrimony and accusation as does Dinah and Adam's courtship in *Adam Bede*, but without drawing on familial ballast or leading to marriage. Neighbors, even those opposed to the Dissenting Reverend, uniformly express satisfaction in "the fact that Janet Dempster was a changed woman—changed as the dusty, bruised, and sun-withered plant is changed when the soft rains of heaven have fallen on it—and that this change was due to Mr. Tryan's influence" (325). The acceptance of Tryan, apparently because of rather than in spite of his extramarital tie to Mrs. Dempster, is a public triumph in the way the downfall of Barton had been a public sin. But the triumph is not the result of clerical "indirectness" of the kind described by Chapman; Eliot, who in all other writings both fictional and epistolary would bemoan the impossibility of direct communication,[34] confirms Janet's comprehension of Tryan's utterly lucid words: "I believe everything he says at once," Mrs. Dempster declares. "His words come to me like rain on the parched ground. It has always seemed to me before as if I could see behind people's words, as one sees behind a screen; but in Mr. Tryan it is his very soul that speaks" (295).

If the pair successfully achieve direct soulful communication that is because Eliot has refined their relationship to such a degree that there is nothing left of them to speak *but* their souls. The Tryan/Dempster relationship is couched in a series of negations that must inevitably leave them with no form of secular human contact. Tryan's death and ascent to heaven are inevitable stages in the process by which Mrs. Dempster can prayerfully follow him there; he is merely an emblem of "human sympathy" preparing "her soul for that stronger leap by which faith grasps the idea of the divine sympathy" (321).[35] At an early stage, the narrator declares that "the time was not yet come for her to be conscious that the hold he had on her heart was any other than that of [a] heaven sent friend. . . ." When she has become his nurse during his final sickness, "no one could feel that she was performing anything but a sacred office." The process has refined the nature of the affection down to the most infinitesimal portion of anything that might be seen as "more than" friendship. And Eliot will admit even that much only at the last moment in which the two are shown together, when Mrs. Dempster's "full life-breathing lips [meet] the wasted dying ones in a sacred kiss of promise" (333). The kiss functions as a last-second pledge of transcendent union, a characteristic Victorian promise familiar from *The Ring and the Book* and elsewhere, that delivers almost nothing to signal earthly heterosexual affection. The narrator goes so far as to call Tryan in the story's final words a man "whose lips were moved by fervent faith" (334)—as if dedicated to sanctifying even the slightest labial movement in Tryan's last earthly moment.

By the time Eliot presents Mrs. Dempster trailing the coffin of her "beloved friend and pastor" (251), none of the suspicions that had attended the phrase "priest and friend" in *The Ring and the Book* may be admitted;[36] but absent too are any of the positive assertions for the relationship's earthly function that Browning's couple had held to until the end. That loss is sizable, perhaps even more politically consequential than the termination of Dinah Morris's preaching career. For the period after Janet's repentance and before

Edgar's illness had seen them involved in reformist activities, both religious and social; he had urged her to pursue a life of energetic "charitable exertion" and "social intercourse" (324). Now, as she waits to join him in "eternal repose," the coming years "stretch before her like an autumn afternoon, filled with resigned memory. Life to her could never more have any eagerness; it was a solemn service of gratitude and patient effort" (333–34).

If Janet Dempster's life centered on "resigned memory" has left her passive, that may well be because she can draw little life from the memory; the relationship has been presented in terms of what it has excluded far more than what it has provided. All these clarifications of what the relationship's earthly status is *not* may tempt readers to provide their own content for it. For all Eliot's restraint, the *Literary Gazette* reviewer believed that the relationship's real nature was transparent, and in that way disappointing:

just as life is ebbing, it flames out into love for his kind and devoted nurse. This *denouement* is perhaps to the taste of young ladies who can never be content with a popular preacher unless they can have him to preach to them at all times and places; but to our mind that is disappointing. That a clergyman should not be able to hear the confession of a handsome penitent of the other sex, without straightway wishing to marry her, is not heroic. It is artistically a mistake to lower the reader's estimate of Mr. Tryan's moral greatness just at the end of the book.

More recently, Derek and Sybil Oldfield have recognized the same element in "Janet's Repentance," though they see it more sympathetically:

Other critics have been embarrassed that Tryan should come to love Janet, but it is made so clear that she is the outstanding human being in the first place, and her looks and plight had so struck Tryan from the beginning, that it would seem far more unnatural and forced if Tryan had maintained his rôle of merely spiritual guide to the last.[37]

Like the critics who wish to praise Browning as a Victorian admirably willing to acknowledge sexuality, the Oldfields, in their defense of Eliot, translate her complex negotiations into more conventional assertions about what was "natural" to heterosexual relations. They credit Eliot's decision to bar earthly marriage between Tryan and Mrs. Dempster as a way of resisting "false optimism at the end"; the *Literary Gazette*, in contrast, denounced her for lowering the reader's sense of "moral greatness at the end of the book." Neither reading is comfortable with Eliot's refusal to admit to the extrawordly union anything additional, not the slightest intrusion of worldly "falling in love." But Eliot has suffused it all in purity; and no speculation on the merits, shortcomings, or implications of the romance Eliot has never described can save the bond's social significance from having been refined, wholly, out of existence.

But not for good. Twenty years later Eliot resurrected the same plot—at least in outline—for *Daniel Deronda*, this time limiting the priestly relation to what it could or could not do for the female penitent on earth. Once Gwendolen Harleth's "feelings [have] turned this man [Deronda], only a few years older than herself, into a priest" (401), her situation has come to match Janet Dempster's: a wife, beautiful and sinful, trapped in a ghastly marriage, struggling hopefully with the counsel of a priestly figure who urges her to seek solace through dutiful immersion in community. The twin situations also issue in the same consequences, with the evil husbands' violent deaths intensifying the guilt-ridden widows' dependence and isolation, and accordingly, the priests' wholly lucid urgings.[38] When the stories finish with the priests' departing for grand destinations, the widows are left morally sound and hopeful of comparable grand ends for themselves. The two conversion narratives have defined their central relationships in terms of redemption more than romance; the futures to which the stories point are in both cases far more momentous than any domestic marriage.

They are futures that project far beyond Eliot's plots and settings, representing nothing less than the extremest ends of the priestly careers they will fulfill: for Tryan, who has ministered to Janet as a Christian, eternal heavenly salvation; for Daniel, who has suggested to Gwendolen a life defined by communal impulses, the chance to realize his beliefs in the founding of a new holy nation. That these goals have markedly different effects on women in comparable situations is due to more than just Tryan's being a clergyman by profession, and so having Christian salvation to offer, while Daniel is a "priest" only by posture. The more important difference is that Tryan's transcendent goal is one Janet can look to equally, if passively, while Daniel's goal—intellectual, social, political—must painfully exclude Gwendolen, however ambitious her intents. Whereas "Janet's Repentance" ends with the assurance that the pair will meet in heaven, Gwendolen leaves her novel with a much vaguer assurance, telling Daniel again, "*It is better—it shall be better with me because I have known you*" (754).

"Again," since Gwendolen exits stammering for a fourth time, here in writing, the same words she had spoken to Daniel half-way through the novel and repeated twice at their last meeting.[39] With those words she had responded to the first of his many recommendations of "faith or fellowship" (421): if "It is better—it shall be better with me because I have known you" are the defining words for the relationship, as their repetition and final position suggests, then Eliot's text could not convey more dramatically a sense that language has only incompletely articulated the nature of the communion here conceived. As the foregoing pages should have suggested, this rocky pattern of repetition[40] and refusal is unique to *Daniel Deronda* among Eliot's fictions. She had shown herself remarkably adept at resolving gender relations according to models of transcendent faith or marital companionship. In her final novel, she settles upon none of these models to characterize the final state of the most important heterosexual bond.

The avoidance is especially impressive because of the explicitness with which *Daniel Deronda* has summoned the categories she had used earlier, only to renounce them. At one point, the narrator characterizes the "mission of Deronda to Gwendolen" with a Christian family idiom reminiscent of Dr. Kenn's, noting the way "our brother may be in the stead of God to us" (709); at another, Daniel clasps Gwendolen's hands "as if they were going to walk together like two children" (643), the model of innocence that had failed to mediate desire between Maggie and Tom Tulliver. But these stray references are no more than that. And Eliot is far more emphatic in discounting the possibility of a marriage plot:

> [Gwendolen's] imagination had not been turned to a future union with Deronda by any other than the spiritual tie which had been continually strengthening; but also it had not been turned towards a future separation from him. Love-making and marriage—how could they now be the imagery in which poor Gwendolen's deepest attachment could spontaneously clothe itself? (717)

Deronda has, early on, come to recognize Gwendolen's motives to be free from "vulgar flirtation" (405). The narrator confirms him too as "blameless in word and deed" (692), much as Browning's Pope had confirmed the priest Caponsacchi "guiltless in thought, word and deed." Such confirmation seems necessary, for the world of *Daniel Deronda* is far closer to that of "Amos Barton," *The Mill on the Floss*, and *The Ring and the Book* than to that of "Janet's Repentance," in its tendency to suspicious scrutiny. Even positive figures like Daniel's future wife, Mirah, and Lady Mallinger assume a courtship between him and Gwendolen; the characters with the least moral authority, such as Grandcourt and Hans Meyrick, voice these assumptions more overtly. Perhaps their most arch expression comes from Daniel's guardian, Sir Hugo, who conflates Daniel's priestliness with "flirting":

> "I don't think you ever saw me flirt," said Deronda, not amused.
> "Oh, haven't I, though?" said Sir Hugo, provokingly. "You are always looking tenderly at the women, and talking to them in a Jesuitical way. You are a dangerous fellow—a kind of Lovelace who will make the Clarissas run after you instead of your running after them." (332–33)

It is Meyrick who prompts Daniel's most emphatic denial:

> ". . . let me say, once for all, that in relation to Mrs. Grandcourt [Gwendolen], I never have had, and never shall have, the position of a lover. If you have ever seriously put that interpretation on anything you have observed, you are supremely mistaken." (729)

But the novel expends only as much energy discounting these licentious readings as it does disclaiming the possibility that Daniel may end up in the taintless clerical role through which Tryan had served Mrs. Dempster.

> She was bent on confession, and he dreaded hearing her confession. Against his better will, he shrank from the task that was laid on him: he wished, and yet rebuked the wish as cowardly, that she could bury her secrets in her own bosom. *He was not a priest.* He dreaded the weight of this woman's soul flung upon his own with imploring dependence. (642; emphasis added)

That Eliot's narrator must finally insist on explicitly disqualifying Daniel's priestliness indicates how insistently and self-consciously the novel has used it to characterize his relation to Gwendolen. But by this point his priesthood has been revealed as deriving from a source different from Tryan's offer of Christian salvation: it is inconceivable, in the novel's terms, that the Jew's spiritual tie with

Gwendolen would consummate in heavenly union. Though it could still end in "love-making and marriage"—the novel's perfunctory account of the socially accepted marriage between the Klesmers, a Jewish male and a woman of the English elite, makes that clear— Eliot will not let it. The priestly model thus provides but an incomplete alternative to courtship in characterizing Gwendolen and Daniel's bond, and one that will not issue in transcendence or in any other model of consummation.

The denials that permeate *Daniel Deronda* are at once more various and more precise than those of "Janet's Repentance." And whereas such denials had entirely constituted the representation of the central relationship in the earlier story, here they are complemented by detailed attempts at a positive description. "Janet's Repentance" attempted to define its central relationship according to the absence of sexuality; it had followed the same negative strategy as unsuccessful mid-Victorian attempts that positioned "friendship" as distinct from courtship and desire. *Daniel Deronda* does not discount sexuality as an element of the relationship: the narrator admits, albeit somewhat reluctantly, that what Daniel and Gwendolen feel for each other might legitimately be called "love":

It was no treason to Mirah, but a part of that full nature which made his love for her the more worthy, that his joy in her could hold by its side the care for another. For what is love itself, for the one we love best?—an enfolding of immeasurable cares which yet are better than any joys outside our love. (741)

Mighty Love had laid his hand upon her; but what had he demanded of her? Acceptance of rebuke—the hard task of self-change—confession— endurance. If she cried towards [Deronda], what then? (717–18)

In the presence of these kinds of affection, much-doubted "friendship" could hardly hold ground. In any case, derivations of "friendship" in *Daniel Deronda* always lack conviction or emotional force when applied to heterosexual relations: the future Mrs. Klesmer invokes the typical formula when she doubts, incorrectly, that her beloved can have "more than a friendly regard" for her (222); Gwendolen's evil husband Grandcourt calls himself her only "friend" (319), and the "chivalrous" and cynical Sir Hugo Mallinger is eager to offer himself as Gwendolen's "friend" once her husband has died (705); the "friendly pressure" of Daniel's hands on Gwendolen's is, at a late moment, wholly disappointing (716). When the novel provides its most precise characterization of the element of attraction that is central to the non-courtship of Daniel and Gwendolen, "friendship" is explicitly set aside in favor of a more complex "feeling":

In the wonderful mixtures of our nature there is a feeling distinct from that exclusive passionate love of which some men and women (by no means all) are capable, which yet is not the same with friendship, nor with a merely benevolent regard, whether admiring or compassionate: a man, say—for it is a man who is here concerned—hardly represents to himself this shade of feeling towards a woman more nearly than in the words, "I should have loved her, if——:" the "if" covering some prior growth in the inclinations, or else some circumstances which have made an inward prohibitory law as a stay against the emotions ready to quiver out of balance. The "if" in Deronda's case carried reasons of both kinds; yet he had never throughout his relations with Gwendolen been free from the nervous consciousness that there was something to guard against not only on her account but on his own—some precipitancy in the manifestation of impulsive feeling—some ruinous inroad of what is but momentary on the permanent chosen treasure of the heart—some spoiling of her trust, which wrought upon him now as if it had been the retreating cry of a creature snatched and carried out of his reach by swift horsemen or swifter waves, while his own strength was only a stronger sense of weakness. How could his feeling for Gwendolen ever be exactly like his feeling for other women, even when there was one by whose side [his wife's] he desired to stand apart from them? (579)

Far more ambitious than the terse negations of "Janet's Repentance," and more assured than the doubtful evasions of "Amos Barton" and *Mill on the Floss*, this account creates ambiguity through what it admits and subordinates rather than what it sublimates or represses. Sexual attraction is acknowledged, but it is not made definitive: that "nature" can produce "wonderfully mixed" motives complicates any attempt to align the relationship either within or in complete defiance of conventional courtship; but the same complexity bars flat application of priestly purity—as it will be Gwendolen's "wonderfully mixed consciousness" that prevents her from falling upon her knees before Deronda in an attitude of worship (647). Also reiterated is the speculation about what would have happened "if" Daniel and Gwendolen had met under other circumstances (712). But "his feeling for Gwendolen" is explicitly distinct from his "feeling for other women" and equally distinct from his feeling for his wife. Those elements of attraction are, the novel insists, subordinate to others that constitute the "permanent chosen treasure of the heart," the center of Daniel and Gwendolen's relationship. Attraction is less important than a larger continuum clearly distinguishable from a narrative of "love-making and marriage."

Daniel Deronda can achieve its unconventional subtlety because it defines its central heterosexual relation according to a different version of "passion"—what Eliot refers to as "social passion," which, once focused, can make "fellowship real" (336). This communal motive is offered as the alternative for the "many lives" whose passion is "spent in [a] narrow round, for want of ideas and sympathies to make a larger home for it" (421)—that is, trapped in domesticity and courtship. Its grounding in a model of "personal duty and citizenship" (476) links this "social passion" to what Tryan had urged for Janet Dempster: "See what work there is to be done in life. . . ." But in *Daniel Deronda*, unlike "Janet's Repentance," the narrative never resolves or transcends the dynamic of "social intercourse and charitable exertion" (*Scenes*, 324). Rather, that dynamic makes all "consequences passionately present" (*Deronda*, 420) and remains the defining element in the relationship to the end, and beyond.

It is necessarily a tragic element.[41] While both Daniel and Gwendolen grope for a role through which to become "an organic part of social life" (336), Daniel is able to find it in Zionism, whereas Gwendolen, who has had "no . . . thought" of "the fermenting political and social leaven which make a difference in the history of the world" (718), is barred from any such vehicle. In the end, the novel insists that Gwendolen's growing awareness of this "larger" world (747), and of her inability to determine some active relation to it, is the principal source of her misery. Insofar as *Daniel Deronda*'s concluding pages focus on Gwendolen, they are concerned almost exclusively with her doubt as to whether she will ever be able to realize a vision of social duty like that Daniel has suggested to her.[42] That focus represents the book's retroactive proof, of sorts, that the relationship has throughout subordinated courtship to a common impulse toward the "social," albeit an impulse unevenly fulfilled—the proof, that is, that the novel may find its full resolution only in the kind of "future" in which earlier feminists had hoped heterosexual "friendship" could displace the hegemony of courtship. Daniel's departure to join his fellow Zionists is presented as causing Gwendolen pain less because she loses him romantically, or even personally, than because she loses the embodiment of her "hope for moral recovery," because she has "identified him with the struggling regenerative process in her" (717) that depends on her finding some source of "duty" (715). The "shock" Gwendolen suffers at the thought of separation from him goes "deeper than personal jealousy," says the narrator, because she loses Daniel to something like what he has taught her to crave for herself, "something spiritual and vaguely tremendous that," because she possesses no equivalent, "thrust[s] her away" (748). The news of his intention to marry Mirah causes deeper pain still, but largely because it is the most emphatic sign of her permanent exclusion from his task, the converse of the way in which his marriage allows him "the very best of possibilities . . . —the blending of a complete personal love in one current with a larger duty" (581).

That Daniel's extrasexual "passion" is "social" rather than spiritual means that the yield of his relationship with Gwendolen must be found, if it is to be found, on earth. This is not a "friendship" meant to lead to some transcendent "duty" of the kind Josephine Butler would aspire to. This can not even be called a "friendship," at least not according to any mid-Victorian understanding of the word. Not only has this relationship admitted sexual attraction, but it has focused exclusively on secular strivings—it is not meant to be consummated at all.

But if there is a role available to Gwendolen in England that would match what the selfless and married Mirah is destined to find elsewhere,[43] it has not been designated by the well-meaning Daniel or by anyone else in the book. Gwendolen's closing letter to Daniel points to this continuing lack and also, however ingenuously, to his corresponding failure: "*I have remembered your words—that I may live to be one of the best of women, who make others glad that they were born. I do not yet see how that can be, but you know better than I*" (754). The reference to what Gwendolen can't yet "see," and to what Daniel presumably must, echoes the terms of their earlier negotiations—Gwendolen had wondered whether he had "some way of *looking* at things which might be a new footing for her," and he had urged her to "*look* on other lives besides [her] own" (400, 416; emphasis added). Such visual idioms would become important to later figures capable of achieving what Gwendolen could not;[44] in Gwendolen's letter they are but a mark of final futility. She has attained neither "personal love," nor the "larger duty" toward which Daniel in his priestly role has pointed her, and neither is anywhere in sight.

Eliot's readers might have spurned the priestly bond as a model for "friendship" in any case, since Victorians assumed equality to be essential to friendship of any kind, whereas priests had to be assumed superior to their penitents, at least in knowledge.[45] Eliot insists from the moment she introduces the priestly model into *Daniel Deronda* that its benefits are reciprocal, its effects perhaps even "often stronger on the one who takes the reverence" (401) than on the penitent worshiper. But that imbalance is perhaps too well confirmed in Daniel's relation to Gwendolen: if their relationship can be defined, from his point of view, by the way it has consolidated his social passion, then he has reaped all the tangible benefits, while she can only repeat her unrewarded faith in him; the relationship she is left with is difficult to name.

It Shall Be Better: *Daniel Deronda*'s Concluding "Blank"

Where Eliot left finally unnamed the bond "distinct from exclusively passionate love . . ., which yet is not the same with friendship, nor with a merely benevolent regard," she preserved the possibility of its naming. Like Julia Wedgwood, Eliot believed such a relation to be one that only "some men and women (by no means all)" could manage; like Wedgwood, Eliot believed that present circumstances militated strongly against it in any case. Gwendolen's repetition, in writing, of her earlier "it is better—it shall be better with me because I have known you" indicates that the narrative has not generated the conditions necessary to the emergence of a satisfactory idiom; at the same time, the repetition indicates a continued refusal to concede or misname. The dash can be read as preserved for the missing idiom, akin to the "blank" in Janet Dempster's life to which Eliot had repeatedly referred[46] before filling it with religious "love" (293). But syntactically, no version of "love," religious or romantic, or of sterile "friendship," unconvincingly defined as the exclusion of passion, can fit in the blank re-asserted by Gwendolen: what belongs there is not a name for a relationship but a proof of the relationship's fulfillment of its purpose: *how* it is better, by what consequence; some adverbial phrase modifying the act of improvement.

That the conclusion of *Daniel Deronda* so slightly substantiates that proof may be explained partly by reference to Eliot's own isolation. To the end of her life, she bemoaned her inadequate involvement in social action but distanced herself from the movements through which women had achieved cooperative roles alongside men.[47] Her political reticence was surely reinforced by social circumstance: those movements, aware of their vulnerability to accusation and doubt, looked to her class for women who represented a kind of respectability that it would have been difficult for Marian Evans Lewes, or even for Gwendolen Harleth Grandcourt, to bestow. But if Eliot's "social passion" thus remained unexpressed, it also remained, in her final novel, uncompromised, in ways that the impulses of the contributors to *Women's Work and Women's Culture*, wholly ready to appropriate conventional signs to give legitimacy to their social innovations, had not.

A novel's mere refusal to compromise would seem to contribute little to social change. *Daniel Deronda*'s ending has often been faulted for hinting at but not depicting its vision of progress. For Suzanne Graver, Gwendolen's fate is a failed subversion of the institution of marriage: "Although the criticism of social institutions in *Daniel Deronda* is vigorous, it has no vent in action where the portrait of English life is concerned." Accordingly, Graver says, Eliot's version of community "remains an important, not an embodied ideal." John Kucich comes to a similar conclusion when discussing *Daniel Deronda* in the context of the rest of Eliot's work: "What is missing in Eliot is . . . the truly social, interdependent vision she tried so hard to create." For Cynthia Chase and Ellen Rosenman, Eliot's solution is not so much missing as displaced: Chase notes that *Deronda*'s "text banishes the decisive performance to a fictive future beyond the story's end," while Rosenman faults Eliot for the "gap" between her "fictional world and the real one" in which women's opportunities were dramatically improving. Sally Shuttleworth is but a bit more sympathetic when she locates the decisive gap within the text, conceding that "perhaps the strength of *Daniel Deronda* lies in George Eliot's willingness to leave [its fundamental question about the status of women] unresolved."[48]

Critical disappointment about what is *not* realized in *Daniel Deronda* descends from F. R. Leavis's interest in the Jamesian Portrait of Gwendolen that Eliot never wrote. As Leavis did, Graver, Kucich, and others see a great unwritten novel latent in *Daniel Deronda*, though of a very different kind. Critics interested in Eliot's treatment of social situations have tended to credit the ending of *Daniel Deronda* with good intentions and failed execution; but those like Leavis who have focused on the novel's irresolution as a problem of novelistic structure rather than of social realism have often been considerably more harsh in their judgments. Leavis indeed saw the end of *Daniel Deronda* as indicating "the absence of the great novelist," a "failure of creativity" with "calamitous consequences." A more recent analysis by Philip Weinstein, in his *Semantics of Desire*, characterizes "the irresolution of Gwendolen's future" as "vacuous rather than rich with implication." "Of all Eliot's novels, *Deronda* alone is not a coherent whole . . .," complains Mary Doyle: "If we have here a deliberate irresolution of plot, it is not clearly purposeful. Why should Gwendolen's life-role be left more uncertain than Deronda's? And how shall we respond to her indefinite and possibly dismal fate?" Doyle finds these deficiencies particularly troubling in the light of Eliot's emphatic defense of the novel's method, recorded in her letters. "The critic is boggled by such a phenomenon," says Doyle, "and deeply puzzled that George Eliot, the author of *Middlemarch*, could not see what she had done."[49]

But there is more than adequate evidence for the purposefulness of Eliot's ending. The author was indeed insistent about the care with which she had composed *Daniel Deronda*: "I meant everything in the book to be related to everything else," she wrote to Barbara Bodichon. Earlier she had complained repeatedly to her publisher, John Blackwood, about readers who disapproved of her not granting the outcomes they anticipated for her characters. She mentioned in particular "one reader [who] is sure that Mirah is going to die very soon and I suppose will be disgusted at her remaining alive." She continued, "Such are the reproaches to which I make myself liable. However, that you seem to share Mr. Lewes's strong feeling of Book VII [the penultimate] being no falling off in intensity, makes me brave. Only, endings are inevitably the least satisfactory part of any work in which there is any merit of development." [50]

The "disgusted" reader presumably anticipated that Mirah's death would free Daniel to marry Gwendolen, thus providing the novel with the conventional marital consummation. "Poor psychologists are they who are so little able to follow the subtle development of these two characters, as to feel disappointed when they are not united at the end," wrote Rabbi David Kaufmann, in a minority opinion Eliot and Lewes liked so well they got Blackwood to have it translated and published. [51] But that disappointment was the understandable product of Victorian literary convention, which had made the notion of novelistic ending almost inseparable from marriage. [52] Eliot even inscribed that expectation in *Daniel Deronda*: late in the novel, Mrs. Meyrick explains her enjoyment in reading the *Times*'s marriage lists as "giving her the pleasant sense of finishing the fashionable novels without having read them, and seeing the heroes and heroines happy without knowing what poor creatures they were" (675). In the context of such assumptions, Blackwood was right in acknowledging the concluding "situation of Gwendolen and Deronda" to be "so new . . . and oh so delicately handled." [53]

Eliot's closings prior to *Daniel Deronda* would presumably have been more satisfying to Mrs. Meyrick, for they had relied on the two commonplace alternatives, marriage and death. *Middlemarch*, for instance, has come to be viewed as the ultimate expression of the Victorian impulse to resolve. [54] Studies of novelistic closure have assigned *Daniel Deronda* the opposite position: in conjunction with Eliot's comment from early in her career that endings were "the weak point of most authors . . . some of the fault [lying] in the very nature of a conclusion, which is at best a negation," *Daniel Deronda* has come to be seen as the ultimate counterexpression against the impulse epitomized in *Middlemarch*. [55] Marianna Torgovnick, in her extended reading of *Middlemarch*, finds more "consolatory" the "open" ending of *Daniel Deronda*; the later novel suggests to her the "possibility of a new society structured along religious and humanitarian lines," in contrast to

the way the final paragraph of *Middlemarch* . . . unblinkingly evaluates Dorothea's life in terms of the reduced possibilities [Eliot] assumes exist for the nineteenth century man or woman. Perhaps because religious impulse has the potential to build a new society at the end of *Deronda*, there is no need for the consolatory, didactic kind of ending in *Middlemarch*. Deronda's after-history is not supplied for the reader; his fate and Gwendolen Harleth's remain "open." [56]

Boone too praises the way "the ending of the Daniel plot has certain, though circumscribed, affinities with what is 'open' about Gwendolen's uncertain future," such that, "by exposing wedlock as something less than a happy conclusion, this rich and innovative novel succeeds in calling into question the social order underlying the traditional order of fiction itself." [57]

Whether they generate notions of absence, vacuousness, or openness, these studies of *Deronda*'s ending *as ending* credit Eliot mainly with negation: "there is nothing like unmarriage, an idea that realists have always toyed with, to express openendedness," notes Alexander Welsh,[58] in a comment that can serve to show *Deronda*'s mere formal avoidance of marriage to be, in itself, neither particularly original nor disruptive. Eliot's own remark disparaging "conclusion" as "at best a negation" suggests that she would hardly have been satisfied with credit for a nullity. Moreover, *Daniel Deronda* does not entirely negate the gestures of traditional closure: "there is marriage (Daniel and Mirah's) and a death (Mordecai's)," Boone notes, and one may go further to say that Deronda's marriage has all the closing familial munificence of Adam Bede's and that Mordecai's death is enwrapped in all the transcendent promise of Edgar Tryan's. The continued irresolution of Daniel and Gwendolen's relationship in the midst of traditional closing gestures makes it very hard to characterize the precise effect of the novel's ending: Shuttleworth, for instance, describes the novel as wholly avoiding "the compromise of marriage" in the same sentence in which she mentions Mirah's "complete fulfillment." [59]

With such exemplary gestures of closure and anticlosure existing side by side, not only within the same career but within the same novel, closure seems at best an uncertain measure of Eliot's achievement. Boone's reference to "the lack of a romantic denouement" is no truer to Eliot's language than his reference to an "unconventional friendship"; it misses the mark to the same degree as the Victorian *Spectator*'s praise for *Daniel Deronda*'s "subtlety" in describing "relations which have never in any way been those of passion" or the *The Gentleman's Magazine*'s assurance that Gwendolen "is still young, and it is reasonable to suppose that she will find some heart-free individual who can make her drink the waters of Lethe." [60] These renderings account for what hasn't happened, sexually or romantically, in the novel's plot, but not for what the novel has painstakingly described.

Such approaches slight the "decisive performance" to which *Daniel Deronda* devotes so much energy: its "nice distinctions" of idiom, [61] its intense negotiations, not only with structures, but with phrases that Eliot had deployed readily at earlier stages of her career. What is missing is not the conventional closing gestures—which are wholly, even doubly present—but the corresponding labels that would assimilate Gwendolen in some comfortably named role. Having discredited "passionate love," "friendship," or "merely benevolent regard" would not prevent Gwendolen's affection from being dubbed that of a sibling-in-law (a second Seth's or Chettam's) or that of a heavenly spirit (like Milly's or Tryan's), or prevent it otherwise from exploding the plot, ever unbridled (like Maggie Tulliver's). The final chapter of *Daniel Deronda* may be said to have all these legitimizing formulas at its disposal, separately or in combination, [62] but none is positioned to denominate the book's central relation. They therefore issue in a supremely conventional formal ending that nevertheless retains a repeated, disconcerting blank in its midst, a blank that is emphasized in the text but unaccounted for in the plot. Gwendolen's italicized letter, arriving in the midst of Daniel and Mirah's wedding plans and just prior to Mordecai's death, neither participates in the narrative nor disrupts it; every other paragraph in the chapter connects tightly to those around it, but the letter passes almost as a kind of ghostly voice-over that in no way affects the narrative, before or after. Within that odd space is the smaller one of Gwendolen's written stammer: "It is better—it shall be better with me because I have known you." The repetition and preservation of an incomplete moment in speech asserts that moment's static survival independent of narrative progress, as if the phrase has been drawn out of time. [63]

The result does not seem to me the same as merely postponing the problem to some inconceivable future. The blank within that unassimilated section of text is more than a vacuous opening: a wide variety of possible fillers has been rejected; the novel has been very precise about what *should not* reasonably go there. (Boone's sense of "circumscribed" possibilities is very much to the point here.) In accounting for the rare "feeling" distinguishable from other conventional or trivial ones, the novel has made clear that there is as yet no precise idiom that can suitably occupy that blank, as there is yet no representable result for the relationship it anticipates between Gwendolen and Daniel. But the dash stands as a preserved place within which the idiom, and the activity it might name, could appear. Eliot creates a text open to future events she cannot depict: *Daniel Deronda* does not require a sequel of the sort that was written for it (as for *Adam Bede*); it is, as Boone says, distinctly and "unexpectedly modern"[64] or even post-modern, in so far as it invites a kind of future writing-in of the missing idiom. A novel's disturbance of the social order can only be described as significant if it summons, at least implicitly, some productive action: *Daniel Deronda*'s resistance of the marriage plot for its central relationship cannot be said to urge the avoidance, or even the undercutting, of marriage, since the novel so happily affirms that institution for Daniel and Mirah. But the novel's resistance of comforting idioms calls for a new gesture of naming. There is something that hasn't been said, the repeated blank testifies, that yet needs saying. *Daniel Deronda* calls for the advancement of an idiom it has but half-created.

It is unlikely that Eliot or any writer sympathetic to Gwendolen's fate would have conceived of Gwendolen's missing idiom as parallel to "friendship," a term that offered perhaps less promise than any other. As long as "friendship" was defined unconvincingly as sexlessness, any attempt to occupy ground with it was destined to be ephemeral, to interrupt conventional narratives less tangibly even than did Gwendolen's letter, always to be displaced in favor of other more acceptable terms. In banishing "friendship" along with those other idioms that had served to categorize the prevailing fictions of her time, Eliot left a silence. Yet in emphatically preserving that silence, she made the strongest possible case for the needed idiom, for the name that would account for heterosexual interaction of a truly productive kind. The narrative fates of *Daniel Deronda*'s characters are what make that need seem compelling and disconcerting and what give that need clear human significance. But it is Eliot's experiments with idiom that alert her readers to what is needed—an alternative to discursive restrictions in the presentation of heterosexual relations—and that might caution readers against asserting false or compromising alternatives of the kind she rejected: the kind that, in a mid-Victorian context, inevitably sen-tenced heterosexual relations to either the most unacceptable or the most commonplace realms.

Part II

"Intensities and Avoidances": Male Novelists in an Awkward Age, 1895–1913

3

Friendship and New Women

Late-Victorian Phrasings

My first two chapters showed that heterosexual friendship, defined mainly according to the absence of sex, had only an ephemeral status in mid-Victorian discourse, as an inconstant overwhelmed by terms pertaining to other relations more readily acknowledged. With the grandiose implications of "Platonic" love discredited, cross-sex "friendship" between the unmarried functioned in public discourse as a "mere" negation, a "pure and simple" space that inefficiently banned sexuality and was itself empty of signification. Where extramarital relations neither transcended that space (in extraworldly triumph) nor sank below it (in sin), they were resigned to dubiety, to continual displacement. The most frequently chosen legitimizing formulas, borrowed from the realms of the family and clerical life, furthered rather than countered that continual resignation of friendship; responding to those formulas, even the most sympathetic modern criticism has made little progress toward suggesting an alternative.

Yet those representations of relationships I have examined thus far do suggest a positive function for friendship. Each pair (the Mills, the "exceptional" man and woman imagined by Julia Wedgwood in *Women's Work and Women's Culture*, Browning's Pompilia and Giuseppe, and Eliot's Daniel Deronda and Gwendolen Harleth) is associated with cooperation of a specific kind, and cooperation provides the relationships with a positive dynamic other than (or more important than) courtship and sexuality. They are structured by shared activity, actual or intended. As such they might be plotted according to their degree of cooperative energy and production, not just mutual attraction.

Remarks by the Mills, Wedgwood, and others indicate that mid-Victorian feminist interest in friendship had been prompted by the wish to end courtship's hegemony over bourgeois heterosexual relations. Later in the century, increased cooperation between the sexes in commonly represented activities encouraged the New Woman to subordinate the requirements of courtship to new modes of work: where heterosexual cooperation was necessary, as it had long been among the working classes, "friendship" might be thought of as a necessary daily fact.[1] Narratives concerned with heterosexual relations might now dwell, at least temporarily, on the immediate activity of relationships—on their attempts at cooperation and communication—rather than on their inevitable progress toward or resistance to subsequent consummation, and idioms like "friendship," "comradeship," and "fellowship" might seem legitimate and authentic.

It was the first time Jessamine had tasted real comradeship with a man. Comradeship is impossible where sex is predominant, and in the refined world which she had forsaken sex stands opposite to sex, the stronger with the stirrings of an exhausted sensuality, the weaker comporting itself as a *recherché* morsel which knows its price. But here all was changed. This stalwart peasant saw her only as a serviceable human being; he shouted orders in a peremptory tone as he ran hither and thither, and she made every effort to obey them, sending back shrill retorts when necessary, her voice forsaking in the exigency of the moment that sweet lowness which is an excellent thing in drawing-rooms.[2]

Even when such displacements of sexual desire turn out to be as temporary or compromised as had their mid-Victorian equivalents (the working relationship cited above, from Emma Frances Brooke's *A Superfluous Woman* [1894], does soon after become mainly passionate) the fact that they even tentatively propose a positive definition is crucial. For by the 1890's, "friendship" had changed its function and become something other than a term of negation—though not because working "comradeship" had successfully displaced sex. On the contrary, "friendship," however unstable, had now to account for both work and sex. The suggestion posed by Eliot in *Daniel Deronda*, that a male/female cooperative relationship outside of marriage could accommodate elements of sexual attraction even when no idiom superior to faulty "friendship" existed to designate them, developed by the end of the century into the belief that heterosexual friendship *necessarily included* sexual relations. In New Woman novels of the 1890's, friendship is no longer that which is not sex; sex indeed seems sometimes to inhere in "friendship," so the category in opposition to which friendship is defined is not sex but marriage and related social conventions.[3]

The two chapters that follow concern characteristic rhetorical gestures in the works of several turn-of-the-century male novelists who were reacting to changes in the representable gender roles. Although their texts include more sustained consideration of male / female friendship than their mid-Victorian predecessors' had, these writers make little more progress toward producing a viable idiom for it. This failure—and its status as a recognized or recognizable failure is evident in the eventual collapses or capitulations of idioms they do deploy—follows from the texts' inadequate demarcation of any sphere of shared heterosexual activity that might provide adequate grounding for viable terms. Instead, friendship in these novels is the object of a continuous idiomatic crisis, demanding constant repetition and qualification of the words that are used to label it.

With the incorporation of sex into friendship, the relationship that had once seemed opposed to sex now takes on a narrative position almost identical to sex: an object endlessly contemplated as a secret.[4] Novels of the 1890's are obsessed with naming heterosexual relations, even at the expense of plotting. Yet the social worlds (within the novels) in which "friendship" is evaluated rarely allow characters to enact it, either publicly or privately, so their experiments produce few helpful results. They suggest, frequently, only another discursive impasse, this one perhaps more troubling than the one Eliot had conveyed at the end of *Daniel Deronda*: for where Eliot had hopefully preserved a space for the emergent relation and its idiom, these later writers imply that a new form of friendship has now become possible but is still unaccompanied by the words necessary to give it legitimacy. When these texts circumscribe friendship, they do not consign it to an open space for future representation. Instead, they shut off that space *from* representation.

These confident but despairing male writers' sense of thorough recognition allows them to provide the period's clearest placing of friendship's relation to more conventional heterosexual relations. Their novels offer the best opportunity for defining a discrete (if, finally, suspect) place for "friendship" within the discourse of the period. Their confidence that they can comprehend and fully (if but implicitly) resolve the new social conditions distinguishes the men's writings from that of their female contemporaries, which seem much less apt to hint that they have achieved a self-satisfying vision of male/female friendship, articulable or otherwise. The suggestions in the male-authored texts about to be discussed, that friendship is assuredly imminent or inevitably doomed, differ significantly from the "anguished uncertainty" at the end of Sarah Grand's *The Heavenly Twins* (1893) or the bitter disappointment at the end of Ethel Arnold's *Platonics* (1894). An alternative study focusing on women writers from the years prior to World War I would, I think, find few or no claims to novelistic progress toward satisfactory idioms for heterosexual friendship. If, in the face of such Victorian continuities, New Woman novels by women "flaunt their anger," as Ann Ardis has suggested,[5] that evident rage distinguishes their work from the odd combinations of surety and resignation evidenced by the male New Woman novelists and their successors, who flaunt instead a sense of their own heady experimentation and heroic defeat.

I argue in this chapter that New Woman writers Grant Allen and Thomas Hardy manage both smugness and constant equivocation in conveying their visions of new relations between the sexes; nowhere is that combination more apparent than when they invoke, as an emblem for their own discoveries, the figure of Percy Bysshe Shelley, whom the Victorians associated with every gender-related tension and ambiguity. The late-Victorian advocacy of Shelley's example seems at once atavistic and progressive, returning to an early-nineteenth-century figure to move "friendship" beyond its mid-century connotations toward ones that would include rather than exclude sex. As such, Victorian Shelleyans' position on "friendship" is less modernizing than muddling: it is a means for commentators to validate ostensibly novel social models without distinguishing them from earlier models of transcendence and sin—without, in fact, delineating them at all.

And even a writer known to be extremely precise in his negotiations with English idiom may ultimately contribute little toward the realization of "friendship." This chapter—and my treatment of the nineteenth century—ends by considering Henry James's 1899 novel *The Awkward Age*. Rather than merely hinting at and concealing a claimed resolution, James's book shapes an image of retreat from the discursive pressures of the new era: unwilling to renounce male / female "friendship," however unlikely and ephemeral it may seem, James gives it a place to run home to, though not a place he even pretends to be able to present.

Delicate Distinctions in
The Woman Who Did

The impulse to snicker, knowingly, at the title of Grant Allen's 1895 novel *The Woman Who Did* is entirely appropriate, on both historical and textual grounds. The titles of sequels such as *The Woman Who Didn't* and *The Woman Who Wouldn't* indicate that late-Victorian readers snickered[6]—just as the book asked them to, by continually inviting them to demand "Did what?" and to assume the response, that what the woman did was to have sex. Even the author seems to be snickering, smugly, as he presents his novel's subject matter: *The Woman Who Did* smacks of self-satisfaction. Allen announces his marital and moral complacency with twin dedications, one inscribed to his "dear wife" (to whom he says he has "dedicated [his] twenty happiest years") and a second, presumably inscribed to himself, which declares the book to have been

> Written at Perugia
> Spring 1893
> For the first time in my life
> Wholly and solely to satisfy
> My own taste and my own conscience

Immediately after, his two sentences of Preface declare his distinctive prescience:

> "BUT surely no woman would ever dare to do so," said my friend.
> "I knew a woman who did," said I; "and this is her story."

The title phrase points also to the topicality of Allen's wisdom, for *The Woman Who Did* eponymously claims to have accomplished what Victorian readers knew the Novel and the New Woman lately and remarkably to have been doing. Allen's novel followed a series of books on similar subjects, all as strikingly and self-consciously polemical, emotional, and sexually candid.[7] The

genre's protagonists were understood to mirror the careers of contemporary females: the New Woman Novel offered the public a
chance to see the much-discussed "wild women" in action.[8] Readers
sought the private experiences behind a public controversy.

Allen's title would accordingly provoke both the prurient question and the understood answer at the head of a reading experience
that sustained their interplay—an inexhaustible alternation of "Did
what?" and "Did this."[9] For *The Woman Who Did* demonstrated
that the New Woman controversy could disclose what the New
Woman was *not* doing far more volubly than what she was doing;
the controversy was far more efficient at eliciting further questions
than at providing definitive answers. Margaret Oliphant's famous
attack on Allen and his novelistic and actual accomplices as "The
Anti-Marriage League" incorporated the same tantalizing mechan-
ics as Allen's title. Short of spending their whole lives refusing
marriage proposals, what were the New Women doing?

It is . . . important to ask what is the result of the struggle of the woman who
did, and of others who have followed her. Its result is to select, as the most
important thing in existence, one small (though no doubt highly important)
fact of life, which natural instinct has agreed, even among savages, to keep
in the background, and which among all peoples who have ceased to be
savage is veiled over by instinctive reticences and modesties of convention
as well as by the everlasting truth of Love. . . . I do not choose to sully my
lips with the name which the lesser passion thus selected bears, and it is
painful to me, as a woman, to refer to it; but it seems necessary to point
out to the public what is the immediate result of the crusade against marriage now officially organized and raging around us. It is to displace love
altogether . . . and to place in its stead the mere fact which is its seal, one
incident in life, but not more. To make this the supreme incident, always
in the foreground, to be discussed by young men and women, and held up
before boys and girls, and intruded upon those from whom circumstances
or choice have shut it off, or who have outlived the period in which it is
interesting, seems to me an outrage for which there is no justification.[10]

Did what? Even if premised on the same "matter-of-fact" confidence about human "nature" that mid-Victorian commentators had
held, the New Woman controversy throve on fixing the unnarrat-
able as the center of its narratives.[11] Allen's novel accounts for the
consummation of the woman who did's unmarried relationship as
follows:

The door was opened for him by Herminia in person; for she kept no servant,—that was one of her principles. She was dressed from head to foot in a simple white gown, as pure and sweet as the soul it covered. A white rose nestled in her glossy hair; three sprays of white lily decked a vase on the mantel-piece. Some dim survival of ancestral ideas made Herminia Barton so array herself in the white garb of affiance for her bridal evening. Her cheek was aglow with virginal shrinking as she opened the door, and welcomed Alan in. But she held out her hand just as frankly as ever to the man of her free choice as he advanced to greet her. Alan caught her in his arms and kissed her forehead tenderly. And thus was Herminia Barton's espousal consummated. (77)

Allen's sixth chapter so concludes: with a teasing reticence, to be sure, but at the same time with an implicit claim to have told all, if to tell all is to disclose consummation. One may be expected to know what happened in the same way one may know (and hear) the word Mrs. Oliphant won't speak. The sense of the novel's having fully comprehended (even if it won't exactly say) all the New Woman has done and has meant to do is reasserted throughout Allen's text, both in Herminia's own unflappable assurance that she knows what she wants and in the narrator's insistent confirmations of her sapience. To further emphasize his proprietary enlightenment, the author leaves to his namesake, Alan, the male protagonist (evidently a younger, less enlightened version of Allen himself), the role of the benighted observer who is unable to read Herminia's intents and acts. Though Alan is above all understanding, in the sense of sympathetic, and is in fact introduced into the text as a "kindred soul" to Herminia (36), when he has to articulate or act upon what he understands he is utterly baffled. He commits, first of all, the terrible blunder of proposing marriage, then the second error of doubting that Herminia has considered what her preference for remaining unmarried entails.

Herminia looked up at him, half hurt. "Can't have thought of what it entails!" she repeated. Her dimples deepened. "Why, Alan, haven't I had my whole lifetime to think of it? What else have I thought about in any serious way, save this one great question of a woman's duty to herself, and her sex, and her unborn children? It's been my sole study. How could you fancy I spoke hastily, or without due consideration on such a subject? ... Could you suspect me of such carelessness?—such culpable thoughtlessness?—you, to whom I have spoken of all this so freely?" (38–39)

In elaborating what she has pondered, as the scene continues, Herminia confidently adopts "friendship" as the name for the relation she desires. She uses the word, and Allen confirms its use, as perfectly lucid, conveying a clearly conceived union, Herminia's alternative to marriage. The term that Victorians had used, uncomfortably, to designate the exclusion of sex from extramarital relationships serves Herminia matter-of-factly to declare sex's inclusion in her extramarital relationship: the "friendship" Herminia proposes with Alan, Allen asserts, "was but the due fulfilment of her natural functions" (70). But however much Allen and Herminia claim to know exactly what they have in mind, Alan remains stunned.

> Alan stared at her, disconcerted, hardly knowing how to answer. "But what alternative do you propose, then?" he asked in his amazement.
>
> "Propose?" Herminia repeated, taken aback in her turn. It all seemed to her so plain, and transparent, and natural. "Why, simply that we should be friends, like any others, very dear, dear friends, with the only kind of friendship that nature makes possible between men and women."
>
> She said it so softly, with some womanly gentleness, yet with such lofty candor, that Alan couldn't help admiring her more than ever before for her translucent simplicity, and directness of purpose. Yet her suggestion frightened him. It was so much more novel to him than to her. Herminia had reasoned it all out with herself, as she truly said, for years, and knew exactly how she felt and thought about it. To Alan, on the contrary, it came with the shock of a sudden surprise, and he could hardly tell on the spur of the moment how to deal with it. He paused and reflected. "But do you mean to say, Herminia," he asked, still holding that soft brown hand unresisted in his, "you've made up your mind never to marry any one? made up your mind to brave the whole mad world, that can't possibly understand the motives of your conduct, and live with some friend, as you put it, unmarried?" (39–40)

Throughout Alan and Herminia's relationship, Allen and Herminia insist on her confidence about the clarity and naturalness of the bond she envisions; it is that assuredness that makes the book's references to "friendship" remarkable. More tentative uses of the word to designate a relationship inclusive of sex were becoming common: the philosopher Edward Carpenter would write in the following year, "people are beginning to see . . . that Love and Friendship—which have been so often set apart from each other as

things distinct—are in reality closely related and shade impercep-
tibly into each other"; the third installment of a *Westminster Review* exchange entitled "Friendship Between the Sexes" soon issued
in contributor L. Keith Stibbard's acknowledging, "Experience and
observation have taught me that just as sex influences other relations, so, in at least as large a degree, it must impress its character
upon friendships." [12] But no sense of imperceptible shades or uncertain influence troubles Herminia: she knows what she wants, what
she thinks she must have, and what she thinks she can have.
Alan, on the other hand, never quite grasps it.

> He took it for granted that of course they must dwell under one roof with
> one another. But that simple ancestral notion, derived from man's lordship
> in his own house, was wholly adverse to Herminia's views of the reason-
> able and natural. She had debated these problems at full in her own mind
> for years, and had arrived at definite and consistent solutions for every
> knotty point in them. Why should this friendship differ at all, she asked,
> in respect of time and place, from any other friendship? (69)

Yet in spite of his alter ego's constant and painful bafflement, Allen
continually upholds Herminia's right to withhold full explanation.

> It was not, she explained to him further, that she wished to conceal any-
> thing. The least tinge of concealment was wholly alien to that frank fresh
> nature. If her head-mistress asked her a point-blank question, she would
> not attempt to parry it, but would reply at once with a point-blank answer.
> Still, her very views on the subject made it impossible for her to volunteer
> information unasked to any one. Here was a personal matter of the utmost
> privacy; a matter which concerned nobody on earth, save herself and Alan;
> a matter on which it was the grossest impertinence for any one else to make
> any inquiry or hold any opinion. They two chose to be friends; and there,
> so far as the rest of the world was concerned, the whole thing ended. (73)

Herminia's simultaneous wish to maintain a private discourse while
making a public statement on behalf of "her sex" offers the reader
the possibility of sharing Alan's privileged incomprehension; the
novel provides special access to a silence.

Yet within the story's context, Herminia's refusal to provide
complete clarification does little to limit public discussion. Like
Giuseppe and Pompilia's claim to be "friends," Herminia's claim
about her relationship with Alan becomes only a cipher to be displaced by various conventional labels. Alan fears from the begin-

ning that "base souls would see . . . only the common story of a trustful woman cruelly betrayed by the man who pretended to love her . . ." (54–55). Ultimately, he confronts this view directly when it is voiced by his own father, in a conversation reminiscent (in subject if not in tone) of Daniel Deronda's rebuttal of his guardian:

> ". . . Why the devil couldn't you marry her outright at first, instead of seducing her?"
>
> "I did not seduce her," Alan answered stoutly. "No man on earth could ever succeed in seducing that stainless woman."
>
> Dr. Merrick stared hard at him without changing his attitude on his old oak chair. Was the boy going mad, or what the dickens did he mean by it?
>
> "You *have* seduced her," he said slowly. "And she is *not* stainless if she has allowed you to do."
>
> "It is the innocence which survives experience that I value, not the innocence which dies with it," Alan answered gravely.
>
> "I don't understand these delicate distinctions," Dr. Merrick interposed with a polite sneer. . . .

Alan is unable to offer any delineation that can withstand his father's conventional rendering. He repeatedly refers to Herminia's objection to marriage, but is unable to explain the alternative she favors. "I came to tell you the difficulty in which I find myself, and to explain to you my position," he insists. "If you won't let me tell you in my own way, I must leave the house without having laid the facts before you."

"As you will," his father replies, and Alan does go, though not without Allen's assuring us that "Alan made one more effort. In a very earnest voice, he began to expound to his father Herminia's point of view" (93–95). None of this final attempt is disclosed in the novel's text, and Allen has provided no suggestion that Alan has any functional vocabulary at his disposal. The word "friendship" has not arisen during this dialogue, appropriately not, since it is Herminia's word, and Allen's; not Alan's, and not that of public discourse—not that of any situation other than the couple's private conversation, where it recurs constantly. In public it is consistently suppressed. Addressed as Alan's wife in a Milanese hotel,

Herminia longed to blurt out the whole simple truth. "I am *not* his wife. I am not, and never could be wife or slave to any man. This is a very dear friend, and he and I are travelling as friends together." But a warning glance from Alan made her hold her peace with difficulty and acquiesce as best she might in the virtual deception. (102–3)

For all the assurance with which "friendship" is introduced to designate "the whole simple truth" of *The Woman Who Did*, the word's undermining by convention is as steady as Herminia's downfall. When Alan dies in Perugia, he has left "absolutely everything of which he died possessed 'to my beloved friend, Herminia Barton,' " in a will unsigned and hence invalid (128); the word "friend" of course underscores the extralegality of their bond, and thus of the will, from which she gets nothing.[13] When she returns to England, still thinking of him as her "only friend" (133), their story is "retold by each man or woman after his or her own fashion," most of them seeing "nothing but material for a smile, a sneer, or an innuendo" (132). And when, years later, Herminia rejects a marriage proposal from a new "friend," she articulates no alternative of the kind she had suggested to Alan. " 'No, no,' she said firmly, over and over again. 'You must take me my own way, or you must go without me.' " The man's response indicates the degree to which "friendship" has reverted to its mid-Victorian status: " 'Herminia,' he said, before they parted that afternoon, 'we may still be friends; still dear friends as ever? This episode need make no difference to a very close companionship?' "

"It need make no difference" (169), she responds, evidently having renounced her earlier understanding of "the only kind of friendship that nature makes possible between men and women" (39). Allen rhetorically confirms that renunciation, ending the sixteenth chapter, "And from that day forth they were loyal friends, no more, one to the other" (170). "Friendship," hitherto invoked in defiance of convention, has been relegated to suggesting only chaste failure: a minimal relation to which "more" would have to be added in order for it to become significant. Nor has the novel provided any moment at which the content and meaning of "friendship" would become apparent, though the reader has continually been assured that it is being presented and tested. The capacity of "friendship" to designate a bond inclusive of sex has had the same fate in the novel as sex itself: continually affirmed but never plainly chronicled; claimed and withheld.

Shelleyans and Anti-Shelleyans

As it attempted to chronicle changes in gender relations, the New Woman novel insisted on New-ness.[14] Yet nowhere are both the energy of Herminia's claims and their fragility more apparent than in her recourse to two famous precursors, George Eliot and Percy Bysshe Shelley. Though she tells Alan, first of all, "When George Eliot chose to pass her life with Lewes on terms of equal freedom, she defied the man-made law," she nevertheless thinks Eliot's example badly compromised, because "as soon as Lewes was dead, George Eliot showed she had no principle involved, by marrying another man" (47).[15] Herminia recalls this concession again when she rejects her second suitor, fearing, "If I were to give way now, as George Eliot gave way, . . . I should counteract any little good my example has ever done or may ever do in the world" (167–68). In having her reject Eliot, Allen cuts off Herminia from all comparable figures—she acknowledges "brave women" before her who have "avoided marriage" but doubts that they acted "from principle, and from principle only" as she means to (46–47). But in the process he does link her positively to a male exemplar:

I can never quite forgive George Eliot—who knew the truth, and found freedom for herself, and practised it in her life—for upholding in her books the conventional lies, the conventional prejudices; and . . . I can never admire Shelley enough, who, in an age of slavery, refused to abjure or deny his freedom, but acted unto death to the full height of his principles. (102)

Where Eliot is denounced for a further contradiction, Shelley is praised as a hero of consistent idealism. He is in fact the only predecessor for whom Herminia ever expresses enthusiasm; she calls him nothing less than "the prophet and interpreter of the highest moral excellence" (101). Through her praise for Shelley, Allen brings Herminia closest to a positive assertion as to the nature of the relationship she envisions. Not that she says anywhere what she thinks Shelley's example entails, but her praise for Shelley represents her one link to an explicit set of statements about relations between the sexes.

It places her, moreover, on one side of a passionate late-Victorian debate, whose terms may serve as an index to the idiomatic crisis in the best-known New Woman novel. The fin-de-siècle Shelley controversy, replicated in *The Woman Who Did* and then in *Jude the Obscure*, demonstrates that conventional terms for gender relations were persisting but were, at the same time, blending together. Under such circumstances, Thomas Hardy could no more render "friendship" explicable than could Herminia.

Since the mid-1880's, when his family's bundles of biographies and editions had driven Shelley to new prominence, controversy about his status as exemplar had become increasingly heated. By 1892, *The Fortnightly Review* could declare Shelley "the only personage of his time over whom intelligent and candid men still see fit to lose their tempers." In the same year, Henry Salt's pro-Shelley work *Shelley's Principles: Has Time Refuted or Confirmed Them?* quoted the explorer H. M. Stanley as warning Shelleyans that they were "playing . . . with fire." Though acknowledging that "Mrs. Grundy has now substituted for the grim old notion of a diabolical Shelley that pleasanter picture of an 'ineffectual angel,'" Salt referred approvingly to Karl Marx's calling Shelley "essentially a revolutionist." "There are more than the first mutterings of that revolution in the Golden City of Divine institutions prophecized of by Shelley in *Laon and Cythna*," warned Shelley biographer John Todhunter.[16]

Todhunter went on to envision "a good many Cythnas ready to rush about on their black Tartarian hobbies, of whom Mrs. Mona Caird [one of the earliest and most prominent of New Woman writers] is the one who has recently made most noise"; New Woman writing often invoked Shelley in its attacks on marriage.[17] This connection was one readers were prepared to find and to fear, since late-Victorian anxieties over Shelleyan "freelovers and freethinkers" had already been sparked by Cordy Jeaffreson's admonitions against Shelleyanism in his 1885 *The Real Shelley*. Fresh from having portrayed another insidious Romantic, *The Real Byron* (1883), Jeaffreson warned of the increasing influence of "The Shelleyan Socialists," those "conscientious though misguided persons, who . . . regard with various degrees of approval or tolerance Shelley's daring . . . proposal for abolishing lawful marriage, and replacing it with the Free Contract. . . ."[18] Not everyone in 1885 was sure who these "fiends" were or why Jeaffreson's attack was so vituperative.[19] But in ensuing years, some of Jeaffreson's warnings must have seemed justified as Shelley and the opponents of marriage became more explicitly associated, even if never as explicitly as he had pictured.

Jeaffreson condemned Shelley chiefly for being "the author of *Laon and Cythna*," and for having tried to demonstrate therein "that incest was nothing but an imaginary sin; . . . that instead of being loathsome, nauseous, hideous, unutterably repulsive and sinful, the conjugal union of a brother and sister under the Free Contract was permissible . . . and compatible with moral purity." Shelley's attack on marriage, seen thus, encompassed the consummate perversion of familial "delicacy," not through an aversion to either marriage or family but through a conflation of them. And Jeaffreson saw *Laon and Cythna* as on the verge of provoking a modern crisis, since "Fate" had "determined that a poem, which a committee of men of the world declared unfit for circulation during the profligate Regency, should be produced *verbatim* for the moral edification of the men, and women, and young people of Victorian England." *The Real Shelley* closed by pointing to the insidious potential of Shelley's rise to eminence.

Now that *Queen Mab*, with its anti-matrimonial note, is put into the hands of our boys; now that *Laon and Cythna*, with its monstrous doctrine, is seen on our drawing-room tables; now that the author of so reprehensible a book is proclaimed a being of unqualified goodness, who, under auspicious circumstances, 'might have been the Saviour of the World,' it is time for the world to be told that the recent efforts to win for Shelley a kind of regard, to which he is in no degree whatever entitled, are only part of a social movement, that, so far as the extreme Shelleyan Socialists are concerned, is a movement for the Abolition of Marriage,—in accordance with the spirit and purpose of his Social Philosophy.[20]

For Jeaffreson, texts like *Laon and Cythna* embodied an immense confusion at the heart of English understandings about social relations. But Jeaffreson's own assessment of Shelley partook of some of the customary contradictions. He considered *Epipsychidion*, after all, to be "the finest love poem in the literature of the universe," the product of "a powerfully imaginative brain . . . [which had] perfected its conceptions with the self-concentrated energy of a power, wholly disconnected from the animal that possessed it." Its subject Shelley had endowed "with all the conceivable virtues of womankind," in order to produce "a being that was less a reality than the offspring of his fancy." In Shelley, the two extremes at which Victorians had commonly placed heterosexual love—those of sin and salvation—seemed vexingly to merge.[21] Shelley could be cited to underwrite either or both of two extremes: ethereal sublimation on the one hand and social and sexual revolution on the other.

Accordingly, when *The Woman Who Did* invokes Shelley, whose notion of "friendship," was anyway, unlike Herminia's, a sexless one,[22] the novel never makes clear whether he is being praised for having ineffectually and angelically transcended "the conventional prejudices" through an idealist adherence to principle or for having violated those prejudices through particular practices. And the other New Woman novel most closely associated with Allen's makes the complications inherent in Shelley's example a key subject of discussion—the late-Victorian confusions that Shelley had brought into focus become, in fact, what the novel is *about*. *Jude the Obscure*'s references to Shelley are part of the book's continuous struggle with the difficulties of naming extramarital relations. Far from helping to reconcile this crisis, Shelley serves in the novel to articulate contradictory impulses, to maintain the tensions that follow from them, and to hinder their reconciliation in speech. Whereas Jeaffreson had feared that opponents would use Shelley's model to validate new alternatives, Shelley serves instead in *Jude the Obscure* to make clear that the New Woman's vision can't be clearly expressed.

Thomas Hardy, a longtime Shelley enthusiast, had marked his copy of Jeaffreson "most unjust."[23] His particular admiration for *Laon and Cythna*, the poem whose influence Jeaffreson most despised, surfaced repeatedly in the novels that followed upon Jeaffreson's warnings. *The Woodlanders'* Fitzpiers "rhapsodizes" a full stanza of Laon's words while thinking of his beloved; in the serialized *Pursuit of the Well-Beloved*, a phrase from the poem (which eventually became the novel's epigraph) emblematizes the object of Pearston's affection. But Hardy's references to Shelley during this period usually summon those elements Jeaffreson had tersely approved in *Epipsychidion*; from *Laon and Cythna*, as from elsewhere in Shelley, Hardy took words that evoked not sexual license but blessed incorporeality.[24] The borrowings sometimes entailed odd adjustments of Shelley's original context, as when Pearston's ideal beloved, reappearing in various persons, is referred to as "his Shelleyan 'One shape-of-many-names,'" words that in *Laon and Cythna* describe "the Spirit of Evil." But if Hardy's use of the phrase appears to shed the direness of Shelley's intent, that is consistent with Hardy's general tendency in these novels to quote Shelley one-sidedly, as an authority on "female forms, whose gestures beam with mind," the seer of Woman as "an irradiated being" (Hardy's words) "robed in such exceeding glory / That he beheld her not . . ." (Shelley's, quoted by Hardy immediately after). When Hardy quotes Shelley to express adoration of woman as "Idea, in Platonic phraseology," the verse not only deliberately restores "platonic" love's connection to Plato but proclaims, in its conspicuous Romantic diction, a kind of affection that requires extraordinary forms of expression.[25]

Such extraworldliness contributes little to the novels' attacks on those worldly institutions of which Jeaffreson labeled Shelley the great adversary. In *The Woodlanders* and *The Well-Beloved* ethereal Shelleyanism makes in fact an ironic contrast to the prosaic lives of the women to whom Fitzpiers and Pearston apply it, and to the social constraints that shape those women's careers. Though it is the Shelleyan Pearston who voices the latter novel's attacks on marriage, they come in those moments when he seems least inspired by Shelley, periods when he is renouncing his Platonic attachments. In these books, Shelley is invoked on behalf of conventionally Victorian spiritual relations, not to undermine them.

But in *Jude the Obscure* Shelley seems to serve both purposes, as Jeaffreson's contradictory remarks had suggested he might. At the end of Part IV, the section of the novel in which the struggle to name Jude Fawley and Sue Bridehead's extramarital bond becomes most intense, Shelley is twice invoked to provide a last word, a final modification of proffered terms. On the first occasion, Phillotson, Sue's husband, approaches his friend Gillingham to rehearse his public explanation for having allowed Sue to join Jude:

"she has not distinctly implied living with him as wife, though I think she means to. ... And to the best of my understanding it is not ignoble, merely animal, feeling between the two. . . . I found from their manner that an extraordinary affinity, or sympathy, entered into their attachment, which somehow took away all flavour of grossness. Their supreme desire is to be together—to share each other's emotions, and fancies, and dreams."

"Platonic!"

"Well no. Shelleyan would be nearer to it. They remind me of—what are their names—Laon and Cythna. Also of Paul and Virginia a little. The more I reflect, the more *entirely* I am on their side!"

"But if people did as you want to do, there'd be a general domestic disintegration. The family would no longer be the social unit."

"Yes—I am all abroad, I suppose!" said Phillotson, sadly. (247)

Phillotson's discrimination of the "Shelleyan" from the "Platonic" marks a departure from the identification of the two in Hardy's preceding novels. It seems impossible to declare with certainty what Phillotson means by it. But one may note that he has offered two shades of discrimination from "living . . . as wife" in marriage (rather than from sexual attraction or relation, as a mid-Victorian might be expected to do). It seems therefore worthwhile to accept the New Woman novel's gambit of posing a fundamental question and providing a fictional answer that only stimulates the question further—that is, it seems worthwhile to hazard a few guesses as to what Phillotson might have in mind. He might mean the "Shelleyan" to imply a sexual element, however "flavour-less," that would be absent from the "Platonic." He might also wish to counter Gillingham's general cynicism and the implications of a word that Victorians could hardly use seriously with one that had some force, however controversial. Because Phillotson has already acknowledged that he thinks his wife "means to" live with another man "as wife," Gillingham's "Platonic!" could indicate lack of attention, comprehension, or seriousness. "Also of Paul and Virginia" would seem at best to add to the confusion: although those figures might be expected to represent a model of sexlessness, the phrase syntactically reinforces the Shelleyan against the Platonic.[26]

In any case, these attempts at definition only end by being abandoned in favor of a new topic. When Sue invokes Shelley a few pages later, to lend moral authority to her own sense of the relationship, she seems to have in mind a version very different from Phillotson's. She responds in kind to Jude's calling her "you spirit, you disembodied creature, you dear, sweet tantalizing phantasm. . . .":

"Say those pretty lines, then, from Shelley's 'Epipsychidion' as if they meant me!" she solicited, slanting up closer to him as they stood. "Don't you know them? . . . These are some of them:

There was a Being whom my spirit oft
Met on the visioned wanderings far aloft.

. . . . . .

A seraph of Heaven, too gentle to be human,
Veiling beneath that radiant form of woman ...

Oh, it is too flattering, so I won't go on! But say it's me!—say it's me!"

"It *is* you, dear; exactly like you!"

"Now I forgive you! And you shall kiss me just once there—not very long." She put the tip of her finger gingerly to her cheek; and he did as commanded. "You do care for me very much, don't you, in spite of my not—you know?"

"Yes, sweet!" he said with a sigh; and bade her good-night. (259–60)

As John Goode has noted, Sue omits from the *Epipsychidion* passage those lines that suggest the physical and sexual.[27] Whether that indicates imperfect memory or selective quotation on Sue's part, her intent seems clearer than Phillotson's, at least on the matter of sex. Both Jude's words and those Sue quotes point precisely to the conception of the "Platonic" Hardy had associated with Shelley in his anachronistic *Pursuit of the Well-Beloved*. Where Phillotson had opposed the Shelleyan to the questionable Platonic, here they seem back in tandem.

Shelley thus apparently signifies first the sexual and then the sexless in successive, equally unsatisfying scenes in which he is invoked to provide clarification for a proposed definition. In the first case the allusion is apparently meant to make more exact Gillingham's name for the relationship; in the second case it seems to validate Jude's words for Sue's position in it. But the responses Shelley's name or words elicit—further qualification prior to dismissal, desultory acceptance before resigned silence—show that he has provided nothing toward a functional idiom. Jeaffreson had written against Shelleyans "who . . . have contributed or are contributing, by written words or spoken words . . . to the opinion that society should . . . recognize the Free Contract as a kind of marriage. . . ."[28] But Shelley serves Phillotson and Sue only privately, that is, to allow each to affirm his or her own belief in the idea that no one else understands. Hardy's rendering at this point differs from Allen's in leaving the sexual dynamic in the relationship unresolved, but it duplicates the claim of *The Woman Who Did* that a character has found a model that can account for the relationship, even if it has not been made explicit in the novel's text.

Jude includes one more direct reference to Shelley. Fifty pages after the allusions just discussed, as Jude and Sue continue their attempt to find some idiomatic norm for their relationship, Sue argues, "I fancy more are like us than we think!" That statement once again claims an unspoken understanding as to what defines their relationship, as to what they are "like." "Well, I don't know," Jude appropriately responds, but Sue continues.

"We are a little beforehand, that's all. In fifty, a hundred, years the descendents of [those now marrying] will act and feel worse than we. They will see weltering humanity still more vividly than we do now, as

'Shapes like our own selves hideously multiplied,'

and will be afraid to reproduce them."
"What a terrible line of poetry! ... though I have felt it myself about my fellow-creatures, at morbid times."
Thus they murmured on. . . . (299)

Though the line from *Laon and Cythna* now provides the stuff of nightmare, it is again positioned as if it may offer a last definitive word. Yet the quote only launches the argument into the grotesque. Late-Victorian Shelleyans and anti-Shelleyans shared a common ambivalence about the precise function of Shelley as an exemplar for and contributor to discourse on heterosexual relations. He was the talisman by which heterosexual friendship might be granted a kind of cultural centrality, for better or worse. But the way Shelley is used in *Jude the Obscure* suggests that such a touchstone could provide no satisfactory idiom. Rather, it serves to shut such discourse down, though never finally: the morbid murmuring persists for as long as the novel.

Good-Fellowship: *Jude the Obscure*

In having their New Women look to Shelley to validate visions of friendship, Allen and Hardy invoked an emblem for the bewildering condition of discourse on cross-gender relations in their time. Martha Vicinus's observation that "the 1880's and 1890's were marked by the public and private discussion of the weaknesses of marriage, the validity of divorce, and the importance of friendships across gender lines" rightly links these three subjects and suggests the idiomatic problems inherent in their connection.[29] Late Victorians could attack marriage and argue for making it finite, but they could only insist on the "importance" of an alternative, not name it. Shelley represented a recognized challenge to the "current body of opinion, taught as a religious dogma, invariable, inflexible . . . that all forms of intercourse of the sexes, other than lifelong unions, are criminal"; at the same time he epitomized the way those who sought to argue otherwise were limited to the conventional terms. "Spouse! Sister! Angel!" Shelley could be found apostrophizing in *Epipsychidion*.[30] In such Shelleyan phrasings the conventional categories may be found to overlap: sexuality, family, and transcendence (but not work) coincide. Each of these elements could by the 1890's be considered as possible elements of "friendship." But their conflation hardly offers an avenue of escape from conventional categories. On the contrary, those categories seem all the more inclusive and to leave less space than ever for the emergence of a liberating idiom associated with the models of heterosexual activity and cooperation that feminists had striven for.

Sue introduces "friendship" into *Jude the Obscure* as casually as Herminia brings the word into *The Woman Who Did*, but Hardy compromises it from the start by linking it to the kind of false familial terms that had failed Maggie Tulliver in Eliot's *The Mill on the Floss*. *Jude*'s narrator affirms that Sue's initial note to Jude

was of the most artless and natural kind. She addressed him as her *dear cousin Jude* . . . and reproached him with not letting her know [of his arrival]. They might have had such nice times together . . . for she . . . had *hardly any congenial friend*. But now there was every probability of her soon going away, so that the chance of *companionship* would be lost perhaps for ever. (122, emphasis added)

The underscored terms match Jude's anticipations: he has already decided before he hears from Sue that

he would have to think of Sue with only a *relation*'s mutual interest in one belonging to him; regard her in a practical way as some one to be proud of; to talk and nod to; later on, to be invited to tea by, the emotion spent on her being rigorously that of a *kinsman* and well-wisher. So would she be to him a kindly star, an elevating power, a *companion* in Anglican worship, a tender *friend*. (113, emphasis added)

The concluding set of appositives echoes mid-Victorian practice: even having established the barrier of consanguinity, Hardy (and Jude) must nevertheless preface the word "friend" with a string of transcendent modifiers before it can be uttered with any conviction. Those modifiers provide only the briefest stability. They close the chapter, but within two pages Hardy has reduced the familial barrier to a false rhetorical flourish—"She was such a stranger that the kinship was affectation" (115)—and within ten pages he has done the same to spirituality: "For whatever Sue's virtues, talents, or ecclesiastic saturation, it was certain that those items were not at all the cause of his affection for her" (121).

But in the early stages of their acquaintance, Sue reestablishes the terms of Jude's preconceptions. She draws on "friend" and "cousin" for her forms of address, and these are sometimes validated by the narrator, who describes her speaking to Jude "with the freedom of a friend" (123) and recounts their having "shook hands like cronies in a tavern" (172). Further, Sue places Jude as the object of her "elevating power," saying, "I did want and long to ennoble some man to high aims; and when I saw you, and knew you wanted to be my comrade, I—shall I confess it?—thought that man might be you" (172).

Complications set in immediately thereafter, leading to the struggles for definition—by Phillotson, Sue, Jude, and others—already discussed. When Jude first expresses physical desire, Sue acknowledges that their cousinship has always been "merely nominal" (176). When Jude tells Sue of his marriage to Arabella, the narrator declares that "the antagonisms of sex to sex were left without any counterpoising predelictions. She was his comrade, friend, unconscious sweetheart no longer; and her eyes regarded him in estranged silence" (185). But the terms are at this point confounded rather than discarded, as the combining of "comrade" and "friend" with "sweetheart" suggests: "they pretended to persuade themselves that all that had happened was of no consequence, and they could still be cousins and friends and warm correspondents" (187). "Friend" and "cousin" continue to alternate with courtship idioms like "sweetheart" until the contest is settled by an unambiguous kiss:

she had conceded that the fact of the kiss would be nothing: all would depend on the spirit of it. If given in the spirit of a cousin and a friend she saw no objection: if in the spirit of a lover she could not permit it. "Will you swear that it will not be in that spirit?" she had said.

No: he would not. . . . They had quickly run back, and met, and embracing most unpremeditatedly, kissed close and long. When they parted for good it was with flushed cheeks on her side, and a beating heart on his.

The kiss was a turning-point in Jude's career. . . . (233)

It marks an idiomatic turning point as well, for her admission of "the spirit of a lover" now leads Sue effectively to banish "friend" and "cousin" from her relationship with Jude; when a distraught note from Phillotson refers to Jude as Sue's "lover," she does not contest the word (240). But the same sequence makes clear how desperate Sue is to maintain her original terms, as she immediately seeks to reapply them within her marriage to Phillotson: "Oh Richard, be my friend and have pity!" (239).[31] That will not work, for Phillotson's understanding of "friend" is the conventional mid-Victorian one: his pejorative use of the word severs it from Sue's more ambitious associations, including cousinship, when he tells Gillingham

I have been struck with . . . the extraordinary sympathy, or similarity, between the pair. He is her cousin, which perhaps accounts for some of it. They seem to be one person split in two! And with her unconquerable aversion to myself as a husband, even though she may like me as a friend, 'tis too much to bear longer (245).

In the book's penultimate section, these complicated attempts at definition give way again to the predominance of romantic terms. Courtship rhetoric serves first as a negative standard, an indication of what Jude and Sue are not before they have sex, and then a positive one once they have. But once the relationship becomes sexual, Hardy's narrator affirms them "true comrades" (285), a validation reminiscent of Herminia's reference to "the only kind of friendship that nature makes possible between men and women." "Can you keep the bee from ranging . . . ?" Sue sings complacently, as Hardy describes their having entered a "dreamy paradise" (286).

That comradeship is but a private triumph, protected by their public facade of ostensible marriage, and their children's murder/suicide destroys both. In the last stage of their relationship, a series of familiar fictions jostle for authority: Jude sees them as "seducer" and seduced (352, 382), the terms Alan's conventional father had used, while she sees them as "adulterers" (372). But it is clear in any case that the newness of their relations has not let them avoid the familiar pattern of precourtship "friendship," the unconsummated courtship leading to sex legitimized publicly by marriage (and containing sanctioned "friendship"). They have simply followed that pattern awkwardly, while absorbed in pathetic attempts to deny its rules. To name their final relation, Jude insists on terms pertaining to marriage, while Sue tries once again to restore "cousin" and "friend," a reprise that signals the final collapse of their attempt to agree on a viable idiom.

"We'll be dear friends just the same, Jude, won't we? And we'll see each other sometimes—Yes!—and forget all this, and try to be as we were long ago?"

Jude did not permit himself to speak, but turned and descended the stairs. (362)

They part thus:

"Well—don't discuss it. Good-bye, Jude; my fellow-sinner, and kindest friend!"

"Good-bye, my mistaken wife. Good-bye!" (369)

The novel has been occupied throughout less with narrative progress toward the relationship's final resolution or fertile future than with self-reflective tension about how the relationship might be described at any point. Of the episodes here mentioned, only their kiss, which begins their courtship, their act of consummation, which establishes the marital model, and the killing of their children, which undoes all, serve to move the plot. All others center on acts of naming, ways of declaring what their relationship represents at each stage. The desire to name seems insatiable, with every proposed idiom intensifying the equivocation—an idiomatic version of what Leo Bersani has called "insistent stasis," a pocket of linguistic indulgence rather than a path toward conceivable issue. Indeed, the earlier serialized version of *Jude* published by Hardy in *Harper's Magazine* had remained a story of unconsummated courtship, strung out doggedly without even the novel-version's minimal plot adjustments. To give that version of the relationship legitimacy, Hardy had relied far more heavily on the familial terms— no doubt aware of the irony in his having to maintain such terms to keep his ideal couple respectable, whereas Shelley had had to *delete* comparable terms from *Laon and Cythna* toward the same end.[32] In the novel version, Jude and Sue succeed only in making the conventional romantic plot a temporary torture: told of their final passionate rendezvous, Phillotson responds, "O—the old story" (401), a fit last word on the couple's long-sustained, embattled, and finally futile efforts to produce some original controlling fiction.[33]

But at their best they have briefly discovered one, grounded in cooperation. During their period as "true comrades" disguised as spouses, Hardy has Sue join Jude at work "to see what assistance she could render, and also because they liked to be together." Though they are at work repairing an image of the Ten Commandments, the scene does not partake of Sue's rhetoric of religious fellowship—as adulterers they are in violation of one of those commandments anyway, and along with religion the family idioms drop away too.[34] Instead, Hardy emphasizes how Sue's well-honed skills contribute to a moment of perfectly shared work:

standing on a safe low platform erected by Jude, which she was nevertheless timid at mounting, [Sue] began painting in the letters of the first Table while he set about mending a portion of the second. She was quite pleased at her powers; she had acquired them in the days she painted illuminated texts for the church-fitting shop at Christminster. Nobody seemed likely to disturb them; and the pleasant twitter of birds, and rustle of October leafage, came in through an open window, and mingled with their talk. (312)

Twenty years earlier, Hardy had imaged such cooperation as a rare basis for successful marriage, like Gabriel Oak and Bathsheba Everdene's, in *Far From the Madding Crowd*. He had complained that "this good-fellowship—*camaraderie*—usually occurring through similarity of pursuits, is unfortunately seldom superadded to love between the sexes, because men and women associate, not in their labours, but in their pleasures merely." Though Gabriel and Bathsheba could demonstrate friendship only as an element "superadded" to the completed fact of romance, the novel elsewhere confronted the absence of an independent idiom for extramarital friendship. When her spurned suitor, Boldwood, challenges her, "Do you like me, or do you respect me?", Bathsheba responds: "I don't know—at least, I cannot tell you. It is difficult for a woman to define her feelings in language which is chiefly made by men to express theirs."[35]

In *Jude*, Hardy uses "comradeship," a standard Victorian term for marital affection, to label the missing element in Jude and Arabella's errant marriage (93).[36] Neither that man-made term (etymologically associated with room-mates) nor "good-fellowship" nor any other satisfies Sue in her struggle to name the extramarital relation she desires; but at work, Hardy suggests, Jude and Sue's "talk" can become natural, even indistinguishable from "the pleasant twitter of birds." Here, when Sue and Jude are not negotiating a name for their relationship, the narrator can represent cooperation as the center of their extramarital affinity, in a scene that maintains their defiance of rather than assimilation in marriage.[37]

At *Jude the Obscure*'s most optimistic stage, Hardy gives emphasis to an element of the New Woman's life Allen had hardly mentioned: the tantalizing aspects of *The Woman Who Did* had gone far to obscure any suspicion that what the woman had done was to work. *Jude the Obscure* figures as "true comradeship" an extramarital relation that includes both sex and work. It is the kind of scene Elaine Scarry has celebrated in her brilliant account of the way Hardy inscribes their work onto the bodies of his characters:

That [Hardy's] most radical portraits of the man-materials relation so consistently occur in the context of scenes of human desire and courtship perhaps expresses Hardy's sense that one does, in desiring a person, desire the whole world bodied forth in that person, or to phrase it in another way, one loves not just the person but the world out into which the person projects and inscribes himself or herself. At the same time, however, the context of courtship seems intended to invite the recognition that there is not only between two human beings but between man and his materials an extraordinary intimacy and comradeship, even a wholly asexual love, that each regularly enters the interior of the other, that they sometimes wound each other, but that they also habitually speak on one another's behalf, each routinely expressing the other's hidden attributes and unarticulated vulnerabilities.[38]

"They were not, however, to be left thus snug and peaceful for long," are Hardy's next words after the description of Jude and Sue's happy "talk." Resigned that immoral acts and moralistic conventions must always intrude, Hardy in his novels allows the context of desire and courtship to frustrate the kind of mutuality Scarry describes. To exemplify the way Hardy puts "the body . . . at risk," Scarry herself refers to the way Tess D'Urberville's body is "altered" by her "encounter with Alec": acknowledging that "this particular alteration [Tess's pregnancy] may belong to the realm of desire rather than work," Scarry notes that "the encounter is between an employee and her employer . . . and what happens to her is (as is routinely recognized in the twentieth century and as Hardy deeply understood) a hazard of the workplace, an industrial accident."[39] The vision of work that would admit affection and yet avert such accidents would surely require "an extraordinary intimacy and comradeship," if not "a wholly asexual love." Feminist efforts on behalf of heterosexual "friendship" had been motivated by just such a hope. But the predominance of desire and courtship bars that possibility from Hardy's fiction.

For even Hardy's investment in Jude and Sue's grand cooperative moment may belong "to the realm of desire rather than work," and may reflect personal wish fulfillment more than social vision. Critics have long recognized Jude and Sue as embodying aspects of Hardy's relationship with Florence Henniker, whom he called "preeminently the child of the Shelleyan tradition," and with whom he had co-written a published story—but whom he had apparently failed to seduce. *Jude the Obscure* reflects above all Hardy's willingness to adopt utter resignation when unable to preserve heterosexual relations in just the way he desired. In his poem "Wessex Heights," he wrote of Henniker:

> As for one rare fair woman, I am not but a thought of hers,
> I enter her mind and another thought succeeds me that she prefers;
> Yet my love for her in its fulness she herself even did not know;
> Well, time cures hearts of tenderness, and now I can let her go.[40]

Hardy's peevish willingness to "let her go" was subsequently belied by another thirty years of close acquaintance. His tone in "Wessex Heights" has affinities with Robert Browning's dismissal of Julia Wedgwood and with lines written even more smugly in Hardy's own period by fellow-novelist Samuel Butler:

> . . . like and love are far removed;
> Hard though I tried to love I tried in vain.
> For she was plain and lame and fat and short,
> Forty and over-kind. Hence it befell
> That though I loved her in a certain sort,
> Yet did I love wisely but not well.[41]

Butler's sonnet jokingly celebrates his failure to resolve matters much like the ones over which Hardy had let Sue and Jude agonize; slightly less caustic, Hardy's poem nevertheless relishes his having smoothly recovered from love unexpressed. Such smug dismissal might obscure the frustration of thwarted attraction. Hardy had envisioned a brief private retreat—for Jude and Sue in a church, for himself and Henniker "At an Inn" (as imagined in the poem of that title). But unable to see how such a relationship could hold, Hardy then banished its realization to the unforeseeable future—to a time "fifty, a hundred years" later, when others, as Sue says, would "act and feel worse than we"—and "let it go" for now, in fin-de-siècle resignation, as untenable. "It is a serious lack," as Christine Brooke-Rose has said. "For this of all relationships," she adds, "where so much depends on that mysterious quality called companionship (which is what Sue wanted) the imaginative effort should have been made." [42] Hardy not only refuses such effort, but also preempts its possibility.

Shortly before the publication of *Jude*, Hardy had asked in a public symposium on gender relations "whether civilisation can escape the humiliating indictment that, while it has been able to cover itself with glory in the arts, in literatures, in religions, and in the sciences, it has never succeeded in creating that homely thing, a satisfactory scheme for the conjunction of the sexes." [43] *Jude the Obscure* demonstrates how even the most sustained treatments of "friendship" may, while claiming to authenticate it, ultimately betray it. Hardy could fantasize for himself a homely, temporary, private escape, and in the process depict and even enact heterosexual cooperation. But if he couldn't have it all his way, the deal was off: he would mark friendship a silent thing doomed.

James's *The Awkward Age* and the Full Value of "Friendship"

Such socially futile gestures on behalf of "friendship" might yet be invaluable to their author's self-justifications: even as they ultimately confirmed discursive limits and cast further doubt on "friendship," they could provide private solace. The century expired with Henry James desperately reaching for such verbal comfort. Constance Woolson's apparent suicide had challenged James to wonder (so biographer Leon Edel has argued) whether their fifteen years of sexless relations had caused her unbearable frustration, and thus whether "a defect in his own 'system' of friendship" had become lethal. [44]

In the weeks following Woolson's death, James spent a fair amount of time describing the relationship's dynamics to others. For Frances Boott he recalled Woolson's "chronic melancholy (so that half one's friendship for her was always anxiety)." Two days later the parenthentical aside grew into James's statement to William Baldwin: "Half of my friendship for her was a deep solicitude, a deep compassion, a vigilant precaution, so far as was possible . . ."; on the same day, James wrote to Katherine De Kay Bronson that "one's friendship for [Woolson] was always half anxiety." However the other half of his friendship with Woolson had been constituted, two months later he could collapse it into the first, jotting as an afterthought to his brother William, "*All* intelligent interest in her was an inevitable anxiety" (emphasis adjusted).[45] He soon after went to Italy to dispose of Woolson's effects, among them the letters he had sent to her. Once finished with this task, James complained in his diary of his recent "terrific sacrifice to the ravenous Moloch of one's endless personal, social relations—one's eternal exposures, accidents, disasters." But he wrote at the end of the entry, "*Basta*," considering himself through with all that.[46]

Having sealed off the friendship's private record, he seems to have resumed his public reconsideration of it in his own terms. Edel connects "the burden of Miss Woolson's unfathomed secret" to James's subsequent writings "from this moment on—and for the next five years" about characters "who try to probe the secrets of the world around them, but who do not possess enough facts for their inductions and deductions."[47] The period of *What Maisie Knew*, *The Awkward Age*, and *The Sacred Fount* would lead by 1901 to James's great tragedy of undisclosed affection, "The Beast in the Jungle."

But unresolved gender relations are in this period neither new nor unique to James's fiction; they had always been central to his work and to realist fiction as a whole.[48] The most distinctly English of James's late novels, *The Awkward Age*, is most significant for my purposes because that novel attributes its gendered disaster to societal rather than personal failure; because it judges that failure to be part of a fin-de-siècle apocalypse for English discourse; and because James poses as a "refuge" from the apocalypse a secluded relation that is the surest sign of heterosexual friendship's idiomatic impoverishment at the end of the Victorian era. There is nothing revolutionary in the relation James comes to propose; it includes neither work nor sex, the components that had marked Hardy's defiant idyll. Yet having chastened and refined and isolated his sanctuary, James still won't name the treasured bond. Like George Eliot before him, he withholds or dismisses the conventional and compromised terms for friendship, and he rejects both the illicit and transcendent forms Hardy had found in Shelley. But James gives much less of a sense than Eliot had as to where better terms might be found. In flight, James's survivors (Nanda and Longdon) take nothing from the discursive world whose disintegration they have experienced throughout the novel. *The Awkward Age* marks a final Victorian record of friendship's century-long retreat from public discourse.

The retreat is here precipitated by an unconsummate moment of failure, as Vanderbank, like John Marcher of "The Beast in the Jungle" fulfills his own "dreadfully possible future" by failing to express love for Nanda. By James's standards, these futures are the more tragic because they have been scrupulously watched for, and more tragic still because that careful scrutiny has been the central dynamic in the failed relations. "I'll watch with you," May Bartram promises Marcher at the outset, later adding, "If I've been 'watching' with you, as we long ago agreed I was to do, watching's always in itself an absorption."[49] The idea that James here as elsewhere registers so painfully, of a friendship tragically defined by shared vision, is one that Virginia Woolf would, some years later, translate into a more positive formulation: indeed, the way Bartram and Marcher's shared "watching" creates "the odd rhythm of their intensities and avoidances" places their relationship in a novelistic tradition that can be traced from Daniel Deronda and Gwendolen Harleth through Woolf's Lily Briscoe and Mr. Ramsay, a tradition of visual cooperation that affords some positive content for heterosexual friendship. But in *The Awkward Age* shared watching merely and unsatisfactorily binds the heroine, Nanda, not only to the inadequate hero, Vanderbank, but to two other men who are also watching him—Mitchy, a would-be suitor of Nanda's, and Longdon, a former suitor of Nanda's grandmother's, who wishes to precipitate Nanda and Vanderbank's marriage. This community of watchers is defined by their acute consciousness of the failure they are observing; but the more perceptive these characters become, the more helpless they are to express what they see.

While the tragedy in "The Beast in the Jungle" is private to Marcher and Bartram,[50] that of *The Awkward Age* seems always

communal, a social deficiency in which all participate. The "awkward age" is not personal to Nanda's adolescence, but historical,
a transitional moment in human relations within a community
unequipped to accommodate it. At the climax of Vanderbank's
failure, James summons Longdon as a mute, absent, hypothetical
but representative "observer." It is Longdon's task to measure the
social significance of the private loss Nanda suffers at Vanderbank's
hands. Nanda is coming as close as she can to expressing the unnamed tragedy to Vanderbank, or to offering him the chance to
express it—as close as May Marcher comes at the moment when
she tells Marcher that "the door's open" to him, before she gives
way despairing to "a slow fine shudder" when she knows he won't
respond.[51] In their silence, Nanda and Vanderbank make no greater
claim upon the naming and meaning of their moment than does the
absent Longdon, whose sudden intrusive summoning by James as a
participant in the "defeat" marks him not only as victimized but as
complicit—and identifies him with the position of "all" observers
of the scene, including James and his readers:

". . . There it is [Nanda says to Vanderbank]—it's all out before one knows
it, isn't it, and I can't help it any more than you can, can I?" So she appeared to put it to him, with something in her lucidity that would have
been infinitely touching; a strange grave, calm consciousness of their common doom and of what in especial in it would be worst for herself. He
sprang up indeed after an instant as if he had been infinitely touched; he
turned away, taking just near her a few steps to and fro, gazed about the
place again, but this time without the air of particularly seeing it, and then
came back to her as if from a greater distance. An observer at all initiated
would, at the juncture, fairly have hung on his lips, and there was in fact
on Vanderbank's part quite the look of the man—though it lasted but just
while we seize it—in suspense about himself. The most initiated observer
of all would have been poor Mr. Longdon, in that case destined, however,
to be also the most defeated, and the sign of whose tension would have
been a smothered, "Ah, if he doesn't do it *now*!" Well, Vanderbank didn't
do it 'now,' and the long, odd slow irrelevant sigh he gave out might have
sufficed as the record of his recovery from a peril lasting just long enough
to be measured. . . . (344–45)

Comparison with the endless elaborations in similar scenes created by Allen and Hardy makes James's pantomime all the more
striking: *The Awkward Age* is not a novel registered entirely in dialogue, as James later described in his Preface, but a novel registered

in the moments when dialogue halts. The summoning of initiated observers is entirely necessary, for Vanderbank utterly fails, here and later, to acknowledge in any way the significance of the moment. Some time after Marcher's failure, Bartram informs him that it has passed already unbeknownst to him, perhaps with a " 'name' but oh with a date"; in *The Awkward Age*'s equivalent passage, Vanderbank vaguely remembers the scene quoted above as one when "we had some good talk," while "the talk, Nanda's face implied, had become dim to her; but there were other things" (496). That's the extent of their shared recollection of her relationship. All this culture can express is a silent impasse.

In an analogous scene earlier in the book, Nanda has recalled a prior stage of Vanderbank's inaction as "an age, no doubt—but an age without a name" (214). The phrase not only anticipates May Bartram's emphasis on a precise moment of linguistic inadequacy but also echoes metonymically a comparable recognition in the novel's title. James here too calls upon a hypothetical "spectator" to recognize the "climax . . . to some state of irresolution about the utterance of something" (215). This "age without a name" is rendered awkward by deficient idioms: Nanda and Vanderbank's failed articulation, like all other impasses in this 1899 novel, is conditioned by the "dead" language characteristic of fin-de-siècle discourse. Tony Tanner has aptly described the world of *The Awkward Age* as one where "[i]ndeterminacy of nomenclature becomes total semantic depletion." Tzvetan Todorov similarly has written of the "obliquity" in the novel's having "reached such a degree that it is no longer obliquity; the connecting lines between words and things are [not] merely loose or tangled—they have been cut."[52] James's self-conscious insistence on dialogue without a narrator's intrusion emphasizes that severance, for the resourceless characters are left entirely to their own sparse designs.

Victorian idioms survive among them only faintly and ironically. Fittingly, James's two fleeing survivors bear slight resemblances to the Nineties' "twin apostles of social apocalypse," those who had articulated Victorianism's demise: early on, Longdon is labeled a "dandy," though a dandy who "might also have been a priest" (5); and several of the female characters appear to be, as *The Saturday Review* saw them, "mere caricatures of new women"—none more so than Nanda, victimized for the unutterable things she cerebrates as Herminia and others had been condemned for what they had unutterably done.[53] Linda Dowling has described the way the historical Dandy and the New Woman, though mutually antithetical, both "expressed [their] quarrel with Victorian culture chiefly through sexual means—by heightening sexual consciousness, candor, and expressiveness."[54] Too late, too timid, and too baffled to express such a message, Longdon and Nanda observe consciousness's having been overwhelmed by deceptive and ineffectual sexual discourse that claims to admit everything but bars the revelation of anything.

The Awkward Age's community is so preoccupied, for instance, with evasive figurings of sexuality that one may forget that most of its central relationships are sexless heterosexual bonds. Transient, these indefinite bonds have finite dates, but no definite names: mediated through a language that seems pure surface, they seem less repressive than simply inarticulate. If one surmises that the heterosexual dynamics conventionally central to the novel are here unfortunate trappings for an author who would at some level prefer to engage homosocial relations, then "friendship" seems very apt as a designation of what goes on between men and women in the book: it promises much, provides nothing.[55] "We all call everything—anything," says Vanderbank (274). It is Mitchy who announces the consequences of such belief: "[Vanderbank] has his ideas—he thinks nothing matters. He says we've all come to a pass that's the end of everything" (228).

"The end of everything? One might easily receive that impression," replies Longdon, who will hear Nanda confirming that impression in the novel's final scene: "Everything's different from what it used to be" (544). The reader has been trained by that point to expect no clear referent for Nanda's "it," or for the past and present conditions "everything" might include, any more than for the "that" in Nanda's "I am like that" (543), her description of her fallen state. So there should be little surprise that Nanda and Longdon's relation, James's one defiant response to the apocalypse, remains in the end equally obscure, equally unnamed. Anticipating their retreat to Beccles, Longdon's secluded home, James characterizes their future bond only with Nanda's "I'll come if you'll take me as I am" (538) and Longdon's warning that if she flees with him "it's never again to leave me—or to be left" (541). In what sense

will Longdon "take" her? James has summarily eliminated most of
the conventional possibilities that would give Beccles some moral
sanction: it will be no temple, since he has undercut Longdon's
priestliness by coupling it with dandyism; nor will it be a family
home, since he has rendered familial idioms ridiculous by making
light of Longdon's affection for successive generations of women.[56]
Nanda dismisses both Mitchy's vision of Longdon's coming for
her with "the post-chaise and the pistols" (525) and her mother's
"What do you call that then, I should like to know, but his adopt-
ing you?" "Ah," replies Nanda, "I don't know that it matters much
what it's called" (328).

Because the novel spends most of its energy in futile quests after
names for its relations,[57] the absence in the final pages of even conventional figurings for friendship may signal James's ultimate acceptance of the age's "total semantic depletion." The critical record,
in contrast, has supplied Nanda and Longdon's relationship with
an array of names. *The Literary World*'s reviewer disparaged it as
a "so-called love affair"; Séamus Cooney noted in 1960 that "critics have generally taken it to be an adoption," with Yvor Winters
alone seeing Nanda ready "either to be adopted [by Longdon], or to
marry him . . ."; Oscar Cargill said neutrally that Longdon "offers
her permanent refuge in his home and she accepts"—a version
echoed more banally yet in *The Oxford Companion to American
Literature*'s assessment that "the best solution of the problem is for
her to live permanently in Longdon's country place. . . ." Edward
Wagenknecht brings together all these categories under one other
recognizably Victorian one when he calls Longdon "Nanda's good
angel, who rescues her . . . by providing a refuge for her elsewhere,
and, at the end, virtually adopts her"; Wagenknecht also can fore-
see eventual marriage for Nanda after Longdon's death.[58] Edel and
Tanner elide the practical dilemma of characterizing the relationship by assigning it to James's private psyche: Edel says that "Mr.
Longdon can now do what Henry James has done all his life—har-
bor within his house, the house of the novelist's inner world, the
spirit of a young adult female . . ." and Tanner declares that "Henry
James, in the form of Mr. Longdon, enters his own novel to rescue Nanda, as though recognizing the value of her attitude and the
pathos of her predicament, he could not bear to see her foolishly
undervalued and so callously marooned."[59]

The temptation to rename or abstract the relationship follows from an acknowledged absence of idiom in the novel's finale. "The nature of this relation is deliberately obscure," Cooney observes. "The evolution of Mr. Longdon's feelings for Nanda does take on reality before our eyes," says Todorov, "and yet we have the feeling that we see it through a glass darkly." *The Awkward Age* serves to conceal a sexless relation even more completely than other 1890's narratives had withheld the sexual.[60] James provides the reader with no inroads for conventional condemnation, dismissal, or undermining of the relationship's cogency; he has withdrawn or withheld all compromised terms.

And at the beginning of the novel James has definitively preempted those who would deride "friendship" as untenable:

> "Ah but what becomes of friendship?" Mr. Longdon earnestly and pleadingly asked, while he still held Vanderbank's arm as if under the spell of the vivid explanation supplied him.
>
> The young man met his eyes only the more sociably. "Friendship?"
>
> "Friendship." Mr. Longdon maintained the full value of the word.
>
> "Well," his companion risked, "I dare say it isn't in London by any means what it is at Beccles. I quite literally mean that," Vanderbank reassuringly added; "I never really have believed in the existence of friendship in big societies—in great towns and great crowds. It's a plant that takes time and space and air; and London society is a huge 'squash,' as we elegantly call it—an elbowing pushing perspiring chattering mob." (20)

In spite of Longdon's brief stubborn maintenance of the "full value of the word," the book registers the "semantic depletion" of "friendship" in recognizable stages. Vanderbank proves his cynicism by repeatedly calling himself Nanda's "old friend" and "great friend" (e.g., 17, 206) and then betraying her. Nanda in turn eventually spells out the word's uselessness by leaving a silly epithet in the awkward and futile place "friend" ought to occupy, the place left when all more acceptable relations have been ruled out: when Mitchy dubs himself Nanda's "gentleman whom she can never get rid of on the specious plea that he's only her husband or her lover or her father or her son or her brother or her uncle or her cousin . . .," and thus seems to displace the "only" from his apparent claim to be her "friend," Nanda restores it, saying, "Yes, he's simply her Mitchy" (516–17), a final trivialization of mid-Victorian phrasings like "friendship 'pure and simple.'"[61]

In those final pages, the word is not assigned to Longdon either, except in one isolated and much qualified reference by the narrator, in which Nanda's "old friend" is said to be "keeping his place in the silence . . ." (540). Winters sees James "trying to have it both ways," invoking both adoption and marriage. But with those alternatives already voided, James seems rather to be keeping and consuming some unnamed and unnameable model. Rejecting the idioms for heterosexual relations available to his English social setting, James, like Allen and Hardy before him, claims to have envisioned his desired relationship yet leaves it unarticulated. It resides beyond the novel's temporal limit, as Eliot's "blank" had demanded fulfillment beyond the plot of *Daniel Deronda* and as Hardy's version of "comradeship" would have to be realized in an era after *Jude*. Hardy had anticipated the gap of a full generation; James dates it more immediately with the book's final word, "tomorrow," while still avoiding the question of how it may come to be. These novels thus assign "friendship" a nearly definitive nineteenth-century placing, yet leave it unimaged, hopelessly out of reach.

James was less ready than Hardy to consider cooperative work between the sexes. Millicent Bell notes that James "thought about the subject enough to conceive of a story based on the thesis that the friendship of man and woman could not be easily combined with joint pursuit of the literary goal"; Edel calls it remarkable that James even considered literary collaboration with Woolson, and there is no evidence of its ever having begun. Edel also credits an androgynous James with having safely internalized such cooperation.[62] But the idea of "refuge" seems more significantly realized in James's portrayal of Beccles, Longdon's "unworldly world," his and Nanda's distant retreat.[63] For it was common for writers around the turn of the century to image forbidden single-sex relations as thriving in some imminent time or secluded haven; *The Awkward Age* completes the process whereby novels like *The Woman Who Did* and *Jude the Obscure* closed off comparably subversive cross-sex bonds from any idiomatic reality, while claiming that they had nearly arrived.[64] Heterosexual "friendship" had altered in the 1890's, to be buried again in the novel.

4

Ways of Looking On: Friendship in Early Modernist Fiction

From Salon to the Uttermost Shore:
Joseph Conrad and Agnes Tobin

Sampled and tested, then rejected or at best put off to an impossible future, heterosexual "friendship," as engaged by writers like Allen, James, and Hardy, would seem to have little promise left. Whereas it had once connoted sexlessness, however doubtful, it now might as easily connote the sexual as well; whereas it had once seemed "unnatural" and therefore without a place in English society, it might now seem, in certain forms, entirely "natural" and yet impossible to articulate. But the two novelists discussed in this chapter each confirm, though in very different ways, that heterosexual friendship had nevertheless emerged—that for English writers at the beginning of the twentieth century, it had even become inescapable. Joseph Conrad might treat "friendship" as an oddity, satirize it, and even doubt, as much as earlier writers had, the possibility of describing it clearly; but a male writer whose literary career depended so significantly on collaboration with women, and whose commercial success depended on his making a successful appeal to women readers, could hardly avoid gesturing toward productive and affectionate heterosexual cooperation, at least not without repudiating significant elements of his own career. Unless, that is, he were to take the approach of D. H. Lawrence, as dependent on heterosexual collaboration as any English writer, yet wholly cynical about "friendship" as anything more than a necessary ruse: Lawrence was as desperate as any mid-Victorian to present "friendship" as no more than a deception or a trap. If Conrad's men and women show some of the first signs that "friendship" had come to name a genuine source of cooperative creation, Lawrence's remain locked in a sexual exchange that must always end in victimization and defeat.

Conrad's and Lawrence's experiences of the inevitability of heterosexual interaction follow upon a long literary tradition in which such interaction seemed, at least for men, a profitable option. Because authorship was one of the few professional roles accessible to women, the act of writing had long seemed a possible locus for some form of working interaction between the sexes, though by no means one predicated on equality or mutual respect. Indeed, one readily accepted model of intellectual collaboration had served to establish a safe home (far safer than the one James had set aside to lodge Nanda) for the woman who was friend to men; even Hardy's Henniker had sometimes resided there.[1] English custom maintained the *salon* as a more-than-respectable meeting place for various elites: here a singularly elevated and pristine woman presided over a stable of invariably ingenious males, unsullied by the complications "natural" to other arenas. In 1854, on the verge of her own literary career, George Eliot had praised French salons as the source of that nation's unique development of "womanly intellect"; reversing the usual subordination of "friendship" to "love," Eliot described how Mme. de Sablé had been "a woman whom men could more than love—whom they could make their friend, confidante, and counsellor; the sharer, not of their joys and sorrows only, but of their ideas and aims."[2] The eighteenth-century salon ideal had just then been given fresh currency by Auguste Comte, who, in his dedication to "perfect friendship" between the sexes, urged mid-Victorian England to adopt a conception of society that would depend upon the Positivist salon hostess for its "moral control." The only positive associations "friendship" had achieved in English came when it was subsumed under more recognized categories like domesticity and salvation; the salon might at least make a virtue of such discursive conditions by celebrating the assimilation of "friendship" into a heavenly model of home.

The skeptical feminist response to Comte, which I described in Chapter 1, centered less on Positivism's insistence "that woman's life should still be essentially domestic" than on its making woman, in Frances Power Cobbe's words, into "an idol of clay . . . like all other idols, an image of Repose," a mere powerless "Vice Goddess." The salon was designed, feminists saw, to be an ethereal locus for the ambitious household angel, benign mother of minds. Nevertheless, by the turn of the century a peculiarly English version of the salon Vice Goddess, no less angelic but slightly more active than Comte's, had gained prominence. Unlike her French predecessor, whose "forté was evidently not to write herself, but to stimulate others to write; to show that sympathy and appreciation which are as genial and encouraging as the morning sunbeams" (as Eliot had approvingly reported),[3] the supreme English hostess might perform as a writer without diminishing her household status. Thus the poet Alice Meynell, dubbed by George Meredith "the pencilling Mamma," could be recalled by an "Old Bohemian" as

no ordinary highbrow but a very beautiful woman whose presence, as much as her writing, was an inspiration. . . . She had the face of an angel and alas! a too frail physique. . . . She possessed an instinctively gracious dignity of manner, yet the sense of humour of a frivolous girl. Almost all her guests whom one first met on those delightful occasions one desired to meet again. I remember one Sunday evening, coming out of the house by chance with a woman of the world, more distinguished for her physical charm than for intellect. As we walked towards the Bayswater Road, talking about our hostess as if she had been some minor deity, my companion suddenly remarked, "I feel somehow as if I must go to church and pray."[4]

Meynell's closest friend, a U.S. citizen named Agnes Tobin, was in some respects the typical English salon woman, and in fact sometimes served to draw visitors to the Meynells' drawing room. But she lived in England principally as a rover, outside the salon and all other forms of conventional protection. Agnes Tobin survives peripherally in the literary history of the time, typically noted as follows:

Agnes Tobin, literary member of a San Francisco banking family, was a close friend of such literary figures as William Butler Yeats, Joseph Conrad, Alice Meynell, John Millington Synge, George Meredith, Edmund Gosse, Francis Thompson, Joaquin Miller, and Arthur Symons. In his *Confessions*, Symons describes her as "bright, warm-hearted, very talkative; very amusing; she had an extraordinary charm. And wherever she went, her attraction was so curious that she was not only at home, but that one always felt at home with her. She had a passion for meeting famous writers." Conrad dedicated his *Under Western Eyes* "To Agnes Tobin who brought to our door her genius for friendship from the uttermost shore of the West."[5]

Such accounts give passing acknowledgment to Tobin's writing and point instead to achievements typical of the salon hostess, though made more remarkable still by her having been without a home, or, rather, having brought her sense of being "at home" with her as she traveled. As Conrad's pronouncement acknowledges, her negotiation of friendship in England was remarkable for its being remote, alien.

What mode of private conduct Agnes Tobin's "genius for friendship" managed to authorize is hard to ascertain. The Tobins were raised as Catholics, and it is not impossible that she presented herself as religiously chaste. But given the skepticism that religious couchings of "friendship" had met in Eliot's world and Hardy's, one hardly imagines they would hold in England or among Irish Protestants at the turn of the century. Though Alice Meynell's son Francis characterized Agnes as "a nun," he said more specifically, "a nun in fancy dress on a feast-day." Drawing on a letter from New York literary benefactor John Quinn, Michael Holroyd's biography of Augustus John notes that Agnes Tobin "had been observed to be 'a little bit flighty' "; Holroyd goes on to describe Tobin as "like . . . a jester at Court," "forty-five with the light behind her"—this as of 1911, when she helped rescue the failing Arthur Symons, John's friend—"a woman of the right instincts but the wrong clothes," who, Holroyd adds, "had translated Petrarch." Of John's reaction to Tobin's care, Holroyd remarks only, "He stood up to it well." Zdzisław Najder, Conrad's biographer, describes her as "a rich young [also as of 1911, when she first visited Conrad] California poetess and patron of writers (particularly of Arthur Symons, who lived [nearby])." She is characterized in Najder's book by Conrad's memory of her "delightful scent of intelligence and charm."[6]

Old or young according to the kind of condescension being offered her, Tobin has been granted little to suggest why these artists would have grudged her so much of their time—the usual suggestion being that she flattered them as a slight flirt, a kind of literary groupie. This in spite of the fact that her "patronage" of Symons had consisted chiefly of saving his life, according to John, or that Yeats had named her no less than the greatest American poet since Whitman, calling her Petrarch translations "very delicate, very beautiful, with a curious poignant ecstacy."[7] But such remarks would not bar imputations then any more than now. Synge's assuring his beloved Molly Allgood "you need not be jealous" of Tobin did not prevent a bitter quarrel or Synge's having subsequently to assure Allgood, "There is not of course the remotest sign of flirtation about us but I like her greatly, and value her friendship." Later Synge would write to Allgood that he intended "to write to 'My Dear Friend' [Tobin] again to tell her how I am getting on. . . ."[8] Whatever the source of Synge's caps and inverted commas, they are evidence of care and self-consciousness about the idiom that would designate Tobin's role. In this private instance at least, "friend" would not suit Tobin without qualification.

Yet by 1911 she had been living abroad for most of fifteen years, writing and being written to as "friend" in correspondence with illustrious men, and there is no indication in the surviving letters of any difficulty or misunderstanding. Her usual subject is the material business of writing. She awaits the performance of her *Phèdre* by the Abbey players; she commiserates with Synge over the "disturbance" attendant to the Abbey's performing his *Playboy of the Western World*; she arranges for Quinn to buy Conrad's and Symons's manuscripts; she suggests to Gosse that a Civil List pension be procured for Yeats; she keeps Symons alive, barely. Yeats and Thompson are effusive in their praise for her translations, and she is grateful to them. Some offer sympathy in her episodes of dire illness, and she says she will recover. Just as Conrad was the only one of her correspondents to make public commemoration of her "genius for friendship," only his letters remark repeatedly on that skill. He once goes so far as to relate it to her fragile state, in a letter written several months after the publication of *Under Western Eyes*:

Muy guerida Inez,
Your letter is a great reward. But you are so delightfully imaginative yourself that any man with a vision of his own may be certain of your favor. I am deeply moved by the friendliness of your words; and no less grieved that the improvement in your health seems temporarily checked. Do try to find time to think of yourself a little or else your genius for friendship will be your undoing. . . .[9]

Conrad's sympathetic recognition of difficulties attending Tobin's gift to men of vision is not the sort of insight he is commonly associated with. But in fact the dedication to *Under Western Eyes*, which brings Tobin's "genius" to his threshold but no further, is one of several occasions when he explicitly acknowledged complexities attending heterosexual friendship. As documents pertaining to Agnes Tobin sketch a life outside the salon and other conventional English categories for bourgeois heterosexual relations, Conrad's fictions chart a fellow outsider's ongoing response to those categories. In no sense did he feel "at home" among them, nor would his fictional treatments of "friendship" have entirely underwritten successful negotiation of them by Tobin or anyone else: Conrad's aggregate statement on heterosexual friendship in his novels *Nostromo*, *Under Western Eyes*, and *Chance* is nearly as evasive and discomfited as the dedication to Tobin is forthright and positive. For Conrad's rendering of friendship reflects more than just the limited social and idiomatic conventions of his adopted homeland; it also reflects the ambivalence of an author whom English literary convention required both to confront and to repudiate the inscription of cross-gender relations. Scenes of heterosexual co-operation like those the fin-de-siècle Hardy had sought to banish to the distant future were, as the century turned, necessary material facts of Conrad's writing life, and his fiction reveals his uncomfortable awareness of such dependence. Yet his tribute to Tobin's "genius" is typical of his disposition to acknowledge that male/female relations required careful negotiation and offered powerful imaginative rewards—and Conrad comes closer, I believe, to developing a viable idiom for heterosexual friendship than do any of his predecessors or contemporaries.

Even were Conrad's achievement in regard to idioms for friendship not impressive, he would seem to me worthy of careful attention here for the very reasons that might make his mention in this context seem surprising. My preceding chapters have described how heterosexual "friendship" was, throughout the Victorian period, constantly displaced and how that process is now reinforced by critical tendencies that make "friendship" all the more difficult to recover. Yet, as George Eliot's avoidance of "friendship" and Allen's, Hardy's, and James's intense embraces of it demonstrate, the representation of heterosexual friendship is best fostered by those who treat it with the greatest skepticism, registering discomfort or resistance rather than insisting on its "full value." Conrad, in his attempt to become part of an English literary world that depended so much on readerly interest in heterosexual relations but offered so little to authenticate possibilities like "friendship," tests the limits and openings in that world's gender-related discourse. I will examine evidence relating to Conrad's and Tobin's private experiences a little more closely than I have comparable evidence relating to other figures, but not to prove that Conrad's and Tobin's was somehow a more authentic "friendship"; it is rather to highlight modern readerly assumptions that have militated against accounting for the relationship at all, and to show how Conrad himself confronted such assumptions in his work. Conrad's fiction represents not so much a source of turn-of-the-century idioms for heterosexual friendship as a record of their shadow life, one that suggests why the public negotiation of "friendship" might have required creative "genius" of a most taxing kind.

If Tobin's "genius for friendship" consisted, as Conrad's letter to her suggests, in basing relations with men on "imaginative" appreciation of artistic effort, that was a skill Conrad had benefited from before. His first literary mentor had been a woman, Marguerite Poradowska. She was the one writer among his close acquaintances before he began his own novelistic career; it was Poradowska to whom Conrad announced the completion of his first novel and whom he asked to be the first translator of his work. But Conrad's biographers have been loath to acknowledge her formative role in his career, because it does not suit the established commonplace that Conrad was a misogynist. Frederick Karl acknowledges this incongruity in *Joseph Conrad: The Three Lives*:

> much has been written about Conrad's indifference or even antagonism to his female characters and about his lack of respect for women in general, such views making him into a rough-hewn sailor who preferred male bonding to female companionship. Those who hold to that idea, however, must account for his extraordinary friendship with Marguerite Poradowska, in which he reveals his inner self, bares his most frail longings and hopes, exposes himself without shame or embarrassment, and never indicates any sense of male superiority or feminine dependency. He honors Marguerite for what she is, a woman of some talent intent on establishing an independent life. . . . [He accepted] Marguerite as an equal—not at all as the person Marlow condescends to in "Heart of Darkness" when he brags to his male audience that he has never needed "Women!" [10]

Yet Karl and others "account" for this relation by depicting it as a thwarted courtship that must have climaxed in a "'discreet' stage," during which "their correspondence must have become too intimate." The biographers' chief evidence for that stage is an "abrupt gap" in the extant correspondence between 1895 and 1900, which they assume must indicate a period when Conrad and Poradowska exchanged romantic letters since destroyed—though there are ample reasons to think that their correspondence had simply diminished with the end of his sea career and the expansion of his circle of literary acquaintances as he settled into English life, and his marriage.[11] (See Appendix.)

Whether additional letters ever existed and whether Conrad ever courted Poradowska are matters of limited—strictly biographical—interest; of greater importance is the biographers' common reluctance to plot Conrad and Poradowska's relation as that of literary associates. Najder asks only tentatively if "it is perhaps best to seek the key to the 'Poradowska puzzle' in literature," even while acknowledging both that she was "the only person among [the young Conrad's] acquaintances outside Poland who belonged to his own cultural milieu" and that their correspondence almost from its beginning concerned "literary subjects." Though Najder notes that Poradowska had "already published four novels . . . when Conrad was making his début," his previous paragraph names Edward Garnett, whom Conrad met five years later, as the "first writer in [Conrad's] group of friends." [12] Neither "friend" nor any related term has been deemed adequate to the Conrad/Poradowska relationship. Karl sees Conrad's Victorian-like appropriation of the Polish term of endearment, "auntie," as a "means [by] which Conrad could carry on an apparent flirtation, however serious or frivolous, under the guise of showing respect and obligation toward a member of his family." [13] There is a "gap" here, the product of recognizably Victorian idiomatic limitations that date back to *Daniel Deronda* and before: the biographers find no way to describe the male and female figures' relationship according to its shared participation in an activity other than courtship. Thus the relationship must be charted according to the moment when it became "too intimate" or disparaged for having existed "more on paper than in the flesh"—an odd dismissal for a correspondence between two writers.[14]

Conrad had in fact been a good deal involved in cooperative relations with women before he met Agnes Tobin—not only with his "dear Teacher" Poradowska, but also with Emilie Briquel, who had first translated his work into French; Aniela Zagorska, whom he had authorized to translate all his works into Polish; Helen Watson, who had proofread for him *The Nigger of the "Narcissus"*; and most enduringly Lillian Hallowes, to whom he dictated his books for twenty years. These women all had roles ostensibly subordinate to his central position as the originating author of his works, but they were all almost as essential to the production and distribution of certain editions of those works as Tobin, whose procuring of Quinn's patronage kept Conrad solvent. These women also had the most immediate access to him as a working writer. In 1911, Conrad wrote to Tobin of the "unfortunate, soul-crushing weariness" of his "writing life," then added, "I don't write generally to people in that tone. With you I am frank—but this frankness is for you only. Vous comprenez? It wouldn't do to let the world in behind the scenes. Even Jessie [his wife] herself is not always admitted when darkness descends upon the stage. A quoi bon l'inquieter? N'est-ce pas?"[15]

Conrad's suggestion of intimacy here is expressed less as flirtation than as willingness to permit Tobin to share the private space in which he writes. The wording also closely resembles that of Karl's account of the way Conrad "reveal[ed] his inner self" to Poradowska. Biography reflects some of the narrative pressures of fiction, and it may be that imposing a courtship dynamic on all of his heterosexual relations serves to move the otherwise slow progress of a male writer's life along. But evidence from Conrad's career suggests that it was indeed the demands of his writing life that motivated the hardly flirtatious Conrad's interactions with women. And key moments in his fiction demonstrate just how integral he might have thought the "genius for friendship" he attributed to Tobin was to the telling and circulation of his stories.

Conrad's "Profound Sympathies"

If Conrad scholarship has been reluctant to conceive of his writerly interactions with women as constituting "friendship," that is not because his works don't make the term available—though neither can they be said to offer it as stable or assured. Just after the end of the long retrospect that begins Conrad's 1904 novel *Nostromo*, a pivotal chapter begins with the Frenchman Decoud in the act of writing privately to a female "friend":

It was part of what Decoud would have called his sane materialism that he did not believe in the possibility of friendship existing between man and woman.

The one exception he allowed confirmed, he maintained, that absolute rule. Friendship was possible between brother and sister, meaning by friendship the frank unreserve, as before another human being, of thoughts and sensations; an objectless and necessary sincerity of one's innermost life trying to react upon the profound sympathies of another existence.

His favorite sister, the handsome, slightly arbitrary, and resolute angel, ruling the father and mother Decoud in the first-floor apartments of a very fine Parisian house, was the recipient of Martin Decoud's confidences as to his thoughts, actions, purposes, doubts, and even failures. . . . (223)

The passage is one of a number of early Modernist texts that continue their Victorian predecessors' sullen rejection of male / female friendship: in the year after *Nostromo*, for instance, James Joyce's gloomy *Dubliners* diarist would declare that "friendship between man and woman is impossible because there must be intercourse." [16] (D. H. Lawrence's work in the ensuing years would cast the greatest doubts, as will be described shortly.) But Decoud's denial of heterosexual friendship is unusual for its being so obviously consumed by what it denies, the way Victorian denials of sex had been. Not only does Decoud's rejection of "friendship" preface an exception that conspicuously disproves his rule—his frank letter to his sister will occupy the book's next twenty-five pages—but it follows immediately upon another such exception: his secret conversation with Emilia Gould, which, as Decoud now writes, has proven her "a good ally," who "seizes upon all [his] suggestions with a sure instinct . . ." (245). Decoud will eventually be seen "pressing Mrs. Gould's hand" as he entrusts her with his notebook epistle to his sister (260).

The gesture seems appropriate, since nearly all of *Nostromo*'s comparable moments of intimacy derive from Emilia Gould's "genius of sympathetic intuition" (156). Earlier, Decoud has noted her "subtly devoted, finely self-forgetful . . . readiness of attention," in words that anticipate his definition of friendship. Her gift "in the art of human intercourse" is said, accordingly, to consist in "delicate shades of self-forgetfulness and in the suggestion of universal comprehension" (46), an art she practices in her relations with nearly every male character in the novel—with Decoud, Don Jose,

Viola, Nostromo—except her husband. Conrad makes her seem to have the "fountain of friendship for men" that George Eliot had ascribed to the wedded Dorothea Brooke, but without its flowing to or from marriage and without her taking on the status of a household "angel" like Decoud's sister. Her relationships seem, instead, to depend merely on the "frankness" Conrad would describe as exclusive to his communication with Tobin.

"How was Conrad able to create such a character as Mrs. Gould . . . ?" asks Thomas Moser in the book that has established current critical assumptions about Conrad's portrayal of women. It is a way of asking how Conrad, chronicler of a conspicuously "male world," could depict a woman capable of relating to men in a way that does not hinge on sexuality, the "uncongenial subject" Moser sees as harmful to Conrad's fictional powers. Moser qualifies his praise for the characterization of Emilia Gould by noting that "her courtship is kept safely in the past, that Conrad avoids any close consideration of her married life, and that to the rest of the world she remains an unassailable matron."[17] But those qualifications could, in the context of Moser's central argument about the debilitating effects of sex and romance upon Conrad's fiction, suggest an answer to his own question about the portrayal of Emilia Gould: her role in Nostromo is structured less according to the dynamics of courtship and marital intimacy than according to problems of perception (or "attention") and communication, problems that motivate many of Conrad's most esteemed plots.

Conrad's characters typically emerge through the unreliable perceptions and communications of those with whom they interact—Kurtz and Lord Jim are perhaps the most famous examples in this regard. But Emilia Gould is, like Marlow, one of the exceptional figures whom Conrad allows to participate actively in her self-disclosure: she is "unassailable" sexually, but not perceptually; her thoughts are shared and relatively open. That Conrad could portray a female character with insights stable and interesting enough to share has seemed, according to the prevailing critical line, even less likely than his creating a believable female character. "Conrad's misogyny, present in his work from [his first two novels] onward, derives from his identification of sexual experience with the loss of mental clearness and self-possession," J. Hillis Miller has asserted, applying Moser's findings to the whole of the Conrad canon.[18] In conjoining the novelist's attitude toward women to his attitude toward "sexual experience," Miller severs heterosexual motives from any form of enlightened subjectivity, in a way even Decoud in his "sane materialism" might have found extreme. There seems, in this account, no way to measure Conrad's portrayal of hetero-sexual interactions—or even the mental processes of the male and female characters who interact—except according to the presence or absence of sex.

But Conrad's fiction invites consideration, at least, of other pos-sibilities. At the center of the novel dedicated to Agnes Tobin, *Under Western Eyes*, is a male writer committed to "elevating humanity" by proclaiming that "there is nothing to be done without women" (125, 237). Russian author Peter Ivanovitch is, in the words of the unnamed English narrator, "a revolutionary feminist, a great writer, if you like and—how shall I say it—the—the familiar guest of Madame de S——'s mystic revolutionary salon" (131). Ivanovitch's autobiography and several other works have "preached generally the cult of the woman," his own faith, manifested "under the rites of special devotion to the transcendental merits of . . . Madame de S——, a lady of advanced views" whom the narrator at once com-pares to Mme. de Staël (125). The prophet's "conviction of women's spiritual superiority" leads him to identify the salon of Mme. de S—— as "a unique centre of intellectual freedom and of effort to shape a high conception of our future" (127). Under his system—as under Auguste Comte's *System of Positive Polity*—men would derive from women the spiritual means to universal redemption.

Conrad's "Author's Note" says Peter Ivanovitch and Mme. de S—— are "the apes of a sinister jungle and are treated as their gri-maces deserve" (xiii). The narrator calls the salon "that home of necromancy and intrigue and feminist adoration" (327); its mali-cious functions, like Ivanovitch's hypocritical writing, depend on cruelty inflicted upon Tekla, the woman who is the insidious pair's most obedient confidante.[19] Were the models of heterosexual inter-action heralded and enacted by Peter Ivanovitch the only alterna-tives in the novel to the doomed romance between Razumov and Nathalie Haldin that is at the novel's center, then *Under Western Eyes* would seem to exemplify nothing more than the cynicism or incapacity in the face of cross-gender relations that is customarily associated with Conrad.

But the novel establishes Ivanovitch's villainy by having him enter blandly dismissing a relationship that might seem to be in various ways a genuine version of the kind Ivanovitch himself so grandiosely perverts. "Ah! your English friend," he says to Nathalie Haldin. "I know. I know. That's nothing" (119). Both Nathalie Haldin and her "friend," the narrator, apparently think otherwise. They have, he says, become "excellent friends" (102) in the course of his tutoring her in English literature, such that her mother has come to refer to him as "*l'ami*" (103). Subsequently it is "the warmth of [his] regard for Miss Haldin" (164) that keeps the narrator involved in the political intrigues in which he is less directly implicated than the novel's other characters. And the pair's relationship gives the narrative its being: for the narrator's story derives from Nathalie Haldin's having given him her brother's diary (376), in a gesture accompanied by a handclasp very like that when Decoud passes his notebook to Emilia Gould.

The narrator is explicit about his making "no claim to a special standing for [his] silent friendship" (126); and the one exchange during which he and Nathalie attempt to define their bond ends in resignation, though not great disappointment. In keeping with Conrad's general distrust for ideologues, the scene shows that no firm rhetoric like the one associated with Ivanovitch adheres to this relation. But neither, consequently, does any of Ivanovitch's hypocritical revolutionary fervor. Nathalie Haldin has been accusing the narrator of a decorous English refusal to be "rude" in matters of politics. "You shrink from the idea of revolutionary action for those you think well of as if it were something—how shall I say it—not quite decent." He briefly redirects the conversation to a consideration of their relationship:

> "You are quite right," I said. "I think very highly of you."
> "Don't suppose I do not know it," she began hurriedly. "Your friendship has been very valuable."
> "I have done little else but look on."
> She was a little flushed under the eyes.
> "There is a way of looking on which is valuable. I have felt less lonely because of it. It's difficult to explain." (134)

"Really?" replies the narrator. "Well, I too have felt less lonely. That's easy to explain, though," and he then quickly returns discussion to the nature of revolution. Though he elsewhere wonders "why she should have felt so friendly to me" (118) and characterizes his own "warmth" as "an unselfish sentiment, being its own reward" (164), both seem ready to maintain their "silent friendship" as "a way of looking on" that is pertinent to but not determined by the politics associated with Peter Ivanovitch.

Daniel Schwarz is the scholar who has contributed the most toward revising critical opinion about Conrad's portrayal of heterosexual relations; he has provided, for instance, the strongest explanation for Emilia Gould's role in *Nostromo*. Accordingly, he shows unique respect for the relationship of the narrator and Nathalie Haldin. He describes the narrator both as a foil for Conrad in his "rejection of political commitment in favor of personal relationships and private commitments" and as "a deeply committed friend, capable of perspicacious observation and sensitive to the needs of others," "the epitome of morality and sanity." Schwarz's reading of the teacher seems to me credible but not unimpeachable: Suresh Raval has more recently found the narrator an inadequate observer of "the complex and contradictory moral and political life in Russian society" and noted that "certain narrative moments suggest that [his] interest in Nathalia derives from his impotent and jealous romantic love for her." Raval admits that "these moments are not serious," and Schwarz provides ample illustration for the way the narrator "involves himself in Nathalie's affairs, and befriends her with a sensitivity and responsiveness that her Russian acquaintances lack."[20] But in eliding the ambiguities noted by Raval, Schwarz renders exact that which Nathalie and the narrator leave unclear. And Schwarz's praise for the relationship as "affirming personal values" does not show how it relates to those theories of Peter Ivanovitch's that would make such values the basis of a religion and revolution. Conrad had revised *Nostromo* to end it with a humane act by the emasculated Monygham in service of Emilia Gould:[21] a modest affirmation, even in the context of Nostromo's tragic doom, of a bond very much like Nathalie and the narrator's. But the pair in *Under Western Eyes* manages no such final affirmation, and the book in fact ends with ominous praise for their opponent, with a woman revolutionist insisting, "Peter Ivanovitch is an inspired man."

Inspired with a genius how different from that Conrad attributed to Agnes Tobin in the volume's dedication? The novel does not provide sure terms for answering such a question. Heterosexual friendship is here never clearly validated or discounted; it is defined half by the way Russian "autocracy" perverts human relations and half by the way an isolated couple finds comfort in shared but silent watching. Yet those terms of definition at least ensure that the novel's treatment of friendship falls outside the sex/gender equation Miller implicitly ascribed to Conrad's *oeuvre*; more broadly, they provide an English vocabulary for European gender roles that is not based mainly on the inclusion or exclusion of sexuality. Still, *Under Western Eyes* instances "friendship" only in Ivanovitch's false and immoral theory and in the narrator and Nathalie's wordless application. The strongest evidence of heterosexual friendship's positive value (beyond the "sensitivity and responsiveness" made explicit by Schwarz but not by Conrad) is that Peter Ivanovitch seems so utterly wrong in his dismissiveness—much as the hero of *Nostromo* seems disingenuous or obtuse in his comparable rejection—and more wrong still in his ostensibly superior model. Conrad's texts, in other words, offer "friendship" legitimacy mainly by undermining its most extreme misuse and by countering those who refute its more credible examples. What that leaves—what there is left to friendship—goes mostly without saying.

Of course, the affirmation of friendship in *Under Western Eyes* would have to overcome not only the usual matter-of-fact sexual suspicions, and not only the presence of Ivanovitch's absurd analogue, but also an array of international and transhistorical confusions: an "obscure" (126) and evasive Englishman is employing his nation's deficient idioms in the service of Conrad's recollections from nineteenth-century Poland to describe the interactions of Russian characters against the backdrop of a model derived from eighteenth-century France.[22] And that narrator seems most skeptical about language's representational value in any case; he begins the narrative by denouncing "words" as "the great foes of reality" (3). Cast in terms of these complications and skeptical qualifications, Conrad's tentative achievement seems a good deal more impressive. *Under Western Eyes* moves heterosexual friendship as close to idiomatic and theoretical legitimization as it could without Conrad's offering a flat, unqualified, and (one assumes) necessarily unconvincing statement like, "This friendship has been very valuable as a way of looking on," to paraphrase (slightly) Nathalie Haldin. The energy the novel puts toward keeping such a definition possible, even if it is never quite broached, makes *Under Western Eyes* as crucially *about* the uncertain status of heterosexual friendship as any English fiction since *Daniel Deronda*.

I don't insist that Conrad *intended* to experiment with friendship's idioms: there are enough tensions in language and in the relation between the personal and political in *Under Western Eyes* to generate the "silent friendship" as an incidental yield. Yet there is reason to think of Conrad's career as having become, by 1911, crucially enmeshed in the difficulties of articulating a creative relation between the sexes. *Under Western Eyes* is commonly recognized as the product of the central crisis in Conrad's career, whether a transitional moment preceding a marked decline, as in Moser's view, or a period of revaluation, in Schwarz's. Either way, "in Conrad's later writing," as Najder says, "women occupy far more space than in his works from the years 1897 to 1909." Schwarz sees the change as precipitated by Conrad's wish "to demonstrate that he was an English novelist, not a Slav writing in English, as reviewers implied"—a novelist capable, that is, of writing "English novels of manners and [of exploring] the intricacies of personal relationships in the context of contemporary customs and values." [23] If Conrad was to make himself truly at home in English culture, he would need a wider audience and greater financial stability.

Chance, the novel that followed *Under Western Eyes*, was both the "most English" of his novels [24] and his first popular success. Though the reasons for that success have been explained variously, there seems little doubt that this was the first of his novels to appeal to women readers. That fact left Conrad, who was desperate for money and acceptance, more ambivalent than satisfied. Hitherto typed as writer mainly of sea stories for a small audience of appreciative men, he disparaged *Chance* to his male colleagues as a "girl-novel," "stuff in which I don't believe," yet told his agent of his "confidence" in the book's quality and railed defiantly against his publisher's wish that he return to his old subject matter for the sake of sales: "There aren't ten thousand words of what you want of 'sea' in the hundred and forty thousand of *Chance*," he told Methuen, "not nearly enough to slake that thirst for salt from which it appears you have been suffering so long." Years before, at the time of *The Nigger of the "Narcissus"*, Conrad had told Helen

Watson of his hope that there "may be found a few *men and women* who will see what I have tried to see" (emphasis added).[25] But the reputation he had since created with sea stories like that all-male one might make his subsequent attempt at a new audience seem a betrayal both of his sex and of his commercial base.

Under Western Eyes reflects the tensions incumbent on an author motivated simultaneously to appeal to and to reject women as the public sharers of his vision, those whom he might "make . . . see." [26] Dedicating the book to the writer Agnes Tobin as one who had come from "the uttermost shore of the West," he addressed her almost as a fellow ocean voyager. But the novel itself suggests that there must be something insidious to a male writer's willingness to make grandiose and hypocritical appeals to women; its most positive (if finally ineffectual) model is the man willing simply to observe and mistranslate. In this initial approach to the novel of manners Conrad relies on a setting that shelters him from having to provide almost any direct presentation of people like his English readers. He protected himself further by editing out a number of critical remarks about English institutions uttered by his Russian characters.[27] But he couldn't complicate the novel's "Englishness" more thoroughly than to give centrality to a model of gender relations England had never yet accommodated and to present that narrative through the much-mediated words of an Englishman who would quietly assert that model's provisional existence.

The England of 1911 would in fact have presented Western eyes with a feminism more practically revolutionary than that promised by the narrator or Peter Ivanovitch.[28] And when Conrad acknowledged English feminism explicitly in his next novel, he confronted a far more troubling challenge to his authorial role. "There is a way of looking on which is valuable. . . . It's difficult to explain," Nathalie Haldin had told the English professor, as an evaluation of their friendship. These words would as well suit the self-justifying claims of Marlow, the narrator for much of Conrad's 1913 novel *Chance*. Marlow describes his own capacities for observation as a function of his marginality. Moreover, half of what Marlow recounts in *Chance* is borrowed from women; his bounty comes from his conversations with the English feminist writer Mrs. Fyne and with Flora de Barral, daughter of a failed London tycoon. Marlow is reluctant to admit his dependence—"never mind that. The means don't concern you except in so far as they belong to the story," he snaps at his listener, after diffidently claiming to have been Flora de Barral's confidant (325–26)—much as he had been reluctant to admit his dependence on "women," in the passage cited by Karl above. (Conrad was now depending on the patronage of Quinn that Tobin had procured for him, while writing the novel whose female audience would help him to some greater financial stability.) But in the midst of his various hostile reactions to women's increasing influence, as represented by Mrs. Fyne's feminism, Marlow attributes to women the same position he has undertaken as storyteller and the very skill to which he aspires. Describing Flora's marginality—the fate of "a woman for whom there is no clear place in the world"— Marlow declares:

And this is the pathos of being a woman. A man can struggle to get a place for himself or perish. But a woman's part is passive, say what you like, and shuffle the facts of the world as you may, hinting at lack of energy, of wisdom, of courage. As a matter of fact, almost all women have all that— of their own kind. But they are not made for attack. Wait they must. I am speaking here of women who are really women. And it's no use talking of opportunities, either. I know that some of them do talk of it. But not the genuine women. Those know better. Nothing can beat a true woman for a clear vision of reality; I would say a cynical vision if I were not afraid of wounding your chivalrous feelings—for which, by the by, women are not so grateful as you may think, to fellows of your kind ...

"Upon my word," Marlow's listener responds, "what are you flying out at me for like this?" (281). Critics have accused Conrad of using irony defensively in *Chance* to cover his own inescapable sentimentality, but here the listener's response clearly invites recognition of Marlow's bitter self-defensiveness. If women possess the clearest sagacity, the most unsentimentally realistic perspective, and the information on which Marlow's tale is based, his own powers may be described, in the terms of his own admission, as deriving entirely from *their* marginality. He repeatedly acknowledges "the woman in [his] nature" (53), calling it "that drop of superior essence" (146). His remark about women's possessing the "clearest vision of reality" seems directly in contradiction to Miller's sex/ women/"loss of mental clearness" equation, for Marlow attributes his enabling connection with Flora de Barral to the absence of a sexual dynamic between them.

A young girl, you know, is something like a temple. You pass by and wonder what mysterious rites are going on in there, what prayers, what visions? The privileged man, the lover, the husband, who are given the key of the sanctuary do not always know how to use it. For myself, without claim, without merit, simply by chance I had been allowed to look through the half-opened door and I had seen the saddest possible desecration. . . . (311)

Women as temples, women as "preserving for us certain well-known, well-established, I'll almost say hackneyed, illusions, without which the average male creature cannot get on" (94): Marlow's comments on women in *Chance*, even when they are not openly hostile, often echo the conventional categories that had found their place in Comte's salon and that had disturbed mid-Victorian feminists. But they mark reactions, I am suggesting, not just to Mrs. Fyne's post-Victorian feminism—"Her theory was that they should turn themselves into unscrupulous sexless nuisances" (190) —but to Marlow's anxiety about having to share elements of her situation in order to maintain his own identity as storyteller. He is most insistent on denying women "opportunities" for work— "Women can't go forth on the high roads and by-ways to pick up a living even when dignity, independence, or existence itself are at stake" (172)—but the experiences that *Chance* cedes to its female characters provide Marlow, as he finally admits near the close, with "all the details which really matter in this story" (443), a good number of which are rendered in the women's own voices, however mediated through those of Marlow and the narrator. Marlow's independent struggle for survival, like Conrad's, on the one hand has left him dependent on women, and on the other hand has placed him in the "passive" role he has ascribed to them: that of the observer awaiting the opportunity for "a clear vision of reality." Conrad leaves Marlow facing the possibility that whatever "clear vision" he finds may not be his own. The book's one working woman is a writer.

Chance, first published in 1913, marked Conrad's full confrontation, initiated partly by *Under Western Eyes* but developing since the earliest stages of his career, with the world of the woman reader and with a world in which women who earned their way with their minds were becoming increasingly conspicuous.[29] His approach to the English novel of manners defied some of the conventional patterns of chivalrous domestication and idolization: "A woman is not necessarily a doll or angel to me," he has Marlow say. "She is a human being, very much like myself" (53).[30] Though his earlier grudging acceptance of sibling relations as a unique instance of "friendship . . . between man and woman" and his satire of the "Platonic," as represented by Peter Ivanovitch, had recapitulated typical Victorian reactions, the relationships that give the narratives of *Under Western Eyes* and *Chance* their being provide markedly unconventional models.

Yet the silences and indirections that characterize those relationships show Conrad's affinities with other male writers in the period. It seems to me that behind his ironic views of Decoud, Ivanovitch, and even Marlow, his readers are expected to recognize an author unintervening but in control, who has comprehended what his characters cannot and is at home with his unrevealed vision. Like Allen, Hardy, and James, Conrad leaves his readers to believe themselves in the presence of an author who has resolved for himself matters about which his characters remain uncomprehending, defensive, or simply wrong—in any case, unspeaking. Conrad's fiction suggests that "friendship" as "a way of looking on" is possible, desirable, and even, for the production of certain kinds of narratives, necessary, but not that it can itself be plainly acknowledged or represented. While he would not consign it to the realm of domestic tragedy as did his contemporaries, he would not offer it an alternative space either; and as the other novelists had shown, where "friendship" could find no stable grounding, it would always be vulnerable to absorption or erasure. If Conrad did believe a "genius for friendship" with the opposite sex integral to changing conditions, by 1913 he had lost his acknowledged exemplar of such genius permanently; for Agnes Tobin, whom literary history discards even from its peripheries after the time of *Under Western Eyes*, had returned, deemed incurably mad, to San Francisco, where she would be attended to during her final thirty years at the Fairmont Hotel, at the home of her brother, and among the Sisters of the Holy Family.[31]

Watching for the Vital Part:
Lawrence, Work, and the "Usual Plan"

The year 1913 was the last for a while when England could afford to cast doubt upon working relations between women and men. Yet there appeared in that year D. H. Lawrence's *Sons and Lovers*, famous for making explicit the eroticism of family life, but equally explicit in denouncing heterosexual cooperation and in denying that shared labor could be at the center of cross-sex relations. Lawrence might be the first English writer to have to repudiate "friendship" between the sexes as if it were something his culture might be ready to embrace. But Lawrence can also be seen as re-inscribing the Victorian discursive impulses that had undermined not only "friendship" but all attempts to ground heterosexual relations in work. Elaine Scarry has described Tess D'Urberville's rape by her employer as "a hazard of the workplace, an industrial accident" of a kind "routinely recognized in the twentieth century";[32] *Sons and Lovers* suggests that such incidents ought properly to inhere wherever the workplace includes women.

As "Paul [Morel] Launches Into Life" in the novel's fifth chapter, he comes to the recognition that work divides rather than unites the sexes, and he draws pleasure from that insight:

He liked to watch his fellow-workers at work. The man was the work and the work was the man, the one thing, for the time being. It was different with the girls. The real woman never seemed to be there at the task, but as if left out, waiting (141).

As Paul matures, he develops and expands upon this vision. By the book's final pages he believes he has discovered the secret at its center, when he tells Miriam Leivers, "I suppose work *can* be nearly everything to a man, though it is not to me. But a woman only works with a part of herself. The real and vital part is covered up" (404). Lawrence has already provided some confirmation for these ideas; as Paul has watched Clara Dawes at work, he has seemed quite near to discovering her vital part:

Paul watched her. She sat square and magnificent. Her throat and arms were bare. The blood still mantled below her ears; she bent her head in shame of her humility. Her face was set on her work. Her arms were creamy and full of life beside the white lace; her large, well-kept hands worked with a balanced movement, as if nothing would hurry them. He, not knowing, watched her all the time. He saw the arch of her neck from the shoulder, as she bent her head; he saw the coil of her dun hair; he watched her moving, gleaming arms. (318)

Paul's "not knowing" absolves him, evidently, of responsibility for the scene's sexual energy. In spite of Clara's apparent concentration on what she is doing, Lawrence's account makes sexuality seem to inhere in her activity—Paul passively observes it rather than projects it. He so enjoys his distant vantage point that he will not relinquish it even when Clara comes to work under him: in Kate Millett's words, "although in the time-honored manner of sexual capitalism, he is sleeping with one of his underlings, he insists on a rigid division between sex and business."[33]

That division is nevertheless one *Sons and Lovers* rejects. Though Paul's employment at an artificial-limbs factory means that the human body often appears in the novel segmented, mechanized, and deformed, it is never sexless. Lawrence's pervasive sexualization of the working women's bodies that Paul "liked to watch" is most conspicuous in the treatment of Fanny, a factory "girl" who (aside from her name) would seem the novel's least likely sex object. A paragraph in the "Clara" section recalls that Fanny is a hunchback, twice Paul's age, and beneath him in status; but within a few paragraphs, Fanny, "gazing" at Paul in her "'finishing-off' room" until she has been "overcome with emotion," has "flung her arms round his neck and kissed him vehemently" (328–30).

The scene snubs novelistic decorum, for Fanny's disability, age, and class are attributes that would have authorized an earlier novelist to efface her sexuality: she seems a descendant, for instance, of Philip Wakem in *The Mill on the Floss* and other Victorian characters as harmlessly disabled, aged (e.g., Dr. Kenn in the same novel), or impoverished (that novel's Bob Jakin). Lawrence had in fact written "Maggie Tulliver and Philip" in his copy of Schopenhauer, alongside the words, "Next to old age and disease, nothing disgusts us so much as a deformed shape"; Miriam Leivers's living model, Jessie Chambers, recalled his complaining that Eliot had "gone and spoilt" the book by linking "the vital Maggie Tulliver to the cripple Philip."[34] Fanny's hunchback would seem ordinarily to prevent a novelist's endowing her with sexual vitality, but because she is one of the workers Paul habitually watches, Lawrence has had opportunity to call close attention to her hair (as "something [for Paul] to paint"), her short black bodice, her long "strides," and her hands "excitedly twitch[ing] her white apron, which was spread on the bench in front of her." "I'm going to look," he says. It turns out that Fanny's apron is concealing the working women's gift to Paul, a set of paint-tubes, the tools of his art, which Paul then receives along with Fanny's kiss. Paul's scrutiny of Fanny thus eventually exposes not only her vital part but his as well.

There is reason to think of all such scrutiny as insidious,[35] but its particular significance in Lawrence's writings becomes obvious only in relation to a recurring opposite scene, in which a woman is made to observe—and admire—a man at work. In July 1908, Lawrence set himself thus before his lover, Louie Burrows:

All last week, and all this, I have been in the hay. Hardly do I know myself; I have cast my tender skin-of-college culture (don't dare to say it never grew)—my hands are pachydermatous (Hurray!)—and still jolly sore; my manners are—dear me, dear me, Mrs. Grundy!—my exquisite accent . . . is gone; as the corns rose on my hands so grew gruffness in my speech. You will like me, you hussy.

On the following day Lawrence extended the same scene to Blanche Jennings, a Liverpool postal worker who was assisting him with his first novel, *The White Peacock*:

About half an hour ago I came in from the hay field, where I have been working for the last fortnight. I have had a bath, a delicious cold bath, and have eaten half a fruit pie. Now I am as complacent as a god.

My hands are brown, hard, and coarse; my face is gradually tanning. Aren't you glad? I have really worked hard; I can pick alongside a big experienced man; indeed I am fairly strong; I am pretty well developed; I have done a good deal of dumb-bell practice. Indeed, as I was rubbing myself down in the late twilight a few minutes ago, and as I passed my hands over my sides where the muscles lie suave and secret, I did love myself. I am thin, but well skimmed over with muscle; my skin is very white and unblemished; soft, and dull with a fine pubescent bloom, not shiny like my friend's. I am very fond of myself. I like you because I can talk like this to you.

Lawrence continues this letter by explaining why he "value[s] the friendship of men more than that of women," and his stated reasons form a complement to his descriptions of working women cited above. "You measure a friend by the breadth of his understanding," says Lawrence, but

a woman's soul of emotion is not so organised, so distinctly divided and active in part as a man's. Set a woman's soul vibrating in response to your own, and it is her whole soul which trembles with a strong, soft note of uncertain quality. But a man will respond, if he be a friend, to the very chord you strike, with clear and satisfying timbre, responding with a part, not the whole, of his soul. It makes a man much more satisfactory.

Much as in *Sons and Lovers*, Lawrence divides the sexes according to men's fit involvement and women's desired withdrawal or incorrectly proportioned participation. More importantly, Lawrence takes no responsibility for the reactions he describes: if his are partial and controlled, and Jennings's are total and chaotic, that follows from their sexual identities—not, apparently, from Lawrence's casting their relation in terms of his fondness for himself and the corresponding sensual response he may provoke from Jennings. "In the intervals of writing" the letter, Lawrence discloses near its end, "I have been talking with my [male] friend, who is sitting on the grass beside me . . ., so pardon my scrappiness." The letter itself has created conditions in which, while the male friends share a controlled, cooperative experience, Jennings must process Lawrence's barrage of continuous language on her own, as best she can. Friendship between men is for Lawrence fully cooperative; heterosexual friendship is atomizing, distinctly lonely.

A comparable contrast inheres in the letter's extended celebration of Lawrence's "long fortnight [working] in the hay, with my friends, men, three men, whom I really love" and his curt thanks to Jennings for her "remarks" on his novel-in-progress: "You will be sick of it if you have to read it again," he tells her, "but tell me, please, everything you can think of."[36] As opposed to his wholly mutual experience with his male co-workers, Lawrence continually commandeers the experience of his female readers, both Jennings and Burrows, telling them what their reactions must be ("You will like me"; "Aren't you glad?"; "You will be sick of it"). Yet his pleasure in his labor seems to derive greatly from his being able to prompt the women's entirely predetermined reactions to it. Much of Lawrence's thinking on work and gender may be derived from the hay-harvesting scene, whose central components seem to be the male body admired by the excluded woman: critic Harry Moore notes that it foreshadows various (equally idyllic) harvesting passages in Lawrence's fiction.[37] In *The White Peacock*, Lettie looks on enviously as George scythes his corn.

> "I wish I could work here," she said, looking away at the standing corn, and the dim blue woods. He followed her look, and laughed quietly, with indulgent resignation.
>
> "I do!" she said emphatically.
>
> "You feel so fine," he said, pushing his hand through his open shirt-front, and gently rubbing the muscles of his side. "It's a pleasure to work or to stand still. It's a pleasure to yourself—your own physique."
>
> She looked at him, full at his physical beauty, as if he were some great firm bud of life. (48)

Her sense of exclusion characterizes Lettie throughout the novel; fulfilling farmwork with George, on the other hand, permits the novel's Lawrence figure (Cyril) "an almost passionate attachment" to him, "more perfect than any love I have known since, either for man or woman" (223).[38] All gender relations in *The White Peacock*, including the necessarily unequal access to "friendship," are structured by male communion in and female remoteness from work. These positions are imaged most precisely when Lettie tries to convince George of the merits of the contemporary English painter George Clausen's depictions of agricultural labor:

> "he sees the mystery and magnificence that envelops us even when we work menially. I *do* know and I *can* speak. If I hoed in the fields beside you—" This was a very new idea for him, almost a shock to his imagination, and she talked unheeded. The picture under discussion was a water-colour—"Hoeing" by Clausen.
>
> "You'd be just that colour in the sunset," she said, thus bringing him back to the subject, "and if you looked at the ground you'd find there was a sense of warm gold fire in it, and once you'd perceived the colour, it would strengthen till you'd see nothing else. . . ." (28)

George is utterly unable to conceive of the image of Lettie at work: his initial "shock" seems to deafen him, and Lettie must overwhelm his senses with the scene's other elements to get him to acknowledge it at all. Lawrence never does permit Lettie to complete the image of herself with a hoe. Neither has he chosen to lend her a like image from Clausen, as he could: while Clausen's paintings do often represent men and women cooperating in such tasks, "Hoe-ing" is a painting of two men.[39] Even when she seems to be directing the scene's observations, Lettie is doubly subjected to watching the man involved in work she may not share and having to "know" and "speak" only his physical magnificence, not even her own experi-ence as observer.[40]

In *Sons and Lovers*, women don't watch men's work as intently, but the sexes' relative positions remain the same. It is "a great bitter-ness to Miriam to see herself deserted by Paul for Edgar," George's equivalent, as the men hoe turnips and cut wood (195). Later, as Edgar and Paul unload coal, the latter is "rather self-conscious, be-cause he knew Clara could see if she looked out the window. She didn't look" (284). Paul of course conquers Clara's aloofness, and unlike the rural Lettie and Miriam, she is associated with the factory labor Lawrence depicts as demeaning rather than the farm labor he suffuses in golden light; under those diminished conditions, it is Paul who will be the watcher, she the observed worker.

Work is the measure of all forms of "friendship" in Lawrence's early writings, but work's more important function is to create occasions when one sex can watch the other. While both labor and scrutiny can be intense, neither is ever reciprocal enough to issue in a satisfactory form of "friendship" when both sexes are involved. In a certain sense, Lawrence must explicitly deny the possibility of heterosexual friendship in order to maintain an important ele-ment of his male homosocial relations.[41] He is not interested in an all-male world but rather a carefully divided one, two spheres that each obtain proper meaning from the point of view of the other: women's envious emotions validate but don't intrude upon male absorption in work, and men may scrutinize women's incomplete involvement in work in order to complete the scene. Friendship is here not a shared "way of looking on" but rather a way of being looked upon; and only men benefit from the activity.

One would hardly guess from these scenes that heterosexual co-operation, reciprocity, or friendship could ever have been a part of Lawrence's own laborious watching—that is, of his writing or painting. Yet Lawrence wrote in 1914, "I think the only re-sourcing of art, re-vivifying it, is to make it more the joint work of man and woman"; and strong arguments have been made for his having "genuinely collaborated" with women.[42] I will conclude my consideration of pre-War models of heterosexual "friendship" with a brief discussion the young Lawrence's uses of that word,[43] because the Lawrence of *Sons and Lovers* provides the clearest illustration of how unstable and vulnerable to appropriation "friendship" was just before it came to be wholly embraced, on behalf of militarism and nationalism, during World War I. I have suggested that Conrad's and James's fictions had managed, most tentatively, to figure "friendship" through moments of shared vision, in ways that avoided certain idiomatic compromises; *Sons and Lovers*, in contrast, hands "friendship" over to Victorian conventions that might well have seemed anachronistic by 1913. For instance, the narrator uses the term to denote a delusion that Paul must physically outgrow as he reaches sexual maturity:

He would not have it that they were lovers. The intimacy between them had been kept so abstract, such a matter of the soul, all thought and weary struggle into consciousness, that he saw it only as a platonic friendship. He stoutly denied there was anything else between them. Miriam was silent, or else she very quietly agreed. He was a fool who did not know what was happening to himself; by tacit agreement they ignored the remarks and insinuations of their acquaintances.

"We aren't lovers, we are friends," he said to her. "*We* know it. Let them talk. What does it matter what they say?" (213)

Even in ignorance, Lawrence's male figure consigns his female counterpart to silence or agreement: here "friendship" is the sign of that sexual ignorance, and in its throes Paul can make recognizably mid-Victorian use of it to bespeak the absence of sex. At a later stage, *Sons and Lovers* reflects the more typically late-Victorian collapse of that opposition when the narrator calls Miriam both Paul's "friend" and his "lover" in rapid succession (337). Yet earlier on that same page, the narrator goes on at length affirming Paul's "belie[f] in simple friendship" with Clara: "It was only a friendship between man and woman, such as any civilized persons might have." Later in the novel Paul publicly uses "friend" when telling other men about his adulterous relationship with Clara, gaining no legitimacy from it and apparently expecting none (417); the narrator refers to each of Paul's knowing male "associates" in the scene as his "friend," as if to mark the contrast between false and true uses of the term. *Sons and Lovers*'s references to heterosexual "friendship" thus demonstrate both the mid-Victorian meaning (sexlessness) and the late-Victorian one (inclusive of sex) and compromise both. "Only a friendship" could not seem a more meaninglessly apologetic phrase.

There is of course nothing new in the fact of an author's deriding friendship as unnatural: Dinah Mulock Craik might typically have provided Lawrence with the vocabulary for so doing half a century before.[44] What makes Lawrence's wordings distinct from their mid-Victorian equivalents is the way the displacement of friendship implicates everything men and women do together. Not only does friendship seem false and ineffective in suppressing sex, but it seems equally false and ineffective in authorizing key activities that run idiomatically parallel to "mere friendship." The fact that Paul can "only give friendship" accords with the fact that Miriam "would never let herself want him. She would *merely* see"; Paul illustrates that they are "only friends" by saying that "it's *only* words that go between us" (271, 398, emphasis added). The functions to which Lettie had asserted her rights ("I *do* know and I *can* see"), rights over which Lawrence's letters to Burrows and Jennings had seized control, are here entirely disparaged. In the context of heterosexual relations, vision and language are as inconsequential as friendship, and insufficient to withstand the same prior forces.

Those priorities held true in the collaboration that produced Lawrence's novel. That Miriam's real-life model, Jessie Chambers, contributed much to *Sons and Lovers*, has already been thoroughly documented[45] and need not be detailed again here; I wish only to add that the novel's rejection of Chambers's "friendship" (as Miriam's) corresponds idiomatically to the rejection of her contributing vision and "talk," elements Lawrence had readily appropriated. In her memoir Chambers recalled as "the death-blow to our friendship" Lawrence's decision "to give a recognizable picture of our friendship [in *Sons and Lovers*] which yet completely left out the years of devotion to the development of his genius," the years of their "devotion to a common end." In neither her account nor Lawrence's novel does Chambers appear to have had much invested in "friendship" except insofar as Lawrence forced it upon her. She says she "had no faith in or even desire for a friendship in which love was ruled out in advance," and she associates the word with Lawrence's having "continually [tried] to find some basis for a relationship between us other than the natural one of love and marriage."[46] Lawrence's betrayal, from Jessie Chambers's point of view, was in rejecting the cooperation that he negatively associated with "friendship" and that she saw as appropriate to courtship. Ultimately, Lawrence would say, "Friendship between a man and a woman, as a thing of first importance to either, is impossible, and I know it,"[47] and he would grant as little credit to any activity he associated with "friendship." And Jessie Chambers, who seems to have maintained a Victorian understanding of "friendship" to the end, would find no reason for asserting her independent part in a relationship so termed.

The fact that Lawrence's novel still flourishes while Jessie Chambers's fiction of their relationship was destroyed unpublished is appropriate to the notion of cooperation they shared. If they were to work together it was to be toward "the development of *his* genius." From Mill to James, English male representations of "friendship," whether hopeful or skeptical, had often seemed built around women's contributions to the products of male genius. Conrad had been unusual in placing a male "friend" in a subordinate, observant role in relation to an active female protagonist. Lawrence, in life and work, literalizes women's secondary role by making them spectators to his act of creation. Victorians like Mill and Lytton had found great "value" in the assistance a "really superior woman" could give her intellectual spouse. Lawrence demanded such support from a whole range of women whose assistance he recruited in the years before he met Frieda Weekley, his wife-to-be. What Lawrence seems always to have assumed when working with Jennings, Burrows, Chambers, or Helen Corke was the principle he enunciated to Corke: "I always feel, when you give me an idea, how much better I could work it out myself!"[48] Lawrence accordingly appropriated and reshaped their materials to suit his designs, while the women's manuscripts were suppressed, deferred, or destroyed.

The argument that has been made for Lawrence's collaboration with women must account for a great deal of bullying. Yet rejection of that argument must account for Lawrence's having self-consciously sought practical aid exclusively from women beginning in the earliest stages of his career. While *The White Peacock* was still in manuscript, he mentioned to Blanche Jennings that his novel's "circle of feminine acquaintance is soon to be quite large; she has not a single male friend, poor child." Several weeks later he told Jennings emphatically that he would not show the work to his male friends: "I talk to them about intellectual things, sex matters, and frivolities, never about anything I care deeply for." But in fact, the novel, his "little girl," seems, when he describes it to Jennings, to be made up entirely of such trivia:

In the first place it is a novel of sentiment—may the devil fly away with it— what the critics would call, I believe, an 'erotic novel'—the devil damn the whole race black—, all about love—and rhapsodies on spring scattered here and there—heroines galore—no plot—nine-tenths adjectives—every colour in the spectrum descanted upon—a poem or two—scraps of Latin and French—altogether a sloppy, spicy mess. Now madam—I offer you the dish. You will do me honour if you will taste.

But when he goes on to ask her help with the manuscript, his language anticipates that of the letter describing his working man's body.

If you would be so good, you would make a really good judge of it on the emotional side, I believe. I would not ask you to criticise it so much as a work of art—by that, I mean applying to it the tests of artistic principles, and such-like jargon—don't smile too soon, my head is not very swelled, I assure you;—but I would like you to tell me frankly whether it is bright, entertaining, convincing—or the reverse. Don't base your conception of its lucidity on the style of this letter—I hold that parentheses are by far the most important parts of a non-business letter—and don't be afraid of my feelings. If you say something violently nasty I shall say 'Dear me, the woman's taste and judgment are not yet well cultivated'—and I shall become quite fond of you, seeing in myself the person meet to cultivate in you the requisite amount of good taste and discrimination.[49]

"I am very fond of myself. I like you because I can talk like this to you," Lawrence would write to Jennings at the end of his hay-working effusion. The precondition of his liking her after she has read the novel—that she will prove herself deficient in "taste and judgment"—are already established when he dissociates her from "artistic principles," when he tells her how to read his "letter," and when he makes clear that the letter is anyway a matter of "non-business." The aesthetic bullying and narcissism leads, whether Lawrence is pointing to his body or to his text, to an offer of affection: the end result is not to be realized in the resultant work but upon his body, Lawrence in effect using labor to reveal his own "vital part" to Jennings. One adjective that may be used for this dynamic—the one used by the editor of Lawrence's letters—is "flirtatious," but that word seems adequate only when hinged to Eliza Lynn Linton's mid-Victorian sense of dangerous deception.[50]

Lawrence's contention that work reveals man and excludes the "real woman" suggests that work may leave him vulnerable, unless he can shift its subject / object terms to make the women who watch him vulnerable instead. He undertakes this reversal constantly. Male work he presents as an end in itself, immediate and creative, vulnerable to no troubled talk and no complicated sight lines; it can make, per the title of the hay-working chapter in *The White Peacock*, "A Poem of Friendship." But where men and women meet over work, relations are always distanced, objectified, and preliminary to another act of real consequence; the eroticism is constant, voyeuristic, and predatory.[51] Lawrence suggests that heterosexual relations cannot be defined by working reciprocity because work inherently places men and women in distinctly different roles, with different stakes and priorities. Yet Lawrence favors, and depends on, women's presence in the workplace, for it is in the sexualization of Lawrence's work that he may achieve his own apex as both object and subject. Friendship is, for Lawrence, a ruse well worth maintaining, because its consummation might let a man achieve utter predominance in the working world.

Lawrence's scenes of observed work thus refigure the commonplace image of separate spheres into a subject/object split, bridgeable always, only, and absolutely through sex. Even Freud's writings, pervaded by an "atmosphere of sex" and becoming known to Lawrence's readers at around the time *Sons and Lovers* was published, wouldn't cast that sort of light on the everyday life of 1913 England.[52] There is in any case a great difference between Freud's argument for a "large . . . contribution" of "an erotic factor to friendship and comradeship, to *esprit de corps* and to the love of mankind in general" and Lawrence's certainty that heterosexual friendship was ultimately "impossible." In fact, Freud from the outset demonstrated a fairly conventional insistence on preserving, idiomatically, "bounds of friendship";[53] as I will discuss in Chapter 6, his innovative contributions to sexual discourse can be seen as having helped preserve a space for friendship rather than as having overwhelmed it. Lawrence's strategy, in contrast, was built on resignation. He assumed from the outset that gender relations could be plotted only according to Victorian custom. When suggesting to Jessie Chambers in 1906 that they each begin a first novel and then compare notes, Lawrence declared his intention to rely on "the usual plan" of the courtship novel, generally preferred by George Eliot and others: "to take two couples and develop their relationships." [54] That plan is replicated in *The White Peacock*, and it is augmented in *Sons and Lovers* only to the extent of giving his alter ego a place in both couples and confining one of those couples more closely than usual to the family home.

Lawrence's limited images for heterosexual cooperation deny the breadth of his own experience, for his early years were closely connected to reforms that made it more possible for women and men to conceive of common tasks, chances for them to think together. His first significant job, for instance, derived from the Education Act of 1902, an important step in the history of English coeducation. Women were his colleagues at the Croydon school, at suffragist rallies, and at socialist meetings where socialism was claimed to enable "men and women to meet on a footing of perfect freedom and perfect equality. They have no material obligations to one another, the non- or imperfect fulfillment of which, culpable or otherwise, can breed jealousy or debate. There is left to them their spiritual fellowship and all that it implies." [55] On the verge of war, skepticism about heterosexual friendship required stubborn resistance to contemporary conditions; but Lawrence's writings suggest that heterosexual friendship still was a dubious category and that resistance to it could still be voiced in recognizably Victorian terms. Lawrence seems a kind of ultimate spokesman for that resistance, first because he presents heterosexual friendship not only as publicly unnegotiable but as privately untenable and even immoral, and second because his rejection of friendship's idioms, in favor of the names he prefers, also entails rejection of the very activities that might otherwise give friendship validity. Lawrence leaves nothing but the couple locked in mutual regard. Unlike Hardy's, James's, or Conrad's, Lawrence's man and woman never really watch or work on anything together: "we shall always be more or less each other's work," Paul tells Miriam as they separate (362), each able to see only the other.

Part III

The War and Its Aftermath

5

Friendship in Wartime

Wartime Phrasings: Scenes of Friendship

A pair of photographs from 1917 shows a group of Oxford-shire farm workers smiling and leaning on their spades. Most are women. One is Clive Bell, author of *Art*; his urbane presence aside, these images resemble hundreds produced in England during the second half of World War I, after Conscription, when working men and women-at-work-with-men became treasured spectacles of the English life at home.[1] And thus did "friendship," a relationship whose very existence had been denied by the mid-Victorians (as discussed in Chapters 1 and 2) and that had received only tentative and implicit acknowledgment at the turn of the century (as discussed in Chapters 3 and 4) suddenly attain prominence, praise, and patriotic support. Images and accounts of contented, affectionately linked workers gave England assurance of a united wartime workplace that had eliminated the barriers of sex. Gilbert Stone completed his 1917 survey of *Women War Workers* by "ventur[ing] to express the hope that full effect will be given to the view there is full friendship between man and woman. . . ."[2] The following year Ethel Alec-Tweedie's *Women and Soldiers* confirmed that hope's fulfillment: "The war, it is true, has brought about a comradeship between the sexes that is to be encouraged, for the more men and women meet as companions and friends, the less they will meet to the harm of both." Such statements flouted allegations of unproductive sexual attractions or hostilities. Alec-Tweedie acknowledged that male factory workers at the outset "didn't exactly encourage women to take their places. . . . But all jealousy must cease in sex-comradeship," she insisted:

The sexes were meant to work together, and our factories and public offices have proved how easily they can do it. There is no sex in brains and work. Men hated women workers before the war. They were rivals. Men admired women workers after the war began. They were equals and comrades.[3]

Confirmation of this sociability came from a variety of sources. Though Wartime issues of *The Woman Worker* often deplored instances of "Man's Inhumanity to Women," the periodical could still declare of the union it represented, "Though the Federation is a woman's organization, its policy has always been to work with the men." It then went on to applaud new working relations in traditional Victorian (i.e., familial and romantic) terms: "The men of the factories are not an alien race. They are our fathers, brothers, and sweethearts, just as the boys in the trenches are: and anyone who attempts to cause division between us is no friend, but a foe to the workers...."[4] "[W]e stand, men and women, working together as a united nation!" wrote Viscountess Wolseley in *Women and the Land*. The Women's Farm and Garden Union and the Women's National Land Service Corps concurred, quoting their workers as saying, "The few men and boys that were left were excellent to work with, and welcomed us heartily," and "I found the men and the boys on the farm very easy to get on with: I was known as 'our lady.'"[5] Even if such reports had to acknowledge the occasional "cropping up once more [of] the old foolish sex jealousy,"[6] they were emphatic in counteracting the old assumption that promiscuity must inevitably result when men and women met outside safe, traditional domestic roles. Rumors against the WAACs and the Women's Land Army surfaced but were refuted. The Ministry of Labor, for instance, noted "the advantage to the soldiers of the possibility of frank and wholesome comradeship of women of their own race and the graver social dangers which such comradeship tended to avert."[7]

A significant amount of distortion was necessary to convince the English public that the new forms of interaction were uniformly beneficial. Arthur Marwick has described the Wartime press's concentrated and exaggerated attention to the fact of women's labor: he cites the complaint of *The Women's Industrial News* that "the press paragraphs referring to the replacement of men by women upon farms have been calculated to give an erroneous impression to the unknowing public."[8] In fact, images of contented women in agricultural costume, though widely circulated by the government in order to lure additional female workers, concealed the disappointments women were experiencing from farmers unwilling to take them on. But where women did work the land, members of the press eagerly distorted their prosaic activities into idyllic fiction. A Women's Farm and Garden Union leaflet remarked,

There seems to be one class of (supposedly) able-bodied men which has somehow escaped the recruiting net. This is the photographer. . . . Each and all of these has his fling just now at "Women on the Land." But they seem to have one peculiarity in common, that is, that woman as she really is when doing real work is unsuitable for artistic purposes. The "artist" decrees they must assume impossible attitudes, or appear to be performing such tasks as never fall to them. This is a distinct nuisance and a constant cause of trouble, by leading those who have not seen the workers to imagine that they and their teachers consider these positions and operations to be the proper thing. . . . We now hear of a photographer who declined to represent certain students at their regular jobs, but insisted on one taking an axe and pretending to be engaged in felling a tree, on a branch of which another student was asked to pose.

The leaflet urged resistance against such manipulation; it argued that women should not "allow themselves or their work to be thus caricatured," and suggested that they "decline to be photographed at all, unless when doing their ordinary work in the ordinary manner."[9]

But there was little chance of resisting the trend: England was committed to celebrating all forms of women's work as extraordinary. "After three years of war it became the fashion to say, 'The women are wonderful.' Soldiers, politicians, everyone repeated it again and again . . ." recalled Alec-Tweedie in 1918. Attention was insistently called to women's thriving in tasks they had previously been denied, or, as often, in tasks they had always carried out without public acknowledgment. Whether the war had actually produced the reported dramatic increase in the number of women laborers remains a source of debate, for the number of clerical jobs for middle-class women had already been increasing and women had long worked in factories and on farms.[10] It was, in any case, always apparent that wartime employment gains would be relinquished to returning soldiers;[11] and even Alec-Tweedie acknowledged that those who repeatedly proclaimed women "wonderful" only "very, very reluctantly promised some of them the vote in the near future."

The war inspired a new and ephemeral set of heterosexual tableaux, hailed throughout England for their novelty and sanctified by their patriotic utility. David Mitchell has described the characteristic reaction of wartime journalists who visited munitions plants and other places where women were hard at work: "apparently forgetting that hard labor had always been the lot of working-class women, [the reporters] were duly and continually astonished by it all." The newspaper accounts described in detail the "incongruous . . . spectacle of women operating masses of powerful machinery," declaring women to have "wooed and won this new kind of male monster." [12] Such sudden journalistic attention sprang in part from factory labor's being newly undertaken by middle- and upper-class women. A part of the much-noted process whereby the war was to have brought "about free and more natural intercourse between different types of people" previously separated by sex and class,[13] the zealous enthusiasm of leisure-class laborers has led even as recent a commentator as Sandra Gilbert to think of the war years as a time of celebration for women.[14] But the most significant change for working-class women was doubled hours, signaled more often by random praise than by pay. And they heard their new colleagues being called "wonderful" for carrying out the same tasks they had performed thanklessly for many years. The continuities were perhaps greater than the innovations: "the effect of the war," according to Deborah Thom's recent study, "was to accentuate the trends of thought current in the pre-War period." [15]

But for representations of heterosexual friendship, the shift from uncertain acceptance to triumphant celebration marked a dramatic change. "Friendship" and "comradeship" were now sanctioned via accepted activities by which they might be positively imaged: war work could embody friendship, much in the way courtship and domestic ritual had enacted romance and familial affection. Friendship between the sexes thus acquired an idiomatic stability it had previously lacked. This general change did not necessarily apply to specific instances of gender relations: "friend" did not take on the cogency of "friendship." As exemplified by the passage from *The Woman Worker* quoted above, men continued to be designated in relation to women with the terms of romantic and familial love; Alec-Tweedie referred to male workers as the "husbands, sons, brothers, or sweethearts" of the working women. Joyce Berkman has provided an apt description of the easy ideological shift whereby old terms of endearment became more generally applicable: in wartime, she has observed, "mothering required not simply mother-care but guarantees that the state be safe for children, and *strong*. . . . Women must serve the community beyond the family—protect the nation from its enemies."[16] Thus, May Bradford, who spent the war writing letters for wounded soldiers, recalled that nearly from the outset "the men took to calling me Mother." Other women were given male designations: Flora Sandes's active military service allowed her to be "Brother" to her "comrades"; at home, women who worked at remounting mules and horses came to be called "lads."[17] "Mother" and "Brother" were equally effective in showing that women were meeting men in one large united family, to which sex was irrelevant. Wartime conditions thus energized the old idiomatic formulas meant to preclude suspicion of sexual attraction or activity. What had once been thought insidious or absurd was now unimpeachable.

After Conscription, sex-free cooperative relations on the home front might seem all the more plausible because of the kind of males likely to be left working alongside women. Almost any man still at home was assumed to be too old, young, or otherwise incapacitated for war or sex. Returning soldiers who took to the fields were implicitly sanitized by acquired infirmities: at a National Land and Home League meeting the contention that "the average woman is as good as an average farm-labourer" was interrupted with "As he is now, not before the War."[18] Then there were the conscientious objectors, exempted from combat and assigned to various forms of "productive labor." Their masculinity might be visibly impugned by the application of a white feather, and was in any case greatly doubted.[19] It was among this emasculated community that the photographers who manipulated women war workers into unlikely poses could seem to represent the "one class of (supposedly) ablebodied men which has somehow escaped the recruiting net." All the visible images of men and women were understood to represent the undistracted, maximally productive "comradeship" that could serve the war effort better than any other imaginable dynamic.

Thus text and cameras fabricated and endlessly re-produced images that had formerly been obscured. As never before, Anne Wiltsher has noted, women "were *seen* to be doing skilled and/or heavy work. . . ."[20] Indeed, being watched became a common element of the women workers' experience, whether photographers were present or not. Ina Scott, having volunteered to "set" potatoes, recalled, "We frequently had a group of spectators watching us work—singularly enough, nearly always composed of men, generally old men, but sometimes a farm-hand or two. . . ." Scott's experience was matched by women in a variety of occupations, most of whom knew watching to be coupled with subordination. The postal worker Mary Hughes, for instance, remembered "old gentlemen of no occupation [standing] at their windows on the look-out for some peccadillo committed by the new hands. . . ."[21] In Chapter 4 I described the young D. H. Lawrence's intense observation of female labor, his effort to expose the woman's withholding her "vital part" from her work. Now, a temporary agricultural worker reported, "The whole time one could only feel we were on trial, and even though they were so short-handed, it required a great deal of tactful persuasion to convince the employer that he could go off to another part of his farm, and not find, on his return, that the work would be standing at the same point as he left it."[22] In wartime factories, male "line watchers" were appointed to inspect women's industrial work.[23]

There is also evidence that, again as Lawrence would have it, the women who were the objects of such regard were considered to lack the observational skills certain specialized jobs demanded. One of Lloyd George's Munitions Girls recalled that women who were skilled at machine work were nevertheless thought unqualified for service as "viewers," that is, for checking that the shells had met specifications: "They lack the fine sense of accuracy which the work requires," she admitted, "no doubt due to the difference in the upbringing and early education of a boy and a girl."[24] The war's new images of heterosexual cooperation and sexless "comradeship" were by no means proof against conventional assertions of sexual difference. Newly legitimized "friendship" was, on the one hand, a merely temporary assertion of equality and, on the other, a way of obscuring the same kind of unequal dynamics that had haunted the workplace in peacetime.

Bloomsbury's Alternatives

Clive Bell's employers too thought themselves affirming a version of friendship, but what went on in their fields was in explicit opposition to the war. That men like Bell could now farm instead of fight was partly due to the efforts of Liberal M.P. Philip Morrell and his wife Ottoline, who, before the war, had introduced various intellectuals to Prime Minister Herbert Asquith: cases such as Bell's and the economist Gerald Shove's were on Asquith's mind when he argued for a definition of conscientious objection flexible enough to cover a variety of intellectual demurrals.[25] With the war's arrival, the Morrells turned their country home, Garsington, into "a center . . . for those who were still under the control of reason, who saw the War as it really was, not through a false emotional madness, and the intoxication of war fever."[26] Here various men could complete their alternative war service by working on the Morrells' farm, immersed, as they were supposed to be, in a sexually mixed working society. It seems ironic, given D. H. Lawrence's prewar skepticism about such cooperation, that he was the Morrells' first invitee, in February 1915; Lawrence even envisioned a "new community" taking shape at Garsington, but a series of squabbles shortly resulted in his looking elsewhere.[27] Nevertheless, by the spring of 1916 a group of painters, writers, and students, united by opposition to the war, if not by the "control of reason," had found refuge at Garsington.

There they were urged by Ottoline Morrell to pursue a kind of cooperative intensity as fervent as that promoted by the war propagandists. But one central attribute of the Morrells' version of cooperation was a kind of sexual license exactly opposite to what mainstream commentators were calling appropriate to wartime gender relations. Dora Carrington thought Lady Ottoline's concerted "attack on the virgins"—as for example her intense efforts to get Carrington to sleep with fellow painter Mark Gertler—to be "like the worst Verdun onslaught."[28] Such campaigns, central to the Garsington way of life, could have chaotic results. Gertler, who was in love with Carrington, suggested that Ottoline Morrell invite her and Lytton Strachey to Garsington to discuss his (Gertler's) paintings—only to have Carrington fall tragically in love with the amiable and unresponsive Strachey.

The war propaganda might, of course, have led one to expect other kinds of bonds to develop. Strachey had by this time drafted the "Florence Nightingale" section of his *Eminent Victorians*, and he had written therein of the wartime "friendship of a man and woman," Sidney Herbert and Nightingale, whom Strachey saw as

intimately bound together by their devotion to a public cause; mutual affection, of course, played a part in it, but it was an incidental part; the whole of the relationship was a community of work. Perhaps out of England such an intimacy could hardly have existed—an intimacy so utterly untinctured not only by passion itself but by the suspicion of it.[29]

Perhaps out of Wartime England Strachey would have found no vocabulary from which to draw this ironic characterization, its terms so assuredly ingenuous as to be entirely atypical of those the Victorians would have written of themselves. But Strachey could mouth a widely accepted chaste ideal of English "community of work," so much desired for the Front and the munitions factories, with the confidence of a man whose personal experience of community depended to a large degree on an insistence on sexual explicitness. Garsington perpetuated the free discussion of sexuality that Virginia Woolf considered Strachey responsible for having initiated in Bloomsbury. (Strachey had begun thinking about the insidious Florence Nightingale at the time a convalescent Virginia Woolf was volunteering to type his pornographic *Ermyntrude and Esmeralda* "and anything else chaste or otherwise.")[30] "Suspicion of passion" was pervasive and eagerly acknowledged in cooperative endeavor among the "colony of artists hived in the [Morrells'] great barn,"[31] as well as among Garsington's officially recognized wartime guests, the Conscientious Objectors—like Clive Bell—whom the Morrells allowed to perform required alternative service on their farm.

Their true focus, of course, was supposed to be war work. But the Morrells struggled to create a form of labor consistent with both the government's requirements and the C.O.s' limited skills; inevitably, they assigned men to what had become typical "women's work" as other wartime employers were assigning women to "men's." "It was no easy matter to find work on the farm that was simple and light for these inexperienced men to do," Lady Ottoline would recall. "Generally they worked with the village women, at hoeing or light work." This was the second farm Gerald Shove served at, and he found his work at Garsington "from the physical standpoint far more successful." His wife, Fredegond, Virginia Woolf's cousin, recalled "very lovely scenery with true country people living around us, and [residing] in comfortable lodgings kept by an Oxford undergraduate landlady" whom Gerald won over in spite of her "one day throwing his shoes across the floor with a mutter about conscientious objectors." He was evidently less successful winning over his supervening landlady, for Ottoline Morrell recalled his doing "the minimum of work," and even that "slothfully and doggedly and unwillingly." Fredegond Shove remembered that "Gerald never complained in any of his time on the land," but Lady Ottoline clearly came to resent him, not least for his unsuccessful attempt to unionize her regular farm laborers.[32]

His "Rabelaisian flirtations with the old village women who worked on the land" apparently met no objection. These are the chief sorts of activity with which Clive Bell's farm service is associated in memoirs of the time. Garsington resident Dorothy Brett remembered Bell as one "whom the farmers loved though he never did a lick of work, giving birthday cakes to the farmers' wives." Fellow C.O. David Garnett deemed Bell "the most popular figure on Philip Morrell's farm." According to Garnett, Bell possessed the

qualities that the working classes like best in a gentleman. The men could imagine that they would have been like Clive if they had had the opportunity; the women wanted just such qualities in a husband or a lover. When he was in the hay or harvest field there were jokes and laughter and the work went quickly.[33]

The two photographs I mentioned earlier suggest this levity, and if Bell's evident awkwardness with his tool is coupled with a sense that the workers' smiles are in fact flirtatious, the pictures stand as effective parodies of the widely publicized wartime comradeship. They are companion pieces to Strachey's ironic comment on the "community of work . . . utterly untinctured not only by passion itself but by the suspicion of it." Friendships were developing in the fields of Garsington, across class and between the sexes, but not on the terms the government had designated.

Clive Bell's grin implicitly conveys a further level of defiance against the newly aligned conventions, since his wife was at just this time living with two other conscientious objectors at another farm a good distance away. "The new ideal of comradeship in marriage will certainly make smoother the task of parenthood," Alec-Tweedie had promised; but though their son Quentin has since described the Bells' marriage as having become a "union of friendship" during the prewar years, its adjustments during the war were not of the kind Alec-Tweedie had in mind.[34] Vanessa Bell and her two children had been living with Duncan Grant and David Garnett since early in the war; Grant would eventually become her lover and Garnett would earnestly try to. After Conscription she had arranged for them all to take a farm together at Wissett Grange in Suffolk so that the men might begin the required farm work; shortly after they moved in, Clive Bell had visited with his new lover, Mary Hutchinson, and brought folding chairs.[35]

In 1915 Vanessa Bell had written to her former lover, Roger Fry, "I don't know how to describe the whole arrangement between the 3 of us." By 1917 Fry would praise her for having negotiated personal relations that were more complex and defiant than anything occurring at Garsington.

My dear it would take ages to tell you all I do admire you for but you see I think you go straight for the things that are worthwhile—you have done such an extraordinarily difficult thing without any fuss, but thro' all the conventions kept friends with a pernickety creature like Clive, got quit of me and yet kept me your devoted friend, got all the things you need for your own development and yet managed to be a splendid mother. . . .[36]

And Fry wasn't the only one to think Vanessa Bell had managed something remarkable at Wissett. Having returned from a visit there "so stiff with weeding and herding geese that I can hardly walk," her sister Virginia Woolf wrote to Lytton Strachey, "Wissett seems to lull asleep all ambition—Don't you think they have discovered the secret of life? I thought it wonderfully harmonious." Strachey responded, "Is it the secret of life or of . . . something else . . . I don't know what? . . . Oblivion? Stupor? Incurable looseness?— that they've discovered at Wissett? I loved it, and never wanted to go away." To her sister Woolf wrote,

I've seldom enjoyed myself more than I did with you, and I cant make out exactly how you manage. One seems to get into such a contented state of mind. I heard from Lytton who feels the same, and says he would like to live with you forever. He's rather off Ottoline, I gather—at any rate he doesn't mean to live with her. . . .[37]

The mention of Ottoline Morrell is significant: where aspects of the Bell-Garnett-Grant arrangement were difficult to explain, its contrast with Garsington provided a central point of definition. That contrast may now serve to highlight Wissett's more substantial defiance of both wartime conventions and earlier ones. A paper by Strachey describing a day during his Wissett visit refers to "a long and rather fierce argument as to whether [Ottoline Morrell] had any artistic capacity, and whether she was 'creative'; I said that she was, and that Garsington proved it; but all the others were against me." Biographer Frances Spalding says of Vanessa Bell that "her intense interest in Garsington [at this time] suggests that she regarded it as a rival outpost." Bell told Fry of her disagreement with Strachey, saying that what Ottoline had "was different from having any creative power—but Lytton thinks Garsington a creation. ... To me it seems simply a collection of objects she likes put together with enormous energy but not made into anything."[38] Spalding emphasizes Vanessa Bell's sense of artistic superiority and financial inferiority to the resources developed by the Morrells. But there were other differences pertinent to the attempt at Wissett, and then at a second farm, Charleston, to shape wartime activities integrally "into" something. Most importantly, art and farm work blended at Wissett and Charleston to form the center of daily life, whereas they often seemed peripheral to Garsington's festivity and intrigue. Vanessa Bell's life then seemed to her sister to consist of "the dirt, the itch, the brats, the paints . . ."; Virginia Woolf also imaged Duncan Grant as repeatedly "covered with mud and manure."[39] David Garnett's autobiography recalls,

I began to work very hard at Wissett: the orchards badly needed pruning, the blackcurrant bushes were infected with "big bud." I dug all day and planned new operations late into the evening. I was young and strong and that was my first falling in love with working on the land. I made plans, scoured the countryside for bees, went to market-day auctions at Halesworth and bought chickens, ducklings, and goslings.

Duncan worked hard too, but I am glad to say that he often spent either the morning or the afternoon in painting. Our future was uncertain; it was highly probable that I should be uprooted from Wissett even before I had taken root—but ignoring such possibilities I worked with love.[40]

Woolf wrote to Katherine Cox in March 1916:

[Duncan] is out picking Big Bug [sic] off the currant bushes for 8 hours a day: sleeps all night, paints on Sundays. I dare say he will paint better, though I think he's very good; but sitting over one's work in Fitzroy Street, with a pat of butter turning yellow in a painter box seems to me infernally dreary. Nessa is going to keep house for him perhaps all the summer. So you see, Bloomsbury is vanished like the morning mist.[41]

Vanessa Bell's experience of wartime farm work consisted neither of idle Rabelaisian banter between intellectuals and villagers nor of the domesticity of Ottoline Morrell's "salon." This last word figures importantly in the comparison between the two sites; it also helps characterize the Bloomsbury that had, as Woolf said, "vanished." From Bloomsbury's point of view, Ottoline Morrell was a surviving type of the English Salon Hostess, that presiding figure of heterosexual friendship who (as described in earlier chapters) had been known since the eighteenth century to English thinkers and visitors including John Stuart Mill, George Eliot, and even Joseph Conrad and W. B. Yeats. Back in 1907 Virginia Woolf had seen her sister in the salon hostess's sanctified role: "Nessa and Clive live, as I think, much like great ladies in a French salon," she had written to Madge Vaughan: "they have all the wits and the poets; and Nessa sits among them like a Goddess." Clive Bell himself later applied the term more hesitantly, remembering Bloomsbury's "reading society" as a "*salon*—if that be the word." But by 1916, Vanessa Bell could see herself as distinctly removed from that context, writing to Strachey of Mary Hutchinson's visit, "Mary I think is made for salons. Her exquisiteness is not lost upon us but it ought really to be seen by the polite world." If the war had "disintegrated" Bloomsbury, as Clive Bell would later recall, it was the circumstances attendant to Conscription that had collapsed its salon structure in the process. Woolf illustrated Bloomsbury's having "pretty well exploded" by citing not only its dispersal to Wissett, and all that entailed, but also the fact that "the whole of our world does nothing but talk about conscription, and their chances of getting off, and they are all taken up with different societies and meetings and wire pulling. . . ."[42] In wartime England, even such activities as keeping men out of the military could only be conceived as involving the work of both sexes; the tableau of a salon of intellectual men hostessed by one or two women—as Bloomsbury had originally been constituted[43]—would have seemed an impossible anachronism after Conscription.

"It was the war, in fact, which enabled Bloomsbury to catch up with heterosexuality," Robert Skidelsky remarks in his biography of J. M. Keynes, and the change entailed more than just the new sexual pairings and "domesticity" that Skidelsky describes.[44] Vanessa Bell would indeed "keep house" for Grant and Garnett, but she would also establish a life-style in explicit avoidance of the era's dominant vision of sexless, uniform, male-controlled gender relations and in implicit avoidance of the gentlemanly games of the "polite world" that her husband was negotiating at Garsington. Woolf reported, "Nessa seems to have slipped civilization off her back, and splashes about entirely nude, without shame, and enormous spirit. Indeed, Clive now takes up the line that she has ceased to be a presentable lady—I think it all works admirably." The success was remarkable principally for the conditions under which it had been achieved. "It is amazingly remote from the war and all horrors," Vanessa Bell wrote to her husband on the day after she arrived at Wissett. "How absurd it seems that people shouldn't be allowed to live this kind of life in peace. One could be perfectly happy like this I believe."[45]

Her keeping house, moreover, meant fostering a productive, creative, integral, if inevitably temporary home. She and Grant famously collaborated on designing Charleston's interiors, while each of them, and Garnett as well, continued independent production of art in his or her chosen form. As several commentators have recognized, the chief virtue of the Bell-Grant-Garnett arrangement was, in Spalding's words, "the peaceful working existence it produced"—what Jane Marcus calls "the freedom to work."[46] These phrases aptly reflect the way the three had created working conditions that would suit the authorities while still resisting abhorrent wartime zeal.

This working compromise was even harder to maintain than that managed by the Morrells. The Wissett farm laborers underwent scrutiny like that described by the women workers: "Every Sunday," Garnett recalled, "groups of village people strolled up to Wissett Lodge and looked for a long time over the paddock gate to see what new folly we had committed." Neighborly watchfulness could take its toll. Though the "follies" consisted mainly in the employment of unorthodox but practical methods, local "hostility" eventually seems to have influenced the War Agriculture Committee's decision to order Grant and Garnett from Wissett to undertake work it thought more appropriate. The move to Charleston subjected them to harder labor and harmed Grant's health, such that his service had eventually to be reduced in the winter of 1917–18 to half days of farm work.[47]

In February 1918 Grant began *Interior*, a painting that was both result and image of the working relations he was sharing (see frontispiece). To the left is Vanessa Bell, shown painting objects that are on a table at the picture's center; to the right is David Garnett, seated at the table, writing. The two working figures are angled with their backs and shoulders sloping downwards towards the bottom center. They thus form a triangle with the unseen painter (or viewer), and were Garnett looking up, rather than down at his paper, the gazes of all three would be directed at the same central point. But they are not so directed. Though Bell and Garnett's eyes are at the same level[48]—which takes some distortion, since the top of her painting, level with her head, is appreciably higher than the table over which he is leaning—they share only a working area, not a task. The effect is of eyes that partly meet and partly turn toward the central objects, but that mainly focus on each of the works at hand. It suggests a striking combination of cooperation and independence.

At the same time, what Richard Shone has described as a "highly wrought design of great gravity"[49] makes the painting seem angular and constricted. Creation at Charleston occurred under intense scrutiny that carried with it the continual threat of the C.O.s' being imprisoned; creation at Charleston was itself a kind of enforced labor. Bell, Grant, and Garnett could achieve a working self-liberation by adjusting the terms of their service, but the fact of that service remained an imposition the war required of English women and men. Vanessa Bell would remember these years as a time when "all the world was hostile close round one. . . ."[50] England's insular claim to universal comradeship was based on shared enmity toward those outside, especially those who would not serve in the expected ways; the Garsington / Wissett / Charleston experiments were generated under siege, as delicate alternatives within a pervasive nightmare.

The Best We Know: Woolf's Pastoral
Vision in *Night and Day*

That wartime Bloomsbury was capable of productive experimenting attests to its imaginative resourcefulness under oppressive conditions. "Apart from Virginia's illness, the four years of the 1914 war were the most horrible period of my life," Leonard Woolf wrote in his autobiography.

The five years of the 1939 war were more terrible and they brought the suicide of Virginia, but at least things moved and happened and one was kept keenly alive by the danger of death continually hanging just above one's head. The horror of the years 1914 to 1918 was that nothing seemed to happen, month after month and year after year, except the pitiless, useless slaughter in France. Often if one went for a walk on the downs above Asham one could hear the incessant pounding of the guns on the Flanders front. And even when one did not hear them it was as though the war itself was perpetually pounding dully on one's brain, while in Richmond and Sussex one was enmeshed in a cloud of boredom.

The passage goes on to mention "one lightening of the darkness": Virginia Woolf's health improved in the last two years of the war, so that she "was able, with cautious restraint, to live a social life," and to work steadily on *Night and Day*.[51] She seems to have conceived of her second novel after her contented visit to Wissett in August 1916. The same letter that passed on her and Strachey's admiration to her sister concluded, "I am very much interested in your life, which I think of writing another novel about. It's fatal staying with you—you start so many ideas."[52] The novel was her principal activity for the remainder of Virginia Woolf's War.

She would eventually complain of the Armistice Day celebrations' disturbing her work on the final chapter.[53] If that suggests that in composing *Night and Day*, Woolf had sealed herself off from contemporary energies, and events, then it is possible to find confirmation of such removal in the book itself: her fellow fiction writer Katherine Mansfield condemned *Night and Day*, in a contemporary review, as annoyingly impervious to "what has been happening." Describing the book as "in the tradition of the English novel" but unresponsive to contemporary debate on the genre, Mansfield gave first voice to the still dominant opinion that the book is trivially conventional. Privately, Mansfield rejected it as an exercise in artistic and historical irresponsibility: "I don't like it, Boge," she wrote to John Middleton Murry:

My private opinion is that it is a lie in the soul. The war has never been: that is what its message is. I don't want (G. forbid!) mobilization and the violation of Belgium, but the novel can't just leave the war out. There *must* have been a change of heart. It is really fearful to see the 'settling down' of human beings. I feel in the *profoundest* sense that nothing can ever be the same—that, as artists, we are traitors if we feel otherwise: we have to take it into account and find new expressions, new moulds for our new thoughts and feelings. . . . Inwardly I despise them all for a set of *cowards*. We have to face our war. They won't. I believe, Bogey, our whole strength depends on our facing things. I mean facing them without any reservations or restraints.[54]

Jane Marcus has offered the strongest defense of *Night and Day*, principally as a Mozartian comic opera but also as a negotiation of biographical and historical realities. I will quote Marcus's description of the novel at length here, both because of its usefulness, particularly for readers unfamiliar with this lesser-known novel's characters, and because of Marcus's understandable imprecision when accounting for the complex heterosexual relations Woolf portrays:

The pastoral idyll, which her sister Vanessa seemed to be living in the country with Duncan Grant, was Woolf's inspiration for the novel. What most impressed her was that their domestic arrangements allowed them the freedom to work. It was a scene of great creative outpouring. The perceptive novelist shows in *Night and Day* a brilliantly accurate historical portrait of the differences in attitudes towards work of middle-class Edwardian men and women. William Rodney begrudges every minute of drudgery in his government office which keeps him from his poetic drama. Ralph Denham chafes at the bonds of domestic responsibility which keep him in his law office. To the women it is another matter altogether. Katharine [Hilbery] daydreams about marriage (first to William and then to Ralph), with no thought of sex but with a deep longing for the opportunity to work. . . .

And Mary [Datchet], with her discipline and decision, goes from that time-honored condition of women, volunteer work (even though the cause is women's suffrage), to become the salaried secretary of a movement for greater social change. . . . She suppresses her personal relationships as well as her writing in a conscious effort to find salvation in work. . . .

This is one of Woolf's amazing political perceptions: that the ideal of the female utopia was to be in paradise alone, to work.[55]

Marcus's account suggests how many different elements are at stake in *Night and Day*, and how difficult they may be to integrate. First of all, Marcus must merge Bell and Grant's cooperative wartime "idyll" with pre-War understandings of work. Then she must derive that sense of the idyllic by attributing to the "perceptive" Woolf a wholly naive interpretation of what she had found at Wissett.[56] Lastly, Marcus implies but does not examine the pronounced gap, at the novel's conclusion, between the resolutions reached by the woman worker (Mary) and the engaged couple (Katharine and Ralph). And it is that gap that makes apparent just how much *Night and Day* ultimately leaves unresolved: as a whole, the novel expresses "political perceptions" that extend beyond the available models for relations between the sexes. Though the original couples, Katharine/Rodney and Ralph/Mary, comically re-sort themselves by the end of the novel, Mary's solitary work never does become satisfactorily redemptive for her; but neither does the novel suggest that marriage is the all-encompassing solution, for Katharine and Ralph's visibly fails to account for the worker's world.

Marcus gives appropriate emphasis to the productive activities of the novel's female protagonists: she sees Mary as representative of the "aspiring young woman who needed work and discipline when her male counterpart was rejecting those Victorian values." But when Marcus says that "we expect [the novel's] marriages to produce not babies but books,"[57] she is implicitly attributing to *Night and Day* a further level of affinity with "Victorian values": as I noted in Chapter 1, the Victorians readily saw books and the like as by-products of happy marriage. It seems to me that what is original and impressive about *Night and Day* is not its echoing of the conventions available in either Victorian or Edwardian discourse but its depiction of cooperative relations outside courtship, home, and the workplace as customarily conceived. *Night and Day* is a novel that looks toward the future by denying the strictures of the present and past.

Woolf's novel is both more and less conventional in its presentation of heterosexual cooperation than Marcus suggests—or rather, it represents a more complicated dialectic with convention, because of its relation to Wartime discourse. *Night and Day* is a War novel in the way Lawrence claimed his *Women in Love* was: "a novel which took its final shape in the midst of the period of war, though it does not concern the war itself. I should wish the time to remain unfixed," said Lawrence, "so that the bitterness of the war may be taken for granted in the characters."[58] More than wartime "bitterness," *Night and Day* reflects Bloomsbury's contradictory senses of dissatisfaction and festivity, of confinement and escape, of public defiance, and, most of all, the need for refuge. These qualities are evident also in Lawrence's novel, but whereas Lawrence spent the war in fruitless quest for a separate peaceful place and used *Women in Love* to turn on Ottoline Morrell for failing to provide him with it, Bloomsbury managed to construct its sanctuary. *Night and Day* is an emblem of that fragile shelter. Those who "faced" the war, as Mansfield demanded, inevitably came to serve the war by getting caught up in its desperation: many English feminists and even Conscientious Objectors decidedly did that. But Vanessa Bell was so caught up perhaps less than anyone, having "slipped civilization off her back," in Virginia Woolf's words—having "done such an extraordinary thing without any fuss," as Roger Fry had said. Woolf wrote in June 1918 of the war's "horrible sense of community," expressing a view that differed greatly from the way the nationalists saw the widely proclaimed mixing of heterogeneous English men and women; only after Armistice would she declare with relief, "We are once more a nation of individuals."[59] She owed her husband's escape from service in part to the mental fragility that made it impossible for her to be absorbed in the war's conflations.[60] In any case, with what was left of Bloomsbury, she refused. *Night and Day* expresses that refusal while speculating on versions of community distinguishably less "horrible" than the war's.

The novel is "pastoral," but only in Louis Montrose's complex sense of the word, indicating a form "capable of embodying some of the contradictory values and premises of . . . social life."[61] Though *Night and Day*'s world is not the England of wartime, neither is its Arden more than deceptively idyllic. The countryside around Lincoln, the setting for the novel's pivotal middle chapters (15 to 19), lulls the central characters into believing they have resolved their London courtship problems in perfect friendship: Ralph thinks

Mary's family's country home "the best place in England," and the two achieve there "a sagacious kind of comradeship, the most complete they had attained in all their friendship . . ."; Katharine and Rodney's country walk seems equally productive, alerting her to the "lapse" she has committed in accepting his proposal (212) and leading him almost to prefer "the steady good sense, which had always marked their relationship, to a more romantic bond" (246). But before they leave the country, their crises have been thoroughly intensified: Ralph soon proposes to Mary and so causes their "old friendship" to "crumble" (250); Katharine agrees to marry Rodney, but soon it will become clear that she won't. This Arden provides neither easy retreat nor resolution.

Still, the countryside remains the place of refuge to which Ralph Denham persistently plans to go, "to throw up his profession and live in a little cottage and write books" (187). That cottage in fact becomes the specific sign of the working independence to which Ralph and Katharine together aspire; in the end she flatly reminds him, "Oh, that cottage. . . . We must take it and go there" (502). But their contemplated answer is evidently only as tentative as the others that have occurred in the rural environment:

Together they groped in this difficult region, where the unfinished, the unfulfilled, the unwritten, the unreturned, came together in their ghostly way and wore the semblance of the complete and satisfactory. . . . Books were to be written, and since books must be written in rooms, and rooms must have hangings, and outside the windows there must be land, and an horizon to that land, and trees perhaps, and a hill, they sketched a habitation for themselves . . . and still, for both of them, it swam miraculously in the golden light of a large steady lamp. (506)

To Woolf, wartime cooperation in the countryside seemed at least this new and incomprehensible, and she looked upon it with persistent interest. In June 1916 the Woolfs had "been asked to get people interested in these Women farmers," Leonard having already visited a cooperatively run farm. The following summer at Asham Virginia Woolf noted in her diary, "Home by the fields. A great deal of the corn has to be cut by hand. Men still working & women too at 7." In the subsequent days she recorded that corn's being cut and carted. A week later she noted that the corn was now being harvested by a new and different constituency, German prisoners of war: she listened to their songs, once greeted them in the road, and chronicled their process of cutting and carting clover. In the last summer of the war the conversation of two farm-laborers at their enforced work so impressed her that she decided that "the existence of life in another human being is as difficult to realize as a play of Shakespeare when the book is shut"; so she thought when she saw her C.O. farm-working brother Adrian

talking to the tall German prisoner. By rights they should have been killing each other. The reason why it is easy to kill another person must be that one's imagination is too sluggish to conceive what his life means to him— the infinite possibilities of a succession of days which are furled in him, & have already been spent. . . . The prisoner, who looks very lean & hopeless, seemed to like talking; I met him later & we smiled, but the sentry was not there.[62]

Where there seems such a small distance between comradeship and murder, and where even tentative friendship arises under such close scrutiny, there can seem little hope of productive talk. It is not surprising therefore that Woolf barred from *Night and Day* the specific wartime circumstances that surrounded her. Instead, the novel's rural population is rendered only superficially, through the image of "two or three men hoeing in a turnip-field," an image that the narrator acknowledges could easily be taken as in "keeping with the Middle Ages" (178). It is this vision, more suggestive of the illusions of eclogue than of Grant's and Garnett's sometimes difficult war work, that seems to fuel Ralph's confused speculations about his cottage. Yet Woolf also makes Ralph's attainment of his fantasy depend entirely on his converting his troubled relationships with Mary and Katharine into some satisfactory form of interdependence. The result will be an image of cooperative work, but one that depends neither on the Lawrentian model of male farm labor described in Chapter 4 nor on the "female utopia" described by Marcus. ("The pure essence of either sex is a little disheartening," Woolf had written on her return from a "prosaic, reasonable & unconcentrated" suffrage rally in March 1918.)[63] Woolf's characters instead negotiate a complex alternative heterosexual relation that logically extends the Wissett/Charleston group's subversion of the forms of wartime "comradeship."

That alternative requires a mixture of privacy and communion— a combination especially difficult to conceive of under wartime conditions but typical of Woolf's fictional resolutions throughout the remainder of her career.[64] The most obvious and pertinent mark of autonomy is Mary's: even if Mary does not achieve a "female utopia," she does indeed manage to be "alone, to work," as Marcus says, and to be acknowledged by the others as such. In *Night and Day*'s final chapter, Ralph leaves Katharine standing beneath Mary's window while he goes to tell Mary that he and Katharine are engaged. When Katharine observes Mary's light in the window above, "a sign of triumph shining there for ever" (505), it now seems to have affinities with the "great lamp" that was to illuminate Ralph and Katharine's shared vision. But Ralph ascends only to find himself unable to confront Mary, so she is spared having to align herself in relation to Ralph and Katharine's weddedness.

Mary is thus granted a privacy beyond any that, for instance, had been available to the undomesticated and forward-looking heroine of *Daniel Deronda*, to cite the example I have considered most closely in this study: Mary "has her work" (505) where Gwendolen had been left desiring it. Yet Mary is also less isolated, from compatible men as well as women. Gwendolen Harleth's tenuous link to Daniel Deronda's "social passion" had been theoretical and abstract. But by the time Katharine wonders about Mary, "Is she alone, working at this time of night?" (505), the answer has been rendered uncertain by Mary's relation to a character named Horace Basnett. He has lately hired Mary to work on his "scheme for the education of labor" and further social reform (355); moreover, he has "almost persuaded [her] that she, too, was included in the 'we'" responsible for motivating that scheme (356). Under Ralph's pressure, Mary has decreed Basnett "too uncompromising" (389), but the novel has presented him as a fit co-worker for her, possessed of "an intelligence in his face which attracted her intelligence" (357). Ralph had once seemed to offer Mary such mutuality, but this is different: no romance inheres in the new relation. Basnett is part of her "work," which, Mary is sure, "is the thing that saves one" (391). That work is, in any case, the thing that brings her an independent salary, without the "lapses" of courtship that have hitherto constrained both her and Katharine.

But in *Night and Day* too "much depend[s] on the interpretation of the word love" (313), and its counterparts, for the novel to give primacy to a notion of work wholly distinct from sexual attraction. If Woolf's narrator seems to have contempt for

Katharine's mother as "the champion of married love in its purity and supremacy" (409), little more sympathy goes to the entirely antiromantic "champions of the cause of women" (261) among Mary's acquaintances. With these absolute poles equally discredited, the book's explicit affirmations regarding gender relations must be found among the more complex discourses that Ralph and Katharine develop together on their own. "There are different ways of loving," Katharine asserts late in the novel (423), in the only "interpretation of the word love" that seems telling amid the array of words for heterosexual relations that *Night and Day* takes up and sets aside.

"I could undertake at this instant," Ralph declares to Katharine, "to lay down terms for a friendship which should be perfectly sincere and perfectly straightforward." The terms are set out with a rationality appropriate to the kind of relationship they define:

"In the first place, such a friendship must be unemotional," he laid it down emphatically. "At least, on both sides it must be understood that if either chooses to fall in love, he or she does so entirely at his own risk. Neither is under any obligation to the other. They must be at liberty to break or to alter at any moment. They must be able to say whatever they wish to say. All this must be understood." (337)

Katharine's ready acceptance of these terms is predicated on the pair's having generated a "common language," capable even of accounting for their "lapses" of "romance" (473). Yet their agreement remains, as Katharine tells her father, "nothing that I can explain to a third person" (476). Her hopeful mother is willing to believe that "names aren't everything; it's what we feel that's everything" (480), but that placidity is shaken by Katharine's asking, "Why, after all, isn't it perfectly possible to live together without being married?" (482). Mr. Hilbery meanwhile believes "the whole position between the young people" to be "gravely illicit" (475); "I will have no more of these equivocations," he declares (476).

At such moments, the world of *Night and Day* seems hardly different from that of, say, the mid-1890's world of *The Woman Who Did*. There, as presented in Chapter 4, comparably inarticulate attempts to define heterosexual "friendship" capable of accommodating sexuality met with comparable parental opposition. In fact, Katharine's parents badger Ralph into accepting not only marriage but its inequities: "He wished to dominate her, to possess her," Woolf's narrator says, as Ralph imagines marrying Katharine in order not to lose her (489). But Katharine and Ralph have treated the rituals of courtship and marriage as at most incidental to their affection; they seem to anticipate a life of working together well before they concede to be engaged. When Ralph reaches Katharine with the new resolution her parents have talked him into, the question of marriage immediately becomes irrelevant. The book will climax not with marriage but with whatever new definition of their relationship the pair can arrive at together.

That project requires an idiom distinct from the terms of courtship and marriage. In their stead, Woolf intensifies in the final pages a vocabulary of cooperative visual perception that has been building throughout the book. The success of relationships has seemed, all along, measurable by the clarity with which pairs see together: the insufficiency of Ralph and Mary's bond even at its best has been evident, for instance, in the way they see "nothing of the hedgerows, the swelling plowland, or the mild blue sky" that surround them in the fields (219). When Ralph turns from her, Mary's "clear vision of the way to face life" is threatened (277). In contrast, the center of Ralph and Katharine's relationship from the beginning is vision mutually empowered. At an early stage he tells her, "I've come to believe that we're in some sort of agreement; that we're after something together; that we see something" (299). Later, it is the "sight of her gazing from his window" that gives him "a peculiar satisfaction" (380) while she wonders, "Was he not looking at something she had never shown to anybody?" (383).

If Mrs. Hilbery is indeed partly right in saying that in this novel's world "names aren't everything," that is because language seems deficient to account for people's shared seeing: "what more did he see?" Katharine wonders, "looking at him in silence, with a look that seemed to ask what she could not put into words . . ." (383). Jean Guiguet has declared that *Night and Day* is "about silence,"[65] and the novel in fact includes dozens of such references to gaps in speech. But the couple is not finally entirely mute. The narrator says that their "sounds were inarticulate; no one could have understood the meaning save themselves" (492). They test public, then private, language diligently, only to find words lacking—most notably when Ralph attempts to write Katharine a letter. The process of writing leads Ralph more and more to accept the visual basis of their relationship, and to seek a means of communication that will account for that basis adequately.

It was a difficult matter to put into words. . . . In an infinite number of half-obliterated scratches he tried to convey to her the possibility that although human beings are woefully ill-adapted for communication, still, such communion is the best we know; moreover, they make it possible for each to have access to another world independent of personal affairs, a world of law, of philosophy, or more strangely a world such as he had had a glimpse of the other evening when together they seemed to be sharing something, creating something, an ideal—a vision flung out in advance of our actual circumstances. . . . Making every allowance for other desires, on the whole this conclusion appeared to him to justify their relationship. But the conclusion was mystical; it plunged him into thought. The difficulty with which even this amount was written, the inadequacy of the words, and the need of writing under them and over them others which, after all, did no better, led him to leave off before he was at all satisfied with his production, and unable to resist the conviction that such rambling would never be fit for Katharine's eye. He felt himself more cut off from her than ever. In idleness, and because he could do nothing further with words, he began to draw little figures in the blank spaces, heads meant to resemble her head, blots fringed with flames meant to represent—perhaps the entire universe. (487)

While Ralph is thus coming near to renouncing the verbal for the visual, Katharine is working at her favored occupation, mathematics. When they next meet, they spontaneously find themselves reading "each other's compositions in silence" (492). Now, when altogether without words they achieve their most significant instant of communication, she is as surprised by Ralph's reaction—"she looked to see whether Ralph smiled, but found his gaze fixed on her with such gravity that she turned to the belief that she had committed no sacrilege but enriched herself, perhaps immeasurably, perhaps eternally"—as he is by hers:

Did she smile? Did she put the paper down wearily, condemning it not only for its inadequacy but for its falsity? Was she going to protest once more that he only loved the vision of her? But it did not occur to her that this diagram had anything to do with her. She said simply, and in the same tone of reflection:

"Yes, the world looks something like that to me too." (492–93)

Words serve here only to confirm an ongoing action, as the scene dramatizes and extends the tribute to shared vision enacted in Duncan Grant's *Interior*: agreement of vision is confirmed in the convergence of independent creations, with a corresponding validation of both autonomy and mutuality. *Interior* is implicitly (compositionally, that is) about the relation of its figures; the climactic scene of *Night and Day* is no more explicit in naming Ralph and Katharine's relationship, for, like *Interior*, it centers instead on what they see.

That Woolf declared *Night and Day* to be related to the painterly life lived by her sister and Grant at Wissett provides one explanation for the novel's insistence on vision, and on privacy. But the significance of those related themes seems to me to extend well beyond the simply biographical. The degree of autonomy *Night and Day* preserves for its characters seems proof against the war's "horrible sense of community," for the shared vision remains individualist in a way speech can never quite be, and in a way the rituals of marriage or of wartime "work" could never be either. Just as importantly, the abstract object of each of the characters' visions is far removed from England's wartime insistence on utility—on comradeship's producing, under constraint, visible results. Woolf concentrates not on created matter but on the shared *action* of sight. The privacy and gravity of *Night and Day*'s vision is very much like that maintained by Grant's painting but very different from the spectacle of Clive Bell and his cohorts mugging for the eager camera. The war had put the bodies of men and women to work in the service of "terms of friendship" that seemed "perfectly straightforward" but far from "perfectly sincere," a vision of "comradeship" Woolf and her friends despised. *Night and Day*, like the living arrangements that inspired it, resists all trace of the war's poses. It undertakes, however incompletely, "to lay down terms for a friendship" that are both "perfectly sincere and perfectly straightforward" because, finally, uncontaminated by the war's idioms. Katherine Mansfield was right in saying that the novel didn't "face" the war—for it looked, defiantly, away.[66]

Night and Day's self-consciousness and experimentation at the level of idiom is not obviously replicated at the level of novelistic structure. The book does end in marriage, and in so doing takes on attributes of a conventional romantic comedy, though the significance of that fact can be measured quite variously. One reader of the novel, Lucio Ruotolo, has suggested that *Night and Day*'s "resolutions" are so "pro forma" as to be untrustworthy.[67] Marcus, in contrast, thinks that the novel's pre-vision of productive, working marriage marks the ending as demonstrably anti-conventional. Like earlier novels concerned with setting "terms" for heterosexual "friendship," *Night and Day* inevitably sends conflicting signals to students of narrative closure; again like in those other novels, there can be little doubt that its relation to idiom is at least tense and deliberative, and probably defiant.[68] There is no good word, the novel goes to great lengths to make clear, that can adequately name what Ralph and Katharine manage at their moment of shared vision: in its final utter avoidance of English idiom, *Night and Day* may seem comparable to Henry James's *The Awkward Age*, which ends in silence and retreat, suggesting that some new post-Victorian male/female friendship has indeed developed but without any adequate name to express it. But Katharine's assenting "the world looks something like that to me too" suggests a moment of genuine communication of a kind James's world would never have allowed and an assurance that Conrad's "way of looking on" had not made available. At that stage, *Night and Day*'s constant concern with defining heterosexual relations not only places it in the tradition of idiomatic crisis I have described but makes it that tradition's first success. This novel has presented, and never compromised, successful heterosexual cooperation.

Two months after both the war and *Night and Day* were finished, Woolf recorded in her diary her intention "to spend the evenings of this week . . . in making out an account of my friendships & their present condition, with some account of my friends' characters." Evidently having already told others of her "projected work on friendship," she began it the following day and kept at it for six weeks only to deem it "laborious" and "rather misleading" and to drop it for good.[69] That Woolf should have begun her account so soon after the novel and the Armistice suggests a need to evaluate friendship under new conditions, with the war's pressure on friendship newly released. Woolf had almost certainly experienced the "change of heart" Mansfield had accused her of avoiding, but she was not willing to offer a new "disquisition" on "friendship" as such.

One explanation is that in the wake of the war's false insistence on the value of sexless relationships, Woolf would have seen herself obligated to define and illustrate "friendship" with a sexual explicitness she was not prepared to undertake. Her novels would never shy from acknowledging "lapses" of sexual attraction between men and women, but neither would their portrayals of sexuality in friendship become more detailed than that of, say, *The Woman Who Did*. Woolf acknowledged that avoidance as a kind of deficiency in *Night and Day*, in her response to a now-lost letter from Strachey: "I take your point about the tupping, and had meant to introduce a little in that line, but somehow it seemed out of the picture—still I regret it. Never mind; I've an idea for a story where all the characters do nothing else—but they're all quadrupeds."[70]

But Woolf's more likely and more significant realization about the representation of friendship—and in any case the one I will expand on in the final chapter of this study—is that "friendship," as a subject unto itself, was now bankrupt. On the one hand, it had been compromised by wartime falsifications and constraints; on the other hand, even more importantly, it had become almost irrelevant to the credible representation of productive relations between women and men. Bloomsbury was certainly past the point of feeling required to *name* its modes of unconventional heterosexual relations in order to practice them in creative working environments; and Woolf herself may be thought to have passed that point when she managed to represent Ralph Denham, Katharine Hilbery, and Mary Datchet in moments of promising, productive union without having found a word for what she was representing. The absence of a viable name for the relationships seems less important, at such moments, than Woolf's successful representation of enacted cooperation: a great deal more depends on what the characters together see than on what one might call the relationship they achieve when seeing together. It is in these and subsequent portrayals of moments of shared vision that Woolf's greatest achievements in representing friendship may be found.

Seeing Together: Woolf, Fry, and Friendship After the War

A Power of Attention: Sight and Sexuality in *Mrs. Dalloway*

By the end of the war, Woolf was nearly through with "friendship," named as such. When her subsequent fiction, drawing on Bloomsbury's anti-conventional negotiations with bourgeois discourse, seeks to validate cooperative heterosexual relations, it finds little more use for words like "friendship" and "comradeship" than had earlier novelistic experimenters like Eliot. England had been willing to valorize such terms only as long as they seemed suitable to the war effort, so Woolf's postwar fiction engages a period when they have lost all possible cogency. *Mrs. Dalloway* and *To the Lighthouse* authenticate a kind of bond "friendship" had sometimes been invoked to signify—extramarital, extrafamilial, based on a dynamic other than courtship—but they avoid the discursive and literary conventions that had compromised "friendship" before the war as well as the false qualifiers that had underwritten the word's recent brief legitimacy. The vocabulary Woolf summoned in these 1920's fictions served her too at the end of her career, as she composed the biography of her friend Roger Fry; by that point she had found a way of describing heterosexual relations not only between individuals but also in collectives. Woolf produces in these texts an enabling and creative alternative to the words that had so long gone awry.

I have already introduced the idiomatic source Woolf drew on, in reference to the way "friendship" was defined by a male novelist for whom Woolf had particular sympathy[1]—that is, Conrad's rendering of "friendship" as "a way of looking on." A link between gender relations and occasions of shared vision inheres in the twentieth-century artistic tradition of which Conrad's and Woolf's fiction and Fry's art criticism were a part, for Modernism's shift "from linearity to multi-perspectivity" served to undermine dominant bourgeois ways of perceiving, a central attribute of which had been the establishment of an exclusively patriarchal point of view.[2]

Chapter 5 suggested why the politics of seeing would have been a particular priority for interwar thinkers concerned with the possibility of productive heterosexual relations: the right to "see" work, and to see as work, had been granted at most unevenly during the short-lived labor experiments of World War I. But Woolf's writings do considerably more than merely reposition the sex-based lines of sight mapped by Lawrence and the war propagandists, so I here must say a little about the way I mean to position words like "seeing," "vision," and "looking," as I trace Woolf's deployment of them to name the central activity in her representation of normative relations between men and women.

In the *Oxford English Dictionary* "vision" is defined consecutively as "the action or fact of seeing or contemplating something *not actually present to the eye*" and then "the action of seeing *with bodily eye*" (my emphasis). The act of "seeing" may thus, in short succession, either be removed from the body and its senses or assigned to them. Other idioms suggest comparable ambiguities—"sight," for instance, generally being the property of the eyes, but "foresight" and "insight" being independent of them. Woolf's interest in moments of "vision" seems to pertain interchangeably to bodily perception and imaginative projection; because I am concerned with representations of human beings in their acts of cooperation, I am more likely to be interested in perceptible actions (of which the act of seeing is one), and I thus run the risk here of sometimes reading references to "sight" literally when they might more obviously be read as referring to figurative seeing, the production of imagined mental images.

I would not be the first to employ such literalism, or to recognize its arbitrariness.[3] But much of my discussion of "vision" as a category centers on actual acts of viewing—such as specific occasions when women are watched while at work, as described in Chapter 5, or when women watch acutely, or when men and women see together. Versions of cooperative sight, I will argue, stand as a significant way of saying what heterosexual friendship is, or might consist in; the vision-related idioms will, I hope, emerge as a valuable alternative, drawn from the working world of actions and recognitions, to the evasive, speculative, and untenable uses of "friendship" and its counterparts.

Woolf conceived of *Mrs. Dalloway* as "a study of . . . the world seen by the sane and the insane side by side." She would defend the novel's unity by declaring that she "certainly did mean that" Clarissa Dalloway and the mad Septimus Smith, who never meet, "should be entirely dependent upon each other." *Mrs. Dalloway* has structural affinities with an unwritten play Woolf conceived at the age of twenty. It was to be a collaborative project with a friend, Jack Hillis: "I'm going to have a man and a woman," she said,

—show them growing up—never meeting—not knowing each other—but all the time you'll feel them come nearer and nearer. This will be the real exciting part (as you see)—but when they almost meet—only a door between—you see how they just miss—and go off at a tangent, and never come anywhere near again.[4]

While it can't quite be said that Clarissa Dalloway and Septimus Smith "almost meet," the moment when Clarissa senses some sympathy between herself and Septimus—about whose suicide she overhears—and then chooses another path, is arguably the book's most climactic, innovative, and "exciting part."

It might be argued that Clarissa and Septimus hardly relate enough for the novel's presentation of them to be discussed under the heading of "gender relations."[5] But comparing *Mrs. Dalloway* with *Night and Day* shows that in Woolf's fiction, unlike Lawrence's, the significance of heterosexual relationships is not confined to immediate, mirroring, self-absorbed communication between isolated pairs, but rather is dispersed in perceptions shared among some wider community. Near the end of *Night and Day*, Katharine Hilbery continues to think with Ralph Denham as she watches Mary Datchet's window; at a comparable late point in *Mrs. Dalloway*, Clarissa has her intuition of Septimus's thoughts in mind as she observes an anonymous "old lady" from her window (283). Katharine's subsequent "Yes, the world looks something like that to me too" anticipates not only Clarissa's tentative sense of sharing Septimus's dying vision and her visual exchange with her older counterpart but also Peter Walsh's closing recognition of what Clarissa has seen. Each of these moments represents a kind of mediated intuitive contact, usually a pair's observing not each other but a third person whose vision extends what the pair sees to more significant generalizations and thus renders the moment thematically profound: Katharine and Ralph come to meditate not just on their future but on *the* future, while the old woman helps Clarissa to the realizations about Septimus that will lead her to return to her party instead of undertaking Septimus's escape.

As contemporary reviews noted, *Mrs. Dalloway* is built around the visual.[6] Its pivotal scenes are moments of shared vision, from the early collective observation of "the face in the motor car" (23–24) and the skywriter (29–31) to a succession of pairs watching others at Clarissa's party at the end. Such viewing is only inconsistently affirmed. When Septimus Smith's wife worries that "people must notice; people must see" (22), she fears that urban citizens will inevitably and unfortunately notice idiosyncrasies that, in fact, they are all too likely to miss. But when Clarissa thinks of her guests, "They looked; that was all. That was enough" (269), she articulates the triumph of someone who has encouraged a certain level of visual engagement among an assembled group. Ultimately, the novel does seem to suggest that shared "looking" is "enough," insofar as one such moment, uniting Septimus and Clarissa, marks its climax, and another, linking Clarissa and Peter, ends it.

If Woolf's earlier speculation about "a man and a woman . . . never meeting" but still serving as the center of a drama had represented a self-conscious swerving from courtship conventions, the visual priorities of *Mrs. Dalloway* allow the novel to enact that avoidance from start to finish. *Night and Day* had been built so much around "interpretation of the word love" that marriage had been its necessary (if not most important) condition of closure; *Mrs. Dalloway* closes in an avoidance of consummation that yet seems, because of the presence of shared vision, a full triumph. It is the kind of union Peter and Clarissa have been tending toward from the book's opening pages, when Clarissa first muses on their relationship's durability:

For they might be parted for hundreds of years, she and Peter; she never wrote a letter and his were dry sticks; but suddenly it would come over

her, If he were with me now what would he say?—some days, some sights
bringing him back to her calmly, without the old bitterness; which perhaps
was the reward of having cared for people; they came back in the middle of
St. James's Park on a fine morning—indeed they did. But Peter—however
beautiful the day might be, and the trees and the grass, and the little girl in
pink—Peter never saw a thing of all that. He would put on his spectacles,
if she told him to; he would look. (9)

The phrase "some days, some sights" (perhaps a playful echo of
"night and day,") equates their shared experience with their shared
watching. For far from being unseeing, Peter is visually omnivo-
rous. His "susceptibility to impressions" leads him to comment
especially on the "richness" and "greenness" of the trees and grass
in Regent's Park (107), where he distinguishes himself by his care
to the same kind of little girl to whom Clarissa would have claimed
him oblivious. Remembering her much as she does him—"it was
Clarissa one remembered. Not that she was striking . . . ; there
she was, however; there she was" (115), he recalls, anticipating his
words that will conclude the novel—Peter spends a great deal of
the book thinking of Clarissa and looking at her London.

The process that brings her finally before him has as much to do
with the way she leads him to look at the world as with his desire
for her; the process depends, therefore, on a third party or parties
who can help give confirmation to her vision of reality. For Peter's
watchfulness has its lapses. At first he smugly and self-indulgently
ponders on the ambulance carrying Septimus's body as "one of the
triumphs of civilisation." But he soon checks himself: "... Ah, but
thinking became morbid, sentimental, directly one began conjuring
up doctors, dead bodies; a little glow of pleasure, a sort of lust too
over the visual impression warned one not to go on with that sort of
thing any more—fatal to art, fatal to friendship. True" (229). Delineating thus the reasonable limits to the attractions of the "visual"
leads Peter to think of Clarissa's "odd affinities" with people she
has seen but "never spoken to, some woman in the street, some man
behind a counter"—an assertion that in turn leads him to confirm
Clarissa's "transcendental theory" of mutual influence, according
to which the "unseen" part of the self

might survive, be recovered somehow attached to this person or that. . . .
    Looking back over that long friendship of almost thirty years her theory
worked to this extent. Brief, broken, often painful as their actual meetings

had been . . . the effect of them on his life was immeasurable. . . . She had influenced him more than any person he had ever known. And always in this way coming before him without his wishing it, cool, ladylike, critical; or ravishing, romantic, recalling some field or English harvest. He saw her most often in the country, not in London. One scene after another. . . . (232–33)

Clarissa's again coming before Peter in the book's final lines both gives final authorization to the theory Peter has assimilated and proves his perspicacity, bringing them, according to their own shared terms, together. But their union has depended throughout on their common experience of the more general set of connections to other people randomly and commonly perceived, especially Septimus. Finally, it has less to do with the consummation of their relationship ("it would not have been a success, their marriage," Peter concedes [236], and adultery seems out of the question, even if the "ravishing" and the "romantic" are part of what they share) than with the confirmation of what they have seen.

That confirmation comes in *Mrs. Dalloway*'s final moment. Once Clarissa has "looked" at, "see[n]," and "watch[ed]" the old woman and felt "somehow very like . . . the young man who had killed himself" (283), Clarissa's theory of communion needs only to be reapplied by her former suitor, as it is in the book's last lines. "But where is Clarissa? ... Where's the woman gone to?" Peter Walsh has asked Sally Seton (284), presumably at just the moment when Clarissa has seen "the old woman" put out her light, plunging both herself and Clarissa into darkness. As Peter wonders, "What is this terror? what is this ecstasy? . . . What is it that fills me with extraordinary excitement?" the novel's implied response is that Peter has come to some intuitive sense of Clarissa's own revelation about her affinity with Septimus. "It is Clarissa," Peter answers for himself, fulfilled by what he then sees. "For there she was," the book's final words, render the visual image complete. Where *Daniel Deronda* had repeated its uncertain claim as to the value of its principal heterosexual bond in order to show that that value had yet to be adequately proven, *Mrs. Dalloway*'s repetition of "there she was" serves as full confirmation that visual union is sufficient and strong. The moment is reminiscent of a most conventional kind of novelistic consummation, the physical arrival of the beloved. In fact, Walsh's sensations on the occasion resemble those he has experienced in an earlier moment of casual lust, when he has followed an unknowing young woman through the London streets.[7] But here seeing is enough.

Yet as the phrase describing "a sort of lust . . . over the visual impression" makes clear, Woolf has not banished sex. What is remarkable about this closing scene, compared to those of other novels, is that Woolf has felt the need to define her ending neither in terms of the displacement of sex nor in terms of sexual consummation: she has found another idiom around which to build her phrasing of her conclusion. The effect is that of collective fulfillment; that is, the ending is based on conjoining not just two figures but several—Clarissa, Peter, Sally, perhaps other observant watchers at the party, and even, implicitly, Septimus, whom Clarissa's "theory" could reasonably include. These others do not function as panders or mediators for the central pair,[8] but rather as fellow participants in the moment of vision. They maintain a status like that of the painter/viewer in Grant's *Interior*, permitted their own absent, autonomous but connected perspectives on what the pairs come to see. Consummation, such as there is, depends on the sense that one has shared one's vision. Sexual desire may be assimilated into that process, but it does not hold sway.

Bloomsbury was familiar with such triumphs. Clive Bell would recall:

I remember spending some dark, uneasy winter days during the first war in the depth of the country with Lytton Strachey. After lunch, as we watched the rain pour down and premature darkness roll up, he said, in his searching, personal way, "Loves apart, whom would you most like to see coming up the drive?" I hesitated a moment, and he supplied the answer: "Virginia of course."[9]

The collaboration of Bell and Strachey in this moment would, from Woolf's point of view, have been quite telling, for the two men made opposite contributions to her view of heterosexual friendship. *Mrs. Dalloway*'s persistent but subordinated maintenance of sexual desire—duplicated nicely in Strachey's casual phrase, "loves apart"—reflects one of Woolf's own decided preferences at middle age. But she thought that only one of the two men who together desired her appearance could answer to that preference. While she recognized that she had reached a level of relative ease in all her

friendships with men—"it's a great thing to have done with copulation," she declared—Woolf repeatedly remarked upon Clive Bell's
being "enough of my old friend, & enough of my old lover, to make
the afternoon hum." But of her much-loved Strachey she would say,
"though he is in some ways perfect as a friend, only he's a female
friend"; elsewhere she would describe their relationship as "strictly
and even cynically Platonic." [10]

She had learned to think of the element of sex as necessary to
the idioms of Bloomsbury friendship: "A little colour is added to
taste. We have our embrace; our frill of sentiment. Impossible, as
Nessa says, to talk without it." [11] In contrast, Woolf noted in her
essay on "Old Bloomsbury" that though "the society of buggers
has many advantages—if you are a woman," it also had for her a
crucial "drawback":

with buggers one cannot, as nurses say, show off. Something is always
suppressed, held down. Yet this showing off, which is not copulating, necessarily, nor altogether being in love, is one of the great delights, one of
the chief necessities of life. Only then does all effort cease; one ceases to
be honest, one ceases to be clever. One fizzes up into some absurd effer-
vescence of soda water or champagne through which one sees the world
tinged with all the colours of the rainbow. It is significant of what I had
come to desire that I went straight . . . from the dim and discreet rooms of
James Strachey at Cambridge to dine with Lady Ottoline Morrell at Bedford Square. Her rooms, I noted without drawing any inferences, seemed
to me instantly full of "lustre and illusion." [12]

There is significant irony in Woolf's having thought that its lack of
sexual possibility undermined her friendship with Strachey, for she
thought him responsible for sex's having become an essential part
of her "talk." [13] But Bloomsbury's wartime "discovery" of heterosexuality (as noted by Robert Skidelsky) came only after its male
members had thoroughly assimilated and imported a college language of friendship that was for use exclusively between men. [14] If
certain sexual dynamics were thought "impossible" to forgo in
satisfactory heterosexual "talk," not all of Bloomsbury's modes of
conversation would function between its homosexual men and its
women—as much because of idiomatic habits treasured within an
all-male discourse as because of heterosexual idioms that underscored sexual difference and attraction.

As Bloomsbury assimilated elements of sex into friendship while still insisting that cooperative visionary creativity would be the center of friendship, two different traditions came into play. English discourse had long authenticated the creative value of male friendship, and Bloomsbury men drew on the example of the Greeks for making that dominant model accommodate male homosexuality. But wherever discourse had introduced sex into the English idioms of heterosexual friendship, all other factors had been vanquished: once admitted, sex became the central defining fact. As illustrated most visibly in the title and phrasings of *The Woman Who Did*, heterosexual "friendship" inclusive of sex quickly became focused exclusively on the issue of sex, at the expense of anything else heterosexuals happened to do, including, say, work. This tendency for "friendship" to be defined according to the presence or absence of sex—the central fact in the modern English history of the idioms relating to heterosexual friendship—is what Woolf's Bloomsbury experience had served remarkably to counteract. For as a rule Bloomsbury seems to have taken sexual attraction within cross-gender relations as liberating cooperative creativity rather than overwhelming it. Vanessa Bell's "slipping civilization off her back" had helped create Charleston and its products; "frill"-ish Clive Bell had long managed to assist Virginia Woolf's own writing processes in a way no one else could. Meanwhile she complained about what she and her "cynically Platonic" friend Strachey could not quite accomplish together: "I don't see Lytton far enough away to have a clear view of him." [15]

With Bloomsbury's assistance, Freud was helping to render explicit the mechanisms that tended to flood sex into English discourse; in so doing, he was also helping to draw boundaries to the areas so saturated. [16] Similar explicitness in Bloomsbury fostered cooperative freedom, in which sex helped to ratify heterosexual relations that convention would elsewhere uniformly undermine or, in unusual circumstances (as during the war), falsely and opportunistically underwrite. I am arguing, in other words, that by demystifying the process whereby English discourse persistently exploited sex as its central *secret* and so displaced "friendship" as a mere temporary barrier, Bloomsbury made significant progress toward attaching friendship to dynamics other than, or with higher priority than, the sexual. Not that Bloomsbury could entirely eliminate Victorian idiomatic habits: sex had, as at Garsington, almost obsessively to be summoned in talk in order to be properly subordinated in action; disappointed visitors were amazed at the degree to which Bloomsbury's sexual candor did not lead to physical consummation.[17] Perhaps indeed Bloomsbury participated rather conventionally in the modern tendency to connect sexuality and selfhood, and perhaps that tendency is unavoidable for all those who situate themselves as post-Victorian.[18] Woolf's disqualifying herself from cooperative communion with male homosexuals demonstrates, in any case, a decidedly conventional—and, given her own attraction to women, untenable—set of prejudices as to the way sexual orientation might shape gender relations. But Bloomsbury generally thought its insistence on the presence of sex could be part of the process whereby other valued dynamics could be given a new discursive legitimacy. "If you could say what you liked about art, sex, or religion," Vanessa Bell remembered, "you could also talk freely and very likely dully about the ordinary doings of daily life."[19]

That might hold in Bloomsbury's public writings as well as in its private conversations: *Mrs. Dalloway*'s ending provides perhaps the best illustration. Woolf's refusal either to displace or to prioritize sex helps maintain a steady sense of the ordinary in the nevertheless climactic moment of vision Clarissa Dalloway shares with Peter Walsh—who, as Clive Bell would for Virginia Woolf, has remained enough of her old friend, and enough of her old lover, to have made her afternoon hum. Given Freud's function in enabling such phrasings, it is ironic that the analyst Bradshaw should be the one endowed with an obscure "evil" characterized by his being "without sex or lust" though "extremely polite to women" (281). It is Bradshaw and his wife who represent an utterly barren vision, as Woolf has them redundantly "look" at a picture at Clarissa's home for three consecutive sentences, the idiomatic stasis suggesting what that couple cannot together accomplish.[20] They depart characterized by their lack of what Peter and Clarissa share. Between Peter and Clarissa, "lust" is a significant element, but affirmed, shared perception is the more significant one.

A Little Triumphant: *To the Lighthouse*

Particular phrases in Woolf's *To the Lighthouse* seem to me the English novel's best realizations of alternative terms for heterosexual friendship. Yet these do not, any more than do comparable moments in *Mrs. Dalloway*, explicitly reauthorize the word "friendship" or words like it. Such words might by now reasonably seem past the point of redemption, and their subsequent appearances in Woolf's fiction are little more than incidental. Even though the war had provided English discourse with acceptable images and idioms for friendship between the sexes, that discourse had only temporarily stored away, not abandoned, its inheritence of attendant Victorian innuendos, conventions, and images. The war had authenticated "friendship" as referring to cross-sex relations based on cooperation, but with the war's passing, such cooperation had lost the occasion of its legitimacy, leaving the word and others associated with it muddled (in sex and sexlessness, as at the turn of the century) and without recognized signification. Given Woolf's own expressed satisfaction in "having done with copulation," the confusion surrounding "friendship" may be best illustrated in her query to Ethel Smyth about T. S. Eliot in 1936: "how necessary do you think copulation is to friendship?"[21] Such uncertainty suggests how utterly impossible "friendship" had become as a viable alternative to the idioms of courtship and sexuality. Just as I have proposed Woolf's 1918 novel *Night and Day* as a partially successful conclusion to the tradition of attempts to end novels in "friendship," I propose 1919, the year of the soldiers' full return to their prewar working roles, as an unhappy end point for English attempts to validate the word "friendship" in heterosexual relations.[22]

But the defeat of "friendship" does not mean the end of experiments in social idiom. The verbal defeat might in fact energize the search for new means. Lucio Ruotolo states in his discussion of *Mrs. Dalloway,*

Typically for Woolf, human intercourse occurs on the boundary of the mind's knowledge, some obscure communion deeper than ideology and more fundamental than sex. The experience tends to point beyond language itself and, insofar as it remains susceptible to description, urges her toward a special rendering of the novel as a vehicle for communication.[23]

My comments on *Mrs. Dalloway*'s ending are meant to suggest how Woolf's reach beyond the limitations of sex—and "friendship"—result in both generic and idiomatic innovation, through recourse to an empowering alternative. Shared vision does more in Woolf than just expand the possibilities for heterosexual closure in the novel, a significant adjustment in itself; it also offers hints of an idiomatic strategy that might serve social discourse beyond Woolf's novels.

That Woolf would choose to give special authorization to moments of cooperative vision should not seem surprising in the light of the way wartime descriptions of heterosexual cooperation and women's labor had placed women both as observed object and unobservant subject. During the war, women's visual capacities had been assigned to their separate sphere, granted merit in terms of the immediate and actual but denied competence for sustained observation or imaginative oversight. Such evaluation had disqualified them both as "viewers" (in the munitions factories) and as planners on a large scale, and had marked them peculiarly fit for relatively limited tasks. Such limitations were enforced even more emphatically in the interwar period: Deidre Beddoe has described the conditions matter-of-factly as ones in which "housewives were confined to small spaces and the danger was they became small-minded." [24] Feminist historian Ray Strachey suggested in *Our Freedom and Its Results*, published by the Woolfs' Hogarth Press in 1936, that women's confinement to short-range tasks had served to reify their perceptual limitations:

women . . . possess a power of attention to detail which is nearly always of great commercial value. So far is this gift carried that it is often said that they lack all capacity to grasp fundamental principles, and that they fail to see the wood for the trees. Whether this is true or not cannot be judged until enough women have been placed in positions where they are required to look at things in their larger aspects. [25]

Writers arguing for expansion of women's employment opportunities in the first third of the century repeatedly stressed the visual. As the war had drawn particular attention to women's actual physical capacities, affirmation of feminine vision had taken on more literal applications. In *Through a Woman's Eyes* (1917), Beatrice Heron-Maxwell devoted a chapter to "Women as Film Censors," declaring, "It seems as if this wholly modern appointment is especially fitted to the present-day woman, and she particularly qualified for success in it." Where a man was apt to take "a broad view that reduces certain points in the play to a proportion that is too small," a woman would "detach vision from experience and the mature level of memory and mental digestion resulting from it; [she would be] a critic who with a guiding intuition and insight [could] enter into a child's mind, with its limitations and its parodoxically wide horizon, and see with a child's eyes."[26]

But not all advocates of women's work accepted such literal "limitations" or proposed applying them to implement further restrictions. Olive Schreiner had qualified her *Women and Labour* as providing "not only . . . not a general view of the whole vast body of phenomena connected with women's position, but . . . not even a bird's eye view of the whole question of women's labour"; yet Schreiner had argued for changes that would allow the New Women to "see a new earth" built around "the love of comrades and co-workers." "[I]s it only a blindness in our eyes," Schreiner asked in her conclusion, "which makes us see far up the river . . . a clear golden light? Is it only a delusion of the eyes . . . ?"[27] By 1928, Ray Strachey could provide a clear answer, associating tentative postwar advances with a flourishing of the "widening of outlook" that, to her mind, had always been a central feature of the women's movement.[28]

The extremes represented by Heron-Maxwell and Schreiner suggest that sexually differentiated notions of sight could be invoked to justify either the limitation or the expansion of women's "mental industry." Neither alternative was inherently empowering: if literal claims to short-range acuity could confine women to narrow functions, then Comtian claims about women's capacity for the visionary might be used to argue that women's contribution ought rightly to transcend (i.e., bypass) the workplace entirely. Schreiner's argument for "the entrance of women into new and intellectual fields of labour" seemed designed to combat both these dangers, in its emphasis on "the intellectual capacity, the physical vigour, the emotional depth of women," mutually compatible qualities that had been falsely partitioned by the past history of labor. Confronting a time when "the need for [women's] physical labour having gone, . . . mental industry [had not] taken its place," Schreiner sought to validate women's intellects without rendering them bodiless or sexless.[29]

"Vision" marked a category in which body and mind might be made, idiomatically, to meet. Validation of women's "power of attention" would depend, as Ray Strachey would write two decades after Schreiner and Heron-Maxwell, on women's being "placed in positions where they are required to look at things in their larger aspects." In granting such a position to Lily Briscoe, *To the Lighthouse* demonstrates the capaciousness of her vision without denying her physical competence. Moreover, Briscoe's visionary moments draw her into cooperation with men in a fully enabled role: her final moment of shared vision rejects domestic confinement for imaginative breadth, validating "terms of friendship" more definite than those provided by *Night and Day*. Seeing here comes fully to displace courtship as the basis for heterosexual interaction.

The process is not entirely painless, occurring as it does at the expense of Mrs. Ramsay, a version of the cooperative but myopic angel Victorians (and Comtians) had readily embraced. It is the "short-sighted" Mrs. Ramsay's relation to her "long-sighted husband," [30] the center of the novel's first section, that must give way in the end to Lily Briscoe's successful attempt to combine her vision with Mr. Ramsay's. The Ramsays' marital union has been defined by their watching together: "So that is marriage," Briscoe declares of them, "a man and a woman looking at a girl throwing a ball" (110). But that shared vision hardly seems creative, and the first section climaxes with the Ramsays' gazes limited to each other:

Then, knowing that he was watching her, instead of saying anything she turned, holding her stocking, and looked at him. And as she looked at him she began to smile, for though she had not said a word, he knew, of course he knew, that she loved him. He could not deny it. And smiling she looked out of the window . . . (thinking to herself, Nothing on earth can equal this happiness)— (185–86)

Short-sighted Mrs. Ramsay's look out the window can only reflect what is inside. The habitual result of her finding "herself sitting and looking, sitting and looking" is for her to "bec[o]me the thing she looked at," with a sense of "her own eyes meeting her own eyes" (97). This visual solipsism is both a figurative analogue to Mrs. Ramsay's wish to see others' lives in the image of her own (in the image, that is, of her marriage) and a literal rendering of the perceptual limitations that make such projection her only recourse. In a world of watchers, Mrs. Ramsay's insistently mentioned short-sightedness isolates and debilitates her.

The irony is that Mrs. Ramsay's urge for control has taken the form of a desire "to take people by the scruff of their necks and make them see" (89). As had been characteristic of Clarissa Dalloway, in her impatience with Peter Walsh, that desire is coupled in Mrs. Ramsay with a misunderstanding of a male's perceptual powers: "Did he notice the view? No," she thinks of her husband (107). The abruptness of that dismissal will give way in the final section to Cam and Briscoe's sustained involvement with Mr. Ramsay's focused vision. But Mrs. Ramsay is enough shut out from what he sees to attribute his "never [looking] at things" to a quirk of the intellectual life from which she is excluded (108).[31]

And Mrs. Ramsay's absorption in marriage causes her to miss the meaning when she has the kind of experience *To the Lighthouse* valorizes. Her dinner table is one of the book's great occasions for shared observations, a climax of which occurs when she and the poet Augustus Carmichael gaze at the dish of fruit in the middle:

to her pleasure (for it brought them into sympathy momentarily) she saw that Augustus too feasted his eyes on the same plate of fruit, plunged in, broke off a bloom there, a tassel here, and returned, after feasting, to his hive. That was his way of looking, different from hers. But looking together united them. (146)

The book's first moment of community follows from this, as "all" become "conscious of making a party together," participating in a "common cause" (147). Mrs. Ramsay has contributed most to the moment, but soon her obsession with the Rayleys' becoming man and wife allows the larger bond to dissipate into petty chat over Minta's brooch and Mrs. Ramsay's beef. The "spell" cast by Mrs. Ramsay's marital mania dissolves the united group into a series of possible couples.

Yet while Mrs. Ramsay neglects the purple and yellow tableau with which she had drawn gazes to the table's center, its significance is not lost upon Lily Briscoe, who remembers her intention to "move the tree rather more to the middle" (154) of the painting commemorating the period. Briscoe will not neglect perceptually significant moments like the one Carmichael and Mrs. Ramsay have shared: she will acknowledge them as turning points, albeit painful ones, with enough collective force to counter Mrs. Ramsay's attempt to draw her into marriage.

And Lily will arrive at visionary alternatives precisely opposed to what Mrs. Ramsay has had in mind for her. William Bankes's attempt to share Lily's "power of . . . vision" by gazing at her picture seems at first a violation: "[I]t had been seen; it had been taken from her. This man had shared with her something profoundly intimate" (82–83). But Briscoe comes to maintain her relationship with Bankes, "without any sexual feeling," as an affirmation of her artistic labors: "He has his work, Lily said to herself. She remembered, all of a sudden as if she had found a treasure, that she had her work. In a flash she saw her picture and thought, Yes, I shall put the tree further in the middle; then I shall avoid that awkward space" (128). His own fascination with Mrs. Ramsay leads Bankes to think "that friendships, even the best of them, are frail things. One drifts apart" (135). Yet Bankes and Briscoe will disprove that in their shared defiance of Mrs. Ramsay's domesticating pressure. "Thanks to his scientific mind he understood," Briscoe thinks of Bankes in the final section, continuing, "One could talk of painting then seriously to a man. Indeed, his friendship had been one of the pleasures of her life. She loved William Bankes" (262–63).

Even the relationship that has seemed, in the first section, to confirm Mrs. Ramsay's priorities turns out to uphold those that Lily Briscoe connects with Bankes. The adjustment of the Rayleys' marriage into one like the Bells' serves to confirm Katharine Hilbery's suspicion that it should be "perfectly possible to live together without being married," for the couple Mrs. Ramsay had been so proud of bringing together develops after her death a relationship like that Katharine and Ralph had aspired to in *Night and Day*. Lily recalls her recent visit to the Rayleys, when

the car broke down and Minta had to hand him his tools. He sat on the road mending the car, and it was the way she gave him the tools—businesslike, straightforward, friendly—that proved it was all right now. They were 'in love' no longer; no, he had taken up with another woman, a serious woman, with her hair in a plait and a case in her hand (Minta had described her gratefully, almost admiringly), who went to meetings and shared Paul's views (they had got more and more pronounced) about the taxation of land values and a capital levy. Far from breaking up the marriage, that alliance had righted it. They were excellent friends, obviously, as he sat on the road and she handed him his tools. (259)

Still, for all its comfortable defiance of Mrs. Ramsay's expectations, the scene puts precise limitations on the extent of the Rayleys' "friendship." Like wartime "friendship," the apparently innovative relation maintains old inequities. The compromised marriage preserves the structure of its origins in courtship. "He would prove what he could do," Paul Rayley had promised, imagining himself "always leading" Minta (118), and the conversion of those fantasies into "business-like, straightforward" activity has not altered his position of dominance. Minta is three times characterized by her act of handing him his tools. Her role as a nonessential partner in Paul's manual work is far different from Lily's role in her moments of cooperation: Lily knows "she would feel a little triumphant, telling Mrs. Ramsay that the marriage had not been a success" (260), and that is partly because she can also afford to feel superior to Minta Rayley, not only in having avoided marriage, but also in having kept hold of her tools. She has recognized early on that "she could not show [Bankes] what she wished to make of [the scene before them], could not see it even herself, without a brush in her hand" (82). Her persistent hold on her implement—an emblem of the way her visionary capacities are tied to the corporeal—is essential to the satisfaction she takes from her relations with Bankes and Carmichael.

Briscoe's most thorough triumph over Mrs. Ramsay, marriage, and the manual emerges in her final bonding with Mr. Ramsay. In yet another of Woolf's triangulated scenes,[32] Lily is joined by Carmichael, whose participation in shared vision Mrs. Ramsay had neglected but whom Lily will credit with having "crowned the occasion" of her union with Mr. Ramsay. Carmichael's presence will assure Briscoe of having achieved not only a far-sightedness comparable to Mr. Ramsay's but also the practical immediacy of vision that will allow her to complete her painting (309). The need for both these perspectives becomes evident as soon as Lily begins to resolve her relationship with Ramsay.

So much depends then, thought Lily Briscoe, looking at the sea . . . , so much depends, she thought, upon distance: whether people are near us or far from us; for her feeling for Mr. Ramsay changed as he sailed further and further across the bay. It seemed to be elongated, stretched out; he seemed to become more and more remote. He and his children seemed to be swallowed up in that blue, that distance; but here, on the lawn, close at hand, Mr. Carmichael suddenly grunted. She laughed. He clawed his book up from the grass. He settled into his chair again puffing and blowing like some sea monster. That was different altogether, because he was so near. (284)

Woolf considered distance a requisite fact of successful perception.[33] She thought it essential to writing; and, as noted above, she thought its lack a shortcoming in her relationship with Lytton Strachey: "I don't see Lytton far enough away to have a clear view of him." If the long-sightedness necessary to make distance empowering were taken to be an exclusively male privilege, meager limits would be set on vision shared between the sexes. But their "common hilarity" in the inspection of "distant views" is a central fact of Lily Briscoe's dispassionate relationship with William Bankes (34), and it is prerequisite to her negotiating an alternative to marriage with Mr. Ramsay that subordinates but does not deny sexuality. In a remark that echoes Woolf's reservations about what she missed from Strachey, Lily has acknowledged with disappointment that her "relationship" with Ramsay has been "reduced . . . to something neutral, without that element of sex in it which made his manner to Minta so gallant, almost gay" (254). But any face-to-face confrontation between the widower and the woman artist would envelop their relation in the requirements of courtship. For Lily "to give him" what he wants to, she will have not to exchange immediate gazes with him as Mrs. Ramsay had,[34] or to share his commanding view at his side, but to watch with him from her own established position, at a substantial remove from his. This is the condition of their seeing. His daughter Cam, alongside Ramsay as he approaches the lighthouse and then looks back at the island, wonders "What could he see?" but it remains for her "all a blur" (307). Lily, meanwhile, is confident of having matched his perspective from far off. Her exhaustion at the moment she thinks, "He must have reached it," results from both "the effort of looking at it and the effort of thinking of him landing there" (308). Her imaginative effort is confirmed when the novel discloses that Ramsay has, in fact, reached the lighthouse; but the vision requires the ratification of Carmichael's standing by her side and sharing it, before she recreates it in her painting.[35]

Her interactions with Ramsay and Carmichael effectively liberate Lily's "vision," giving her the long-sought courage to affirm, "But this is what I see; this is what I see" (32). In the end, comfortable participation in a communal vision overcomes the difficulties of individual confrontations. The sense of "fifty pairs of eyes [being] not enough to get round that one woman [Mrs. Ramsay]" (294) has hitherto stood as a final barrier to Lily's art.

It was some trick of the painter's eye. For days after she had heard of [Mrs. Ramsay's] death she had seen her thus. . . . But always something—it might be a face, a voice, a paper boy crying *Standard*, *News*—thrust through, snubbed her, waked her, required and got in the end an effort of attention, so that the vision must be perpetually remade. (270)

Briscoe turns from the persistently reappearing figure of Mrs. Ramsay as she tries to envision Mr. Ramsay, but the vision she comes to share with him includes his wife. As Ramsay turns toward the island, an equally distant perspective permits Lily to "get round" Mrs. Ramsay, who finally becomes a figure in the window, like Mary Datchet or Clarissa Dalloway's old woman, a confirming but independent additional perspective. "I have had my vision," the book's final words, are rendered as singular, but the vision has been realized only through its being shared.[36]

Visual power was Woolf's metaphor for successful fiction. "I strike the eye," she had proclaimed triumphantly in 1920; a "wonderful eye" was the key distinction she attributed to the novelist she admired most.[37] Making others see was a commonly expressed goal for the novelists of Woolf's day,[38] but in her case it might serve particularly well both to express and to illustrate the convention that a woman's visionary capacities were equal to the best of men's. In *A Room of One's Own* Woolf records her desire to be "most multitudinously eyed"; her affirmation of women's "power of vision" there stands in opposition to women's traditional role as men's mere "looking-glasses."[39] She liberates Lily Briscoe's "small," "dim" eyes by granting her a communion that bars the conventions of courtship—conventions that might well have been expected to consume a novel that ends by linking a widower, a younger friend of his wife's, his children, and his wife's benign memory.[40] *To the Lighthouse* demonstrates that a novel may conclude in a heterosexual bond independent of hierarchical domestic rituals. Moreover, it proves that idioms like "friendship" are at most incidental to representing such relationships, for those so named—the final quasi-marital "friendship" of the Rayleys, the long-sustained "friendship" between Lily and Bankes—are finally less significant than those unnamed relationships that are more thoroughly portrayed. What has been achieved by the end of *To the Lighthouse* is more than just novelistic "openness" in anticipation of some more productive future: a significant and unconventional human relationship has been confidently figured.[41] *To the Lighthouse* prioritizes vision—not the product of that vision, but its actual cooperative enactment—as the link between its women and men. A painter's stroke enacts the discursive meshing of mental and manual. Not only could a woman "talk of painting then seriously to a man," but man and woman could be mutually enabled by visions shared, kept autonomous, and put in practice. Talk could be authenticated in art, if from a distance; Woolf had experienced that herself.

Intensities: Virginia Woolf and Roger Fry

When Roger Fry died, in 1934, Woolf mourned him as "the most heavenly of men . . . —so rich so infinitely gifted—and oh how we've talked and talked—for 20 years now." Her record of their "talk" together—in her diaries, letters, and *Roger Fry: A Biography*—is filled with scenes of shared vision: seeing together stands in Woolf's writings as the characteristic activity of their relationship. She noted of a party following Fry's funeral, "Well I thought I can see this through Roger's eyes: it's right to enjoy every tint. And yet how can one? This has gone out of the day. . . ." But the loss was only temporary, and a few years later she noted of a National Gallery visit, "I looked at Renoir, Cezanne & c.: tried to see through Roger's eyes: tried to get some solidity into my mind." Once she had published Fry's biography in 1940, she found herself feeling "very much in his presence at the moment; as if I were intimately connected with him; as if we together had given birth to this vision of him: a child born of us."[42]

That image of cooperation, partly new and partly traditional, suited a time when old and unwelcome idioms were making their return. English men and women were again being asked to pull unromantically together as England prepared for another war. On her way into the National Gallery Woolf heard a public announcement urging the acquisition of gas masks, for fear of a possible German invasion. She had recently celebrated being able to think "of Roger not of Hitler" while at work on the biography, later adding, "If it is war, then every country joins in: chaos. To oppose this with Roger my only private position. Well that's an absurd little match to strike. But it's a hopeless war this—when we know winning means nothing. . . . 1914 but without even the illusion of 1914. All slipping consciously into a pit."[43]

Woolf was determined once again to articulate a "private position" uncontaminated by the war's homogenizing of discourse; once again, this would leave her vulnerable to accusation. Three weeks after *Roger Fry* was published, Woolf faced an attack on Fry from art historian Ben Nicolson, similar to but even harsher than that Katherine Mansfield had leveled against *Night and Day*, "I am so struck by the fools paradise in which [Fry] and his friends lived," Nicolson wrote to Woolf.

He shut himself out from all disagreeable actualities and allowed the spirit of Nazism to grow without taking any steps to check it. . . . This intensely private world which Roger Fry cultivated could only be communicated to a few people as sensitive and intelligent as himself. . . . [The artist's] mission is now more vital than it has ever been. He will still be shocked by stupidity and untruth but instead of ignoring it he will set out to fight it; instead of retreating into his tower to uphold certain ethical standards his job will be to persuade as many other people as possible to think and behave in the same way—and on his success and failure depends the future of the world.

Woolf's response to Nicolson shows just how much she was willing to stake on shared vision and the sharing of vision: "Who on earth did that job more incessantly and successfully than Roger Fry?" she wrote.

Didn't he spend half his life, not in a tower, but travelling about England addressing masses of people, who'd never looked at a picture and making them see what he saw? And wasn't that the best way of checking Nazism? Then I opened another letter; as it happened from Sebastian Sprott, a lecturer at Nottingham; and I read how he'd once been mooning around S. Kensington Museum "... then I saw Roger. All was changed. In ten minutes he caused me to enjoy what I was looking at. The objects became vivid and intelligible. ... There must be many people like me, people with scales on their eyes and wax in their ears . . . if only someone would come along and remove the scales and dig out the wax. Roger did it. ..."
    Then the raiders passed over. And I thought I can't have given Ben the least notion of what Roger was like. I suppose it was my fault. Or is it partly, and naturally, that he must have a scapegoat? I admit I want one. I

loathe sitting here waiting for a bomb to fall; when I want to be writing. If it doesn't kill me it's killing someone else. . . .

But what I'd like to know is, suppose we both survive this war, what ought we to do to prevent another? I shall be too old to do anything but write. But will you throw up your job as an art critic and take to politics? And if you stick to art criticism, how will you make it more public and less private than Roger did? [44]

These were not new questions for Woolf. In the book she had written simultaneously with *Roger Fry*, she had taken on the question of what men and women might do "to prevent war." In the final section of *Three Guineas*, Woolf had met the return of the old wartime rhetoric: "The word 'feminist' is destroyed," she ironically echoed; "the air is cleared; and in that clearer air what do we see? Men and women working together for the same cause. . . . The daughters and sons of educated men are fighting side by side." Her response had been to refuse to "merge" female "identity" in the male's, to insist on maintaining autonomy and difference. "[T]hough we look upon that picture [of war casualties] from different angles," she had responded to her fictional male correspondent,

our conclusion is the same as yours—it is evil. We are both determined to do what we can to destroy the evil which that picture represents, you by your methods, we by ours. And since we are different, our help must be different. . . . But . . . we can best help you to prevent war not by joining your society but by remaining outside your society but in co-operation with its aim. That aim is the same for us both. [45]

What Woolf is proposing is very different from "fighting side by side." It obviously isn't "friendship," at least not as the English understood it during the wars. But the suggestion of both autonomy ("remaining outside") and engagement ("co-operation") extends qualities of her novelistic resolutions, [46] and in *Roger Fry* that combination characterizes the way her friend Fry sees, the way Woolf sees Fry, and the way she and Fry see together. Woolf claims repeatedly that Fry effectively shared what he saw, yet did not require full compliance from his fellow viewers. And the biography's imaging of her own relation to Fry illustrates that same freedom in participation—autonomy like that I earlier associated with Duncan Grant's *Interior*, though without the painting's intense reflection of wartime constraint.

The recurrence of the First World War's heterosexual idioms [47] marks the last stage in the historical process described in this book: we have slipped back into a discursive situation we've seen before. Indeed, *Roger Fry* registers the idiomatic accretions of male/female friendship from Victorian times through the interwar period. But *Roger Fry* also intensifies the pattern of avoidance whose parallel history I have been tracing: here is a work that does not ultimately depend on compromised terms for its imaging of cross-gender affection. It resorts instead to alternative idioms newly charged. The broader application of those terms is the subject of my final pages; here I want to explain how *Roger Fry* serves to generate and authenticate them.

For Roger Fry, Woolf says, art criticism meant "seeing pictures."[48] This phrase recurs throughout the book, almost always in association with the important proviso to the effect that "to have another pair of eyes to see with, another brain to argue with, was a very necessary process in making up [Fry's] mind" (121).[49] These references to shared vision generally suggest conflict as much as unanimity, a combination Woolf had long insisted on in relation to Fry. Seeing with him meant complement (appropriate to Modernist interest in multiple perspectives and decentralized points of view), not assimilation. In 1925 she had deemed Fry's "praise about painting always . . . the best worth having—not that one agrees with him, but that his honesty is so incorruptible, and his perceptions so fine"; when she defended Fry against Nicolson in 1940, Woolf insisted "my own point of view [was] entirely different from his." So when "seeing pictures" begins to share prominence with "friendship" in the biography's final chapter, the point is not merely adherence to a common cause:

> if, in order to write and lecture, it was necessary to see pictures "as if for the first time," it was almost equally necessary to see friends. Ideas must be sketched on other people's minds. Theories must be discussed, preferably with someone, like Charles Mauron, who could demolish them. But even if the friend was incapable of demolishing them, they must be shared. "He was so sociable that he could never enjoy anything without at once feeling the need to share it with those around him," as M. Mauron says. It was the desire to share, to have two pairs of eyes to see with, and somebody at hand, or at least within reach of the pen, to argue with. . . . (266)[50]

Such passages challenge a practical fact about the relation of shared vision to the spoken word. It would seem that mutuality of vision can never be expressed spontaneously: one party must always first propose what he or she sees in order to initiate a union that the second party may then confirm. When shared vision is not self-limiting—that is, when it is focused beyond a pair's absorption in looking at each other[51]—it is recognizable only through the mediation of speech (precisely because the two people are now looking away from one another, elsewhere). Dependence on language would seem inevitably to privilege the contribution of the person who initiates the conjoining terms. *Night and Day*'s climactic scene illustrates this problem, for although Katharine has been at work on her own independent visual image, her verbal participation consists only in confirming Ralph's vision: "Yes, the world looks something like that to me too." But *Roger Fry*'s comparable moments never require that kind of full concurrence. They are remarkable, first of all, as drawings back, refusals to consummate sight as closure; but more important is their repeated insistence that Fry's critical act of initiating vision never obligates his fellow perceiver(s) to echo him.

That claim is consistent with one of the book's most emphatic lessons: "in all this protracted and difficult business of revelation and reconstruction" says Woolf, "the critic's own identity has been consumed. Never does [Fry] draw attention by irrelevance or display to his own share in the work of reconstruction" (285). Woolf had long demanded such restraint in her own writing. But in recent years, she had come to associate the principle with Fry. While at work on the biography she remembered as "the best criticism I've had for a long time" Fry's saying "that I poetise my inanimate scenes, stress my personality." In *Roger Fry*, Woolf would take such cautions to heart: she later declared the book "an experiment in self suppression; a gamble in R's power to transmit himself."[52]

Woolf thus saw the book as enacting a perceptual intimacy that did not impose one self upon another. In renewed opposition to wartime insistence on unanimity, Woolf presents cooperation that affirms and maintains the idiosyncrasies of autonomous points of view rather than absorbing them in the making of a singular predictable product. The composition and meaning of *Roger Fry* depend upon gestures comparable to Woolf's refusal in *Three Guineas* to sign the already-made male manifesto with which she has some sympathy: "we can best help you to prevent war not by repeating your words and following your methods but by finding new words and creating new methods." [53] Just as the *Three Guineas* solution distinguishes itself from wartime "friendship" in not requiring forced and one-sided self-suppression, *Roger Fry* reflects Woolf's experience that she and Fry could seek related ends without either artist requiring grave concessions or silences from the other.[54]

What do such reticences leave to "friendship" in *Roger Fry*? To the word itself, not much—even though the book explicitly attacks the Victorian conventions that had made marriage "the only solution" for Roger and Helen Fry (95) and favors instead Fry and Helen Anrep's lawless postwar relation (255): Woolf doesn't use "friendship" to designate the latter, apparently because, as in the late-Victorian texts I discussed in Chapter 3, the word would clarify too little. It would have to be assumed both to include and to exclude too much. "Friend" in *Roger Fry* again designates both explicitly sexual and sexless relations. That might seem a tribute to the openness with which Bloomsbury friendship accommodated sex, were the word not also the means in *Roger Fry* for concealing a central fact. Woolf records that later in Fry's life

people mattered more and more. How much they mattered, how from one end of his life to the other he lived in his friendships, how in letter after letter he broke into praise of his friends—all that is not to be conveyed by lists of names. If certain friends—Lowes Dickinson, Desmond MacCarthy, Vanessa Bell, Philippa Strachey, the Maurons, his sister Margery[—]stand out, they are surrounded by so many others from so many different worlds, talking so many different languages, that to choose from among them or to say what it was that he got from each of them is impossible. (269)

Woolf's discrediting the "list of names" is itself disingenuous, for what she had found truly impossible to describe in the book was what Fry *hadn't* gotten from her sister. Vanessa Bell had, since just before the First World War, been Fry's principal source of sexual and romantic frustration; Fry had admitted to Helen Anrep, as Woolf knew, that his brief prewar "little married life" with Bell had been "the intensest thing in his life." [55] But on this matter the whole book is silent. In an act of concealment the Victorians would have distrusted every bit as much as their chronicler Strachey, Woolf uses "friendship" to subsume the object of Fry's passion in a list that includes male relations and his sibling. Ironically, the book does not suppress quotations indicative of Dickinson's homosexual jealousy regarding Fry's heterosexual interests; and while preparing *Roger Fry* Woolf even recorded a conversation about "Roger & [his sister] Margery's incestuous love."[56] The list demonstrates the most thorough cynicism about the way "friendship," with its random signification, might publicly seal and sanitize heterosexual relations.

"Friendship" then contributes very little to *Roger Fry*'s public presentation of heterosexual pairs. Neither does it figure in the book's more significant consideration of collectivity. Woolf quotes Fry as saying "the greatest art has always been communal, the expression—in highly individualized ways no doubt—of common aspirations and ideals" (173), and she shows the same factors to adhere to his own triumphs, as for instance at the 1910 Post-Impressionist exhibition, about which she writes, "His excitement transmitted itself. Everybody must see what he saw in those pictures—must share his sense of revelation" (152). But no name emerges for the deep feelings produced by these shared moments, not even when, near the end of the book, Woolf records one of Fry's victories from twenty years later, one of the occasions when she too shared his visual responses. The process is detailed, but the bond it generates remains always just beyond denomination:

And then he went on to make the audience see—"the gem-like notes; the aquamarines; and topazes that lie in the hollow of his satin gowns; bleaching the lights to evanescent pallors." Somehow the black-and-white slide on the screen became radiant through the mist, and took on the grain and texture of the actual canvas.

All that he had done again and again in his books. But here there was a difference. As the next slide slid over the sheet there was a pause. He gazed afresh at the picture. And then in a flash he found the word he wanted; he added on the spur of the moment what he had just seen as if for the first time. That, perhaps, was the secret of his hold over the audience. They could see the sensation strike and form; he could lay bare the very moment of perception. . . .

For two hours they had been looking at pictures. But they had seen one of which the lecturer himself was unconscious—the outline of the man against the screen. . . . That was a picture that would remain in memory together with the rest, a rough sketch that would serve many of the audience in years to come as the portrait of a great critic, a man of profound sensibility but of exacting honesty, who, when reason could penetrate no further, broke off; but was convinced, and convinced others, that what he saw was there. (262–63)

Woolf withholds "the word [Fry] wanted" and found, and then declares the vision incomplete. Even the audience's confirming vision
remains only "a rough sketch." But she insists on the fact of the
bond between Fry and his audience, for which no word is necessary
in her account because the all-important action of seeing receives all
the idiomatic stress: "to make the audience see," "he gazed afresh,"
"what he had just seen," "they could see the sensation strike and
form," "the very moment of perception," "they had been looking
at pictures," and so forth. What the audience members feel for Fry
and what Fry feels for them need not be called "friendship" or anything else. An insight from *Mrs. Dalloway* could serve to summarize
Woolf's method: "They looked; that was all. That was enough."

Woolf here places herself in Fry's audience. Elsewhere, when she
emerges as a distinct individual with a particular relation to Fry,
the same reluctance to name the central bond holds. The relationship goes unnamed because the stress falls on the action of seeing.
Woolf dubs herself for this purpose "the common seer, to coin a
counterpart to Dr. Johnson's Common Reader" (105).[57] This "common seer" Woolf describes as "the ordinary non-visual human being
to whom pictures are far more inaccessible than books or music"
(226). The phrase allows Woolf to place herself, with increasing
frequency, as a characteristic but distinct member of Fry's audience
without having to name herself as "I." In the penultimate section of
the final chapter Woolf comes forward more and more as an individual presence, though always concealed by passives and the third
person. As this moving section climaxes, or rather resists climax,
her self-suppression does not prevent the emergence of a keen sense
of its author as Fry's affectionate fellow observer, who has come
to apply her own chosen idioms to ways of seeing she has learned
from Fry.

Sometimes, though not by a conscious effort, people also are seen as if for
the first time. One such occasion—it was the last, as it happened—comes
to memory. It was a summer evening, late in July 1934, and a friend had
brought a picture upon which he wanted Roger Fry's opinion—was it by
Degas, or a copy only? The canvas was stood on a chair in front of him. . . .
Again his eyes fixed themselves with their very steady and penetrating gaze
upon the canvas. Again they seemed to carry on a life of their own as they
explored the world of reality. And again as if it helped him in his voyage
of discovery he turned and laughed and talked and argued about other

things. The two worlds were close together. He could pass from one to the other without impediment. . . . He made goodness seem desirable, as he sat laughing with his friends and looking at the picture. But how describe the pure delight "of watching a flower unfold its cup of red"? Those who knew him best will attempt no summing up of that sensation. They can only say that Roger Fry had a peculiar quality of reality that made him a person of infinite importance in their lives, and add his own words, "Any attempt I might make to explain this would probably land me in the depths of mysticism. On the edge of that gulf I stop."

But it was late; his mind was made up; and once more he was off. (296–97)

That last quotation—"On the edge of that gulf I stop," the last words of Fry's *Vision and Design*—is one Woolf has repeated in her book, just as she has repeated the comparably anticlimactic last words of Fry's *Transformations*.[58] Woolf's refusing with Fry to name the object of attention emphasizes instead the scene's true center: the active realization of a bond between the fellow observers. Woolf aestheticizes her recollection of her last, communally shared moments with Fry, in the manner of one of Fry's own visualizations. But cooperation becomes her explicit subject only at the moment when she renounces naming it, as improper to the relation: there is no way to speak of the moment except to reapply Fry's words for it, and Woolf speaks with Fry's voice only so they may together ban conclusive speech. The name for the relationship is superfluous because the cooperative moment itself, in all its glee and worth, has already been rendered, and it is the point. Its center is the shared act of seeing.

That achievement, rather than any private negotiations between Woolf and Fry, is the one I think we should grant the greatest importance. For the purposes of this study it represents an alternative to naming "friendship," as "friendship" or as anything else. The alternative is instead to enact effective heterosexual cooperation and to represent, as exemplary, the shared acts of creation or vision. Woolf's writings provide evidence that we may think of this model as more than merely a product of a brilliant novelist's skill at wordplay and speculation. It was indeed something she had experienced, though not without effort. "I'm sending you my novel tomorrow— a little reluctantly," Woolf had written to Fry in 1922.

It has *some* merit, but it's too much of an experiment. I am buoyed up, as usual, by the thought that I'm now, at last, going to bring it off—next time. I suppose one goes on thinking this for ever; and so burrowing deeper and deeper into whatever it is that perpetually fascinates. Why don't you come back and explain it?—you are the only person who ever does.[59]

Consistent with Woolf's self-conscious refusal in the biography ever to name what she and Fry saw together, her letters make no references (as they do so often regarding Clive Bell, Lytton Strachey, and others) to the sexual or nonsexual status of her and Fry's relationship.[60] They are neither "mere friends" nor anything else along that continuum.[61] Their correspondence continually acknowledges sex as an element in Fry's (and even Woolf's) relations with Vanessa Bell, and Woolf's letters express a good deal of interest in Fry's other loves; but sex, as presence or absence, never shaped the idioms describing what Woolf and Fry were to each other. Seeing did that, and did it even more effectively when they were among others than when they were alone. In her diary in 1921 she noted

Roger's visit went off specially well. I mean we are grown rather intimate, & sit talking at our ease—practically of everything. This was not so a year ago. It is partly the good effect of having friends in common—not, as used to be the way, my seeing Roger alone, while Leonard stayed at home. I see in this one of the good effects of middle age. Roger had [a book] in his pocket & read a passage aloud which started us off, & Leonard made him stand to his guns; & then on to all the usual things. Roger grudges every minute now that he doesn't paint. So we reflected upon these strange, on the whole merciful, dispensations, by which Roger always sees masterpieces ahead of him & I see great novels.[62]

From such autonomous and creative affections may emerge not just an alternative model for heterosexual relations, but an alternative idiom with which to describe them.[63]

Conclusion: Seeing and the End of Friendship

Far from attempting to give legitimacy to "friendship" as a name for heterosexual relations, this study has meant to suggest why that use of the word would better be abandoned. Indeed, any noun that calls attention to the mere fact of cooperative relationships between unmarried, unrelated men and women seems likely only to invite old assumptions about sex's primacy in heterosexual relations. If our idioms continue to refer to the heterosexual relationship as a subject unto itself, then we are unlikely to be able to provide enabling accounts of occasions when men and women are drawn together primarily by a shared interest in what they may accomplish. For we will continue to focus on the odd, uncertain nature of the interaction, rather than on what men and women together achieve.

My phrasing assumes, of course, that there are occasions, indeed many occasions, when sexual attraction is not the dynamic we may most productively or accurately use to gauge the value of heterosexual relations: if that assumption is false, then most heterosexual relationships—in nearly all working and social environments—must of course be adjudged unconsummated failures. But that is what our idioms suggest. Common, and recognizably Victorian, phrases—"just friends," "only friends," "mere friends"—still define friendships negatively, pointing chiefly and almost explicitly to what relationships pretend to exclude, except in the case of "girlfriend" and "boyfriend," which point equally clearly to what the relationships include and to what therefore disqualifies them from being considered even "mere" friendships.

Feeling compelled to invoke sex when naming cross-gender relationships can cause a great deal of private frustration and inconvenience, as many of us have experienced. Moreover, such conventions limit the discursive possibilities even for the most self-conscious analysts of heterosexual relations: in sociological and psychological research, where "cross-sex friendship" has received the most frequent attention, the category is still defined mainly by negation.[1] In public discussion of the workplace, we find ourselves in the same dilemma as those Victorian feminists who first elaborated the inequities and liabilities inherent in sexuality and courtship's constituting the only nameable center for heterosexual relations: either describe a workplace utterly devoid of affection, or risk suggesting that co-workers' affectionate bonds must always lead "to something else"—that is, back to the realm of courtship and domestic bonds from which, it is commonly assumed, women have but recently arrived. "Women *when named as a sex* . . . cannot escape being the incarnation of gender as strange or temporary workers," Denise Riley has observed;[2] cross-gender working relations, when named as such, cannot escape seeming the responsibility of women who are assumed to have introduced heterosexuality, and thus sexuality, into the workplace. The ironic results have already been suggested above in Elaine Scarry's reference to incidental victims of sexual "industrial accidents" (like Hardy's Tess), in Kate Millett's comment on the "time-honored" practice of sexual harassment by male overseers (like Lawrence's Paul Morel) who declare women responsible for disruptive desires, and in the common practices of wartime supervisors who scrutinized women workers with every intention of finding evidence of error made inevitable by sex. Attention to specifically sexual dynamics and differences among workers will always lead to the work itself being scrutinized unevenly, with a concomitantly unequal distribution of deprecation.

And since "friendship" and all comparable nouns carry so little credibility, clarity, and coherence as signifiers for specific relations or actions involving men and women—since they seem to be able to designate almost anything—they are obviously exceedingly easy to appropriate. The example of World War I should serve to illustrate how easily heterosexual "friendship" may be used to serve the purposes of propaganda. Indeed, our own recent experience of the way a shadowy ideal of male "friendship" and "bonding" has been appropriated to sell beer, cars, military service, and so on makes apparent how easily manipulable our names for affection now are.[3]

I have meant for the preceding pages to demonstrate that "friend-ship," when applied to heterosexual relationships in England during the first years when the workplace came to be represented as includ-ing both sexes, never held ground. In short: when, in mid-Victorian England, "friendship" stood for mere sexlessness, it lacked credi-bility; when, near to the turn of the century, it could indicate both sexless and sexual relations, it lacked clear connotation; when it apparently gained clarity in wartime, it served as a temporary and misleading rallying cry. Various commonplace ways of giving the idiom credibility and legitimacy have been shown to be ineffec-tive or deceptive: familial and spiritual idioms, even in the rare cases when they successfully defer sexual suspicion, merely trans-late friendship into conventional domestic or religious bonds; high-falutin claims for "perfect friendship" merely conceal oppression; silence and evasion concede the relationships to the usual assump-tions.

Not that the Victorian and Modernist representations described here should be summarily dismissed. Even if Mill's *Autobiogra-phy* and *Subjection of Women* concede much to the model of friendship-giving-way-to-marriage, they do not readily capitulate to the Comtian hyperbole they might well have, and they go a long way toward representing writerly collaboration *in action*. Even if *Women's Work and Women's Culture* sees "friendship" as a mere step toward the establishment of a universal Christian family, it still describes heterosexual cooperation in many practical forms, including (like Mill's *Autobiography*) its own collaborative compo-sition. If Browning's *The Ring and the Book* stands as a record of all the ways in which "friendship" could be displaced by other more authoritative categories, the urgency of Giuseppe and Pompilia's argument for "friendship" as the "simple thing it claims to be" re-mains striking for its insistence on unconventional affection in the face of overwhelming opposition. As for Eliot, her early fictions illustrate the ordinary conventions for representing heterosexual conventions as well as any set of mid-Victorian texts; yet *Daniel Deronda* stands as the most impressive novelistic defiance of those conventions, and the text that most visibly looks forward to new innovations.

And as for the male novelists at the turn of the century dis-cussed in Chapter 3, while they show "friendship" to be in an awful muddle, they yet go a long way toward illustrating its modern condition, and they suggest that new possibilities may be at least considered—if only speculatively and privately in *The Woman Who Did*, or in a brief scene of artistic collaboration in *Jude The Obscure*, or in a silent retreat in *The Awkward Age*. By the time of the Modernists, "friendship" may either be tentatively realized, as in Conrad, or emphatically rejected, as in Lawrence, but in either case the novels reflect a deep (and troubled) awareness that new heterosexual relations have emerged.

Yet in the war years "friendship" must be considered nothing less than a weapon, to be deployed mainly against England's military enemies but also, in effect, against Conscientious Objectors and, ultimately, against women workers sentenced to brief, scrutinized, controlled labor. In retrospect, it seems best to mark "friendship," during World War I and ever after, as a false category to be mainly avoided or entirely re-invented, whether during wartime experiments among Bloomsbury's noncombatants or in Woolf's various texts centering on heterosexual cooperation. As I have already said, wartime and postwar experience suggests that the word has become bankrupt; and there seems no better name.

The alternative toward which this study has been tending is to name not relationships but cooperative actions—to forgo "friendship" or any comparable noun in favor of some accounting of what working friends of opposite sexes *enact*. When considering that goal, one particular defect of "friendship" and words like it becomes clear: there is almost no action—no plot—inherent in the nouns "friendship" and "friend"; words like "love" and "lover" connote recognizable activities when applied to heterosexual relations, but "befriend" evokes nothing specific enough to be confidently visualized or represented. The terms of "friendship" withhold from the relationships they name any definitive practice.[4]

Of the many near-synonyms for "friendship," one requires particular mention. Nearly all the authors I have discussed in this study resort at times to a word that may be considered an exception to the tendencies I've been describing: "sympathy," for all its eighteenth- and nineteenth-century liabilities, is worthy of consideration if only for its syntactic function, as something men and women are said to "have" together or something one person can have for another. In its adjectival form, "sympathetic," it can be used to modify a relationship to suggest the priority of feeling, feeling that until the early twentieth century was not understood to be either condescending or pitying. The word seems mainly to have denoted mutual understanding—"feeling together," as its etymology suggests. Its emphasis on emotion to the exclusion of physical action saddles it, of course, with the same sorts of dangers as "friendship": one can imagine compromised idioms like "mere sympathy" or "only sympathetic" that would represent no progress. Still, Richard Sennett has lately made a strong argument for "sympathy," in the context of a larger argument on behalf of certain forms of visual perception,[5] and I think the word worthy of mention if only because it is the noun form for which the best case is made in the texts I have presented.

But the practice that seems to gain most authority from the Modernist writers discussed in the second half of this book would be either to define "friendship" according to the actions that give it meaning—"friendship" as "a way of looking on," in Conrad's case, for instance—or to displace the noun entirely in favor of a description of friends' actions. Woolf and others discussed here offer representations of heterosexual relationships in which, though sexuality is not absent, other dynamics seem more important, and in which the name of the relationship seems far less important than a sense of what the participants have concurrently accomplished as a result.

I would assign a great deal of value to the private notation, cited above, in which Woolf says she has realized, in the presence of her husband, that as a result of her relationship with Fry she may "see great novels" as he "sees great masterpieces." Woolf's casual rendering of that moment highlights her and Fry's cooperation and independence in concurrent imaginative actions—not what they or others called their relationship, and not the products of their practices. If Woolf's account does not seem especially self-conscious or thoughtful, that may be because her experience in a cooperative heterosexual community had accustomed her, by the early 1920's, to avoid the idiomatic habits she had seen seized upon during the war and had given her, in their place, a ready set of alternatives.

In any case, it is worth noting two key differences between Woolf's phrasing and the wartime claims to "friendship." First, the results of Woolf and Fry's cooperation are forward-looking, unrealized, and inexact. Rather than being committed from the outset to specific, preordered products, its benefits are to be determined in outcomes freely arrived at. "Action without the need of completion, action without domination and mastery: these," Sennett has declared, "are the ideals of a humane culture."[6] They are also the ideals to which cooperative action must be directed if its activities are going to be free and creative rather than predetermined. It is true that credible accounts of heterosexual interaction probably need to be defined according to some named end, in order to forestall or replace the assumption that their "natural" end is sex: the blank space that left open the consequence of Daniel Deronda and Gwendolen Harleth's relation must in some way be accounted for. But the example of the war shows that when cooperation's ends are entirely dictated, then the nature of the relationships stands to be preemptively constrained and falsified. While Conrad and Woolf, as Modernists, may rightly be associated with a high premium on the production and preservation of artistic *objects*, the example I would borrow from them here is their acknowledgment of the shifting and uncertain nature of such objects during acts of creation. Woolf's account of Fry's teaching is especially instructive, because she emphasizes throughout its incompleteness and indefiniteness. "On the edge of that gulf I stop," Woolf repeatedly quotes Fry as saying; she thus insists, with him, that the last determining word for the goals of cooperative endeavor must be the word never uttered.

The other key element of Woolf's account of her and Fry's concurrent vision is autonomy. At the most simple level, Woolf sees "novels" while Fry sees "masterpieces," just as in the painting *Interior*, Vanessa Bell paints while David Garnett writes. While relationships may find validation in cooperative creation of a single object, such combined effort carries idiomatic liabilities. As I described in relation to the climax of *Night and Day*, when the cooperation of pairs or groups is limited to one predefined end, then it seems that one party must dictate the primary and defining terms and the visions of the second and subsequent parties must fall into belated and inherently inferior positions: "Yes, the world looks that way to me too." Independence *and* mutuality are more probable when there is evidence of both parties' visionary contributions; when each party can envision or create individually, subordination no longer seems inevitable. The best lesson of *Night and Day*'s account of collaboration would be in the way the novel keeps Ralph and Katharine apart in the early stages of composition so that they may create independent works that, one hopes, may be revised, developed, and re-created, as a result of their interaction. "The aim of free seeing," Mary Ann Caws has said, "would be a flexibility of function able to accommodate images both ordinary and askew, straight or with perceptual shifts, and to translate them liberally into nourishment for new ways of seeing."[7] The distance Woolf insisted on between herself and her friends, as between Lily Briscoe and Mr. Ramsay, seems a necessary factor in the encouragement of unconstrained creativity. Again, the wartime example indicates how easily "friendship" can become an occasion for domination; such abuse may be prevented only if cooperative structures sanction autonomy among the participants.

While the model of independent acts of seeing served Woolf as an alternative to the most insidious implications of "friendship," vision carries its own idiomatic liabilities; and I must be cautious in recommending that phrases like "we are seeing together" or "they see together" displace phrases like "we are just friends" or "they are not screwing around"—no matter how much authority I would want to claim for the careful literary delineations of affection cited in this study. Richard Rorty, whom Caws invokes in making her case for "intersubjectivity" and "community of seeing," is in fact most emphatic in saying, "We must get the visual . . . metaphors out of our speech altogether." For Rorty, visual idioms are associated with a desire to indicate "accurate representation" and "objective truth," elements that foreclose rather than sustain genuine "conversation"; indicative of a stable center, correctly *seen* reality, they are obstacles rather than catalysts to creativity and freedom.[8] But, as I have been saying, the danger of truly enforced unanimity seems to reside more in nouns than verbs: a "community of seeing" may perhaps be assumed all to see the same thing, but a pair or group "seeing together" is involved in work-in-process, as illustrated in Woolf's account of the participation by Fry's audiences and friends. Woolf and Fry would surely have been sympathetic with Rorty's epistemological concerns: their "seeing" was conducted under the assumption that the objects of sight were in unyielding motion and that the act of seeing had itself to be the object of constant debate, but Woolf was also aware of passionless, consensual, domineering "looking" like that she attributed to the Bradshaws in *Mrs. Dallo-*

way. The difference between the "looking together" that "united" the guests at Mrs. Ramsay's dinner table and the Bradshaws' static looking is great, but the wording is similar and thus should encourage precision in our phrasing and intents.

Still, no matter how carefully invoked, the general category of "sight" may, like the class-specific emphasis of this study, serve to obscure a fundamental fact of working cooperation: that most people's work is hardly motivated by the visionary. Though I have suggested that "vision" is a useful category for collapsing distinctions between mental and manual labor and investing all cooperative work with a combination of the imaginative and the physical, the fact is that such a description offers little to workers who experience the intellectual deprivation and physical strain of much alienated labor. If "seeing together" is to serve as a model for viable or valuable idioms for heterosexual affection and interaction, it ought to be used with care and deliberateness: first, where possible, by those whose seeing and working is being described, and otherwise by those qualified to declare that in the activities described there indeed inheres at least the possibility of shared "seeing," of cooperative imaginative potential. In wartime, men and women's together building, digging, and readying the machines of battle became scenes of friendship. Characterizing them as scenes of "seeing together" does not mark an improvement unless the ennobling idioms of sight carry with them specific, testable connotations.

As I have no interest in restoring or inventing heterosexual "friendship," neither have I intended in this book to create a category such as "heterosexual friendship in literature." But in my emphasis on heterosexual dynamics that subordinate sexual desire, I have meant to suggest that there is a good deal more to be found in scenes of heterosexual interaction than literary criticism has yet marked. That scenes of working and imaginative cooperation between the sexes may be more interesting for what they stand to create than for the sexuality they repress, express, or sublimate is by no means a new understanding in literary study; but it is an understanding that has received less expression than its opposite.

My primary interest has been the consideration of particular idioms, and my chief literary-critical purpose here is to offer an example of a somewhat different relation to such idioms. That relation has two interconnected parts: first, careful attentiveness to historically specific idioms; and second, increased acceptance of professional responsibility for the fate of those idioms.

Throughout this study, I have argued for attention to the particular ways in which nineteenth- and early-twentieth-century texts use "friendship" and other words that adhere to it. As I noted in the Introduction, the very fact of attention to heterosexual friendship as a category represents something of a novelty in literary study; but reference to the category does not in and of itself imply close attention to the idioms with which literary texts have negotiated it. In my discussion of the central relationship in *Daniel Deronda*, I noted the way one of the critics most attentive to the importance of the novel's central heterosexual relationship referred to it as "friendship," despite the text's specifically rejecting that term when defining the affection involved. I have, I know, exaggerated the significance of that misnaming, and indeed my own claim that the same text is significant to the history of "idioms for heterosexual friendship" in effect duplicates the error, if error it is. But my point is precisely to call attention to the way the limitations of our own terminology can be productively highlighted by comparison with literature's precise and troubled handling of analogous vocabulary. In contrast, the common abandonment of earlier literature's generically and historically specific linguistic precision in favor of the wholesale application of contemporary critical terms must inevitably constitute a loss. It is hard to judge whether we lose most from ignoring the literature's linguistic complexity or from snubbing critics' discipline-specific training in close attention to literary language. The dire result, in either case, is the reification of scholarly language in its present, illusorily self-sufficient state, rather than the establishment of a dialectic between past and present idioms.

If critics have been slow to establish such a dialectic, then that may be because of a failure to recognize its potential consequences. The present study has made little argument that the texts it has studied exerted any particular "social force" on the idioms of their day, other than to suggest that these texts gave some indication of what it was and wasn't possible to say in the particular periods. But it has presumed throughout that the energetic deployment of certain idioms in writing and speech might now stand to open new possibilities.

I am not proposing that others should mimic, repeat, or otherwise participate in the distribution of the idioms highlighted here. The present study has isolated particular textual moments that invoke "friendship" and idioms analogous to it; I don't assume that every reader of this study would derive from those moments the conclusions I have about the relative uselessness of "friendship" or the desirability of idioms relating to vision and other forms of action. But the acknowledgment that past texts stand as a valuable resource for idiomatic conscientiousness, innovation, and dialectic should lead, I hope, to our shared acceptance of responsibility for what becomes of common idioms in present and future. Our creative re-invention of "friendship," and many other categories with comparably uncertain histories, might stimulate cooperative activities and representations we have yet to see, but can, as speakers and writers usefully contribute to, by the creation of a now unwritten glossary.

Appendix

Appendix
The Conrad / Poradowska Correspondence

The willingness to read courtship into the Conrad / Poradowska relationship even in the absence of any empirical evidence—indeed to derive courtship from a break in the historical record—seems to me a telling example of modern scholarship's having inherited Victorian assumptions about heterosexual relations. The chief support for the theory of suppressed correspondence between Conrad and Poradowska is a set of letters from Conrad's uncle Tadeusz Bobrowski warning Conrad against "flirting" with her. Jocelyn Baines notes, however,

There is no evidence to support Bobrowski's suspicion at this time [1891]. Certainly the letters which Conrad was writing to Marguerite Poradowska do not read like love letters. It seems incredible that he should have been having an affair or even flirting with a woman whom he was calling "Chère Tante" or "Très Chère Tante" and to whom he signed himself "Votre neveu très dévoué, J. Conrad"; he also used the "vous," not the "tu" form of address.

Yet Baines adds, "What happened later is another matter," and he eventually suggests that

it is just possible, and this is the merest conjecture, that he had wanted to marry Marguerite Poradowska and been refused. Throughout 1894 and for the first six months of 1895 Conrad had written to her approximately once a week; an affectionate letter dated 11 June 1895 has been preserved and then there is an abrupt gap until 1900, when there is a letter from Conrad to his "Très chère et bonne." Without question he wrote letters to Marguerite Poradowska during this period which she either destroyed or which have been withheld, and it is not unreasonable to presume that these letters contain matter which she thought was better not revealed.[1]

Zdzisław Najder's sense of the "discreet stage" of Conrad's relationship with Poradowska is similar to Baines's.[2] Even Frederick Karl, who notes that "Tadeusz's remarks were made . . . in ignorance of Conrad's interest in writing and in Marguerite as an established writer," eventually speculates about "an erotic attachment," wondering not whether Conrad was refused but whether he contemplated marriage and withdrew.[3] Bernard Meyer doubts the possibility of Conrad's having proposed chiefly because he believes Conrad to have been too intimidated by Poradowska's maternal power.[4]

The preface to *Letters of Joseph Conrad to Marguerite Poradowska, 1890–1920* shows the following pattern to the number of letters from Conrad to Poradowska in the surviving correspondence:[5]

1890	10	*1895*	11	*1908*	5
1891	24	*1900*	4	*1910*	1
1892	6	*1904*	1	*1912*	1
1893	9	*1906*	2	*1913*	2
1894	32	*1907*	1	*1920*	1

It seems to me this adapted chart can be read as indicating a general diminishing of the correspondence record after 1895 just as credibly as a pronounced break between 1895 and 1900. In the letters after the turn of the century there are references to other letters now lost, but also clear evidence of a falling off in the frequency of correspondence (compared to that of the early 1890's), such that Conrad writes to Poradowska in early 1904 reviewing the entire preceding year, and in January 1908 reviewing the preceding few months: "I bitterly regret my negligence in writing to you," he says.[6] Meyer guesses that with "the prospect of a new career and of a new and distinguishable 'self' " at this time Conrad "could afford to relinquish his child-like grasp on his 'Aunt.' . . ."[7] A review of Conrad's general correspondence during this period suggests similar "long silences" between letters to his Polish cousins, the Zagorskas, and others.[8]

Reference Matter

Notes

Complete bibliographic information for all sources not cited in full in the Notes is given in the Selected References.

Introduction

1. Karen Peterson, "Buddy System Is a Battle for the Sexes," *USA Today*, July 17, 1989, 1D; Bruce Weber, "Can Men and Women Be Friends?" *New York Times*, July 9, 1989, 2: 11. Once the film became well-known, the advertising strategy shifted to presenting the protagonists as (according to a promotional poster) "longtime friends who decide to risk it all by taking a chance on romance."

2. *When Harry Met Sally . . .* , Castle Rock Entertainment, 1989.

3. Dinah Mulock Craik, *A Woman's Thoughts About Women, By the Author of 'John Halifax, Gentleman' &c, &c.*, 177.

4. Maxine Berg's summary account of scholarship's "prevailing assumption" that this separation occurred "at some point during industrialisation" is included in her "Women's Work, Mechanisation, and the Early Phases of Industrialisation in England," in Patrick Joyce, ed., *The Historical Meanings of Work*, esp. 64–66. Berg cautions that it is hard to designate the precise moment of this division (and equally hard, as her essay emphasizes, to measure its consequences for women workers), but there is much evidence that tensions relating to perceptions of this division were pervasive in Victorian and Modern England.

5. See the respective sections in Walter Houghton, *The Victorian Frame of Mind, 1830–1870*.

6. See Richard Altick, *The English Common Reader: A Social History of the Mass Reading Public, 1800–1900*.

7. Chapter 1 presents 1869 as a kind of climax to the Victorian discourse of sexuality, the parameters of which have been described by Steven Marcus, *The Other Victorians: A Study of Sexuality and Pornography in Mid-Nineteenth Century England* (New York: Basic Books, 1966); Jeffrey Weeks, *Sex, Politics, and Society: The Regulation of Sex Since 1800* (1980); Judith Walkowitz, *Prostitution and Victorian Society: Women, Class, and*

the State (1980); Peter Gay, *The Bourgeois Experience: Victoria to Freud,* vol. 1: *The Education of the Senses* (1984). Foucault echoes Marcus's title in calling the first chapter in *The History of Sexuality,* vol. 1: *An Introduction,* "We 'Other Victorians.' "

Weeks raises the important question of what distinguishes Victorian discourse on sex "from what went before" (23); one may also ask what distinguishes English accounts of heterosexuality from contemporaneous U.S. ones. Studies that share some of the interest of this one (for instance Carroll Smith-Rosenberg's and Joseph Allen Boone's, cited below) have merged American and English accounts of "Victorian" discourse, but English texts that describe "friendship" often make persistent apology for their recourse to U.S. examples or treat those U.S. examples as decidedly alien. See for instance Josephine Butler's 1869 essay collection *Women's Work and Women's Culture* (which I discuss in detail in Chapter 2), xlvi, 57, etc., and the epigraph to Joseph Conrad's *Under Western Eyes* (discussed in Chapter 4). Martha Vicinus has noted that the "importance of friendships across gender lines" became an increasingly significant consideration as the century went on (*Independent Women: Work and Community for Single Women, 1850–1920,* 290).

8. Robert Gray, "The Languages of Factory Reform in Britain, *c* 1830–1860," in Joyce, ed., *The Historical Meanings of Work,* 143.

9. See Regenia Gagnier, *Subjectivities: A History of Self-Representation in Britain, 1832–1920,* 61, for the contrast between "middle-class women [who] had professional mediators to speak about, and care for, their bodies, as well as access to an expanding cultural industry about sexuality" and the enforced deprivations of working women. Continued "sexual ignorance" among the English "urban poor" through the 1920's and 1930's is described by Carl Chinn, *They Worked All Their Lives: Women of the Urban Poor in England, 1880–1939* (Manchester, Eng.: Manchester University Press, 1988), 143–45.

10. Lee Patterson, *Negotiating the Past: The Historical Understanding of Medieval Literature* (Madison: University of Wisconsin Press, 1987), 142. Patterson describes how "sanctioned by impeccable authority, the extraordinary language of friendship makes its way into medieval literary culture and becomes (the last thing the authorities could have wanted) lexically indistinguishable from the language of *fine amor*" (135).

11. Osborne continues: "besides it is not to be taught or learned; it must come naturally to those that have it before they can know it" (G. C. Moore Smith, ed., *The Letters of Dorothy Osborne to William Temple* [Oxford: Clarendon Press, 1928], 104). See also the further discussion of such difficulties at 66. James Fitzmaurice and Martine Rey consider "the special meanings" of "friendship" in letters "written by women as women to men"

in "Letters by Women in England, The French Romance, and Dorothy Osborne," in Jean Brink, Allison Coudert, and Maryanne Horowitz, eds., *The Politics of Gender in Early Modern Europe* (Tempe, Ariz.: Sixteenth Century Journal, 1989), 150.

12. John Gregory, *A Father's Legacy to His Daughters* (1774), excerpted in Vivien Jones, ed., *Women in the Eighteenth Century: Constructions of Feminity* (London: Routledge, 1990), 49; Mary Wollstonecraft Godwin, "Love," in her *Thoughts on the Education of Daughters with Reflections on Female Conduct in the More Important Duties of Life* (1787: reprint Clifton, N.J.: Augustus M. Kelley, 1972), 88–89. Catherine Macaulay Graham's *Letters on Education* (1790) argued in favor of the coeducation of children, stating, "By the uninterrupted intercourse which you will thus establish, both sexes will find that friendship may be enjoyed between them without passion" (excerpted by Jones, 114).

13. Robert Browning, "The Other Half-Rome," *The Ring and the Book*, lines 1106–8.

14. Eve Kosofsky Sedgwick, *Between Men: English Literature and Male Homosocial Desire*, 1. Early in *Epistemology of the Closet*, Sedgwick describes a kind of climax in the relationship of a gay man and a woman, "best friends," reached when "it seemed to . . . these friends that permission had been given to the woman to refer to the man, in their conversation together, as a gay man" (3–4).

15. There is almost no discussion of cross-gender friendship in Ronald Sharp's *Friendship and Literature: Spirit and Form* (Durham, N.C.: Duke University Press, 1986). Literary-critical analyses of women's friendships include Janet Todd, *Women's Friendship in Literature* (New York: Columbia University Press, 1980) on eighteenth century fiction, and Tess Cosslett, *Woman to Woman: Female Friendship in Victorian Fiction* (Brighton, Sussex: Harvester, 1988). For the history of single-sex friendships in the Victorian period, see Mark Girouard, *The Return to Camelot: Chivalry and the English Gentleman*, 216–18; Carroll Smith-Rosenberg, *Disorderly Conduct: Visions of Gender in Victorian America*, 39; and Lillian Faderman, *Surpassing the Love of Men: Romantic Friendship and Love Between Women from the Renaissance to the Present*, 159ff. Friendship between men and women has received most consideration from popular social psychologists like Letty Cotton Pogrebin, *Among Friends: Who We Like, Why We Like Them, and What We Do About It* (New York: McGraw-Hill, 1987), and Lillian Rubin, *Just Friends: The Role of Friendship in Our Lives*. The seminal sociological study is Alan Booth and Elaine Hess, "Cross-Sex Friendship." See also Jan Yager, *Friendship: A Selected Annotated Bibliography* (New York: Garland, 1984). The one form of cross-sex friendship that has received particular, isolated attention is that between gay men and

heterosexual women, a construct not available to mainstream discourse until fairly recently; see, for instance, John Williams Malone, *Straight Woman/Gay Man: A Special Relationship* (New York: Dial, 1980). Jacques Derrida's "The Politics of Friendship" considers "the great canonical meditations on friendship" by Cicero, Montaigne, and Blanchot (a list that might also include Bacon). Derrida points to "what one could, as a matter of convenience, call the *history of friendship*." Yet, he adds parenthetically at 642, "a certain friendship could make the most traditional concept of historicity quake." For this reference I am grateful to Cathy Caruth.

16. Frances Bartkowski, "Epistemic Drift in Foucault," in Irene Diamond and Lee Quinby, eds., *Feminism and Foucault: Reflections on Resistance*, 48, 56. Rachel Blau DuPlessis argues that "the point" at which the "basic formations" of relations of "women and men" meet is "the heterosexual couple" (*Writing Beyond the Ending: Narrative Strategies of Twentieth-Century Women Writers*, 1). Sedgwick notes that the word "heterosexual" became popular later than "homosexual" (*Epistemology of the Closet*, 2).

17. Foucault, *The History of Sexuality*, 1: 11; Smith-Rosenberg, *Disorderly Conduct*, 35. For other studies of women's friendships see note 15, above.

18. Foucault, "Power and Strategies" (interview, in *Power/Knowledge*), 142, and *Discipline and Punish: The Birth of the Prison*, 194. Foucault notes in the *Power/Knowledge* interview that "resistances . . . are all the more real and effective because they are formed right at the point where relations of power are exercised" (142). "Discourse" in this study is used in Foucault's sense of an empowered network of expressive acts the effects of which are at most remotely connected to the intentions of any individual; idiom serves as an index to the way singular interventions may disrupt the power of discourse. For a helpful summary account of the way Foucault's "notion that society is a fragmented multiplicity of discourses/practices" serves as "an excellent corrective to many of the impasses of social theory" but fails to "address the issue of the individual," see Mark Poster, *Critical Theory and Poststructuralism: In Search of a Context* (Ithaca, N.Y.: Cornell University Press, 1989), 141. Raymond Williams's account of "hegemony" retains, perhaps, a stronger sense of resistance than does Foucault's account of "power": "A lived hegemony is always a process. It is not, except analytically, a system or structure. . . . The reality of any hegemony . . . is never either total or exclusive. At any time, forms of alternative or directly oppositional politics and culture exist as significant elements in the society. We shall need to explore their conditions and their limits, but their active presence is decisive, not only because they have to be included in any historical (as distinct from epochal) analysis, but as forms which

have had significant effect on the hegemonic process itself. That is to say, alternative political and cultural emphases, and the many forms of opposition and struggle, are important not only in themselves but as indicative features of what the hegemonic process has in practice had to work to control" (*Marxism and Literature* [New York: Oxford University Press, 1977], 112–13).

19. Jana Sawicki, "Feminism and the Power of Foucaldian Discourse," 161, and "Identity Politics and Sexual Freedom" (in Diamond and Quinby, *Feminism and Foucault*), 183.

20. Diamond and Quinby, Introduction, *Feminism and Foucault*, ix.

21. Bruce Boone, "Gay Language as Political Praxis: The Poetry of Frank O'Hara," *Social Text* 1 (1979): 65.

22. Alice Rossi, Introduction, *Essays on Sex Equality: John Stuart Mill and Harriet Taylor Mill*, 10.

23. Mrs. [Ethel] Alec-Tweedie, *Women and Soldiers*, 23.

24. *The Woman Worker*, April 1918, 9.

25. Joseph Conrad, *Under Western Eyes*, 134.

26. Alan Friedman is explicit on this point in *The Turn of the Novel*, 18; so is Barbara Herrnstein Smith when she notes that the novel conventionally ends "at a point when either nothing could follow (as when the hero dies) or everything that could follow is predictable (as when the hero and heroine get married)" (*Poetic Closure: A Study of How Poems End*, 35). "Once upon a time," begins Rachel Blau DuPlessis, "the end, the rightful end, of women in novels was social—successful courtship, marriage—or judgmental of her sexual and social failure—death" (*Writing Beyond the Ending*, 1). Others include Frank Kermode, *The Sense of an Ending*; D. A. Miller, *Narrative and Its Discontents: A Study of Novelistic Closure*; and Marianna Torgovnick, *Closure in the Novel*.

27. Alexander Welsh, "Opening and Closing *Les Misérables*," 22; the *New York Times Magazine*'s summary of the 1990 Modern Language Association Convention listed "closure" as one of those topics that had gone "out" (Anne Mathews, " 'Deciphering Victorian Underwear' and Other Seminars," *New York Times Magazine*, Feb. 10, 1991, 57).

28. Andrew Blake's *Reading Victorian Fiction: The Cultural Context and Ideological Content of the Nineteenth-Century Novel* is one of the most thoughtful analyses of the broader topic of "literature" as "an active constituent of society" (13). Though the archive necessary for empirical study of that process is still in the early stages of being assembled, much has been contributed by descendants of Richard Altick's *The English Common Reader*, especially J. A. Sutherland's *Victorian Novelists and Publishers*, and his *The Stanford Companion to Victorian Fiction* (Stanford, Calif.: Stanford University Press, 1989). The more recent examination of the way

Victorian texts are shaped by the mechanisms of contemporary reproduction has a striking example in Peter Widdowson's *Hardy in History: A Study in Literary Sociology.* See also Jonathan Rose, *The Edwardian Temperament, 1895–1913.* Perhaps the most impressive rendering of the way Victorian novels exerted their influence remains Gillian Beer's *Darwin's Plots: Evolutionary Narrative in Darwin, George Eliot, and Nineteenth-Century Fiction.*

29. Joseph Allen Boone, *Tradition Counter Tradition: Love and the Form of Fiction* 252, 151. Boone explains and acknowledges his dualistic approach at 22; and his search for "a new story" does take him beyond anticlosure to alternative narrative forms, especially that of a "sustaining fiction of female community" (330).

30. Frank Kermode, *The Art of Telling: Essays on Fiction,* 137–38. For this reference, and for suggesting "a dialectical relation between 'the moment' of idiom and narrative dynamics," I am grateful to Mark Wollaeger. D. A. Miller's *The Novel and the Police* ends by describing the novel as presenting the "pattern in which the subject constitutes himself against 'discipline'" as an "open secret" (220).

31. Peter Brooks, *Reading for the Plot: Design and Intention in Narrative.* Brooks considers Russian Formalist "morphology" at 14–15. For a particularly good instance of how the study of narrative endedness may lead to an illuminating account of a particular phrase, see Brooks on the way Kurtz's last words in Conrad's *Heart of Darkness* "answer so poorly to all of Marlow's insistence on summing-up as a moment of final articulation . . ." (249).

32. Sociohistorical studies of the novel have often demonstrated such emphasis; see for instance K. C. Phillipps, *Language and Class in Victorian England* and Ralph Elliott, *Thomas Hardy's English.* Robert Caserio's argument for the value of narrative concludes by saying that "without the narrative representation of action life cannot be apprehended or cared for as continuous, purposeful, or creative . . . and values that measure and determine conduct cannot be fruitfully discriminated or even distinguished" (*Plot, Story, and the Novel: From Dickens and Poe to the Modern Period* [Princeton, N.J.: Princeton University Press, 1979]).

33. Such a way of reading is commonplace in relation to texts considered Postmodern. When approaching *Finnegans Wake,* says John Bishop, "the first preconception to abandon wholesale is that it ought to read anything at all like narrative or make sense as a continuous linear whole. . . . One can, given these terms, start [reading it] . . . anywhere" (*Joyce's Book of the Dark: "Finnegans Wake"* [Madison: University of Wisconsin Press, 1986], 27).

34. Dominick LaCapra, *History, Politics, and the Novel* (Ithaca, N.Y.: Cornell University Press, 1987), 3.

Chapter One

1. For men's friendship, see Mark Girouard, *The Return to Camelot: Chivalry and the English Gentleman*, 216–18. Though some considered women incapable of friendship and others considered women's friendships socially damaging, Victorian romanticization of women's friendships was widespread: see Smith-Rosenberg, *Disorderly Conduct*, 39; and Faderman, *Surpassing the Love of Men*, 159ff. For the "popular debate over female friendships and communities," see Pauline Nestor, *Female Friendships and Communities: Charlotte Brontë, George Eliot, Elizabeth Gaskell* (Oxford: Clarendon Press, 1985), 7–27; some historical factors are summarized by Tess Cosslett, *Woman to Woman, Female Friendship in Victorian Fiction* (Brighton, Sussex: Harvester, 1988), 5–8.

2. Smith and Jameson are quoted by William Rounseville Alger in *The Friendships of Women*, 131. Alger's chapter on "Platonic Love, or, The Marriage of Souls" (114–256) is the most extensive Victorian compendium of observations about heterosexual friendship; he also has chapters on marital relations and father / daughter relations. Smith-Rosenberg calls Alger's "the most famous example of romanticization of women's love for one another," and says the book "circulated widely among educated women and feminists of the time" (*Disorderly Conduct*, 39).

3. Craik, *A Woman's Thoughts About Women*, 175, 177.

4. Craik, 176. Charles Darwin's distinction between "natural selection" and "sexual selection" was unusual in drawing a precise distinction between "natural" and "sexual" dynamics, but it also served to show their close relation. The distinction is clarified in the concluding chapter of *The Descent of Man* (in Philip Appleman, ed. *Darwin*, 204).

5. Foucault, *History of Sexuality*, 1: 35.

6. The quoted warnings are from, respectively, Weeks, *Sex, Politics, and Society*, 23, and James Kincaid, "What the Victorians Knew About Sex," 91–100.

7. Judith Walkowitz, *Prostitution and Victorian Society: Women, Class, and the State*, 86–89; Weeks, *Sex, Politics, and Society*, 20.

8. Weeks's discussion of Victorian discourse on sex (19–21) refers to Laurence Stone's identification of the 1860's as a key transitional moment. Eric Trudgill, lacking Weeks's caution, calls the 1860's "a renaissance of blatant amorality" (*Madonnas and Magdalens, The Origins and Development of Victorian Sexual Attitudes* [New York: Holmes and Meier, 1976], 228). For Peter Gay's broader claim that "in the nineteenth century . . . inti-

mations of the body . . . were everywhere," see *The Bourgeois Experience*, 1: 329. Stephen Heath describes the origin of "sexuality" and other related terms in the nineteenth century, in *The Sexual Fix* (New York: Schocken Books, 1984), 8–16.

9. Eliza Lynn Linton, "Flirting," *The Saturday Review*, June 26, 1869, 837–38, reprinted in Linton, *The Girl of the Period and Other Social Essays* (London: Richard Bentley & Son, 1883), 1: 289, 283, 285. In a subsequent essay on "Old Friends," Linton argued, "In fact, this whole question of friendship wants revision" (2: 308).

10. Godwin, "Love," in *Thoughts on the Education of Daughters*, 88. George Henry Lewes, *Biographical History of Philosophy*, 5th ed. (London, 1880; orig. pub. 1845–46), vol. 1, 268. Godwin declared herself "convinced" of the existence of "friendship between persons of different sexes," but warned that "we cannot extirpate our passions, nor is it necessary that we should, though it may be wise sometimes not to stray too near a precipice, lest we fall over before we are aware. We cannot avoid much vexation and sorrow, if we are ever so prudent . . ." (88–89).

11. See Arnold Cooley, *Dictionary of the English Language* (London and Edinburgh: W. and R. Chambers, 1861), which defines "Platonic" as "pure, spiritual, unmixed with carnal thoughts or desires (as love)" or Joseph Emerson Wincester's *Definitions of the English Language* (Philadelphia: J. B. Lippincott, 1859), which gives "a love between the sexes wholly spiritual or unmixed with carnal desires." For "upper class" prohibitions against use of the (obviously unlikely) word "fellow" for heterosexual relations and for the use of familial terms like "sister" and "aunt" in forms of address (e.g., "Sister Deane" or "dear Aunt"), see K. C. Phillipps, *Language and Class in Victorian England*, 46, 163; Phillipps characterizes the Victorian use of these phrases as "provincial" rather than "urban." George Eliot's frequent recourse to these terms will be considered in Chapter 2.

12. Bulwer Lytton quoted in Alger, *Friendships of Women*, 130. Bulwer Lytton also praises "pure friendships—those in which there is no admixture of the passion of love, except in the married state." Ralph Elliott notes the common nineteenth-century use of "comradeship" to describe the basis of a happy marriage in *Hardy's English*, 319–20. By the end of the century, the use of "friend" to describe a lover or paramour of the opposite sex would become commonplace; see Chapter 3.

13. Beatrice Webb, *My Apprenticeship* (London: Longmans, Green and Co., 1926), 458.

14. The *OED*'s only citation for "companionate" was from 1657. (The present century's second edition of the *OED* adds the phrase "companionate marriage," and cites a series of examples from an eight-year period beginning in 1924.) The *OED*'s definitions for "companion" all pointed

to specifically male roles, mentioning "a fellow" or "a fellow-soldier" as analogous terms, the one exception being its use to refer to "some specific or legal relation," in which case it was "often, like 'partner' or 'consort,' applied to a wife"—though that use was labeled "obsolete." But see Lawrence Stone, *The Family, Sex, and Marriage*, 363, for Francis Place's description of his deceased wife as his "friend" and "companion." J. S. Mill would use the same pair of terms to describe the good intentions of Harriet Taylor's husband; see F. A. Hayek, *John Stuart Mill and Harriet Taylor: Their Correspondence and Subsequent Marriage*, 55. See also John Boyd-Kinnear, "The Social Position of Women in the Present Age," in Josephine Butler, ed., *Women's Work and Women's Culture*. A. James Hammerton, in "Victorian Marriage and the Law of Matrimonial Cruelty," *Victorian Studies*, Winter 1990, 269–92, qualifies some of the claims made by Stone in pp. 325–404 of *Family, Sex, and Marriage*.

15. See Martha Vicinus, *Independent Women: Work and Community for Single Women 1850–1920*, who mentions the "importance of friendships across gender lines" at 290; Carol Bauer and Lawrence Ritt, eds., *Free and Ennobled: Source Readings in the Development of Victorian Feminism* (Oxford: Pergamon Press, 1989), 136–65, 276–94; Patricia Hollis, *Women in Public: The Women's Movement 1850–1900*, 45–132; and Janet Horowitz Murray, *Strong-Minded Women and Other Lost Voices from Nineteenth-Century England* (New York: Pantheon Books, 1982), 257–384.

16. Mrs. Alexander Ireland, ed., *Selections of Letters from Miss Jewsbury to Jane Welsh Carlyle* (London: Longmans, Green, 1892), 347–48. Vicinus's selective quotation of this passage (*Independent Women*, 9) excludes the references to friendship with men, thus making the phrase "friends and companions" seem to refer exclusively to friendship between women.

17. For George Eliot's reliance on these conventions in *The Mill on the Floss*, see Chapter 2; see also D. H. Lawrence's comment on Eliot, cited in note 34 to Chapter 4. Amid all her skepticism about ruses that could be perpetrated upon the young Girl of the Period, Linton suspected no sexual deceit (only inconvenient presumptuousness) among "Old Friends," an idiom generally accepted when applied to the old but looked upon skeptically when applied to the young. See also Craik's particular concern about friendship "between a young man and a young woman."

18. See Hayek, *John Stuart Mill and Harriet Taylor*, 80.

19. Hayek, 85.

20. Indeed, John Taylor's death in 1849 did not seem to his wife or to Mill a happy convenience, but rather, in Harriet Taylor's words, a "sad sad tragedy" (Hayek, 161).

21. Mill, "Nature," *Three Essays on Religion*, 402. For Mill's work on "the Nature" in 1854, see *The Later Letters of John Stuart Mill 1849–1873*, 149.

22. Hayek, *John Stuart Mill and Harriet Taylor*, 92.

23. The most explicit rendering of the Mill/Taylor relationship as love story appears in the title of Josephine Kamm's *John Stuart Mill in Love*—though that title belies the seriousness and excellence of the book's research. Phyllis Rose, who studies the Mills' relationship in the context of Victorian "marriages," is, admirably, the commentator perhaps most honest about her own readerly motives: "I would like to think it was lust fueling Mill's hyperbolic attachment" (*Parallel Lives: Five Victorian Marriages*, 124). For Rose's characterization of the *Autobiography*, see the quotation at note 45 to this chapter.

24. For the attribution of statements to a discursive position, available textually and conditioned by reception and history rather than intention, see Michel Foucault, *The Archaeology of Knowledge*, 94–95, 200.

25. Hayek, *John Stuart Mill and Harriet Taylor*, 190.

26. Hayek, 194. Michael St. John Packe emphasizes the privacy of the Mills' lifestyle and their "more than normal dread of being talked about" (*The Life of John Stuart Mill* [London: Secker and Warburg, 1954], 321).

27. Hayek, *John Stuart Mill and Harriet Taylor*, 197.

28. Hayek, 196.

29. Jack Stillinger, ed., *The Early Draft of John Stuart Mill's Autobiography*, 171 and note, 191. The excised portion appears at 237 of the *Autobiography*, as printed in volume 1 of *The Collected Works of John Stuart Mill*, cited hereafter as *Autobiography*. For the early draft, I will continue to cite Stillinger's separate publication, which indicates Harriet Mill's emendations more clearly than does the facing-page version presented in the *Autobiography*.

30. Mill, *Autobiography*, 193.

31. Hayek, *John Stuart Mill and Harriet Taylor*, 81, 86, 80.

32. "Intimate" retains its euphemistic function and thus its uncertain role as a modifier for "friendship," but current references to "intimate friendship" abound. Janice Carlisle, for instance, refers to J. S. Mill's "choice of Harriet Taylor, first as his intimate friend and later as his wife" ("J. S. Mill's *Autobiography*: The Life of a 'Bookish Man,'" 141). That current commentary has inherited the Mills' problem (i.e., the absence of adequate English terms for their relationship) is illustrated in Alice Rossi's recourse to another language, to the effect that "Harriet made an apt characterization when she told Gumperz that from 1831 on, her relationship both to her husband John Taylor and to John Mill was that

of 'Seelenfreundin'"—soul friend ("Introduction," 10). She cites Hayek, *John Stuart Mill and Harriet Taylor*, 56, 291, as her source for the word.

33. *Autobiography*, 197, 251, 199.

34. Mill, *Later Letters*, 149.

35. Auguste Comte, *System of Positive Polity*, 1: 189. Anna Jameson quoted this passage in her commonplace book before going on, in the statement I quoted in the beginning of this chapter, to confirm its regrettable inapplicability to English convention (*A Commonplace Book of Thoughts, Memories, and Fancies* [London: Longman, Brown, Green, and Longmans, 1854], 253).

36. Stanislav Andreski, "Introduction," *The Essential Comte*, trans. Margaret Clarke (London: Croom Helm, 1974), 8; Comte, *System*, 1: xliv, 103, 100–101.

37. Mill, *August Comte and Positivism*, in *Three Essays on Religion*, 343. The *Autobiography* saw the "spiritual and temporal despotism" of Comte's *System* as comparable to elements in the work of Ignatius Loyola (221).

38. "I bought a cottage as close as possible to the place where she is buried, and there her daughter (my fellow-sufferer and now my chief comfort) and I live constantly during a great portion of the year. My objects in life are solely those which were hers; my pursuits and occupations those in which she shared, or sympathized, and which are indissolubly associated with her. Her memory is to me a religion, and her approbation the standard by which, summing up as it does all worthiness, I endeavor to regulate my life" (*Autobiography*, 251).

39. *Autobiography*, 249; Stillinger, ed., *Early Draft*, 196; *Autobiography*, 251.

40. In private correspondence, J. S. Mill did address Harriet as "my blessed angel"; see *Later Letters*, 287. Susan Groag Bell mentions Comte while arguing that "Mill's extravagances on Harriet's behalf are of a piece with other romantic descriptions of womanhood"; "The Feminization of John Stuart Mill," 87.

41. See Comte, *System*, 1: xxvi. Comte's assertion that women's "mission" can be "summed up in one word, Love" (*System*, 1: 204) echoes Sara Ellis's 1842 exhortation to *The Daughters of England*: "Love is woman's all—her wealth, her power, her very being" (in Patricia Hollis, ed., *Women in Public, 1850–1900: Documents of the Victorian Women's Movement*, 15). In 1854, the same year that saw the last volume of Comte's *System*, Coventry Patmore published the first volume of his *The Angel in the House*, the lengthy poem that epitomized Victorian England's elevation of woman-worship.

42. Frances Power Cobbe, "The Final Cause of Woman," in Josephine Butler, ed., *Women's Work and Women's Culture*, 8 (discussed at length below); Mill, *Auguste Comte and Positivism*, 310; H. A. Page, "The Old Morality and the New," *Contemporary Review* 9 (1868): 64; Stillinger, ed., *Early Draft*, 197–98. For a typical mention of the assumption that "there can be no entire friendship where there is no real equality" see Caroline Norton, *A Letter to the Queen on Lord Chancellor Cranworth's Marriage and Divorce Bill* (1855), in *Selected Writings of Caroline Norton* (Delmar, N.Y.: Scholars Facsimile Reprints, 1978), 92.

43. Mill, *Autobiography*, 249, 257–59. Regenia Gagnier argues that Mill's having "made" Harriet Taylor Mill "his collaborator" in the *Autobiography* shows the "consistency of Mill's private desire and political project" (*Subjectivities*, 256). Avrom Fleishman's declaration that "Harriet Taylor can symbolize Mill's higher self or ego ideal because she is herself a process" oddly combines Comtian and progressive vocabularies (*Figures of Autobiography: The Language of Self-Writing in Victorian and Modern England* [Berkeley: University of California Press, 1983], 152).

44. In considering Mill's "amateurism," Janice Carlisle observes: "Precisely by defining himself as a writer and theorist, he set for himself a life's work in which Harriet Taylor could participate, one that, indeed, by mid-century her gender had come to define" ("Mill's *Autobiography*," 141). Carlisle proceeds in a way that partly anticipates the next stage of the present argument; by linking a reference in Mill's *Logic* to "the lot of the philosopher presumed to have no capacity for business" to the limitations in the *Autobiography*'s depiction of Harriet, Carlisle notes the limits of writing as a "powerless," amateur activity (141–42), as opposed to the more powerful work of the professions. She goes on to suggest that these gestures would have been unnecessary had Mill "achieved his earlier ambitions for active political service." But in saying that Mill in the *Autobiography* "continually attributed the motive force of his writings to Harriet Taylor—she proposed, he disposed," and in suggesting that Mill contributes to a model whereby "women observe, men participate," Carlisle slights the *Autobiography*'s presentation of active physical cooperation, however limited, and the degree to which the *Autobiography* is itself the material result of such cooperation. Chapter 1 of Cathy Shuman's "Different for Girls: Narrative Disruption as Social Containment in Three Victorian Texts" (Ph.D. diss., Yale University, in progress) provides an illuminating account of the use, by both Mill's *On the Subjection of Women* and John Ruskin's *Sesame and Lilies*, "of problematically obsolete class categories to describe women's position."

45. Stillinger, ed., *Early Draft*, 197; Rose, *Parallel Lives*, 132.

46. Mill, *The Subjection of Women*, 270, 330, 331. Subsequent citations appear in the text.

47. Gagnier, *Subjectivities*, 256. On various occasions in the *Subjection*, Mill looks beyond marriage to the conditions of widowed or unmarried women; see, e.g., 338.

48. The phrase describing the focus of *Women's Work and Women's Culture* appears in E. Moberly Bell, *Josephine Butler: Flame of Fire* (London: Constable, 1962), 64. Citations from *Women's Work and Women's Culture* appear in the text, giving essay author and page number for the following essays: Josephine Butler, "Introduction"; Jessie Boucheret, "How to Provide for Superfluous Women"; John Boyd-Kinnear, "The Social Position of Women in the Present Age"; Sophia Jex-Blake, "Medicine as a Profession for Women"; Julia Wedgwood, "Female Suffrage, Considered Chiefly with Regard to Its Indirect Results"; Elizabeth Wolstenholme, "The Education of Girls, Its Present and Its Future." Butler established early in her introduction to the volume (ii) that nearly all the essays in the book had been written before the publication of Mill's *Subjection*.

49. For the successive Married Women's Property Acts of 1870 and 1882, see Lee Holcombe, *Wives and Property: Married Women's Property Law in Nineteenth Century England*, 166–252.

50. Rachel Blau DuPlessis describes this other narrative convention, that of "quest," which serves to sublimate "the desire for achievement into a future generation"; see chapter 1 of *Writing Beyond the Ending*.

51. The dual appeal to religious authority and practical duty could not have been better designed to appeal to Victorian moral convention (especially when grounded within familial idioms, as described below): "Except for 'God,' the most popular word in the Victorian vocabulary must have been 'work,' " says Walter Houghton, at the beginning of his discussion of Victorian attention to that latter term (*The Victorian Frame of Mind*, 242).

52. Boyd-Kinnear's chosen idioms for describing improved relations within marriage centered on "companionship": he suggested, for instance, that men whose first priority in looking for wives was the search for "agreeable companions" preferred educated women (362). That argument would shortly be echoed by Darwin who would describe "Man" as "impelled by nearly the same motives as the lower animals, when they are left to their own free choice, though he is in so far superior to them that he highly values mental charms as virtues" (Appleman, ed., *Darwin*, 207).

53. See E. M. Bell, *Josephine Butler*, 103 (note 48, above).

54. A decade earlier, Anna Jameson had proposed an ideal "communion of labor" as the guiding principle for political change leading to expanded employment for women; see *The Communion of Labor* (Boston: Ticknor

and Fields, 1857), 30. One idiomatic source for combining religious priorities with those of "friendship" could be found in language associated with the Quakers; Butler's introduction to *Women's Work and Women's Culture* made one extended reference to the Quaker "Society of Friends" (xiv–xlvii).

55. Josephine Butler, *Personal Reminiscences of a Great Crusade* (London: H. Marshall & Son, 1896), 405.

56. *Times*, June 22, 1870, 6, and paraphrased by Holcombe, *Wives and Property*, 174.

57. These were the same losses faced by a man whose wife committed adultery; they were the reasons why a wife's adultery was legally considered much more damaging to a husband than vice versa. See for example David Morris, *The End of Marriage* (London: Cassell, 1971), 26.

58. Butler (xxv) echoes, in order to reject, this typical description of "the most fervent advocates of woman's cause."

59. James Fitzjames Stephen, *Liberty, Equality, and Fraternity* (London: Smith, Elder & Co., 1874, orig. pub. 1873), 222; cited in Kamm, *John Stuart Mill in Love*, 199.

60. So "the accusers shriek" according to "The Other Half-Rome" (*The Ring and the Book*, ll. 1106–8). Subsequent citations appear in the text by book and line number(s). (Browning's poem is in twelve books, most entitled with the names of their principal speakers.)

61. Richard Altick and James F. Loucks's note on nineteenth-century reiterations of papal infallibility is a partial exception; *Browning's Roman Murder Story*, 327–28.

62. James's "The Novel in 'The Ring and the Book,'" in *Notes on Novelists* (New York: Charles Scribner's Sons, 1914), 410, is the standard authority for those who wish to focus on the relationship; for Philip Drew's opposing claim that James's emphasis "destroys at a stroke the grand design of Browning's poem," see *Robert Browning: A Critical Introduction* (London: Methuen & Co., 1970), 392.

63. *Saturday Review*, Apr. 3, 1869, 461; Holcombe, *Wives and Property*, 144. Sue Lonoff's declaration that "Browning's 'Roman murder-case' of 1698 seems remote from the world of its audience in its characters as well as its settings" could be rephrased to acknowledge a significant class element—that is, a gap between the aristocratic setting for the poem's domestic brutalities and the lower-class settings in which readers were being accustomed to look for such violence; see Lonoff, "Multiple Narratives and Relative Truths: A Study of *The Ring and the Book*, *The Woman in White*, and *The Moonstone*," in Gerhard Joseph, ed., *Browning Institute Studies*, vol. 10 (New York: The Browning Institute and the City University of New York, 1982), 144. Nancy Tomes has connected the passage of

legislation protecting battered women to "increased middle-class concern" ("A 'Torrent of Abuse': Crimes of Violence Between Working-Class Men and Women, 1840–1875," *Journal of Social History* 11, 3 [1978]).

64. *Times*, Jan. 15, 1869, 9. The events Susannah Palmer described as comprising "the hell in which she had been compelled to live" included her husband's repeated acts of violence against her and his "improper advances" to her 18-year-old daughter.

65. John Addington Symonds, *Macmillan's*, Jan. 1869, 262.

66. See Dorothy Stetson, *A Woman's Issue: The Politics of Family Reform in England* (Westport, Conn.: Greenwood, 1982), 20. The available information on John and Effie Ruskin's sex organs, through texts relating to her annulment suit, is a late but typical product of Victorian judicial procedure, presented in Mary Lutyens, *Millais and the Ruskins* (London: John Murray, 1967), 188–93, and Rose, *Parallel Lives*, 90–91.

67. J. R. Mozley, *Macmillan's*, Apr. 1869, 546–47.

68. Park Honan, "The Murder Poem for Elizabeth," in Roma A. King, Jr., ed., *Victorian Poetry: Issue Commemorative of the Publication of 'The Ring and the Book,'* 216.

69. Ann Brady, *Pompilia: A Feminist Reading of Robert Browning's 'The Ring and the Book,'* 13; Brady suggests the poem's relation to the "equally patriarchal society" and to "the myths of virility" in Browning's "own world of Victorian England" at 126 and 129, respectively.

70. The reference to "what he styles his sister's voice" is not the poem's only example of falsely familial rhetoric: Giuseppe admits to having misrepresented Pompilia as his "sister" during their flight ("Giuseppe Caponsacchi," 1302).

71. Brady, *Pompilia*, 105.

72. Roy Gridley describes Giuseppe as imagining himself as Pompilia's husband: "Browning's Caponsacchi: 'How the Priest Caponsacchi Had His Say,'" in King, ed., *Victorian Poetry: Commemorative*, 290. Honan rehearses in full the identification of Giuseppe and Pompilia with the Brownings ("Murder Poem for Elizabeth," in King, ed., *Victorian Poetry: Commemorative*, 216–17). The St. George parallel is generally seen as authorized by Browning because he adjusted the dates from the original source to make the escape coincide with St. George's Day. According to Charles Phipps's influential study, "whenever Browning is representing the 'true' interpretation of the story, he thinks of Caponsacchi in terms of Perseus or St. George" ("Browning's Canon Giuseppe Caponsacchi—Warrior-Priest, Dantean Lover, Critic of Society," 712). Gridley attests that Giuseppe serves Pompilia as "a Saint George . . . 'for a splendid minute and no more'" (294). The first time (chronologically) that the St. George parallel is introduced is in the passage just cited in the text, when Giuseppe

is called "the true Saint George" by Guido's cousin, a sardonic and unrepentant pander; Giuseppe himself associates the myth with the judgment of the court at its most cynical in his lines 1768–72.

73. Phipps, "Browning's Canon Giuseppe Caponsacchi," provides the most thorough application of the Dantean; see especially his page 710. Gridley's somewhat similar argument puts more emphasis on Giuseppe's fantasy of a "romantic love" for Pompilia as a "fleshly woman" ("Browning's Caponsacchi," in King, ed., *Victorian Poetry: Commemorative*, 290).

74. E. Warwick Slinn sees Giuseppe failing in an attempt to transform his role of priest into that of "cavalier and courtly lover" (*Browning and the Fictions of Identity* [London: Macmillan, 1982], 120). William Buckler emphasizes the compromising and "unmistakably sexual overtones" in the attempt by Giuseppe ("priest turned cavalier turned St. George") to describe his religious conception of Pompilia; Buckler also attempts to sexualize Pompilia's motives (*Poetry and Truth in Robert Browning's 'The Ring and the Book'* [New York: New York University Press, 1985], 146, 135, 83).

75. Altick and Loucks, *Browning's Roman Murder Story*, 119.

76. "Not that there was any belittling of love's physical aspects— Browning was not a Platonic lover . . . ," says Phipps before describing the "mystical love-union" ("Browning's Canon Guiseppe Caponsacchi," 710, 713). Altick and Loucks describe their view of the case's Christian significance in *Browning's Roman Murder Story*, 359.

77. Phipps, 708; Altick and Loucks, 124. Gridley says, "The intricacies of Caponsacchi's sense of what Pompilia means to him defy verbal formulation" ("Browning's Caponsacchi," in King, ed., *Victorian Poetry: Commemorative*, 284). W. David Shaw at first compares Pompilia's "great love for Caponsacchi" to "Juliet's for Romeo," but then says that it "goes in the only way it can go—out of this world, which is also the way Christ's love went. The hermeneutical dilemma facing Browning's Pope is that his faith in the resurrected or redeemed Pompilia, which is his equivalent of the Gospel's proclaiming faith in the risen Christ, does not involve any assent to a verifiable proposition" ("Browning's Roman Murder Mystery: *The Ring and the Book* and Modern Theory," 83–84).

78. Shaw (92) argues that "the individual reader turns out to be the real hero of *The Ring and the Book*."

79. Shaw (83) notes that the Pope's rendering ironically places Guido "in a sense" in "the role of priest, sacrificing his wife so that she can die without blemish."

80. The range is truly enormous, but for examples of the kinds just listed see, respectively, note 72 above (Saint George), "Half-Rome," 795–97 (Apollo), "Giuseppe Caponsacchi," 559, and "Pompilia," 1154 (Myrtilla), and "Pompilia," 1588–89 (Giuseppe as lamb, Guido as serpent).

81. The Pope confirms this description at his 1168. Gridley notes Giuseppe's "negative mode" in which "he may not yet have terms to define what he *is*, but he has terms for what he definitely is *not*" ("Browning's Caponsacchi," in King, ed., *Victorian Poetry: Commemorative*, 285).

82. Altick and Loucks, *Browning's Roman Murder Story*, 121. Pompilia at her 1329–35 describes this process thoroughly in regard to the repetition of Giuseppe's name by others. Browning similarly vexes another of the terms used to define the relationship, "elope," by describing Giuseppe in Book 1 (379–80) as "The priest, declared the lover of the wife, / He who, no question, did elope with her." These lines seem to establish identity between what has been "declared" and what is without question: but see the *OED*'s second, "general" definition of "elope" as meaning only "to run away, escape, abscond."

83. Brady gives priority to the "love of *caritas*" (*Pompilia*, 121). See also Phipps's various references to "love."

84. Giuseppe's role as *amicus curiae* is one of Browning's conspicuous additions to his sources. Judge John Marshall Gest in 1925 chided Browning for having "missed the opportunity of portraying the majesty of the Law, as the controlling force, the savior of human society, ruling and overruling the passions of men and women, even the strongest of all, the sex impulse" (*The Old Yellow Book, Source of Browning's 'The Ring and the Book'* [Boston: Chipman Law Publishing, 1925], 628).

85. Phipps, "Browning's Canon," 718, 713. Though I do not share Phipps's sense of triumph in rendering Giuseppe and Pompilia's relationship as ultimately transcendent, my debt to him is large. Phipps's is the most productive study of the relationship: its affinities with portrayals as different as Buckler's and Altick and Loucks's are impressive; it was also the first to consider the relationship's political implications.

86. Richard Curle, ed., *Robert Browning and Julia Wedgwood: A Broken Friendship as Revealed by Their Letters* (New York: Frederick A. Stokes, 1937), 121, 122. This volume contains a good deal of discussion of the private difficulties of maintaining male / female friendship—see esp. 4, 14, 107–8, 117–22, 179–91—and would indeed be a good place to start an alternative to the present study, one that would concentrate on private personal and biographical issues rather than the challenges to public representation being discussed here.

Chapter Two

1. For the novel's use of form and language to reflect "the tendencies of a new world in the making," see Mikhail Bakhtin, "Epic and Novel," in *The Dialogic Imagination: Four Essays*, trans. Caryl Emerson and Michael Holquist (Austin: University of Texas Press, 1981), 7; note that Bakhtin says "the novel is a love story (although the greatest examples of the Euro-

pean novel are utterly devoid of the love element)" (9). That "few of course would dispute that, with Dickens, the English novel for the first time features a massive thematization of social discipline" is a premise of D. A. Miller's *The Novel and the Police*; see ix. For the tendency of novels to end in death or marriage see Barbara Herrnstein Smith, *Poetic Closure*, 35, and Alan Friedman, *The Turn of the Novel*, 18, as well as the studies by DuPlessis, Kermode, Miller, and Torgovnick cited in note 26 to the Introduction.

2. Kermode, *The Art of Telling*, 137–38. Peter Brooks describes a focus on "those shaping ends that, terminating the dynamic process of reading, promise to bestow meaning and significance on the beginning and the middle," the focus that "animates us as readers of narrative" (*Reading for the Plot*, 19).

3. Boone, *Tradition*, 184, 186, 176–77, 187. Boone's full phrase at 186 is "the social order underlying the traditional order of fiction itself." Boone also refers to "Eliot's depiction of male-female friendship that need not be sexual to be fulfilling . . ." (216).

4. "Her contemporary readers were intent upon divorcing 'George Eliot' from 'that woman,' who lived with Lewes without benefit of legal marriage," Ruby Redinger has observed; "they made the name inviolate" (*George Eliot: The Emergent Self*, 3–4 and see 333–34, 432). See also Gordon S. Haight, *George Eliot: A Biography*, 490.

5. Haight, ed., *The George Eliot Letters*, 2: 213, 6: 117; cited hereafter as *GEL*. For Marian Evans's having become "extinct, rolled up, mashed, absorbed in the Lewesian magnificence," see *GEL*, 3: 65, 88, 111, 302n4, 396. Alexander Welsh compares the "petty" and unrigorous "concealments" of her "irregular marriage" to the diligence with which she maintained the secret of her identity as author in *George Eliot and Blackmail*, 124–25. Evans and Lewes were of course unable to marry legally because he already had a wife, albeit estranged, on whom see Haight, *George Eliot*, 162–63.

6. Haight, *George Eliot*, 52.

7. *GEL*, 1: lvii, 164, 316, lxiv. For references to Mme. D'Albert-Durade as "always 'maman,'" see, for example, 1: 328, and 4: 277. For other uses of family terms in Eliot's letters see especially her correspondence with Elma Stuart (including 4: 167, 230, 242, 355).

8. But Mark Rutherford fictionalized her relationship with Chapman as that of a niece and uncle. See Redinger, *George Eliot*, 217, who cites Wilfred Stone, *Religion and Art of William Hale White* ("*Mark Rutherford*") (Stanford, Calif.: Stanford University Press, 1954), 129.

9. *GEL*, 8: 50, 56, 61. Haight, as editor, notes the last step in this sequence at 61n2. See also Nancy Paxton, *George Eliot and Herbert Spencer: Feminism, Evolutionism, and the Reconstruction of Gender* (Princeton, N.J.: Princeton University Press, 1991), 17–20.

10. One important exception to this rule about indirect address was her relationship to her "nephew" Johnnie Cross (see note 27 to this chapter).

11. Kathleen Watson notes: "During the period in which the novel is set the diction of Methodists differed from the standard English of the day in vocabulary. . . . Methodists used a number of words in a sense different from that current at the time" ("Dinah Morris and Mrs. Evans: A Comparative Study of Methodist Diction," 284–85). Valentine Cunningham places *Adam Bede* in Methodist history in *"Everywhere Spoken Against": Dissent in the Victorian Novel*, 147–71, but does not acknowledge Seth's placement amid the mass of family idioms, and so sees the book as leaving Seth "oddly stranded" (170). Eve Kosofsky Sedgwick describes Dinah's Methodism as "a two-edged sword in the service of her autonomy" (*Between Men*, 141). For nineteenth-century Methodist emphasis on "family religion," including "daily prayer" at "stated times" comparable to that prescribed by Comte, see Edmund Grindrod, *A Compendium of the Laws and Regulations of Wesleyan Methodism* (London: John Mosher, 1842), 187. For a mid-Victorian Methodist's deployment of family idioms, consider the strategy adopted by Thomas Brown Stephenson in setting up his residence for homeless boys in 1869: "He desired his children to feel that they were a family and that they had a home. When he appointed a couple to be in charge of the Home, he called them its father and mother" (Maldwyn Edwards, *Methodism and England: A Study of Methodism in its Social and Political Aspects During the Period 1850–1932* [London: Epworth, 1943], 141). The use of family terms is of course not unique to Methodists among Christian denominations.

12. The formula appears regularly in Eliot's fiction. See, for instance, *Felix Holt, The Radical*, ed. Fred Thomson (Oxford: Clarendon Press, 1980), for "only friendship" (219) and "more than friendship" (227). Ralph Elliott, *Hardy's English*, 320, cites Eliot's *Romola* as an example of the use of "comradeship" to describe marital happiness.

13. Welsh notes the particular sincerity required of Dinah and her coreligionists, who believe that "there is no concealment from God" (*George Eliot and Blackmail*, 138). Nancy Cott has described how nineteenth-century British "Evangelicals linked moral agency to female character with a supporting link to passionlessness" ("Passionlessness: An Interpretation of Victorian Sexual Ideology, 1790–1850," 167).

14. Compare to Giuseppe Caponsacchi's claim in *The Ring and the Book*, cited above: "You know this is not love, Sirs—it is faith."

15. For some "disturbing" implications of this conversation, see Dorothea Barrett, *Vocation and Desire: George Eliot's Heroines* (London: Routledge, 1989), 42; Sedgwick refers to Dinah's preaching as being "chillingly" belittled (*Between Men*, 143). Shirley Foster says that "when the independent voice of Dinah Morris is silenced by marriage at the

end of *Adam Bede*" one may find a clear revelation of Eliot's "ambivalence" regarding marriage ("Female Januses: Ambiguity and Ambivalence towards Marriage in Mid-Victorian Women's Fiction," *International Journal of Women's Studies*, May-June 1983, 227). Cunningham notes that Dinah's marriage was Lewes's "regrettable suggestion" (*"Everywhere Spoken Against,"* 170).

16. Suzanne Graver aptly describes it as "a thriving and extended family so settled and secure as to be able to welcome back an outcast" (*George Eliot and Community: A Study in Social Theory and Fictional Form*, 95).

17. Welsh says that "one reason [*Adam Bede*] is popular is that everything works out so tidily" (*George Eliot and Blackmail*, 140). He also cites U. C. Knoepflmacher's characterization of the ending in terms of "the grandest of pastoral myths," with Adam marrying "a second Eve" and becoming a "Loamshire patriarch whose children will be fruitful and multiply."

18. Wilkie Collins, *The Woman in White*, 628, 435, 581–82, 641, and (for the subsequent reference to Walter Hartright Jr.) 646. *Adam Bede* was published in three volumes on Feb. 1, 1859. *The Woman in White* began its serialization in Dickens's *All the Year Round* at the end of the same year.

19. D. A. Miller, "*Cage aux folles*: Sensation and Gender in Wilkie Collins' *The Woman in White*," 123. This essay is also included in Miller, *The Novel and the Police*, where the corresponding passage appears (without the phrase I have quoted) at 183.

20. "Eliot's Novels," *Quarterly Review*, Oct. 1860, 494; see Cunningham, "*Everywhere Spoken Against*," 170n4, for *Seth Bede, the Methody*.

21. See, for example, *The Mill on the Floss*, 160, 270, 289, 295.

22. Tony Tanner, *Adultery in the Novel: Contract and Transgression*, 72. For more on Eliot and incest see Redinger, *George Eliot*, 45–47, and Eliot's letter to John Blackwood, *GEL*, 5: 403. Robert Polhemus argues that *The Mill on the Floss* "sympathetically portrays, but finally renounces, the incestuous nature of nineteenth-century familialism" (*Erotic Faith: Being in Love from Jane Austen to D. H. Lawrence*, 176). Boone notes that the over-sentimentalization of "the reality of the typical sibling bond" is a "wishful fallacy shared by a variety of Victorian novelists including Austen, Dickens, Eliot, and Gaskell, and exposed in [*Wuthering Heights*] by the negative relations of actual brothers and sisters" (*Tradition*, 154).

23. The two motifs combine in the drowning "embrace," in which Maggie and Tom are described as "living through again . . . the days when they had clasped their little hands in love . . ." (459). Note that "friendship" is part of their childhood language, as in the reference to Maggie and Tom's "getting friends" with each other at 87. Welsh comments on a scene between Maggie and Philip: "Adulthood . . . signifies the unmaking

of a promise and the cessation of friendship" (*George Eliot and Blackmail*, 148).

24. Family terms here become complicit in an exemplary instance of "triangulated desire," as described by René Girard, *Deceit, Desire, and the Novel*. Polhemus says that the incestuous "bias" of Maggie and Tom's relationship "fails to fulfill its cultural purpose—to promote marriages of positive filial feeling and kindred responsibility" (*Erotic Faith*, 182).

25. Mrs. Glegg, at her most objectionable, repeatedly refers to the blood relatives of the financially distressed Tullivers as "friends" (see 183, 186, 223, etc.). The same term is applied to the distraught Maggie's unsympathetic relatives late in the novel (e.g., at 426, 432, 435).

26. *GEL*, 5: 403. Redinger discusses the letter to her publisher in relation to *Brother and Sister* (*George Eliot*, 45–46) and notes: " 'Friendship,' as either word or concept, has no place in the context of the sonnets she wrote about herself and Isaac . . ." (47).

27. The earliest reference to Cross as "nephew" is *GEL*, 5: 301. For her immersion in Cross's family see *GEL*, 7: 341. See also Isaac's congratulatory letter at 7: 280, and her reply at 7: 287.

28. "The Mill on the Floss," *Westminster Review*, July 1860, 24, ascribed to John Chapman in *The Wellesley Index to Victorian Periodicals*, ed. Walter Houghton (University of Toronto Press, 1979), 3: 630. For Marian Evans and Chapman's tumultuous relationship see Gordon S. Haight, *George Eliot and John Chapman*, 2nd ed. (New Haven, Conn.: Yale University Press, 1969), esp. 18–25. She had had a significant early relationship with the Reverend Francis Watts: see her letters to him beginning at *GEL*, 1: 135, esp. 142. Thomas Noble's book on *Scenes* places Eliot's work in relation to historical accounts of Evangelicalism; see *George Eliot's 'Scenes of Clerical Life,'* 165–66n6.

29. Some critics have described Daniel Deronda as "androgynous": see for instance Bonnie Zimmerman, "George Eliot and Feminism: The Case of Daniel Deronda," in Rhoda Nathan, ed., *Nineteenth-Century Women Writers of the English-Speaking World* (New York: Greenwood, 1986), 237.

30. Eliot, "Silly Novels by Lady Novelists," first published in the *Westminster Review*, Oct. 1856 (four months before the first appearance of "Amos Barton"), and included in Thomas Pinney, ed., *Essays of George Eliot* (New York: Columbia University Press, 1963), 318.

31. This matches Foucault's formula, already cited above: "What is peculiar to modern societies is . . . that they dedicated themselves to speaking of [sex] *ad infinitum*, while exploiting it as *the* secret" (*History of Sexuality*, 1: 35).

32. Eliot's interest in "the refinement and differencing of the affectionate relations" (*GEL*, 5: 56) led her to denounce public discussion of incest. For

Browning see his letter to Julia Wedgwood, quoted at note 86 to Chapter 1.

33. Note that the public in "Amos Barton" had also doubted the authenticity of the Countess's relation to the man she called her "brother," who turns out to be "neither more or less than her half-brother" (38). *The Mill on the Floss* includes an idealized conflation of the sibling and priestly bonds in Maggie's temporary fascination with Thomas à Kempis as "the voice of a brother . . ." (254). But Eliot undermines this link in the pages that follow by mentioning Maggie's "exaggeration and wilfulness" in emulating Thomas (256) and by implicitly connecting that emulation to her wish for Philip to be "a brother and a teacher" to her (261). The cleric Mr. Gilfil distinguishes "brotherly affection" for a woman from "love" in "Mr. Gilfil's Love-Story," the middle of the three *Scenes* (135).

34. "Language is a stream that is almost sure to smack of a mingled soil," writes Eliot in *Silas Marner* ([New York: New American Library, 1960], 80); "signs are small measurable things, but interpretations are illimitable" (*Middlemarch*, 24); and, "It is a sad waste of life to write explanatory sheets that end in explaining nothing except the impossibility of mutual understanding" (*GEL*, 4: 375). There are many comparable examples throughout the novels and letters.

35. U. C. Knoepflmacher describes the priestly Daniel Deronda as "fleshless and ethereal," a comment that ill-suits Eliot's emphasis on Deronda's desires but that applies well to his predecessor Tryan (*Religious Humanism and the Victorian Novel: George Eliot, Walter Pater, and Samuel Butler*, 147). Knoepflmacher gives an extensive list of "George Eliot's pastors" at 136.

36. Eliot makes a point of commenting that the "long procession of mourning friends" behind Tryan's coffin includes "women as well as men" (*Scenes*, 333)—a phrase Noble's textual notes suggest she waffled on.

37. *The Literary Gazette and Journal of Belles Lettres, Science, and Art*, Jan. 23, 1858, 83; Derek Oldfield and Sylvia Oldfield, " 'Scenes of Clerical Life': The Diagrams and the Picture," in Barbara Hardy, ed. *Critical Essays on George Eliot* (New York: Barnes & Noble, 1970), 15.

38. Gwendolen sees Daniel as "free from all misunderstanding" (418); more negatively still, the narrator insists, "That Gwendolen's reliance on him was unvisited by any dream of his being a man who could misinterpret her was as manifest as morning" (524). Mary Doyle thinks Deronda a "sermonizing male hero" typical to Eliot's fiction (*The Sympathetic Response*, 159).

39. At 423, Gwendolen says, "It may be—it shall be better with me because I have known you." At 750 she recalls, "I said . . . I said . . . it should be better . . . better with me . . . for having known you," then says, "It shall be the better for me—."

40. In Chapter 3 I consider a "problematics of repetitions" (to use Leo

Bersani's term) in discussions of friendship in the New Woman novel, a genre sometimes seen as descending from *Daniel Deronda*.

41. Tragic, that is, in A. C. Bradley's Aristotelian sense of "waste" that is uplifting for the potential it suggests rather than depressing for the moral loss it enacts (*Shakespearian Tragedy: Lectures on 'Hamlet,' 'Othello,' 'King Lear,' 'Macbeth'*, 2nd ed. [London: Macmillan, 1914], 23); such a sense of unrealized potential is important to my ensuing discussion of the significance of *Deronda*'s ending.

42. Doyle's mischaracterization of the novel's subject as "the search for a role in life, to be found by Gwendolen on the personal level and by Deronda on the social" (*Sympathetic Response*, 160), is useful as a way of identifying the polarization Eliot does *not*, in fact, present. The more apt description is Daniel Mansell's: "Both Deronda and Gwendolen are searching for a duty to submit to, which Deronda at last finds in Zionism, and which Gwendolen never finds" ("George Eliot's Conception of 'Form,'" 74).

43. Mirah, loyal both to her mother's memory and to her community, stands to achieve dual personal/political satisfactions comparable to her husband's. Thus, having repeatedly challenged her authoritarian brother Mordecai, Mirah suggests that Zionism stands to develop roles for women far more enabling than those spurned by Daniel's mother, the Princess. Recent hostility to the "Jewish portion" of *Daniel Deronda* often echoes the terms of anti-Semitic Victorian reviews, ably chronicled by Carol Martin, "Contemporary Critics and Judaism in *Daniel Deronda*."

44. Virginia Woolf and other twentieth-century feminists would demonstrate the particular value of women's ways of seeing; these concerns figure importantly in the discussion of ideas of cooperative vision in Chapters 4, 5, and 6.

45. "Blackmailers and confessors . . . represent more general opinion than their own, else they would have no purchase on the minds of those they hope to influence," says Welsh (*George Eliot and Blackmail*, 291.) Comte's praise for heterosexual friendship, discussed in Chapter 1, is predicated upon a notion of friendship's requiring equality.

46. For references to Janet's "blank" see *Scenes*, 267, 268, 275, 326. Wayne Koestenbaum cites Julia Kristeva's comments on the introduction of "ruptures, blank spaces, and holes into language" and observes, "If 'the moment of rupture and negativity' is feminine, then fissures in a text . . . unseat literary convention *and* patriarchal rule" (*Double-Talk: The Erotics of Male Literary Collaboration* [New York: Routledge, 1989], 113). But Koestenbaum emphasizes the more insidious implications of this strategy, according to which "leaving holes in [a] text" may serve as a "style of seduction" (62); see also his 30 and 137–38.

47. "In my private lot, I am unspeakably happy, loving and beloved. But

I am doing little for others," she noted at the end of 1870 (*GEL*, 7: 144). In the preceding year she had recorded the following vacillations: "I feel too deeply the difficult complications that beset every measure likely to affect the position of women and also I feel too imperfect a sympathy with many women who have put themselves forward in connection with such measures, to give any practical adhesion to them. There is no subject on which I am more inclined to hold my peace and learn, than on the 'Women Question'. . . . But on one point I have a strong conviction, and I feel bound to act on it, so far as my retired way of life allows of public action. And that is, that women ought to have the same fund of truth placed within their reach as men have. . . . I have been made rather miserable lately by revelations about women, and have resolved to remain silent in my sense of helplessness. I know very little about what is specially good for women— only a few things that I feel sure are good for human nature generally, and about such as these last alone, can I ever hope to write or say anything worth saying" (5: 58).

48. Graver, *George Eliot and Community*, 229; John Kucich, *Repression in Victorian Fiction: Charlotte Brontë, George Eliot, and Charles Dickens*, 200; Cynthia Chase, "The Deconstruction of the Elephants: Double-Reading in *Daniel Deronda*," *PMLA* 93, 2 (Mar. 1978): 223; Ellen Rosenman, "Women's Speech and the Roles of the Sexes in *Daniel Deronda*," 253; Sally Shuttleworth, *George Eliot and Nineteenth-Century Science*, 199. Gillian Beer reads all of *Daniel Deronda* as "a novel haunted by the future" (*Darwin's Plots*, 181–209). U. C. Knoepflmacher also notes that *Daniel Deronda* "examines the present, but ardently longs for the future" (*Religious Humanism*, 116).

49. F. R. Leavis, *The Great Tradition*, 85–86, and his introduction to *Daniel Deronda* (New York: Harper, 1961), xvii; Philip Weinstein, *The Semantics of Desire: Changing Models of Identity from Dickens to Joyce*, 102n12; Doyle, *Sympathetic Response*, 160–61, 168.

50. *GEL*, 6: 290, 241.

51. David Kaufmann, *George Eliot and Judaism: An Attempt to Appreciate 'Daniel Deronda,'* trans. J. W. Ferrier, reprint of 1888 2d ed. (New York: Haskell House, 1970), 60. Eliot praised particularly Kaufmann's "clear perception of the relation between the presentation of the Jewish element and those of English Social Life" (*GEL*, 6: 379). Martin notes that the Victorian *Morning Post* was troubled both by Daniel's exclusion of Gwendolen from his Zionist plans and by the fact that the novel's ending would "hinge on the Gwendolen-Deronda relationship" ("Contemporary Critics," 97).

52. Boone discusses Victorian reactions to this issue in *Tradition*, at 183 and in the opening chapter, "Wedlock as Deadlock and Beyond: An

Introduction," 1–30. "The fact is obvious," says Alan Friedman, "that the novel traditionally tends to conclude in marriage or death" (*The Turn of the Novel*, 18); see also Barbara Herrnstein Smith's reference to the genre's conventionally ending "at a point when either nothing could follow (as when the hero dies) or everything that could follow is predictable (as when the hero and heroine get married)" (*Poetic Closure*, 35), and the comment by Welsh given in note 62 to this chapter, as well as the studies by Kermode, Miller, and Torgovnick cited in note 55 to this chapter.

53. *GEL*, 6: 263. While completing her research for *Daniel Deronda*, Eliot "looked into three or four novels to see what the world was reading" (*GEL*, 6: 75).

54. D. A. Miller so affirms (*Narrative and Its Discontents: A Study of Novelistic Closure*, 191), before studying the novel's "uneasiness" with closure at 194.

55. Similarly, Eliot's comment about "conclusion" has become central to studies of novelistic closure. Frank Kermode quotes it at 196 of his *Sense of an Ending*, citing Miriam Allott's *Novelists on the Novel* as his source; D. A. Miller, *Narrative and Its Discontents*, and Marianna Torgovnick, *Closure in the Novel*, quote it at 89 and 22, respectively.

56. Torgovnick, *Closure in the Novel*, 133. Friedman too prefers *Deronda*'s ending as "more powerful" (*Turn of the Novel*, 25). Srilekha Bell considers the ending to be part of Eliot's "piercing and definitive commentary on the unsatisfactory position of women in Victorian England" ("Love, Marriage, and Work in *Daniel Deronda*," *Browning Society Notes 1987–88* 17 [1–3]: 63). John Blackwood ultimately gave his approval too: "There will I know be disappointment at not hearing more of the failure of Gwendolen and the mysterious destiny of Deronda, but I am sure you are right in leaving all grand and vague" (*GEL*, 7: 272).

57. Boone, *Tradition*, 186, 187.

58. Welsh, "Opening and Closing," 22.

59. Boone, *Tradition*, 186; Shuttleworth, *Eliot and Nineteenth-Century Science*, 200.

60. Boone, *Tradition*, 183; *The Spectator*, Sept. 9, 1876, 1132; James Picciotto, *Gentleman's Magazine*, Nov. 1876, 593, reprinted in David Carroll, comp., *George Eliot: The Critical Heritage* (London: Routledge & Kegan Paul, 1971), 413. Boone briefly acknowledges that Daniel is "never quite successful" in his attempt to "suppress the sexual attraction aroused in him" by Gwendolen, but in a corresponding note describes the passage that distinguishes their relationship from "exclusive passionate love" and "friendship" as "deflect[ing] any romantic connotations to Daniel and Gwendolen's friendship" (175 and 353, note 44). Boone comes closest to considering the problem of naming the relationship when he says: "The

principle of 'separateness with communication' that Daniel has in mind for the emergent Jewish national identity must also become part of Gwendolen's personal creed and the model for their own relationship" (184).

61. Even Ellen Rosenman's analysis of "Gwendolen's 'confession' to Deronda" as "a classic instance of female speech, both in what it says and in what it cannot say" is much less occupied with the nature of Gwendolen's language than with the way it "disrupts the coherence of the narrative" ("Women's Speech," 239, 241). But see Rosenman's significant observations about Gwendolen's gaps and their consequences, cited in note 63 to this chapter.

62. When the endings of nineteenth-century novels seek to "satisfy contradictory desires," Welsh has noted, they may in the end choose "marriage for one hero and death for another, or [the contradiction] may be veiled in allegory" ("Opening and Closing," 21).

63. Rosenman notes that Gwendolen's "most powerful responses appear only as gaps, as absence" ("Women's Speech," 241). She concludes that Eliot's central "gap . . . implies the profound disruptions that would occur if women spoke: the replacement of hierarchy with a multivocal world . . ." (253–54).

64. Boone, *Tradition*, 187. Boone cites the last spoken version of the stammer, "It shall be the better for me—" and the narrator's "She could not finish" in order to read the lines as a "breaking-off of speech" that "appropriately symbolizes Eliot's narrative technique . . ." (185). But the subsequent written version, "It is better—it shall be better . . . ," makes clear that Gwendolen only begins her unfinished narrative of what "shall be" because she cannot name what "is."

Chapter Three

1. For the increase of women in middle-class occupations, see Lee Holcombe, *Victorian Ladies at Work: Middle-Class Working Women in England and Wales 1850–1914*, 6. Penny Boumelha notes that New Woman novels were "firmly rooted in the upper middle class" (*Thomas Hardy and Women: Sexual Ideology and Narrative Form*, 137).

2. Gail Cunningham quotes this passage from Emma Frances Brooke's *A Superfluous Woman* in *The New Woman and the Victorian Novel*, 68. The grounding of this instance of heterosexual cooperation in farm labor is reminiscent of the reference to the commonness of such instances in Josephine Butler's *Women's Work and Women's Culture*, and indeed, as Chapter 5 will show, farm labor seems to have been the locus at which representation of heterosexual friendship had the best chance of being placed. Representations of such rural cooperation were, however, not uniformly approving; see Edward Stanhope's report of work "gangs" in Lincoln,

Nottingham, and Leicester counties, which noted "the most horrible immorality and foul language, among even the youngest boys and girls"; cited in H. M. Hyndman, *The Historical Basis of Socialism in England* (reprinted New York: Garland, 1984; orig. pub. 1883), 312–13.

3. The New Woman novel has been studied as having descended from *Daniel Deronda*; see for instance Lloyd Fernando, *"New Women" in the Late-Victorian Novel* (University Park: Pennsylvania State University Press, 1977), 63.

4. "What is peculiar to modern societies, in fact, is . . . that they dedicated themselves to speaking of [sex] *ad infinitum*, while exploiting it as *the* secret" (Foucault, *History of Sexuality*, 1: 35).

5. Ann Ardis, *New Women, New Novels: Feminism and Early Modernism*, 170. Ardis stresses the novels' efforts toward "effecting social change" (117) and cites their Victorian opponents' sense that these books provided "readers with the wrong kind of model to emulate in their own lives" (52).

6. Boumelha mentions these sequels in the context of describing "a kind of industry of rebuttal and parody" inspired by Allen's works (*Hardy and Women*, 137). Ardis emphasizes their "intertextuality"; she also says that "critics . . . recently . . . have commented extensively on the irony of Allen's title," but she cites only Elaine Showalter's 1977 *A Literature of Their Own* (*New Women, New Novels*, 51–52).

7. It is difficult to gauge *The Woman Who Did*'s precise relation to 1890's feminism. The *DNB Supplement* (citing Allen's memoirist, Edward Clodd) says that Allen, generally known as a satirist, "intended the book, in all seriousness, to be taken as a protest against the subjection of women. . . . The lack of humour in it puzzled his friends." Elaine Showalter presents Allen as an enemy to women (*A Literature of Their Own: British Novelists from Brontë to Lessing*, 185 and note). Hilary Simpson calls *The Woman Who Did* flatly "ironical" and "anti-feminist" (*D. H. Lawrence and Feminism*, 22). Satirical intentions would only reinforce the book's claim to have resolved the issues its heroine can't articulate herself, and so would not much alter my current argument, which, concerned with the book's position in late-Victorian discourse, treats Allen's smug distance as straightforwardly moralistic (as at least some Victorian readers seem to have taken it) rather than comical. I also assume, on the basis of the book's dedication, an identification of Allen with his narrator, so I refer to the two interchangeably, particularly to show the odd complementary relation of the narrator/Allen and Alan. It is worth noting that because Allen's novel was read as an attack on marriage, contemporary readers assumed the worst about his own domestic life. Edward Clodd reports: "When an 'interview' with Allen, published in an evening paper, closed with the words, 'He is happily married,' the compositor soothed his doubts thus by punctuat-

ing it: 'He is, happily, married' " (Grant Allen: A Memoir [London: Grant Richards, 1900], 168).

8. See R. Y. Tyrrel, "Jude the Obscure," Fortnightly Review, June 1896, 858; Eliza Lynn Linton, "The Wild Women as Social Insurgents," Nineteenth Century 30 (1891): 596–605. Ardis's New Women, New Novels argues that the New Woman novelists undertook a "reappraisal of realism" rather than a simple mimetic function; that argument is summarized at 3. For a concise summary of New Woman writing prior to The Woman Who Did, see Ellen Jordan, "The Christening of the New Woman: May 1894," 19–21.

9. The ensuing discussion partly adapts the "problematics of repetitions" discussed by Leo Bersani in The Freudian Body: Psychoanalysis and Art. Bersani describes a second half of the story of Freudian sexual narratives: in addition to the "teleological perspective on sexuality" (31), according to which heterosexual adult perversions "become intelligible as the sickness of uncompleted narratives" (32), Bersani notes Freud's suggestion "that the pleasurable unpleasurable tension of sexual stimulation seeks not to be released, but to be increased" (34), so that there inheres in sexuality an interest in sexual tension's being repeated and intensified, not just consistently or finally released. When Bersani says, "It is, in any case, repetition—or what could perhaps be called an insistent stasis—which blocks Freud's attempts to define the sexual" (35), his syntax suggests that Freud must undergo a similar "unpleasurable pleasure" in leaving unconsummated the process of approaching a consummate designation for sexuality. The Woman Who Did and other New Woman writings produce a comparably "insistent stasis" in their self-conscious offer of simultaneous (and repeated) excitation and satisfaction. They replicate this process of unsatisfied repetition in their obsession with particular moments: rather than moving consistently toward consummation, they instead examine a static condition vaguely redefined by isolated (and, in a certain way, ultimately irrelevant) acts of consummation or denial. Bersani's priorities are quite different from mine, here. But the heterosexual temptations of Hardy's and Allen's novels are related, it seems to me, with Bersani's suggestion of a model for reading that depends not on the fate of an impulse toward consummation but instead on the maintenance—masochistic, according to Bersani's model—of a present dissatisfaction. For in each case, plot seems very much subordinate to continuous crises of definition that issue in an achieved but still unexpressed definition.

10. Margaret Oliphant, "The Anti-Marriage League," Blackwood's Magazine, Jan. 1896, 145.

11. The controversy thus exemplifies Foucault's above-cited formula for the modern tendency to speak of sex "ad infinitum while still exploiting

it as *the* secret." The Victorian acknowledgment of sex is discussed in the opening pages of Chapter 1; see especially Craik's comment describing "friendship 'pure and simple.' " For Ardis, the New Woman novelists' "truth-claims about sexuality" as "the core, the center, of human personality" (*New Women, New Novels*, 37, 109) constitute a defiance of Victorian "ideology." Carol Senf summarizes criticism's pointing to the centrality of sex in New Woman writing in " 'Dracula': Stoker's Response to the New Woman," *Victorian Studies*, Autumn 1982, 35–37.

12. Edward Carpenter, *Love's Coming of Age* (New York: Boni and Liveright, 1911; orig. pub. 1896), 121; L. Keith Stibbard, "Friendship Between the Sexes," *Westminster Review*, Nov. 1899, 584.

13. George Henry Lewes's will had left the bulk of his property to "Mary Ann Lewes, spinster" (*GEL*, 3: 212n6b).

14. Jordan notes that the word "new" was "extremely popular" in the period ("Christening of the New Woman," 21).

15. Compare Eliza Savage's condemnation of Harriet Taylor Mill, quoted in note 41 to this chapter.

16. Francis Adams, "Shelley," *Fortnightly Review* 52 (1892): 217; Henry S. Salt, *Shelley's Principles: Has Time Refuted or Confirmed Them?* (London: William Reeves [1892]), 25, 44; John Todhunter, "Shelley and the Marriage Question," *Shelley Society Papers*, vol. 1, part II (London: Reeves and Turner, 1892), 369. Salt also referred to a Shelley Society talk given by Marx's daughter and son-in-law advocating "Shelley and Socialism." On the 1880's as the time when "socialism became an issue for educated people," see Norman Dennis and A. H. Halsey, *English Ethical Socialism: Thomas More to R. H. Tawney* (Oxford: Clarendon Press, 1988), 59. In Victorian times the most notorious fact of Shelley's "Italian wanderings" was his premarital adulterous relationship with Mary Godwin; for Lady Shelley's sponsorship of the various biographies that suppressed this scandalous material, see Sylva Norman, *The Flight of the Skylark: The Development of Shelley's Reputation* (Norman: University of Oklahoma Press, 1954), 224–26. The phrase "ineffectual angel" was famously applied to Shelley by Matthew Arnold.

A hostile paper on Shelley's relation to socialism, delivered to the Shelley Society by A. G. Ross had provoked furious discussion: "MR. BERNARD SHAW," reported the Society's Notebook, "said the paper was the most astonishing he had ever heard, and he combated most of the statements made by the lecturer concerning socialism." Another "SPEAKER, while agreeing with the lecturer that Shelley's ethics were entirely 'rotten,' did not agree with his attack on the street socialists. . . ." Ross in response called the socialists preachers of "the Doctrine of Universal Hate" but "desired to express his regret that he had given offense" (*Note-book of the Shelley*

Society, edited by the honorary secretaries [London: Reeves and Turner, 1888]), 193–95.

17. See Cunningham, *New Woman*, 48, 110.

18. John Cordy Jeaffreson, *The Real Shelley: New Views of the Poet's Life*, 1: 2. On the invocation of Shelley by the previous generation of reformers, see John Killham, *Tennyson and "The Princess": Reflections of an Age* (London: University of London Press, 1958).

19. "If, as Mr. Jeaffreson seems to imagine, certain fiends—advocates of freelove and freethinking—have a scheme to prove Shelley an angel *qua* freelover and freethinker, they are unlikely to have the slightest success except with persons so silly that no refutation is at all likely to produce any effect on them" (review of *The Real Shelley*, *Saturday Review*, June 20, 1885, 828).

20. Jeaffreson, *The Real Shelley*, 1: 12; 2: 336–37, 350, 478.

21. Jeaffreson, 2: 386–87. Recent criticism too has been troubled by Shelley's attempt "to hold simultaneously a spiritual and physical image of human passion." See Richard Holmes, *Shelley: The Pursuit*, 632. In "Compromised Romanticism in *Jude the Obscure*," Michael Hassett notes a point at which "Shelley has trouble . . . because he is talking simultaneously about transcendental communion with Intellectual Beauty and union with a mortal woman" (*Nineteenth-Century Fiction*, Mar. 1971, 440). The sexless Shelley favored by Jeaffreson might be just as well suited to the vocabulary of late-nineteenth-century English socialism as the one he despised; see the vision of socialism represented by London activist James Bronterre O'Brien's quotation from Robespierre in 1885: "We desire an order of things in which all the mean and cruel passions shall be chained down—all the beneficent and generous passions awakened by the laws" (cited in Stan Shipley, *Club Life and Socialism in Mid-Victorian London* [Oxford: History Works, 1983], 10).

22. Shelley's assertion that "friendship" was by definition "exempt from the smallest alloy of sexuality" appears in his fragmentary "Essay on Friendship"; in discussing homosexuality in "A Discourse on the Manners of the Ancient Greeks Relative to the Subject of Love," Shelley speaks of "love" and the "sexual impulse," but not "friendship" (David Lee Clark, ed., *Shelley's Prose, or The Trumpet of Prophecy* [Albuquerque: University of New Mexico Press, 1954], 338, 216–23).

23. Phyllis Bartlett, " 'Seraph of Heaven': A Shelleyan Dream in Hardy's Fiction," 630.

24. Thomas Hardy, *The Woodlanders* (Oxford: Oxford University Press, 1985), 89; in the book version of *The Well-Beloved* the Shelley quotations remain intact, as at 75. Michael Millgate notes that Hardy had considered using a phrase from *Epipsychidion* as the title for what became

Tess of the D'Urbervilles (Thomas Hardy: A Biography, 295). Bartlett notes that Hardy's markings in his 1865 edition of Shelley cluster around "Shelley's idea of the perfect woman, and of ideal love" ("'Seraph of Heaven,'" 624). J. Hillis Miller sees all Hardy's work as exploring this idea; see his *Fiction and Repetition,* 161. He discusses Hardy's Shelley at 148. These ideas stand in Hardy's fiction as an exception or counter-tendency to the rule proposed by Elaine Scarry: "Human consciousness is always, for Hardy, embodied human consciousness: hence all states of being . . . entail reciprocal jostling with the world" ("Work and the Body in Hardy and Other Nineteenth-Century Novelists," 91).

25. Hardy, *The Well-Beloved,* 78, 117, 118. Michael Ryan's reading of the novel as a deliberate spoof of Platonism sees Walter Pater, not Shelley, as the novel's spokesman for the Platonic: "One Name of Many Shapes: *The Well-Beloved,*" in Dale Kramer, ed., *Approaches to the Fiction of Thomas Hardy* (London: Macmillan, 1979), 179–92.

26. For nineteenth-century skepticism about "Platonic" love see the opening pages of Chapter 1. Havelock Ellis said *Jude* was superior to the story of Paul and Virginia precisely because Hardy had admitted sexual passion ("Concerning *Jude the Obscure,*" *Savoy Magazine,* Oct. 1896, 35–49, reprinted in R. G. Cox, ed., *Thomas Hardy: The Critical Heritage,* [New York: Barnes & Noble, 1970], 309).

27. John Goode, "Sue Bridehead and the New Women," in Mary Jacobus, ed., *Women Writing and Writing About Women* (London: Croom Helm, 1979), 107.

28. Jeaffreson, *The Real Shelley,* 1: 2.

29. Vicinus, *Independent Women,* 290. The cruel backlash resulting from these anxieties included increasingly harsh treatment of homosexuals, which in turn put pressure on another form of "friendship": Koestenbaum argues that the Labouchère Amendment, criminalizing all forms of "'gross indecency' between men, whether public or private, consensual or nonconsensual," made "men newly conscious of the sexual implications of close male friendship" (*Double-Talk,* 3, 57).

30. Beswicke Ancrum, "The Sexual Problem, A Rejoinder," *Westminster Review* 143 (1885): 172; Percy Bysshe Shelley, *Epipsychidion,* 130, in Donald Reiman and Sharon Powers, eds., *Shelley's Poetry and Prose* (New York: Norton, 1977), 377.

31. Boumelha provides an apt description of Sue's predicament: "A refusal of the sexual dimension of relationships can seem the only rational response to a dilemma; in revolt against the double bind by which female-male relationships are invariably interpreted as sexual and by which, simultaneously, sexuality is controlled and channelled into a single legalized relationship, Sue is forced into a confused and confusing situation in which

she wishes at one and the same time to assert her right to a non-sexual love and her right to a non-marital sexual liaison" (*Hardy and Women*, 143). Ardis sees Hardy's process as "draining" Sue of "all [her] unpredictable unconventionality" (*New Women, New Novels*, 146).

32. For Bersani, see note 9 to this chapter. For Shelley's "substitution of the words *friend* or *lover* for that of *brother & sister*," the modern reader can turn to Holmes, *Shelley: The Pursuit*, 390, but Hardy would have found ample discussion of this editing in Jeaffreson and other late-Victorian biographers of Shelley. Miller considers Hardy in relation to *Laon and Cythna*'s incestuous elements in *Fiction and Repetition*, 148.

33. Janet Burnstein notes that "the world of men in *Jude* has been impoverished by a loss of meaning in conventional language" ("The Journey Beyond Myth in *Jude the Obscure*," *Texas Studies in Language and Literature* 15 [1973]: 506). William Goetz uses speech-act theory to point to the novel's lack of any alternatives to unacceptable terms ("The Felicity and Infelicity of Marriage in *Jude the Obscure*," *Nineteenth-Century Fiction* [1983], 189–213).

34. For Hardy's use of "the language of theology," see Raymond Chapman, *The Language of Thomas Hardy* (Houndmills, Eng.: Macmillan, 1990), 63–65. For the observation about the scene's religious irony I am grateful to Regenia Gagnier.

35. Hardy, *Far From the Madding Crowd* (originally published in 1874), 419, 376. Hardy's comment on the limits of *camaraderie* closely parallels J. S. Mill's comment that men and women rarely relate in the way of "two friends of the same sex who are much associated in daily life" in *The Subjection of Women* (334), published shortly before.

36. Ralph Elliott discusses nineteenth-century use of "comradeship" to describe the basis of happy marriages in *Hardy's English*, 319–20. But see the *OED*'s suggestion that "comrade" was less likely to be applied to women, as noted in Chapter 1.

37. Hardy made explicit his objections to marriage in his Postscript to *Jude* (29). Patricia Ingham describes *Jude* as having "as its narrative matrix a pattern of recent origin: a woman rejecting marriage" and notes the importance of this pattern for New Woman fiction (*Thomas Hardy* [Atlantic Highlands, N.J.: Humanities Press International, 1990], 89–92). Note that Ingham's description, like Boone's of *Daniel Deronda*, places a negation, rather than an attempt at producing a viable alternative, at the center of these narratives.

38. Scarry, "Work and the Body," 106.

39. Scarry, 95.

40. Evelyn Hardy and F. B. Pinion, eds., *One Rare Fair Woman: Thomas Hardy's Letters to Florence Henniker, 1893–1922*, 14 and frontispiece.

Millgate dates "Wessex Heights" as following the hostile reception of *Jude* (*Hardy: A Biography*). For another tale that incorporates Shelley and Henniker, see Hardy's "An Imaginative Woman." Kevin Moore sees Mrs. Henniker becoming, "as Sue Florence Bridehead, . . . a representative figure for all weak 'Epipsychidions' who dissemble a Shelleyan love to which they are not wholly committed" (*The Descent of the Imagination: Postromantic Culture in the Later Novels of Thomas Hardy* [New York: New York University Press, 1990], 252).

41. Samuel Butler, "Remorse (a)," *The Note-Books of Samuel Butler*, ed. Henry Festing Jones (London: Jonathan Cape, 1926), 424. The sonnet is dated July 30, 1901, in Geoffrey Keynes and Brian Hill, eds., *Letters Between Samuel Butler and Miss E. M. A. Savage 1871–1885* (London: Jonathan Cape, 1935), 359n1. Butler had earlier written of Eliza Savage, "she haunts me, and always will haunt, because I never felt for her love that if I had been a better man I should have felt." Philip Henderson notes that Savage had disliked Aunt Aletha in *The Way of All Flesh*, apparently based on her, and complained to Butler, "You make her like that most odious of women, Mrs. John Stuart Mill, who though capable of surpassing Shelley, preferred to efface herself for the greater comfort of Mr. John Stuart Mill!" (*Samuel Butler: The Incarnate Bachelor* [London: Cohen & West, 1953], 137, 133). Browning's "dismissal" is quoted at note 86 to Chapter 1.

42. Christine Brooke-Rose, "Ill Wit and Sick Tragedy: *Jude the Obscure*," in Lance St. John Butler, ed., *Alternative Hardy* (Houndmills, Eng.: Macmillan, 1989), 37–38. T. R. Wright says, "The New Woman . . . has failed to find an answer to the old problem, not least because, in Hardy's view, there is none" (*Hardy and the Erotic* [Houndmills, Eng.: Macmillan, 1989], 131). For "At an Inn," see Millgate, *Hardy: A Biography*, 339–40.

43. "The Tree of Knowledge," *The New Review*, June 1894, 681; cited by Millgate, *Hardy: A Biography*, 357.

44. Leon Edel, *Henry James, The Treacherous Years: 1895–1901*, 149. See also Edel, *Henry James, The Middle Years: 1882–1895*, 356–72.

45. Leon Edel, ed., *The Letters of Henry James*, vol. 3: *1883–1895* (Cambridge, Mass.: Belknap, 1980), 463, 464, 465, 470. Edel notes that this whole sentence to William "was inserted as an afterthought, and the word 'intelligent' inserted after that" (472). James underscored both "*intelligent*" and "*inevitable*."

46. Edel, *The Middle Years*, 372.

47. Edel, *The Treacherous Years*, 149.

48. For Alexander Welsh's comment on the centrality of "unmarriedness" to realism, see "Opening and Closing," 22.

49. Henry James, "The Beast in the Jungle," in *The Novels and Tales of Henry James: The New York Edition*, vol. 17 (New York: Charles Scrib-

ner's Sons, 1909), 74, 85, and, for the phrase "intensities and avoidances," below, 100. *The Awkward Age*, like many of James's fictions, puts multiple figures in the mediating position within models of "triangulated desire," as described by René Girard (*Deceit, Desire, and the Novel*).

50. At least until Marcher acknowledges his link to his fellow male mourner in the story's final scene, the broader implications of which have been described by Eve Kosofsky Sedgwick in "The Beast in the Closet: James and the Writing of Homosexual Panic," pp. 182–212 in *Epistemology of the Closet*.

51. "The Beast in the Jungle," 105, 106, and, for the reference below to the nameless date, 110.

52. Tony Tanner, *Henry James: The Writer and His Work*, 103; Tzvetan Todorov, "The Verbal Age," 368. Linda Dowling links literary Decadence's "dead language" to a perception that language had become subject to disease or corruption, an idea consistent with *The Awkward Age*'s own sense of belatedness (*Language and Decadence in the Victorian Fin de Siècle*, 148). For historical contextualizations of James's novel see Elizabeth Owen, " 'The Awkward Age' and the Contemporary English Scene," *Victorian Studies* 11 (1967): 63–82, and Hamlin Hill, " 'The Revolt of the Daughters': A Suggested Source for 'The Awkward Age,' " *Notes and Queries*, Sept. 1961, 347–49.

53. The twin apostles are described by Dowling in "The Decadent and the New Woman in the 1890's," 447; *The Saturday Review*'s comments appeared May 13, 1899, 598. As "priest" and penitent, Longdon and Nanda's relationship descends from a typical Victorian model represented by Giuseppe and Pompilia's in Browning's *The Ring and the Book* and a series of couples in George Eliot's fiction (see Chapters 1 and 2).

54. Dowling, "The Decadent and the New Woman," 441.

55. In a talk entitled "Toward a Queer Performativity," at Yale University, Apr. 8, 1992, Eve Kosofsky Sedgwick described James's key terms in *The Art of the Novel* as "having to be specified and despecified at the same time." Sedgwick's account of "shame" as a determining factor in James's life and work provides a context for his response to Woolson's death, particularly as expressed in *The Awkward Age*.

56. Nanda incorrectly guesses that Longdon had had a relationship with her mother rather than with her grandmother (222); the scene is reminiscent of the scene in Hardy's *Well-Beloved* when the youngest Avis asks Pierston, "And were you my great-grandmother's [suitor] too?" (172). The generational issues in the two novels run parallel at a number of occasions.

57. David McWhirter describes James with a vocabulary similar to that derived from Bersani in my earlier discussions of Allen and Hardy: "Love is made problematical in James's fiction, not by its peripheral importance or absence—as some critics have suggested—but by its *insistent and often*

painful centrality" (emphasis added) (*Desire and Love in Henry James: A Study of the Late Novels* [Cambridge, Eng.: Cambridge University Press, 1989], 5).

58. *Literary World*, July 1899, 227, reprinted in Roger Gard, ed., *Henry James: The Critical Heritage* (London: Routledge & Kegan Paul, 1968), 294; Séamus Cooney, "Awkward Ages in *The Awkward Age*," 209; Oscar Cargill, *The Novels of Henry James* (New York: Macmillan, 1961), 268; James Hart, *The Oxford Companion to American Literature* (New York: Oxford University Press, 1983), 47; Edward Wagenknecht, *Eve and Henry James: Portraits of Women and Girls in His Fiction* (Norman: University of Oklahoma Press, 1978), 144, 150.

59. Edel, *The Treacherous Years*, 259; Tanner, *Henry James*, 104. Ruth Bernard Yeazell's description of the reader's relation to James's late style provides a possible explanation for this sweeping range of names: "The late style demands that at every point we sense more than we are yet able to articulate; only gradually do we grow fully conscious of our subliminal guesses" (*Language and Knowledge in the Late Novels of Henry James* [Chicago: University of Chicago Press, 1976], 35).

60. Cooney, "Awkward Ages," 209; Todorov, "Verbal Age," 368. The "solemnity" with which Longdon kisses Nanda's forehead in the final scene (543) seems to me proof of their relationship's chastity, especially in the context of Nanda's repeated rejection of Mitchy's wish to kiss her hand in the preceding scene (524, 530), but mine is, of course, merely a gradually developed "guess" of the kind described by Yeazell, and the novel provides no explicit confirmation.

61. See the opening pages of Chapter 1 for the use of such phrases by Dinah Craik and others.

62. Millicent Bell, *Edith Wharton and Henry James: The Story of Their Friendship* (New York: G. Braziller, 1965), 28; Edel, *The Middle Years*, 318–19, and *The Treacherous Years*, 259.

63. The phrase is Dorothea Krook's, *The Ordeal of Consciousness in Henry James* (Cambridge, Eng.: Cambridge University Press, 1962), 156.

64. Martha Vicinus discusses many versions of "a woman-controlled space" in the period (*Independent Women*, 7). For an all-male counterpart, see James's own "The Great Good Place"—the title of which Edel uses for the section of *The Treacherous Years* that encompasses James's move to Lamb House (the model for Longdon's Beccles) and the writing of *The Awkward Age*.

Chapter Four

1. For Justin McCarthy's recollection of Henniker's house in London, where she established herself as "one of the hostesses . . . who, if she had lived in Paris at a former time, would have been famous as the presiding

genius of a *salon*," see his *Reminiscences*, cited in Hardy and Pinion, eds., *One Rare Fair Woman*, xviii.

2. George Eliot, "Woman in France: Madame de Sablé," *Westminster Review*, Oct. 1854; reprinted in Eliot, *Essays*, 80.

3. Eliot, *Essays*, 74; at 72–73 Eliot comments that Mme. de Sablé, "the valuable, trusted friend of noble women and distinguished men, . . . [had] no ambition as an authoress." In contrast, Mme. de Staël was recognized as both hostess and writer—by, among others, J. S. Mill in *On the Subjection of Women*, 314–15. Both Comte and Cobb are discussed in Chapter 1.

4. Viola Meynell quotes Meredith and Major Fitzroy Gardner's *More Reminiscences of an Old Bohemian* in *Alice Meynell: A Memoir*, 143. For an account of one of the most prominent English salons in the time see Max Egremont, "Lady Desborough, The Souls of London," in Peter Quennell, ed., *Affairs of the Mind: The Salon in Europe and America from the 18th to the 20th Century* (Washington, D.C.: New Republic Books, 1980), 117–30.

5. This summary is representative of various footnotes to collections in which letters to or from Tobin appear: her capsule biographies typically consist of a list of famous "close friends" followed by quotations or paraphrases of Symons's description in *Confessions* and Conrad's dedication. My text gives these last two sources, as does Allan Wade, ed., *The Letters of W. B. Yeats*, 459. Tobin's role as a draw to the Meynells' salon is noted in V. Meynell, *Alice Meynell*, 40–41.

6. Sir Francis Meynell, "A.T. and A.M.," in *Agnes Tobin: Letters, Translations, Poems, with Some Account of Her Life*, xiii; Michael Holroyd, *Augustus John: A Biography*, 1: 315; Zdzisław Najder, *Joseph Conrad: A Chronicle*, 371–72.

7. Yeats's comparison to Whitman is cited by Annette Specht, "Lady of My Delight," *Mundelin Review*, Autumn 1939, 10; his comment on Tobin's translations is given in Wade, ed., *Letters of W. B. Yeats*, 459.

8. Ann Saddlemeyer, ed., *The Collected Letters of John Millington Synge* (Oxford: Clarendon Press, 1983), 1: 251, 255, 316. For the quarrel, see Robin Skelton, *J. M. Synge and His World* (New York: Viking, 1971), 104.

9. The letters mentioned and quoted here appear in *Agnes Tobin*, 71–82. Conrad may have settled on the phrase "genius for friendship" as distinctive to the United States: the *Atlantic Monthly* of September 1891, 432, had headlined a column with the phrase, and the OED ascribed it to James Russell Lowell. Agnes Tobin, as a translator of Petrarch, may have picked up the phrase herself from Maud Jerrold's *Francesco Petrarca: Poet and Humanist* (1909); this use is mentioned by Lorna Strachan, "Agnes Tobin: Translator of Petrarch" (Master's thesis, St. John's University, Brooklyn, N.Y., 1953), 18.

10. Frederick Karl, *Joseph Conrad: The Three Lives*, 279. The passage in "Heart of Darkness" appears at 58 in *'Youth, A Narrative': and Two Other Stories*, vol. 6 of *The Collected Works of Joseph Conrad* (Garden City, N. Y.: Doubleday, Page, 1925).

11. Karl lists the Conrad/Poradowska relationship as one of "Three Problematic Areas in Conrad Biography" in Ross Murfin, ed., *Conrad Revisited: Essays for the Eighties*, 13–30.

12. Najder, *Conrad: A Chronicle*, 150–51, 182.

13. Karl, *Conrad: Three Lives*, 279–80.

14. The quoted phrase is from Bernard Meyer, *Conrad: A Psychoanalytic Biography*, 107, but see also Najder, *Conrad: A Chronicle*, 150.

15. *Agnes Tobin*, 81.

16. Joyce seems to have added Duffy's sullen pronouncement to "A Painful Case" in August 1905; see Hans Walter Gabler, ed., *'Dubliners': A Facsimile of Drafts and Manuscripts* (New York: Garland, 1978), 111, 157. Joyce has another relevant passage in *Ulysses* (New York: Random House, 1986), when Bloom thinks of Parnell and Kitty O'Shea, in the hyperconventional phrasings of "Eumaeus": "First it was strictly Platonic till nature intervened and an attachment sprung up between them till bit by bit matters came to a climax. . . ." (531). Much commonplace cynicism is recorded in the three-part *Westminster Review* series on "Friendship Between the Sexes," 1899, cited in note 12 to Chapter 3; see esp. 334, 584.

17. Thomas Moser, *Joseph Conrad: Achievement and Decline*, 89, 88; the title to Moser's second chapter refers to love and courtship's comprising Conrad's "uncongenial subject." Graham Hough calls Conrad's "largely a male world" in *Image and Experience* (London: Duckworth, 1960), 213.

18. J. Hillis Miller, *Poets and Reality* (Cambridge, Mass.: Belknap Press, 1965), 30. The continuing influence of Moser's strongly argued study is evident in much recent Conrad scholarship, including Najder's biography and Cedric Watts's *Joseph Conrad: A Literary Life* (Houndmills, Eng.: Macmillan, 1989), which cites Moser and Najder at 125. See also Ruth Nadelhalf's feminist analysis *Joseph Conrad* (Hertfordshire, Eng.: Harvester Wheatsheaf, 1991), which treats the characterization of Emilia Gould, as well as that of Nathalie Haldin in *Under Western Eyes*, at 81–108.

19. The extended description of the writer Peter Ivanovitch's cruelty to Tekla as she takes dictation from him (128) seems an ironic reflection on Conrad's own act of dictating *Under Western Eyes* to Lillian Hallowes. Karl (*Conrad: Three Lives*, 658) notes that Conrad had begun dictating the novel but couldn't work fast enough to make it profitable even at Hallowes's low rate. Conrad's son Boris recalled Hallowes's "ability to sit quite silent and motionless in front of her machine, hands resting tranquilly in her lap, for long periods, reacting promptly to a word, a phrase, or a

sudden outburst of continuous speech, hurled at her abruptly as [Conrad] prowled about the room or sat hunched up in his big armchair, as he dictated directly onto the typewriter" (*My Father, Joseph Conrad* [London: Calder & Beyars, 1970], 14). Boris's description of such activities sounds like some of Tekla's scenes, which provide a rare fictional account of the act of writing from the amanuensis's point of view.

20. Daniel Schwarz, *Conrad: 'Almayer's Folly' to 'Under Western Eyes'*, 195, 196, 211; Suresh Raval, *The Art of Failure: Conrad's Fiction* (Boston: Allen & Unwin, 1986), 128. For Schwarz on Emilia Gould, see his 140–41; and for Schwarz's challenge to Moser's assessment of Conrad's misogyny, see "The Continuity of Conrad's Later Novels," in Murfin, ed., *Conrad Revisited*, 151–70.

21. The change is registered in the Signet Classic edition (New York: New American Library, 1960).

22. Moser relates *Under Western Eyes* to "an instance of Anglo-Russian literary relations in late Victorian London," in "An English Context for Conrad's Russian Characters: Sergey Stepniak and the Diary of Olive Garnett," *Journal of Modern Literature*, Mar. 1984, 3–44; Karl (*Conrad: Three Lives*, 645) suggests connections between *Under Western Eyes* and the Poland of Conrad's youth. Eloise Knapp Hay notes the "strange" lack of "critical examination" to which Conrad's text subjects "the teacher's English eyesight": "he stuffily assumes there will be no different opinions from his even among the French and Germans, to say nothing of his fellow Englishmen," and he remains "uncorrected" ("*Under Western Eyes* and the Missing Center," in David Smith, ed., *Joseph Conrad's 'Under Western Eyes': Beginnings, Revisions, Final Forms*, 106–7). Another critical reading of the unnamed narrator, one that sees him as implicated in troubling gender dynamics, may be found in Katherine Snyder, "Bachelor Narrative: Gender and Representation in Anglo-American Fiction, 1850–1914," Ph.D. diss., Yale University, 1992.

23. Najder, *Conrad: A Chronicle*, 362; Schwarz, "The Continuity of Conrad's Later Novels," in Murfin, ed., *Conrad Revisited*, 159.

24. Moser, "Conrad, Ford, and the Sources of *Chance*," *Conradiana* 7, 3 (1976): 207.

25. Najder, *Conrad: A Chronicle*, 390, 375, 374; Karl, *Conrad: Three Lives*, 727; Karl and Laurence Davies, eds., *The Collected Letters of Joseph Conrad*, 1: 334.

26. Conrad's famous passage about his authorial task to "make you see" appears in the Preface to *The Nigger of the "Narcissus"*, vol. 3 of *Collected Works of Joseph Conrad* (Garden City, N.Y.: Doubleday, Page, 1925), xviii.

27. Najder, *Conrad: A Chronicle*, 391.

28. A concise summary (with illustrations) of militant feminism in England in 1910–11 is available in Antonia Raeburn, *The Suffragette View* (Newton Abbot, Eng.: David & Charles, 1976), 46–54.

29. On *Chance*'s commercial success, and its popularity among women readers, see Najder, *Conrad: A Chronicle*, 390. My 1986 Modern Language Association Conference paper arguing for the importance of *Chance* as a significant examination of gender relations was abstracted in *Joseph Conrad Today* 12, 3; I am grateful to Thomas Moser for his generous and insightful response to this paper. See Holcombe, *Victorian Ladies at Work*, for the increase of women in middle-class occupations in the years prior to World War I.

30. Marlow's statement resembles a line about Razumov that Conrad excised from the *Under Western Eyes* typescript: "Women were human beings for him and nothing more. . . ." David Leon Higdon notes that the excised passage "pointedly underlines for Razumov the feminine powers which the novel both simultaneously satirizes and affirms . . ." ("'Complete but Uncorrected': The Typescript of Conrad's *Under Western Eyes*," in D. Smith, ed., *Conrad's 'Under Western Eyes'*, 107).

31. Holroyd describes Agnes Tobin's awareness of her encroaching madness as of 1911 (*Augustus John*, 1: 321). But there are almost no later references to her in the biographies of her distinguished acquaintances. Kevin Starr notes her having some literary interests as late as 1929: "The Papers of Agnes Tobin," *Bancroftiana*, Aug. 1985, 2. In 1938 Yeats responded to a query from Maud Gonne MacBride: "I do not know if Agnes Tobin is still living. . . . She is probably dead. A week ago I was talking to Mrs. Moody, the great tennis player, about the Tobin family. She lives in San Francisco and knows them well, but she had never heard of Agnes Tobin" (Wade, ed., *Letters of W. B. Yeats*, 910). Agnes Tobin did not die until the following year. Obituaries referred to her "long illness," and Starr notes only her having become "a cloistered recluse." For additional information on her final years, I am grateful to her niece, Agnes Albert (interview, San Francisco, 1985).

32. Scarry, "Work and the Body," 95, as cited in Chapter 3.

33. Kate Millett, *Sexual Politics*, 251. Raymond Williams's sympathetic account of Lawrence in *Culture and Society* (New York: Columbia University Press, 1958) ascribes to him the belief "that a common life has to be made on the basis of a correspondence between work relationships and personal relationships . . ." (206).

34. Lawrence's Schopenhauer, as presented by Emile Delevenay, is cited by Edward Nehls in *D. H. Lawrence: A Composite Biography*, 1: 67; the comment from E.T. [Jessie Wood], *D. H. Lawrence: A Personal Record*, is cited in James Boulton, ed., *The Letters of D. H. Lawrence*, 1: 88n3.

35. So have observed, among others, many Lacanian theorists, such as E. Ann Kaplan, "Is the Gaze Male?" in Ann Snitow, Christine Stansell, and Sharon Thompson, eds., *Powers of Desire: The Politics of Sexuality* (New York: Monthly Review, 1983). For a related set of observations, see Peter Berger, *Ways of Seeing*. I consider this issue more thoroughly in Chapters 5 and 6.

36. Boulton, ed., *Letters*, 1: 64–67.

37. See Moore, ed., *Collected Letters of D. H. Lawrence*, 1: 26. Note that subsequent references to Lawrence's letters are to Boulton's edition and not this earlier one.

38. Andrew Robertson's textual note for this passage (386) points to the letter to Jennings quoted above.

39. "Hoeing" is reproduced in Haldane Macfall, *A History of Painting* (London: T. C. and E. C. Jack, 1911), 8: 248. See also *Sir George Clausen, R.A., 1852–1944* (Bradford Art Galleries and Museums of Tyne and Wear County Council, 1980).

40. It might be said that subsequent manifestations of this situation comprise the center of *The White Peacock*, though Lawrence presents the novel's men as experiencing its chief tragedies.

41. Eve Kosofsky Sedgwick introduces the category of the "homosocial" in its "intimate and shifting relation to class" at the beginning of *Between Men*.

42. Hilary Simpson quotes Lawrence's letter to Arthur McLeod (June 2, 1914) and describes the story "Goose Fair" as "the result of some sort of genuine collaboration" between Louie Burrows and Lawrence (*Lawrence and Feminism*, 149).

43. Briefer, anyway, than that I undertook for either *Daniel Deronda* or *Jude the Obscure*, precisely because Lawrence's applications of the term follow conventional plotting so predictably: for more uses of the word "friend" in *Sons and Lovers* not cited in this discussion see 240, 261, 341, 363; for the novel's merging of various conventional categories for heterosexual relations (domesticity, courtship, spirituality) see esp. 296, 307, 347, 387, 431.

44. See Craik's reference to "Platonic" relationships as "contrary to nature" in *A Woman's Thoughts*, 136, and cited in Chapter 1.

45. Keith Sagar gives a chronological account in *D. H. Lawrence: A Calendar of His Works* (Manchester, Eng.: Manchester University Press, 1979), 14–24.

46. Nehls, *Lawrence: Composite Biography*, 1: 147–48, 59, 66.

47. Lawrence to Dorothy Brett, Jan. 26, 1925, in Boulton, ed., *Letters*, 5: 203. Two weeks earlier Lawrence had written to Brett, ". . . I hate 'situations,' and feel humiliated by them" (5: 192), words that seem to ex-

tend Robert Browning's comment to Julia Wedgwood, cited in note 86 to Chapter 1.

48. Nehls, *Lawrence: Composite Biography*, 1:136. Simpson describes the fates of works by Lawrence's various female acquaintances in the course of a defense of Lawrence as practical collaborator. She concludes by declaring it "noticeable that several of the women whom Lawrence knew betray an attitude towards writing very different from his—it is for them a private almost therapeutic affair; often, as in Helen Corke's case, it takes the form of a diary written with no thought of publication. Lawrence is of course himself an intensely personal writer, and one who believed that the artist 'sheds his sicknesses' in books; yet his urge is always to turn the experience into fictive form, and to *publish*." Simpson thus justifies the fact that "frequently, Lawrence seems to appropriate not just material but the creative instinct itself"; see *Lawrence and Feminism*, 143–61. For Mill and Lytton on friendship in marriage, see Chapter 1.

49. Boulton, ed., *Letters* 1: 61, 71, 44. Scott Saunders notes that Lawrence saw the distinction between "manual labor" and "labor of the mind" as a class division: *D. H. Lawrence: The World of the Five Major Novels* (New York: Viking, 1973), 49. Gendered associations inhere in that cherished opposition of Lawrence's, but my point here is that he effectively sexualizes, and disqualifies women from, both kinds of labor. See also James Knapp, *Literary Modernism and the Transformation of Work*, cited in Chapter 6, note 29.

50. Boulton, ed., *Letters*, 1: 2; see Linton, "Flirting," in *The Girl of the Period* (1869), cited in note 9 to Chapter 1.

51. Shirley MacLeod notes, "Here in *Sons and Lovers* the web of misunderstanding between men and women is already thoroughly tangled. Whatever women are and do in themselves is devalued; whatever they are and do in relation to men is overemphasized. A woman cannot be divorced from her sexuality—or rather, from a man's sexual apprehension of her" (*Lawrence's Men and Women* [London: William Heinemann, 1985], 92).

52. "*Sons and Lovers* appeared just when we were beginning to hear about Freud in England . . ." recalled Ivy Lowe Litvinoff (quoted by Nehls, *Lawrence: Composite Biography*, 1: 215), a recollection confirmed by Perry Meisel and Walter Kendrick when they call 1913 "an inaugural moment in the history of psychoanalysis"—though they stress that psychoanalysis had little influence on sexual idiom in pre-War England (*Bloomsbury/Freud: The Letters of James and Alix Strachey, 1924–1925*, 39–40). Meisel and Kendrick note that *The Psychopathology of Everyday Life*'s "attention to daily life was congenial to the English"; the *Saturday Review*'s response to Freud's book (July 11, 1914, 51) supports that contention. The *Athenaeum*'s reviewer of *The Interpretation of Dreams* was troubled, however,

by the sense that "an atmosphere of sex pervades many parts of the book and renders it very unpleasant reading . . . and reveal[s] a seamy side of life in Vienna which might well have been left alone" (Apr. 19, 1913, 424); that phrasing is comparable to the *Times Literary Supplement*'s sense that Lawrence was drawing on "an ugly world" (Dec. 3, 1914, 542). The *TLS* saw the theory of *The Interpretation of Dreams* rendered "perverse" by Freud's "fanatical application of it" (July 2, 1914, 321). See also Nehls, *Lawrence: Composite Biography,* 1: 566n105.

53. Sigmund Freud, "Psychoanalytic Notes on an Autobiographical Account of a Case of Paranoia," in *The Standard Edition,* vol. 12, ed. James Strachey (London: Hogarth Press and Institute of Psychoanalysis, 1958), 61; "Introductory Lectures (Part III)," *Standard Edition,* vol. 16, 425. Freud uses the latter phrase in relation to two men's having had sex together and so having "overstepped the bounds of friendship," but see also "Psychoanalytic Notes ("Dora")," *Standard Edition,* vol. 12: 109, for "more than friendship."

54. Harry Moore, *The Priest of Love: A Life of D.H. Lawrence,* 73.

55. Brougham Villiers, *The Socialist Movement in England* (London: T. F. Unwin, 1908), 310; for the Education Act of 1902 and its relation to Lawrence's life see Holcombe, *Victorian Ladies at Work,* 21–67, and Nehls, *Lawrence: Composite Biography,* 1: 44, respectively, as well as Dina Copelman, "'A New Comradeship between Men and Women': Family, Marriage, and London's Women Teachers, 1870–1914," in Jane Lewis, ed., *Labour and Love: Women's Experience of Home and Family, 1850–1914* (Oxford: Basil Blackwell, 1986), 175–93. (Copelman takes her title from that of an unrecovered talk; her article refers to the experiences of Helen Corke.) For the class rather than gender significance of Lawrence's work as a teacher, see Graham Holderness, *D. H. Lawrence: History, Ideology, and Fiction* (Dublin: Gill and Macmillan Humanities, 1982), 146.

Chapter Five

1. The two photographs, both evidently taken on the same occasion, appear respectively in Sandra Jobson Darroch, *Ottoline: The Life of Lady Ottoline Morrell,* following 86, and Carolyn Heilbrun, ed., *Lady Ottoline's Album* (New York: Knopf, 1976), 52. The captions for both of these photos call attention to the fact that women are at work; only Clive Bell is noticed among the men. One of the most striking of the many photographs of women at work—in this case lifting hay bales with the Army Service Corps—appeared in *The Illustrated London News,* Sept. 29, 1917, 382.

2. Gilbert Stone, "Appreciations and Prophecies," in Stone, ed., *Women War Workers,* 319–20.

3. Mrs. Alec-Tweedie, *Women and Soldiers*, 85, 23.

4. *The Woman Worker*, Jan. 1918, 2, and Apr. 1918, 9. The latter column went on to say that "working women can safely leave" a policy of "anti-man" feminism "to those doctrinaire, theoretical middle and upper-class women, who know no better."

5. Francis Garnet Wolseley, *Women and the Land*, 8; Women's Farm and Garden Union leaflet, Oct. 15, 1915, 1; Women's Land Service Corps, *Interim Report from the Formation of the Corps in February 1916 to September 30, 1916*, 29.

6. Women's Farm and Garden Union leaflet, Nov. 15, 1915, 2.

7. Arthur Marwick, *Women at War: 1914–1918*, 127.

8. Marwick, 74.

9. Women's Farm and Garden Union leaflet, May 15, 1916, 6. The complaint was repeated in the leaflet of Sept. 15, 7.

10. These prewar conditions are described by Anne Wiltsher, *Most Dangerous Women: Feminist Peace Campaigners of the Great War*, 181. Marwick contends that "expansion of job opportunity was the central phenomenon of women's war experience" (*Women at War*, 162). Alec-Tweedie's remark (*Women and Soldiers*, 79) has its contemporary echo in Jane Lewis's refutation of Marwick: "Rather than the war accelerating the entry of women into the labour market . . . it would be more accurate to see the wartime experience as a brief period when male unionists, employers and government (the male workers often under duress) agreed to abandon traditional designations of men's and women's work for the duration of the emergency" (*Women in England 1870–1950* [Sussex: Wheatsheaf, 1984], 180). Gail Braybon says that "the main effect of the war was . . . to bring about the transference of women between the trades, and the return of those previously excluded; there were not really hundreds of thousands of completely new workers in industry as might be assumed at first from the statistics" (*Women War Workers in the First World War* [London: Croom Helm, 1981], 50). Even in 1917 E. N. Thomas noted a dispute over whether the war had produced a relative increase in the number of female agricultural laborers; see his "Women Workers in Agriculture," in A. W. Kirkaldy, ed., *Industry and Finance: War Experiments in Reconstruction* (London: Pitman and Sons, 1917), 151. In her empirical attempt to prove the useful point that "women's war work did not affect women evenly," Deborah Thom oddly conflates Marwick's contention that "women's consciousness was irrevocably changed by the war" with the less contestable assertion that war brought "women's activity in to the light, making them visible" ("Women and Work in Wartime Britain," 316, 297).

11. Deidre Beddoe describes women's post war dismissal from the work-

force in *Back to Home and Duty: Women Between the Wars, 1918–1939*, 12–13, 48–50. Miriam Glucksmann notes an important exception, saying that even as "women trade unionists voiced considerable anxiety about female unemployment as women were ejected from their wartime jobs," there was relatively little consideration of women's opportunities for industrial employment, which actually increased in the interwar years (*Women Assemble: Women Workers and the New Industries in Inter-War Britain*, 8); Glucksmann gives a more standard description of women's postwar ejection from the workplace at 211–12.

12. David Mitchell, *Monstrous Regiment: The Story of the Women of the First World War*, 248. Mitchell's quotation is from a report by Hall Caine that goes on to call the female factory workers "some of the best looking young women in the world."

13. Wolseley uses this phrase to describe the effect of cooperative agricultural work in *Women and the Land*, 112. Eric Leed gives a full account of the European "Community of August" and its effacing of class and sex barriers in *No Man's Land: Combat and Identity in World War I* (Cambridge, Eng.: Cambridge University Press, 1979), 45 ff.

14. See Sandra Gilbert, "Soldier's Heart: Literary Men, Literary Women, and the Great War," in Gilbert and Susan Gubar, *No Man's Land: The Place of the Woman Writer in the Twentieth Century*, vol. 2: *Sexchanges*; orig. pub. *Signs* (1983).

15. Thom, "Women and Work," 301. Mitchell recounts Mary Macarthur's wartime battle to get equal pay for women (*Monstrous Regiment*, 255). The lot of working-class women whose wartime experience consisted mainly of increased working hours is described by Monica Cosens, *Lloyd George's Munitions Girls*, 154. Naomi Loughlin suggested that there were tensions between such women and their new co-workers in "Munition Work," in G. Stone, ed., *Women War Workers*, 36–37.

16. Alec-Tweedie, *Women and Soldiers*, 45; Joyce Berkman, "Feminism, War, and Peace Politics: The Case of World War I." Compare the Victorian argument in favor of heterosexual cooperation on behalf of the universal "human family" in Josephine Butler's 1869 collection *Women's Work and Women's Culture*, discussed in Chapter 1.

17. May Bradford, *A Hospital Letter-Writer in France* (London: Methuen, 1920); Mitchell, *Monstrous Regiment*, 170; Barbara McLaren, *Women of the War* (London: Hodder and Stoughton, 1917), 50. Bradford devoted her final chapter to "My Designation in the Wards." Mitchell (14) notes that when the Victorian Salvation Army regulations describe heterosexual cooperation, they efface sexuality by using only male pronouns.

18. Women's Farm and Garden Union leaflet, May 15, 1918. Note also

D. H. Lawrence's comment on tramcar drivers in the opening paragraph of the story "Tickets, Please": "To ride on these cars is always an adventure. Since we are in war-time, the drivers are men unfit for active service: cripples and hunch-backs" (in *England, My England* [London: Martin Secker, 1924], 99). Lawrence's story is perhaps the plainest illustration of how threatening wartime women's work might seem.

19. Frances Spalding suggests that white feathers, indicating cowardice, were distributed with particular frequency among farm laborers (*Vanessa Bell*, 139). In *Three Guineas* Virginia Woolf describes exaggerated attention to the white feathers as showing "that the male . . . preserves an abnormal susceptibility to such taunts" (182).

20. Wiltsher, *Most Dangerous Women*, 183.

21. Ina Scott, "The Land," and Mary Hughes, "A Postwoman's Perambulations," in G. Stone, ed., *Women War Workers*, 63–64, 67, respectively.

22. Women's Farm and Garden Union leaflet, Oct. 15, 1915, 1.

23. Glucksmann describes the postwar continuation of this practice in *Women Assemble*, 121.

24. Cosens, *Lloyd George's Munitions Girls*, 50.

25. John Rae, *Conscience and Politics: The British Government and the Conscientious Objector to Military Service* (London: Oxford University Press, 1970), 30.

26. Robert Gathorne-Hardy, ed., *Ottoline at Garsington: Memoirs of Lady Ottoline Morrell, 1915–1918*, 84. Heterosexual alternatives to the wartime enthusiasm for cross-sex friendship are described in the pages that follow; another implicit alternative might be found in feminist opposition to the war, which tended, as Wiltsher observes, to be organized by "women only" groups (*Most Dangerous Women*, 53). Berkman notes that "many, but not all feminists concluded that peace politics required exclusively female organizations" ("Feminism, War, and Peace Politics," 154).

27. George Zytaruk and James Boulton, eds., *The Letters of D. H. Lawrence*, vol. 3 (Cambridge, Eng.: Cambridge University Press, 1981), 271. See Darroch, *Ottoline*, 150–51, for the dispute.

28. Darroch, *Ottoline*, 177.

29. Lytton Strachey, *Eminent Victorians* (New York: Capricorn, 1963), 165–66.

30. Nigel Nicolson and Joanne Trautman, eds., *The Letters of Virginia Woolf*, 2: 38 (hereafter cited as *VWL*). Woolf tells the story of Strachey's "one word" ("semen") that broke "all barriers of reticence and reserve" in "Old Bloomsbury," in *Moments of Being*, 195ff.

31. Mary Agnes Hamilton, *Remembering My Good Friends* (London: Jonathan Cape, 1944), 78.

32. Gathorne-Hardy, *Ottoline at Garsington*, 125, 126. Fredegond

Shove, *Fredegond and Gerald Shove* (privately printed, 1952), 33–34. Darroch reports, as a fact pertaining to Gerald Shove, Osbert Sitwell's recollection: "Indeed it was alleged that some cantankerous if cultivated hinds had broken into the Manor House [at Garsington] shouting 'Down with capitalist exploitation' . . ." (*Ottoline*, 214). The pertinent excerpt from Sitwell's *Laughter in the Next Room* is included in S. P. Rosenbaum, ed., *The Bloomsbury Group: A Collection of Memoirs, Commentary and Criticism*, 254.

33. Brett's recollection is from Sybille Bedford, *Aldous Huxley: A Biography*, vol. 1: *1894–1939* (New York: Alfred Knopf, 1973), 72; David Garnett, *The Flowers of the Forest*, 142.

34. Alec-Tweedie, *Women and Soldiers*, 75; Quentin Bell, *Virginia Woolf: A Biography*, 1: 169.

35. For such information I rely on Spalding's *Vanessa Bell*, which in turn relies a good deal on Garnett's *Flowers of the Forest*.

36. Spalding, *Vanessa Bell*, 144, 165. But Fry was in fact less satisfied with this arrangement than his words suggest, as I will discuss in Chapter 6.

37. *VWL*, 2: 106–8, and Michael Holroyd, *Lytton Strachey: A Biography* (New York: Holt, Rinehart and Winston, 1971), 656.

38. Strachey, "Monday June 26 1916" in Michael Holroyd, ed., *Lytton Strachey by Himself* (New York: Holt, Rinehart and Winston, 1971), 146; Spalding, *Vanessa Bell*, 151–52. In her letter to Vanessa Bell, quoted above, Virginia Woolf mentions that she thinks their brother Adrian and Gerald Shove would like "to come to Wissett" for their agricultural service, then adds "but I suppose you don't much want them." Shove subsequently became Garsington's first C.O. farm worker. Quentin Bell points to the tensions in the parallel between Garsington and Vanessa Bell's farm at Charleston in *Virginia Woolf*, 262.

39. *VWL*, 2: 145, 144.

40. Garnett, *Flowers of the Forest*, 113.

41. *VWL*, 2: 83.

42. *VWL*, 1: 318–19; Clive Bell, *Old Friends*, 129, 130; Spalding, *Vanessa Bell*, 145; *VWL*, 2: 102.

43. See Clive Bell, *Old Friends*, 129, for Bloomsbury as a group of men hostessed by the two Stephen sisters.

44. Robert Skidelsky, *John Maynard Keynes: A Biography*, 1: 328.

45. *VWL*, 2: 147; Spalding, *Vanessa Bell*, 150.

46. Spalding, *Vanessa Bell*, 170; Jane Marcus, "Enchanted Organs, Magic Bells: *Night and Day* as Comic Opera," 108.

47. Garnett, *Flowers of the Forest*, 115, 132ff.

48. This seems a common compositional feature in Bloomsbury's multiple-figure paintings, exemplified for instance in Vanessa Bell's "The Dining Room Window, Charleston" and Duncan Grant's "The Dancers."

49. Richard Shone, *Bloomsbury Portraits: Vanessa Bell, Duncan Grant, and Their Circle* (New York: E. P. Dutton, 1976), 179.

50. Vanessa Bell, "Notes on Bloomsbury," in Rosenbaum, ed., *The Bloomsbury Group*, 83.

51. Leonard Woolf, *Beginning Again: An Autobiography of the Years 1911 to 1918*, 197–98.

52. *VWL*, 2: 109. Virginia Woolf would later identify Vanessa Bell with *Night and Day*'s Katharine Hilbery: see *VWL*, 2: 290.

53. "How am I to write my last chapter with all this shindy," Woolf wrote to her sister on Nov. 11, 1918 (*VWL*, 2: 290).

54. Katherine Mansfield, review of *Night and Day*, *Athenaeum*, Nov. 1919, reprinted in Robin Majumader and Allen McLaurin, *Virginia Woolf: The Critical Heritage*, 82; Cherry Hankin, ed., *Letters Between Katherine Mansfield and John Middleton Murry* (London: Virago, 1988), 204; the omitted portion concerns a specific scene in the novel and does not make more clear who exactly "they" are. F. A. Lea provides Murry's concurring reply, "I agree with every word you say about Virginia and the War. . . . The War *is* Life, not a strange aberration of Life, but a revelation of it. It is a test we must apply; it must be allowed for in any truth that is to touch us" (*The Life of John Middleton Murry* [New York: Oxford, 1960], 68).

55. Marcus, "Enchanted Organs, Magic Bells," 108–9. Avrom Fleishman describes the novel as "celebrating love in the comic—particularly the Shakespearian—tradition" (*Virginia Woolf: A Critical Reading*, 22); Fleishman suggests that "some of the *brio* of *Night and Day* derived from the author's response to her recent marriage"—an idea that must surely derive from some enviable understanding of the stamina in marital bliss, as Virginia Woolf had been married since 1912 and had just endured nearly two years of breakdown and convalescence when she first conceived of the book.

56. Marcus describes Woolf's depiction of Bell thus: "Vanessa, the painter, is the eye and the hand, and she, the writer, is the ear and the mouth. If we did not have Quentin Bell's biography, only Virginia's letters, we should see Vanessa as Virginia verbally constructed her, completely inarticulate, deaf and dumb, except with a brush in her hand, a child in her lap or a lover in her arms" (" 'Taking the Bull by the Udders': Sexual Difference in Virginia Woolf—A Conspiracy Theory," in Marcus, ed., *Virginia Woolf and Bloomsbury: A Centenary Celebration* (London: Macmillan, 1987), 166. Spalding (*Vanessa Bell*, 213) describes Woolf's tendency to see only the positive side of Vanessa Bell's life. The following pages are meant to connect Woolf's experiments in idiom with the activities of Vanessa Bell's hands and eyes.

57. Marcus, "Enchanted Organs, Magic Bells," 109; Margaret Comstock concludes her essay " 'The Current Answer Don't Do': The Comic

Form of *Night and Day*" by saying, "Marriage alone does not make the happy ending, for that would be a discredited romanticism. Politics alone do not make the happy ending, for that would be propaganda" (*Women's Studies* 4 [1977]: 169).

58. D. H. Lawrence, "Foreword," *Women in Love* (Cambridge, Eng.: Cambridge University Press, 1987), 485.

59. Ann O. Bell, ed., *The Diary of Virginia Woolf*, 1: 53, 217; cited hereafter as *VW Diary*.

60. See Quentin Bell, *Virginia Woolf*, 2: 31.

61. Montrose, "Of Gentlemen and Shepherds: The Politics of Elizabethan Pastoral Form," 452. The word I've removed by ellipsis is, of course, "Elizabethan." Montrose means his idea to be historically specific, but I would assert the following parallel: that where Montrose sees Elizabethan pastoral as a means whereby "dangerous or impolitic opinions might be voiced obscurely in a style manifestly simple and direct," Woolf's pastoral idyll subverts a dominant discourse (the war's) and suggests simplicity even as it offers complication. The countryside of wartime propaganda was one where men and women met in sexless harmony; Woolf's countryside repeatedly suggests easy contentment but then extends heterosexual crisis.

62. *VWL*, 2: 101; *VW Diary*, 1: 44–46, 49, 186.

63. *VW Diary*, 1: 125.

64. Fleishman uses two quotations to illustrate neatly the "two views of life that Woolf alternately entertained" and expressed in her fiction: "Communication is health" and ". . . we go alone, and like it better so." (*Virginia Woolf*, 95).

65. More specifically, Jean Guiguet identifies *Night and Day* as "that novel 'about silence, the things people don't say' that Terence Hewett [in *The Voyage Out*, Woolf's first novel] wanted to write" (Jean Guiguet, *Virginia Woolf and Her Works*, trans. Jean Stewart [New York: Harcourt Brace Jovanovich, 1965], 213).

66. In *Three Guineas* Woolf would argue "that the daughters of educated men should give their brothers neither the white feather of cowardice nor the red feather of courage, but no feather at all; that they should shut the bright eyes that rain influence, or let those eyes look elsewhere when war is discussed . . ." (109).

67. Lucio Ruotolo, *The Interrupted Moment: A View of Virginia Woolf's Novels*, 67.

68. Susan Leonardi has read *Night and Day* as aspiring to the production of a "woman's sentence" free from "masculine hegemony" ("Bare Places and Ancient Blemishes: Virginia Woolf's Search for New Language in *Night and Day*," *Novel*, Winter 1986, 150–63).

69. *VW Diary*, 1: 234–43; see also *VWL*, 2: 217.

70. *VWL*, 2: 394; for "tupping," the editors' note cites *Othello* I.I: "An old black ram/Is tupping your white ewe."

Chapter Six

1. Woolf's "Mr. Conrad: A Conversation," in *'The Captain's Death Bed' and Other Stories* (New York: Harcourt Brace, 1950), 76–81, concludes with praise for *Chance* as "a great book, a great book."

2. "From linearity to multi-perspectivity" is the central phrase in Donald Lowe's *History of Bourgeois Perception* (Chicago: University of Chicago Press, 1982), which acknowledges Fry to have been the leading proponent in England of "the perceptual revolution of 1915" associated with the French avant garde (110). Mitchell Leaska studies *To the Lighthouse* as a "multiple-point-of-view novel" in *Virginia Woolf's Lighthouse: A Study in Critical Method* (New York: Columbia University Press, 1970); Diane Gillespie describes Virginia Woolf and Vanessa Bell's shared interest in "the relativity of human perception" in *The Sisters' Arts: The Writing and Painting of Virginia Woolf and Vanessa Bell*, 177ff. For the Cubists' undermining of the bourgeois "single eye," see Peter Berger, *Ways of Seeing*, 18; Berger further discusses modern art as questioning the "unequal relationship" between the "individualism of the [male] artist" and "the person who is the object of [his] activities—the woman—treated as a thing or an abstraction" (62–63).

3. Marianna Torgovnick, for instance, has noted "the extent to which all descriptions . . . call upon the visualizing capacity"; she cites Lukács, Derrida, Foucault, and Gombrich as part of a "virtually endless" relevant bibliography (*The Visual Arts: Pictorialism, and the Novel: James, Lawrence, and Woolf*, 24, 228n). Alex Zwerdling discusses Woolf's "fusion of external and internal observation" in the opening chapter of his *Virginia Woolf and the Real World*. Much scientific research on mental imagery would seem to justify drawing some equation between visual and imaginative "seeing": "It has been found that mental images have many of the same physical components as open-eyed perceptions" and "the pathways of [mental] visualization and perception are so similar that the two sometimes occur at the same time," argue Mike Samuels and Nancy Samuels in *Seeing with the Mind's Eye: The History, Techniques, and Uses of Visualization* (New York: Random House, 1975), 57, 59. Not everyone so readily accepts that continuity: Zenon Plyshyn argues for the role of "abstract mental pictures to which we do not have conscious access and which are essentially *conceptual* and *propositional*, rather than sensory or pictorial, in nature," but acknowledges that "the experience of [mental] images cannot be questioned" ("What the Mind's Eye Tells the Mind's Brain: A Critique of Mental Imagery," in John Nicholas, ed., *Images,*

Perceptions, and Knowledge [Dordrecht, Holland: D. Reidal, 1977]). The "debate surrounding visual imagery" and the relation of "mental images" to "visual scanning" is summarized by Glynn Humphries and Vicki Bruce, *Visual Cognition: Computational, Experimental, and Neuropsychological Perspectives* (Hove, East Sussex: Lawrence Earlbaum, 1989), 203–16.

4. *VWL*, 1: 60; 3: 189.

5. Deborah Guth disparages Clarissa's identification with Septimus as a "quasi-mystical interpretation" that "in no way reflects Septimus's own experience." To Guth, "visionary resurrection is but a word" [*sic*], and a destructive one at that: "Clarissa, no less than society, indulges in ritual sacrifice—the sacrifice of an individual reality in favor of the vision" ("Rituals of Self-Deception: Clarissa Dalloway's Final Moment of Vision," *Twentieth Century Literature*, Spring 1990, 36, 39). Guth's hesitations about the extent of Clarissa's individual "transcendence of the onlooker stance" are worthy of careful consideration when evaluating Clarissa in isolation; but Guth's emphasis on personal autonomy and on the need for absolute identification when one individual interprets another's experience seems at least unsympathetic to Woolf's interests in communally shared vision, as described below, and perhaps also finally unreasonable.

6. For a sample, see Majumader and McLaurin, eds., *Virginia Woolf: The Critical Heritage*, esp. 158, 160, 164, 175. Morris Beja emphasizes Woolf's "moments of vision" in *Epiphany in the Modern Novel* (London: Peter Owen, 1971), 112.

7. Walsh's earlier pursuit has been characterized by "this excitement, which seemed even with its back turned to shed on him a light which connected them" (80); his sense of himself as "romantic buccaneer" on that occasion seems in keeping with his "terror" and "ecstasy" in the book's final moment.

8. For contrast, compare the occasions of Girardian "triangulated desire" discussed in relation to Eliot's *Mill on the Floss* in Chapter 2, or the function of the third party in the conclusion to E. M. Forster's *Where Angels Fear to Tread*, in which sexual competition and courtship rhetoric mark Philip (the pander) and Caroline's shared gaze upon Gino as that of a far more conventional romantic triangle.

9. Recounted by Forster in "Virginia Woolf: The Rede Lecture," excerpted in Rosenbaum, ed., *The Bloomsbury Group*, 204.

10. *VWL*, 3: 6; *VW Diary*, 2: 171; *VWL*, 1: 492, 366.

11. *VW Diary*, 2: 173.

12. *Moments of Being*, 194–95. Woolf wrote of Clive Bell to Vita Sackville-West in 1926, "I love him, and always shall, but not in the go-to-bed or sofa way" (*VWL*, 3: 281). The year before, Woolf had remembered the pain produced by the worst stage of her relationship with Bell (in 1908)

as having "turned more of a knife in me than anything else" (*VWL*, 3: 172). That Woolf could continue to celebrate the persisting sexual component of a relationship whose sexual energies had once been terribly disruptive (insofar as they had disturbed her sister) suggests the significance she attached to the sexual "showing off" in the midst of friendship between herself and men.

13. Note that Woolf's account of Strachey's liberation of Bloomsbury conversation (cited at note 30 to Chapter 5) immediately follows the passage in "Old Bloomsbury" just mentioned.

14. For the impact of G. E. Moore on Cambridge men's conversational religion of love, see J. M. Keynes, "My Early Beliefs," in Rosenbaum, ed., *The Bloomsbury Group*, 52–57. Skidelsky is cited above at note 44 to Chapter 5.

15. *VW Diary*, 2: 158. Quentin Bell's biography of Woolf notes his father's position as (in Clive Bell's words) "to some extent her literary confidante"; see also Clive Bell's *Old Friends*, 93.

16. In *The History of Sexuality*, vol. 1, Michel Foucault suggests political consequences of the "Freudian endeavor . . . to ground sexuality in the law" (150). See also Meisel and Kendrick's introduction to *Bloomsbury/Freud*. My discussion of Freud's role in the sexualizing of English discourse appears near the end of Chapter 4.

17. See Quentin Bell, *Virginia Woolf*, 176–77.

18. See Foucault's "Introduction" to *The History of Sexuality*, vol. 2: *The Uses of Pleasure*, and the chapter suitably titled "We Other Victorians" in vol. 1.

19. Vanessa Bell, "Notes on Bloomsbury," in Rosenbaum, ed., *The Bloomsbury Group*, 79.

20. See Leo Bersani's description of "insistent stasis" (*The Freudian Body*, 35), discussed in note 9 to Chapter 3.

21. *VWL*, 6: 59; see also 4: 200: "What is the line between friendship and perversion?"

22. That end to the wartime illusion of sexlessness falls exactly fifty years after the height of the Contagious Diseases Acts controversy had made sex seem inseparable from the discourse of gender relations, as discussed in Chapter 1.

23. Ruotolo, *Interrupted Moment*, 114.

24. Beddoe, *Back to Home and Duty*, 18.

25. Ray Strachey, "Changes in Employment," in R. Strachey et al., eds., *Our Freedom and Its Results, by Five Women* (London: Hogarth Press, 1936), 163.

26. Beatrice Heron-Maxwell, *Through a Woman's Eyes* (London: A. Melrose, 1917), 235, 237, 238. For the early history of film censorship

see Rachel Law, *The History of the British Film*, vol. 1: *1906–1914*, and vol. 2: *1918–1929* (London: George Allen & Unwin, 1949 and 1971). The irony of women's being nominated as film critics for the sake of censorship seems even more pronounced in the light of Beddoe's observation, "It is remarkable too that the feminist *Woman's Leader* introduced a film review column, written by the witty novelist Rose Macaulay, as early as 1921: serious newspapers did not do so for many years" (*Back to Home and Duty*, 117).

27. Olive Schreiner, *Women and Labour*, 14, 208, 247–48.

28. Ray Strachey, *The Cause* (Virago: London, 1978), 390.

29. Schreiner, *Women and Labour*, 131, 80. Regenia Gagnier first alerted me to this crucial (Victorian) distinction between mental and manual labor. For a historical analysis of its relation to Modernism see James Knapp, *Literary Modernism and the Transformation of Work*; I am grateful to Mark Wollaeger for this reference.

30. Mrs. Ramsay is called "short-sighted" at 48 and 109; Mr. Ramsay "long-sighted" at 307.

31. Before Zwerdling's discussion of Woolf's "fusion of external and internal observation" in *Virginia Woolf and the Real World*, critical attention to "vision" in Woolf's writings, and particularly in *To the Lighthouse*, had stressed the word's imaginative sense at the expense of her interest in physical perception. Though A. D. Moody rejects the conclusion's symbolism, he nevertheless discusses the final relation of "Lily's vision" to "Mrs. Ramsay's vision" without ever considering what they have actually seen. Moody's reading is excerpted by Thomas Vogler in *Twentieth Century Interpretations of 'To the Lighthouse'* (Englewood Cliffs, N.J.: Prentice-Hall, 1970), 53–57. William Thickston emphasizes a Wordsworthian idea of imaginative "vision" in *To the Lighthouse* and other novels, though he sometimes discusses the relation of such vision to physical acts of seeing (*Visionary Closure in the Modern Novel* [London: Macmillan, 1988]).

32. Torgovnick notes that "frequently" in *To the Lighthouse* "Woolf establishes triangular patterns of vision and relation" (*The Visual Arts*, 140).

33. Alice Van Buren Kelley emphasizes the "remoteness" of Lily's vision in *The Novels of Virginia Woolf: Fact and Vision* (Chicago: University of Chicago Press, 1971), 143. Jeremy Hawthorn metaphorically discusses emotional distance as central to Peter's final perception of Clarissa in *Virginia Woolf's 'Mrs. Dalloway'* (Brighton, Eng.: University of Sussex Press, 1975), 63. Woolf wrote in her diary, "It is a mistake to think that literature can be produced from the raw. One must get out of life . . . one must become externalized . . . (*VW Diary*, 2: 193). In this regard, Lucio Ruotolo reminded me of the inherent necessity of distance between observer and

object for any reasonably clear visual perception, a point Jacob Bronowski grounds in the history of physics in *The Ascent of Man* (Boston: Little, Brown, 1973), 353–56.

34. At 295, "Lily could see him" precedes a scene in which Lily puts herself in Mrs. Ramsay's place in "an old-fashioned scene" of "ladies [being helped] by the gentlemen." Nancy Topping Bazin characterizes Lily's role as Mrs. Ramsay's surrogate in the concluding "symbolic union of male and female" (*Virginia Woolf and the Androgynous Vision*, 135). For Joseph Allen Boone, "the way in which Lily becomes Mrs. Ramsay's surrogate daughter indicates the degree to which [texts like *To the Lighthouse*] create new models of extended 'family'" (*Tradition Counter Tradition*, 216). Woolf's "Reminiscences" in *Moments of Being* discusses the visual capacities of her mother and sister, who served, of course, as partial models for Mrs. Ramsay and Lily; see esp. 30, 34.

35. John Ferguson's excellent account of Carmichael's significance includes a discussion of "the curious final union of Mr. Carmichael and Lily" as an adjustment of the "Septimus–Mrs. Dalloway bond" ("A Sea Change: Thomas De Quincey and Mr. Carmichael in *To the Lighthouse*," *Journal of Modern Literature* [Summer 1987], 62).

36. Bazin describes the novel's final section as rendering the visions of Mr. Ramsay, Cam, Lily, and James "all . . . androgynous or complete. A fusion occurs in their views of 'reality' as well as in their personal relationships" (*Woolf and the Androgynous Vision*, 136).

37. *VW Diary*, 2: 29; Woolf says of Tolstoy, "Nothing seems to escape him. The wonderful eye observes everything," in a review of *The Cossacks*, *TLS*, Feb. 2, 1917, 55.

38. Torgovnick's introduction in *The Visual Arts* discusses seeing and the modern novelists. The most famous example is of course Conrad's claimed goal to "make you see" in his Preface to *The Nigger of the "Narcissus"*, noted in Chapter 4.

39. Woolf, *A Room of One's Own*, 26, 71, 35. The phrase "power of vision" is Charlotte Brontë's, quoted by Woolf on 71 in the midst of a sentence about Jane Eyre.

40. Rachel Blau DuPlessis comes to similar conclusions: "By the midpoint of the novel, both of the traditional endings—marriage and death—have occurred, a sharp critical statement on Woolf's part that clears the ground of any rival solutions to Lily's plot. The third part of *To the Lighthouse* surpasses these classic resolutions, moving beyond the endings they propose, to brother-sister links, to male-female friendship, and, even more, to a vision that overwhelms all the binary systems on which the novel has been built. . . . The love here is not of the classic novelistic kind: Lily's helpful and genuine admiration for Mr. Ramsay's boots, saving him from yet

another depressive attack, is hardly a prelude to their courtship. But love it is, alluding to familial love, friendly love, comradely ties, some 'of those unclassified affections of which there are so many' " (*Writing Beyond the Ending*, 96–97).

41. Thus Boone's final account of *To the Lighthouse*, which makes Woolf's novel seem to accomplish little different from *Daniel Deronda* in "the very void its absence leaves, for a vision of a different story" (*Tradition*, 214), fails to account for the physical and imaginative actions the later novel has been able to depict in ways unavailable to the earlier one.

42. *VWL*, 5: 330; *VW Diary*, 4: 244, 5: 174, 305. Woolf's diary also recalls a wish to "describe the tremendous feeling at R.'s funeral. . . . I mean the universal feeling: how we all fought with our brains, loves, & so on; & *must* be vanquished" (*VW Diary*, 244). For the relation of Lily Briscoe's work to Roger Fry's aesthetics and Vanessa Bell's paintings, see Henry Harrington, "The Central Line Down the Middle of *To the Lighthouse*," 364. Gillespie's introduction to *The Sisters' Arts* warns against overemphasizing Woolf's debt to Fry but acknowledges his significance for her.

43. *VW Diary*, 5: 167, 170.

44. *VWL*, 6: 413–14. (Woolf quotes excerpts from Nicolson's letter in responding to him.)

45. *Three Guineas*, 102–3, 105, 143.

46. *The Waves*, written a few years earlier, includes moments of shared vision comparable to those I emphasized in *Mrs. Dalloway* and *To the Lighthouse*. But the structure of *The Waves*—a series of relatively independent monologues—makes shared perceptions considerably more difficult to trace, and the idioms of those monologues seem much removed from those of the common discourses of Woolf's time.

47. For World War II's employment opportunities as having afforded women "companionship with other young women and, more important, young men," see Gertrude Williams, *Women and Work* (New York: Essential Books, 1945), 48.

48. Three of the many occurrences of this phrase in *Roger Fry* appear at page 120.

49. In associating *To the Lighthouse*'s conclusion with Fry's aesthetics and Bell's paintings, Harrington reads that ending as a Post-Impressionist "superimposing [of] a second point of view on [a] first" ("The Central Line," 364).

50. *VWL*, 3: 154, 6: 419. *VWL*, 6: 7n1 identifies Mauron as "the half-blind French writer and chemist, [who] had translated Virginia's *To the Lighthouse* and *Orlando*, and collaborated with Roger Fry on his translations of Mallarmé."

51. It is rare for physiological and psychological research on "visual communication" to surpass this barrier, for such study seems to confine itself to occasions when people look at each other (i.e., make "eye contact"); for a synopsis see D. R. Rutter, *Looking and Seeing: The Role of Visual Communication in Social Interaction* (Chichester, Eng.: Wiley, 1984), introduction.

52. *VW Diary*, 5: 200; *VWL*, 6: 417.

53. *Three Guineas*, 143. Despite their obvious investment in individualism, moments like those discussed here have been highlighted by theorists mounting challenges *against* individualism. Thus J. Wyatt, with Julia Kristeva and Hélène Cixous in mind, celebrates Clarissa's "fusion with Septimus" as a triumphant merging and expansion of self: "Avoiding Self-Definition: In Defense of Women's Right to Merge," *Women's Studies* 13 (1986): 115–26.

54. Here I have in mind in particular Woolf's vehement distrust of the impulse toward "Conversion," as associated with Bradshaw in *Mrs. Dalloway* (151).

55. Denys Sutton, ed., *Letters of Roger Fry*, 35, 397. The two sisters and Fry in fact represented a triangle on which Woolf structured the book. For Fry and Woolf as fellow lovers of/rivals for Vanessa see *VW Diary*, 1: 152; *VWL*, 2: 67, 300; and Sutton, ed., 449.

56. *VW Diary*, 4: 285. For Woolf's explicit comment on Dickinson's jealousy see *Roger Fry*, 100. For the purposes of the biography Woolf believed "sodomy & the WC [to be] disinfected" as far as the public was concerned—see *VW Diary*, 5: 256—but she intended from the outset to suppress the relationship between Roger and Vanessa, to which the biography refers in passing as a "friendship" at 162 and on its final page. Another unrevealing reference to the "list" of Fry's friends appears at 267.

57. She is also, of course, coining a counterpart to her own use of the phrase, under which she had published two volumes of literary criticism; she calls herself "the common reader" at 284 when discussing Fry's books.

58. The last words of *Vision and Design* first appear in *Roger Fry* at 229; the similarly anti-conclusive last words of *Transformations*—"It must always be kept in mind that such analysis halts before the ultimate concrete reality of a work of art, and perhaps in proportion to the greatness of the work it must leave untouched a greater part of its objective"—appear in *Roger Fry* at 285–86 and 296.

59. *VWL*, 2: 573.

60. That had evidently been an issue for Woolf and Fry once, as Quentin Bell notes (*Virginia Woolf*, 176). My point is that sexuality did not persist idiomatically in this relationship as it did in Woolf's relationships with Clive Bell and Lytton Strachey.

61. At least not until Woolf eventually refers to their "odd posthumous friendship—in some ways more intimate than any I had in life" (*VW Diary*, 4: 361).

62. *VW Diary*, 2: 150.

63. That is the subject of my final pages; but I should acknowledge here the similarity between vision shared between the sexes, as I have associated it with Woolf and Fry, and Woolf's own description of androgynous vision in *A Room of One's Own* (108). Note, however, the degree to which traditional courtship provides the controlling vocabulary in Woolf's definition of androgyny: "Some collaboration has to take place in the mind between the woman and the man before the act of creation can be accomplished. Some marriage of opposites has to be consummated." Note also that Woolf in that passage concentrates on the fact of the male/female union in and of itself, rather than on any outwardly directed act. I have been suggesting that heterosexual cooperation can only free itself from compromised idioms when language centers on cooperative actions rather than on gender-related denominations: on people working, say, rather than on the fact that women, or women and men, are the performers of the task, or are united by "friendship."

Conclusion

1. The definitive study apparently remains Alan Booth and Elaine Hess's 1974 "Cross-Sex Friendship," which states, in part, "the phrase 'friendship' often implies the absence of overt sexual expression. Note the common expressions: 'He's *only* a friend. They're more than friends.' We are not suggesting here that components such as 'desire' and 'fantasy' are always eliminated from these relationships. Rather, we are arguing that if these components were present in overt behavioral form, the individuals involved in the relationship would not be likely to define it as a 'friendship' " (38n). Popular psychology, which has given the most attention to heterosexual friendship as a category, shares such assumptions: Lillian Rubin asserts, "Most people . . . insist that introducing sex into a friendship is an almost sure way to raise irreconcilable conflicts ("Women and Men as Friends: Mind, Body and Emotion," in her *Just Friends* [New York: Harper & Row, 1985], 151). Robert Bell attributes "the common belief that men and women can be lovers but not friends" to "fears of exploitation in sexual relationships" ("Cross-Sex Friendship," in his *Worlds of Friendship* [Beverly Hills: Sage, 1981], 97).

2. Denise Riley, "Some Peculiarities of Social Policy Concerning Women in Wartime and Postwar Britain," 260.

3. A 1989 magazine ad for Coors Light actually called upon the model of fellow beer-drinkers of different sexes who were "just friends," in order

to produce the slogan, "Coors Light. Just between friends." Indeed, the ad, which showed a smiling woman holding a beer bottle in front of her knees and a grinning male leaning on her shoulder, illustrated the full pattern in which heterosexual friendship commonly participates, from dubious connection with a source of innocence (here childhood) to inevitable admission of a sexual dynamic at the center: "Sam and Me. Me and Sam? We're just friends. Best friends, actually, since Mrs. Ainsley's first grade class when I let the hamster loose and Sam took the rap for me. I mean Sam's seen me in braces and I've seen him eat pizza. There's just way too much history here. Sam's my friend. The one I go to when I really need someone to talk to. I bring the Coors Light and Sam brings his shoulder. And sometimes it's Sam bringing the Coors Light and I'm doing the listening. Me and Sam? Together? I've never even thought about it. Okay, so I've thought about it." For this reference I am grateful to Lon Wilhelms.

4. As noted earlier, "comradeship," "comrade," and "camaraderie" do, etymologically at least, refer to the action of sharing a room. But in the United States in the early 1990's, a majority would surely find these words to have a humorously, sinisterly, or anachronistically communist ring. Family idioms, which have always had their own liabilities (as described in Chapters 1 and 2), must be thought nowadays similarly compromised. Not that such terms don't need recuperation: still, I can't think them the best resource, at present, for the problem considered in this study.

5. Richard Sennett, *The Conscience of the Eye: The Design and Social Life of Cities*, 226–30.

6. Sennett, 248.

7. Mary Ann Caws, *The Art of Interference: Stressed Readings in Verbal and Visual Communication*, 15. Caws considers the "problematics of distance" at 7ff. "This reconstruction of us all," Caws notes, in a statement with which the present chapter should seem in sympathy, ". . . cannot take place until the very speaking core of our interpretive community takes its truest pleasure and deepest joy in the exchange of our ideas taken up and understood together, . . . in our joint understanding and speech and work . . ." (134).

8. Caws, 5, and Richard Rorty, *Philosophy and the Mirror of Nature* (Princeton, N.J.: Princeton University Press, 1980), 371, 377. Note Rorty's own dependence on visual metaphors for thought (e.g., at 378), a factor Torgovnick's account in *The Visual Arts* would suggest is inevitable.

Appendix

1. Jocelyn Baines, *Joseph Conrad: A Critical Biography* (New York: McGraw Hill, 1960), 124, 171.

2. Najder, *Joseph Conrad: A Chronicle*, 183.

3. Karl, *Joseph Conrad: The Three Lives*, 313, 314.

4. Meyer, *Joseph Conrad: A Psychoanalytic Biography*, 107–10.

5. *The Letters of Joseph Conrad to Marguerite Poradowska, 1890–1920*, trans. John Gee and Paul Sturm (New Haven, Conn.: Yale University Press, 1940), xxi–xxiv.

6. Conrad, *Letters to Poradowska*, 111.

7. Meyer, *Joseph Conrad: A Psychoanalytic Biography*, 110.

8. See Karl and Davies, eds. *Collected Letters of Joseph Conrad*, vol. 1, esp. 426, 427.

Selected References

Agnes Tobin: Letters, Translations, Poems, with Some Account of Her Life. San Francisco: Grabhorn Press for John Howell, 1958.

Alec-Tweedie, Mrs. [Ethel]. *Women and Soldiers.* London: John Lane, [1918].

Alger, William Rounseville. *The Friendships of Women.* Boston: Roberts Brothers, 1879.

Allen, Grant. *The Woman Who Did.* London: John Lane, 1895.

Altick, Richard. *The English Common Reader: A Social History of the Mass Reading Public, 1800–1900.* Chicago: University of Chicago Press, 1957.

Altick, Richard, and James F. Loucks. *Browning's Roman Murder Story.* Chicago: University of Chicago Press, 1968.

Appleman, Philip, ed. *Darwin.* New York: Norton, 1979.

Ardis, Ann. *New Women, New Novels: Feminism and Early Modernism.* Brunswick, N.J.: Rutgers University Press, 1990.

Bartlett, Phyllis. " 'Seraph of Heaven': A Shelleyan Dream in Hardy's Fiction." *PMLA* 70 (Sept. 1955): 624–35.

Bazin, Nancy Topping. *Virginia Woolf and the Androgynous Vision.* Brunswick, N.J.: Rutgers University Press, 1973.

Beddoe, Deidre. *Back to Home and Duty: Women Between the Wars, 1918–1939.* Boston: Pandora, 1989.

Beer, Gillian. *Darwin's Plots: Evolutionary Narrative in Darwin, George Eliot, and Nineteenth-Century Fiction.* London: Routledge & Kegan Paul, 1983.

Bell, Ann O., ed. *The Diary of Virginia Woolf.* 5 vols. San Diego, Calif.: Harcourt Brace Jovanovich, 1977–84.

Bell, Clive. *Old Friends.* New York: Harcourt, Brace, 1956.

Bell, Quentin. *Virginia Woolf: A Biography.* 2 vols. New York: Harcourt Brace Jovanovich, 1972.

Bell, Susan Groag. "The Feminization of John Stuart Mill." In Bell and Marilyn Yalom, eds. *Revealing Lives: Autobiography, Biography, and Gender.* Albany: State University of New York Press, 1990.

Berger, Peter. *Ways of Seeing*. London: British Broadcasting Corporation, 1972.

Berkman, Joyce. "Feminism, War, and Peace Politics: The Case of World War I." In Jeane Bethke Elshtain and Sheila Tobias, eds. *Women, Militarism, and War: Essays on History, Politics, and Social Theory*. Savage, Md.: Rowman and Littlefield, 1990.

Bersani, Leo. *The Freudian Body: Psychoanalysis and Art*. New York: Columbia University Press, 1986.

Blake, Andrew. *Reading Victorian Fiction: The Cultural Context and Ideological Content of the Nineteenth-Century Novel*. Houndmills, Eng.: Macmillan, 1989.

Boone, Joseph Allen. *Tradition Counter Tradition: Love and the Form of Fiction*. Chicago: University of Chicago Press, 1987.

Booth, Alan, and Elaine Hess. "Cross-Sex Friendship." *Journal of Marriage and the Family*, Feb. 1974.

Boulton, James, ed. *The Letters of D. H. Lawrence*. Vol. 1: *September 1901–May 1913*. Cambridge, Eng.: Cambridge University Press, 1979.

Boumelha, Penny. *Thomas Hardy and Women: Sexual Ideology and Narrative Form*. Totowa, N.J.: Barnes & Noble, 1982.

Brady, Ann. *Pompilia: A Feminist Reading of Robert Browning's 'The Ring and the Book.'* Athens: Ohio University Press, 1988.

Brooks, Peter. *Reading for the Plot: Design and Intention in Narrative*. New York: Vintage, 1985.

Browning, Robert. *The Ring and the Book*. Ed. Richard Altick. New Haven, Conn.: Yale University Press, 1981.

Butler, Josephine. *Women's Work and Women's Culture: A Series of Essays*. London: Macmillan, 1869.

Carlisle, Janice. "J. S. Mill's *Autobiography*: The Life of a 'Bookish Man.' " *Victorian Studies* 33, 1 (Autumn 1989): 125–48.

Caws, Mary Ann. *The Art of Interference: Stressed Readings in Verbal and Visual Communication*. Princeton, N.J.: Princeton University Press, 1989.

Collins, Wilkie. *The Woman in White*. Ed. Julian Symons. Harmondsworth, Eng.: Penguin, 1974.

Comte, Auguste. *System of Positive Polity*, 4 vols. New York: Burt Franklin, 1951; reprint of 1875 London ed.; orig. pub. in French, 1851–54.

Conrad, Joseph. *Chance: A Tale in Two Parts*. Vol. 13 of *The Collected Works of Joseph Conrad*. Garden City, N.Y.: Doubleday, Page, 1925.

——— . *Nostromo: A Tale of the Seaboard*. Vol. 8 of *The Collected Works of Joseph Conrad*. Garden City, N.Y.: Doubleday, Page, 1925.

——— . *Under Western Eyes*. Vol. 11 of *The Collected Works of Joseph Conrad*. Garden City, N.Y.: Doubleday, Page, 1925.

Cooney, Séamus. "Awkward Ages in *The Awkward Age.*" *Modern Language Notes* 25 (1960): 208–22.

Cosens, Monica. *Lloyd George's Munitions Girls.* London: Hutchinson, [1917].

Cott, Nancy. "Passionlessness: An Interpretation of Victorian Sexual Ideology, 1790–1850." In Nancy Cott and Elizabeth Pleck, eds., *A Heritage of Her Own: Towards a New Social History of American Women.* New York: Simon and Schuster, 1979.

Craik, Dinah Mulock. *A Woman's Thoughts About Women, by the Author of 'John Halifax, Gentleman' &c, &c.* London: Hurst and Blackett, 1858.

Cunningham, Gail. *The New Woman and the Victorian Novel.* London: Macmillan, 1978.

Cunningham, Valentine. *"Everywhere Spoken Against": Dissent in the Victorian Novel.* Oxford: Clarendon Press, 1975.

Darroch, Sandra Jobson. *Ottoline: The Life of Lady Ottoline Morrell.* New York: Coward, McCann & Geohagen, 1976.

Derrida, Jacques. "The Politics of Friendship." *Journal of Philosophy, Law, and Society,* Nov. 1988.

Diamond, Irene, and Lee Quinby, eds. *Feminism and Foucault: Reflections on Resistance.* Boston: Northeastern University Press, 1988.

Dowling, Linda. "The Decadent and the New Woman in the 1890's." *Nineteenth Century Fiction.* Mar. 1979.

——— . *Language and Decadence in the Victorian Fin de Siècle.* Princeton, N.J.: Princeton University Press, 1986.

Doyle, Mary. *The Sympathetic Response.* London: Associated University Presses, 1981.

DuPlessis, Rachel Blau. *Writing Beyond the Ending: Narrative Strategies of Twentieth-Century Women Writers.* Bloomington: Indiana University Press, 1985.

Edel, Leon. *Henry James, The Middle Years: 1882–1895.* New York: Avon, 1962.

——— . *Henry James, The Treacherous Years: 1895–1901.* New York: Avon, 1969.

Eliot, George. *Adam Bede.* London: Dent, 1960.

——— . *Daniel Deronda.* Ed. Graham Handley. Oxford: Clarendon, 1984.

——— . *Essays.* Ed. Thomas Pinney. London: Routledge and Kegan Paul, 1963.

——— . *Middlemarch.* Ed. David Carroll. Oxford: Clarendon Press, 1986.

——— . *The Mill on the Floss.* Ed. Gordon S. Haight. Oxford: Clarendon Press, 1988.

——— . *Scenes of Clerical Life.* Ed. Thomas Noble. Oxford: Clarendon Press, 1985.

Elliott, Ralph. *Thomas Hardy's English*. London: Basil Blackwell, 1984.

Faderman, Lillian. *Surpassing the Love of Men: Romantic Friendship and Love Between Women from the Renaissance to the Present*. New York: William Morrow, 1981.

Fleishman, Avrom. *Virginia Woolf: A Critical Reading*. Baltimore, Md.: Johns Hopkins University Press, 1975.

Foucault, Michel. *The Archaeology of Knowledge*. Trans. A. M. Sheridan Smith. New York: Pantheon, 1972.

———. *Discipline and Punish: The Birth of the Prison*. Trans. Alan Sheridan. New York: Vintage, 1979.

———. *The History of Sexuality*. Vol. 1: *An Introduction*. Trans. Robert Hurley. New York: Vintage, 1980.

———. *The History of Sexuality*. Vol. 2: *The Uses of Pleasure*. Trans. Robert Hurley. New York: Random House, 1985.

———. "Power and Strategies." In Colin Gordon, ed., *Power / Knowledge: Selected Interviews and Other Writings 1972–1977*. New York: Pantheon, 1980.

Friedman, Alan. *The Turn of the Novel*. New York: Oxford University Press, 1966.

Gagnier, Regenia. *Subjectivities: A History of Self-Representation in Britain, 1832–1920*. New York: Oxford University Press, 1991.

Garnett, David. *The Flowers of the Forest*. New York: Harcourt Brace, 1956.

Gathorne-Hardy, Robert, ed. *Ottoline at Garsington: Memoirs of Lady Ottoline Morrell, 1915–1918*. London: Faber and Faber, 1974.

Gay, Peter. *The Bourgeois Experience: Victoria to Freud*. Vol. 1: *The Education of the Senses*. New York: Oxford University Press, 1984.

Gilbert, Sandra, and Susan Gubar. *No Man's Land: The Place of the Woman Writer in the Twentieth Century*. Vol. 2: *Sexchanges*. New Haven, Conn.: Yale University Press, 1989.

Gillespie, Diane. *The Sisters' Arts: The Writing and Painting of Virginia Woolf and Vanessa Bell*. Syracuse, N.Y.: Syracuse University Press, 1988.

Girard, René. *Deceit, Desire, and the Novel*. Trans. Yvonne Freccero. Baltimore, Md.: Johns Hopkins University Press, 1965.

Girouard, Mark. *The Return to Camelot: Chivalry and the English Gentleman*. New Haven, Conn.: Yale University Press, 1981.

Glucksmann, Miriam. *Women Assemble: Women Workers and the New Industries in Inter-War Britain*. London: Routledge, 1990.

Graver, Suzanne. *George Eliot and Community: A Study in Social Theory and Fictional Form*. Berkeley: University of California Press, 1984.

Haight, Gordon. *George Eliot: A Biography*. New York: Oxford University Press, 1968.

Haight, Gordon S., ed. *The George Eliot Letters*. 9 vols. New Haven,

Conn.: Yale University Press, 1954–78. *Cited in Notes and text as GEL.*

Hardy, Evelyn, and F. B. Pinion. *One Rare Fair Woman: Thomas Hardy's Letters to Florence Henniker, 1893–1922.* Miami, Fla.: University of Miami Press, 1972.

Hardy, Thomas. *Far from the Madding Crowd.* London: Macmillan, 1974.

———. *Jude the Obscure.* London: Macmillan, 1975.

———. *The Well-Beloved.* London: Macmillan, 1975.

Harrington, Henry. "The Central Line Down the Middle of *To the Lighthouse.*" *Wisconsin Studies in Contemporary Literature* 21 (Summer 1980): 363–82.

Hayek, F. A. *John Stuart Mill and Harriet Taylor: Their Correspondence and Subsequent Marriage.* Chicago: University of Chicago Press, 1951.

Holcombe, Lee. *Victorian Ladies at Work: Middle-Class Working Women in England and Wales, 1850–1914.* Hamden, Conn.: Archon, 1975.

———. *Wives and Property: Married Women's Property Law in Nineteenth Century England.* Toronto: University of Toronto Press, 1983.

Hollis, Patricia. *Women in Public: The Women's Movement, 1850–1900.* London: Allen and Unwin, 1979.

Holmes, Richard. *Shelley: The Pursuit.* London: Weidenfeld and C. D. Nicolson, 1974.

Holroyd, Michael. *Augustus John: A Biography.* 2 vols. Boston: Heinemann, 1974.

Houghton, Walter. *The Victorian Frame of Mind.* New Haven, Conn.: Yale University Press, 1957.

James, Henry. *The Awkward Age.* Vol. 9 of *The Novels and Tales of Henry James: The New York Edition.* New York: Charles Scribner's Sons, 1908.

Jeaffreson, John Cordy. *The Real Shelley: New Views of the Poet's Life.* 2 vols. London: Hurst and Blackett, 1885.

Jordan, Ellen. "The Christening of the New Woman: May 1894." *Victorian Newsletter* 63 (Spring 1983): 19–21.

Joyce, Patrick, ed. *The Historical Meanings of Work.* Cambridge, Eng.: Cambridge University Press, 1987.

Kamm, Josephine. *John Stuart Mill in Love.* London: Gordon & Cremanes, 1977.

Karl, Frederick. *Joseph Conrad: The Three Lives.* New York: Farrar, Straus, and Giroux, 1979.

Karl, Frederick, and Laurence Davies, eds. *The Collected Letters of Joseph Conrad.* Cambridge, Eng.: Cambridge University Press, 1983–.

Kermode, Frank. *The Sense of an Ending.* New York: Oxford University Press, 1967.

———. *The Art of Telling: Essays on Fiction.* Cambridge, Mass.: Harvard University Press, 1983.

Kincaid, James. "What the Victorians Knew About Sex." In Robert Vicusi, ed., *Browning Institute Studies: An Annual of Victorian Literary History and Cultural History*, vol. 16. Winfield, Kans.: Browning Institute, 1988.

King, Roma A., Jr., ed. *Victorian Poetry: Issue Commemorative of the Publication of 'The Ring and the Book'* 6, 3–4 (1969).

Knapp, James. *Literary Modernism and the Transformation of Work.* Evanston, Ill.: Northwestern University Press, 1988.

Knoepflmacher, U. C. *Religious Humanism and the Victorian Novel: George Eliot, Walter Pater, and Samuel Butler.* Princeton, N.J.: Princeton University Press, 1965.

Koestenbaum, Wayne. *Double-Talk: The Erotics of Male Literary Collaboration.* New York: Routledge, 1989.

Kucich, John. *Repression in Victorian Fiction: Charlotte Brontë, George Eliot, and Charles Dickens.* Berkeley: University of California Press, 1987.

LaCapra, Dominick. *History, Politics, and the Novel.* Ithaca, N.Y.: Cornell University Press, 1987.

Lawrence, D. H. *Sons and Lovers.* Harmondsworth, Eng.: Penguin, 1948.

———. *The White Peacock.* Ed. Andrew Robertson. Cambridge, Eng.: Cambridge University Press, 1983.

Leavis, F. R. *The Great Tradition.* London: Chatto & Windus, 1948.

Majumader, Robin, and Allen McLaurin, eds. *Virginia Woolf: The Critical Heritage.* London: Routledge and Kegan Paul, 1975.

Mansell, Daniel. "George Eliot's Conception of 'Form.' " In George Creeger, ed. *George Eliot: A Collection of Critical Essays.* Englewood Cliffs, N.J.: Prentice-Hall, 1970.

Marcus, Jane. "Enchanted Organs, Magic Bells: *Night and Day* as Comic Opera." In Ralph Freedman, ed., *Virginia Woolf, Revaluation and Continuity.* Berkeley: University of California Press, 1980; reprinted in Marcus, *Virginia Woolf and the Languages of Patriarchy.* Bloomington: Indiana University Press, 1987.

Martin, Carol. "Contemporary Critics and Judaism in *Daniel Deronda.*" *Victorian Periodicals Review*, Fall 1988, 90–107.

Marwick, Arthur. *Women at War, 1914–1918.* London: Fontana, 1977.

Meisel, Perry, and Walter Kendrick, eds. *Bloomsbury/Freud: The Letters of James and Alix Strachey, 1924–1925.* New York: Basic Books, 1985.

Meyer, Bernard. *Joseph Conrad: A Psychoanalytic Biography.* Princeton, N.J.: Princeton University Press, 1967.

Meynell, Viola. *Alice Meynell: A Memoir.* New York: Charles Scribner's Sons, 1929.

Mill, J. S. *The Autobiography of John Stuart Mill.* Ed. John Robson and Jack Stillinger. Vol. 1 of *The Collected Works of John Stuart Mill.* Toronto: University of Toronto Press, 1981.

———. *The Later Letters of John Stuart Mill, 1849–1873.* Ed. Frances Mineka and Dwight Ludley. Vol. 14 of *The Collected Works of John Stuart Mill.* Toronto: University of Toronto Press, 1972.

———. *On the Subjection of Women.* In *Essays on Equality, Law, and Education.* Ed. John M. Robson. Vol. 21 of *The Collected Works of John Stuart Mill.* Toronto: University of Toronto Press, 1984.

———. *Three Essays on Religion.* Vol. 10 of *The Collected Works of John Stuart Mill.* Toronto: University of Toronto Press, 1969.

Miller, D. A. "*Cage aux folles*: Sensation and Gender in Wilkie Collins' *The Woman in White.*" In Jeremy Hawthorn, ed. *The Nineteenth Century British Novel.* London: Edward Arnold, 1986, pp. 95–126. Also included in *The Novel and the Police.*

———. *Narrative and Its Discontents: A Study of Novelistic Closure.* Princeton, N.J.: Princeton University Press, 1981.

———. *The Novel and the Police.* Berkeley: University of California Press, 1988.

Miller, J. Hillis. *Fiction and Repetition.* Cambridge, Mass.: Harvard University Press, 1982.

Millett, Kate. *Sexual Politics.* Garden City, N.Y.: Doubleday, 1970.

Millgate, Michael. *Thomas Hardy: A Biography.* New York: Random House, 1982.

Mitchell, David. *Monstrous Regiment: The Story of the Women of the First World War.* New York: Macmillan, 1965.

Montrose, Louis. "Of Gentlemen and Shepherds: The Politics of Elizabethan Pastoral Form." *ELH* 50, 3 (Summer 1983): 415–59.

Moore, Harry, ed. *The Collected Letters of D. H. Lawrence,* vol. 1. London: Heinemann, 1962.

———. *The Priest of Love: A Life of D. H. Lawrence.* Harmondsworth, Eng.: Penguin, 1974.

Moser, Thomas. *Joseph Conrad: Achievement and Decline.* Cambridge, Mass.: Harvard University Press, 1957.

Murfin, Ross, ed. *Conrad Revisited: Essays for the Eighties.* Tuscaloosa: University of Alabama Press, 1985.

Najder, Zdzisław. *Joseph Conrad: A Chronicle.* Brunswick, N.J.: Rutgers University Press, 1983.

Nehls, Edward. *D. H. Lawrence: A Composite Biography.* Vol. 1: *1885–1919.* Madison: University of Wisconsin Press, 1957.

Nicolson, Nigel, and Joanne Trautman, eds. *The Letters of Virginia Woolf.* 6 vols. New York: Harcourt Brace Jovanovich, 1975–80. *Cited in the Notes as VWL.*

Noble, Thomas. *George Eliot's 'Scenes of Clerical Life.'* New Haven, Conn.: Yale University Press, 1965.

Peterson, Karen. "Buddy System Is a Battle for the Sexes." *USA Today*, July 17, 1989.

Phillipps, K. C. *Language and Class in Victorian England*. Oxford: Basil Blackwell, 1984.

Phipps, Charles. "Browning's Canon Giuseppe Caponsacchi—Warrior-Priest, Dantean Lover, Critic of Society." *ELH* 36 (Dec. 1969): 696–718.

Polhemus, Robert. *Erotic Faith: Being in Love from Jane Austen to D. H. Lawrence*. Chicago: University of Chicago Press, 1990.

Redinger, Ruby. *George Eliot: The Emergent Self*. New York: Knopf, 1975.

Riley, Denise. "Some Peculiarities of Social Policy Concerning Women in Wartime and Postwar Britain." In Margaret Higgonnet et al., eds., *Behind the Lines: Gender and the Two World Wars*. New Haven, Conn.: Yale University Press, 1987.

Rose, Jonathan. *The Edwardian Temperament, 1895–1913*. Athens: Ohio University Press, 1988.

Rose, Phyllis. *Parallel Lives: Five Victorian Marriages*. New York: Knopf, 1983.

Rosenbaum, S. P., ed. *The Bloomsbury Group: A Collection of Memoirs, Commentary and Criticism*. Toronto: University of Toronto Press, 1975.

Rosenman, Ellen. "Women's Speech and the Roles of the Sexes in *Daniel Deronda*." *Texas Studies in Literature and Language* 31, 2 (Summer 1989): 237–56.

Rossi, Alice. Introduction. In Alice Rossi, ed., *Essays on Sex Equality: John Stuart Mill and Harriet Taylor Mill*. Chicago: University of Chicago Press, 1970.

Ruotolo, Lucio. *The Interrupted Moment: A View of Virginia Woolf's Novels*. Stanford, Calif.: Stanford University Press, 1986.

Sawicki, Jana. "Feminism and the Power of Foucaldian Discourse." In Jonathan Arac, ed., *After Foucault: Humanistic Knowledge, Postmodern Challenges*. Brunswick, N.J.: Rutgers University Press, 1988.

———. "Identity Politics and Sexual Freedom." In *Feminism and Foucault, Reflections on Resistance*, eds. Diamond and Quinby.

Scarry, Elaine. "Work and the Body in Hardy and Other Nineteenth-Century Novelists." *Representations* 3 (Summer 1983): 90–123.

Schreiner, Olive. *Women and Labour*. London: T. F. Unwin, 1911.

Schwarz, Daniel. *Conrad: 'Almayer's Folly' to 'Under Western Eyes.'* Ithaca, N.Y.: Cornell University Press, 1980.

Sedgwick, Eve Kosofsky. *Between Men: English Literature and Male Homosocial Desire*. New York: Columbia University Press, 1985.

———. *The Epistemology of the Closet*. Berkeley: University of California Press, 1990.

Sennett, Richard. *The Conscience of the Eye: The Design and Social Life of Cities*. New York: Knopf, 1990.

Shaw, W. David. "Browning's Roman Murder Mystery: *The Ring and the Book* and Modern Theory." *Victorian Poetry* 27, 3–4 (Autumn–Winter 1989): 79–98.

Showalter, Elaine. *A Literature of Their Own: British Novelists from Brontë to Lessing.* Princeton, N.J.: Princeton University Press, 1977.

Shuttleworth, Sally. *George Eliot and Nineteenth-Century Science.* Cambridge, Eng.: Cambridge University Press, 1984.

Simpson, Hilary. *D. H. Lawrence and Feminism.* London: Croom Helm, 1982.

Skidelsky, Robert. *John Maynard Keynes: A Biography.* London: Macmillan, 1983.

Smith, Barbara Herrnstein. *Poetic Closure: A Study of How Poems End.* Chicago: University of Chicago Press, 1968.

Smith, David, ed. *Joseph Conrad's 'Under Western Eyes': Beginnings, Revisions, Final Forms.* Hamden, Conn.: Archon, 1991.

Smith-Rosenberg, Carroll. *Disorderly Conduct: Visions of Gender in Victorian America.* New York: Knopf, 1985.

Spalding, Frances. *Vanessa Bell.* London: Weidenfeld and Nicolson, 1983.

Stone, Gilbert, ed. *Women War Workers: Accounts Contributed by Representative Workers of the Work Done by Women in the More Important Branches of War Employment.* New York: Thomas Crowell, [1917].

Stone, Lawrence. *The Family, Sex, and Marriage in England, 1500–1800.* New York: Harper & Row, 1977.

Stillinger, Jack, ed. *The Early Draft of John Stuart Mill's Autobiography.* Champaign: University of Illinois Press, 1961.

Sutherland, J. A. *Victorian Novelists and Publishers.* Chicago: University of Chicago Press, 1975.

Sutton, Denys, ed. *Letters of Roger Fry.* London: Chatto & Windus, 1972.

Tanner, Tony. *Adultery in the Novel: Contract and Transgression.* Baltimore, Md.: Johns Hopkins University Press, 1979.

———. *Henry James: The Writer and His Work.* Amherst: University of Massachusetts Press, 1985.

Thom, Deborah. "Women and Work in Wartime Britain." In Richard Wall and Jay Winter, eds., *The Upheaval of War: Family, Work, and Welfare in Europe, 1914–1918.* Cambridge, Eng.: Cambridge University Press, 1988.

Todorov, Tzvetan. "The Verbal Age." Trans. Patricia Martin Gibby. *Critical Inquiry* 4 (1977): 351–71.

Torgovnick, Marianna. *Closure in the Novel.* Princeton, N.J.: Princeton University Press, 1981.

———. *The Visual Arts, Pictorialism, and the Novel: James, Lawrence, and Woolf.* Princeton, N.J.: Princeton University Press, 1985.

Vicinus, Martha. *Independent Women: Work and Community for Single Women, 1850–1920*. Chicago: University of Chicago Press, 1985.

Wade, Allan, ed. *The Letters of W. B. Yeats*. New York: Macmillan, 1955.

Walkowitz, Judith. *Prostitution and Victorian Society: Women, Class, and the State*. Cambridge, Eng.: Cambridge University Press, 1980.

Watson, Kathleen. "Dinah Morris and Mrs. Evans: A Comparative Study of Methodist Diction." *Review of English Studies* n.s. 22 (1971): 282–94.

Weber, Bruce. "Can Men and Women Be Friends?" *New York Times*, July 9, 1989.

Weeks, Jeffrey. *Sex, Politics, and Society: The Regulation of Sex Since 1800*. London: Longman, 1980.

Weinstein, Philip. *The Semantics of Desire: Changing Models of Identity from Dickens to Joyce*. Princeton, N.J.: Princeton University Press, 1984.

Welsh, Alexander. *George Eliot and Blackmail*. Cambridge, Mass.: Harvard University Press, 1985.

———. "Opening and Closing *Les Misérables*." *Nineteenth Century Fiction*. Special Issue: Narrative Endings, June 1978.

Widdowson, Peter. *Hardy in History: A Study in Literary Sociology*. London: Routledge, 1989.

Wiltsher, Anne. *Most Dangerous Women: Feminist Peace Campaigns of the Great War*. London: Pandora, 1985.

Wolseley, Francis Garnet. *Women and the Land*. London: Chatto & Windus, 1916.

Woolf, Virginia. *Moments of Being*. Ed. Jeanne Schulkind. London: Hogarth Press, 1985.

———. *Mrs. Dalloway*. New York: Harcourt, Brace & World, 1953.

———. *Night and Day*. New York: Harcourt, Brace & Co., 1948.

———. *Roger Fry: A Biography*. London: Hogarth Press, 1940.

———. *A Room of One's Own*. New York: Harcourt, Brace & World, 1929.

———. *Three Guineas*. New York: Harcourt, Brace & World, 1938.

———. *To the Lighthouse*. New York: Harcourt, Brace & Co., 1927.

Woolf, Leonard. *Beginning Again: An Autobiography of the Years 1911 to 1918*. New York: Harcourt Brace Jovanovich, 1964.

Zwerdling, Alex. *Virginia Woolf and the Real World*. Berkeley: University of California Press, 1986.

Index

In this index "f" after a number indicates a separate reference on the next page, and "ff" indicates separate references on the next two pages. A continuous discussion over two or more pages is indicated by a span of numbers. *Passim* is used for a cluster of references in close but not consecutive sequence.